Noir Affect

Noir Affect

CHRISTOPHER BREU AND
ELIZABETH A. HATMAKER
Editors

FORDHAM UNIVERSITY PRESS
New York 2020

Copyright © 2020 Fordham University Press

All rights reserved. No part of this publication may be reproduced, stored in a retrieval system, or transmitted in any form or by any means—electronic, mechanical, photocopy, recording, or any other—except for brief quotations in printed reviews, without the prior permission of the publisher.

Fordham University Press has no responsibility for the persistence or accuracy of URLs for external or third-party Internet websites referred to in this publication and does not guarantee that any content on such websites is, or will remain, accurate or appropriate.

Fordham University Press also publishes its books in a variety of electronic formats. Some content that appears in print may not be available in electronic books. Visit us online at www.fordhampress.com.

Library of Congress Cataloging-in-Publication Data available online at https://catalog.loc.gov.

Printed in the United States of America

22 21 20   5 4 3 2 1

First edition

CONTENTS

Preface   vii

Introduction: Dark Passages
CHRISTOPHER BREU AND ELIZABETH A. HATMAKER   1

1. Toward *Alphaville*: Noir, Midcentury Communication, and the Management of Affect
   JUSTUS NIELAND   29

2. Public Violence as Private Pathology: Noir Affect in *The End of a Primitive*
   CHRISTOPHER BREU   59

3. Cold Kink: Race and Sex in the African American Underworld
   KIRIN WACHTER-GRENE   78

4. Noir Pedagogy: The Problem of Student Masochism in the Classroom Economy
   ELIZABETH A. HATMAKER   99

5. The Shadows of the Twilight World: Beebo Brinker and the Circulation of Affect
   SEAN GRATTAN   122

6. Peripheral Noir, Mediation, and Capitalism: Noir Form, Noir Mediascape, Sociological Noir
   IGNACIO M. SÁNCHEZ PRADO   137

7. Cyborg Affect and the Power of the Posthuman in the *Ghost in the Shell* Franchise
   PETER HITCHCOCK   156

8. Playing with Negativity: *Max Payne*, Neoliberal Collapse, and the Noir Video Game
   BRIAN REJACK   178

9. Chick Noir: Surveilling Femininity and the Affects of Loss in *Gone Girl*
   PAMELA THOMA   197
10. Surplus Feelings: Neoliberal Noir and the Affective Economy of Debt
    ALEXANDER DUNST   222
11. Capitalism as Affective Atmosphere: The Noir Worlds of Massimo Carlotto
    ANDREW PEPPER   241

Afterword: Melodrama, Noir's Kid Sister, or Crying in Trump's America
    PAULA RABINOWITZ   261

List of Contributors   275
Index   279

PREFACE

This book had its genesis in death. It was supposed to be about death and negation, but in the abstract. Unfortunately, the abstraction did not hold. Death and its negativity became all too real during its writing. Elizabeth Hatmaker was my spouse, intellectual interlocutor, friendly femme fatale, and partner in crime. She was also a brilliant poet, an astute theorist, a sometimes critic, a thinker of the first order, and an all-around funny and beautiful person. We conceived of this book in 2012 or so. I think the germ of the idea was hers, but it came out of our dialogue which had been going on continuously since we first met in 2000. We contacted possible contributors to the collection in 2013. She was diagnosed with ALS in 2015, just when the work on the collection was really swinging into gear. Unfortunately, the disease proceeded swiftly and she passed away two years later. We started out to write about noir and suddenly we were living it. Like a noir novel, the proximity of death produced all kinds of complicated affects in both of us and between us. One imagines that one will be heroic in such situations, but noir tells us otherwise. You get through. And that's what we both did in different ways, me as her primary caregiver and she facing a disease worse than any mere description can convey. If there is an ethics to noir, it is to face such affects head on. It is to recognize death and the anxiety it produces and not look away. We both already believed this for different reasons and to this ethic we were true.

Due to Elizabeth's disease and passing, I have of necessity done much of the writing in the introduction. I also have edited and reworked her essay, which is a different contribution than she initially planned; it is an amazing essay and I am very happy that we can include it here. Make no mistake, though: this book is predicated as much on Elizabeth's vision as it is mine; the kernel of the book, that noir is about negative affect, is hers. Moreover, the ideas in the introduction are as much hers as mine, even as I did the writing. There were times when I would be stuck and she would provide me with a solution from her sick bed. Our collaboration continued almost to the very end. It was her idea too to make this an edited collection.

I had an idea of writing a jointly composed monograph, but she rightly asserted that this would be much better as an edited collection, where we could bring together so many of the brilliant people we know who work on noir. She was, of course, right and the book is their book as much as ours.

Accordingly, I first want to thank Elizabeth for her brilliance, her knowledge of everything noir, her bravery, and her wisdom. This book is dedicated to her. I also want to thank all of our brilliant contributors. You have turned this book into a sum much greater than its parts. I love the way in which the different essays in the book speak to each other and challenge each other. My thanks to Paula Rabinowitz for agreeing to write the powerful afterword for the book. As fans of Paula's work, we were ecstatic to have her agree to write the afterword.

I also want to thank Richard Morrison, editorial director of Fordham University Press. I have worked with Richard on three books now and none was more meaningful and important than this one. I already knew Richard was a fantastic editor and one of the true professionals. While I was undergoing the illness and loss of a partner, Richard was doing the same. We were already close but this made us much closer. So I would like to acknowledge his partner, Tim Hough. I also want to thank all of the editorial staff at Fordham. All of you have made working on this project a pleasure.

There are too many people who play a central role in my intellectual and affective life to list here, but I want to thank a few different communities. First, I want to thank my peeps at my home institution, Illinois State University: colleagues, graduate students, and undergraduates. Somehow you still put up with me even after twenty years. I also want to thank the community of scholars that have formed around the Society for Critical Exchange and the journal *symplokē*, all the participants in the Facebook Comparative Theory Group, my friends and interlocutors from Germany, all my pulp and popular literature peeps, all of those from the University of California at Santa Cruz diaspora, Elizabeth's family, and my sweet, supportive family.

I want to thank the two anonymous readers for Fordham University Press (one of whom I found out later is Kate Nickerson) for providing the best and most supportive feedback a scholar could ask for. What is good about this book is due in no small part to you.

There are a few folks who have been core intellectual interlocutors in recent years and I want to thank them individually: Stacy Alaimo, Carlos Amador, Renée Bergland, Kaitlin Blanchard, Levi Paul Bryant, Jeffrey Di Leo, Carla Freccero, Sean Grattan, Christian Haines, Peter Hitchcock,

Caren Irr, Aaron Jaffe, Anna Kornbluh, Sophia McClennen, José Saldívar, David Schmid (whose insight about all things crime fiction related was crucial in the early conception of this project), Julietta Singh, Nathan Snaza, and Phillip Wegner.

I also want to thank those special folks who helped bring me back to the force and beauty of this impermanent, profoundly messed up, but living world: Robin Baldridge, Tom Banks, Layla Bodet, Scott Davis, Megan Lewis, Erick Longfellow, Josette Lorig, Brian Rejack, Max Rovner, and Gina Stinnett. (Many of these folks are also intellectual interlocutors).

Finally, I want to thank Kirsti Sandy on behalf of Elizabeth. They were best friends, movie lovers, and co-conspirators. I know Elizabeth would be annoyed with me from the beyond (if there is one) if I forgot to mention her.

C. B.

Noir Affect

Introduction: Dark Passages
Christopher Breu and Elizabeth A. Hatmaker

> A married couple is haunted by the fact that one of them killed a blackmailer. The woman, through whose perspective the scene is focalized, doesn't remember killing the blackmailer and suspects her husband of doing the deed. Although we never get the husband's perspective, it appears to be strictly parallel. Both love each other and yet neither can trust nor forgive each other.
>
> —CORNELL WOOLRICH, *I Married a Dead Man*[1]

Noir is elusive. While all critical categories are characterized by debate and disagreement, noir as a category seems particularly prone to fractiousness, dissension, and divisiveness. Almost from the moment Nino Frank first named it and Raymond Borde and Étienne Chaumeton produced their first book-length study of the "noir series" of films, critics debated the term and what it designated.[2] Is noir a genre? Is the term itself a valuable descriptor? Why not use more stable and precise genre descriptions such as detective fiction and film or crime fiction and film? Why use a category that is, as Marc Vernet has argued, more of a retrospective critical construction than a description used by the filmmakers and writers themselves?[3] Of course, all critical categories are, in part, retrospective constructions. Yet something about noir seems particularly belated and arbitrary.

Part of the problem is that it is hard to locate what constitutes noir in relationship to positive qualities. Film theorists have talked about certain kinds of lighting (chiaroscuro, low-key) and cinematographic techniques (the use of the canted frame, expressionism) while film and literature scholars have talked about certain kinds of plots (the psychological crime thriller) or characters (the criminal antihero, the hard-boiled protagonist, the femme fatale, the homme fatale) as definitional. Scholars have even attempted to fix the surface features of the noir plot. Writing in the late 1970s and under the influence of Northrop Frye, James Damico essays the following structuralist account of the noir plot (one that may have contradictions or variations but ostensibly represents the deep structure of the form):

> Either he is fated to do so or by chance, or because he has been hired for a job specifically associated with her, a man whose experience of life has left him sanguine and often bitter meets a not-innocent woman of similar outlook to whom he is sexually and fatally attracted. Through this attraction, either because the woman induces him to it or because it is the natural result of their relationship, the man comes to cheat, attempt to murder, or actually murder a second man to whom the woman is unhappily or unwillingly attached (generally he is her husband or lover), an act which often leads to the woman's betrayal of the protagonist, but which in any event brings about the sometimes metaphoric, but usually literal destruction of the woman, the man to whom she is attached, and frequently the protagonist himself.[4]

While this description certainly fits some noir plots (such as the novel and film versions of *The Postman Always Rings Twice* and *Double Indemnity*, or Jacques Tourneur's *Out of the Past*) there are many noir narratives that do not fit this description (whether it is the film and novel versions of *Mildred Pierce*, Patricia Highsmith's *The Talented Mr. Ripley*, Jim Thompson's *The Killer Inside Me*, Jean-Luc Godard's *Alphaville*, or Koreyoshi Kurahara's *I am Waiting*).[5] And even as Damico names a number of important noir elements (including chance, death, fatal attractions of various sorts), his description doesn't feel like it gets to the heart of the noirs that it effectively describes. In a more thematic vein, American studies, cultural studies, and film studies scholars such as E. Ann Kaplan, Paula Rabinowitz, Frank Krutnik, Robert Corber, Elizabeth Cowie, Christopher Breu, and others have also argued that noir, whatever the surface features of the text or film in question, is about social antagonisms and struggles around gender, class, and race.[6] These scholars are not wrong. Indeed, we will draw on their work in elaborating our own account of racial, class, gender, and sexual antagonism as it is structured by noir affect, but it is hard to situate these features as distinctively noir, since these thematics are also present in other twentieth- and twenty-first-century genres. Similarly, Jennifer Fay and Justus Nieland argue in their excellent *Film Noir: Hard-Boiled Modernity and the Cultures of Globalization* that noir is an ambivalent response to different manifestations of global modernity.[7] This is no doubt true. Drawing, in part, on Fay and Nieland, we too will situate noir as an engagement with modernity. The problem is, though, that the same could be said about a number of forms of cultural production, including the novels and films that are grouped under the banner of modernism. The elusive noir element vanishes yet again, resisting positivization.

Perhaps the reason for this resistance lies in the very negativity of this thing we call noir. In trying to define noir, we encounter the same forms of negativity that characterize the work of the form itself. Noir itself foregrounds fractiousness, divisiveness, conflict, and dissension. Moreover, it is preoccupied with belatedness, retrospection, fatality, inadequacy, and intransigence. It also marks the elusiveness of subjects to definition and even to self-knowledge. As Slavoj Žižek argues, the critics and practitioners of noir (not to mention the characters featured in noir texts) exist in a noir relationship with noir itself.[8]

Noir Affect, Space, and Time

> A middle-class woman has been kicked out of a car and left on the side of a deserted mountain pass by a rich date, because he finds her annoying. A working-class man who she dated a couple of times after meeting him on the internet and who has been stalking her offers her a ride back to town. She refuses his offer, rejecting him in much the same language that she was just rejected. They struggle and the man kills her. The camera works through a complicated set of shots reverse shots indicating the multiple, incompatible points of view.
>
> LEE SANG-IL, *Villain*[9]

An understanding of noir as characterized by negative affect is the central premise of this book. As affect often does, noir affect works virally to inflect (or infect) not only the characters and situations dramatized by the noir text, but also its formal dimensions and the cultural and critical discourses about noir. Noir figures space and time in distinctive ways. Moreover, these figurations are necessarily intertwined. Noir has a specific historical genesis that overlaps with various moments of modernization. As Fay and Nieland, Andrew Spicer, James Naremore, and David Schmid and Andrew Pepper persuasively demonstrate, it is also a transnational and even global phenomenon.[10] Noir may have had its initial genesis in the writings of James M. Cain, Cornell Woolrich, and Horace McCoy in the 1930s as well as in the classic cycle of Hollywood films of the 1940s and

1950s. However, these films were not only produced by European refugees and received filmic and critical homages in French New Wave and Japanese postwar cinema, they also often engaged in a dialogue with continental movements such as existentialism, psychoanalysis, and certain strains of twentieth-century Marxism. As Naremore points out, Albert Camus's *The Stranger* and Cain's *The Postman Always Rings Twice* share both a writing style and a set of themes.

In defining noir in terms of negative affect, then, we are not abjuring historical or spatial context. Indeed, part of the ambit of this project is to situate noir in the twentieth- and twenty-first-century globe. While *Noir Affect* does not present essays on all the different spaces of noir's global efflorescence (the recent explosion of Scandinavian noir and the recent resurgence of noir television in the United States being but two examples), the book does collect a range of essays addressing an array of global locations, from the United States to Mexico, Japan, Italy, and France. We also read noir as an always evolving and self-aware practice. Rather than emerging as discrete practices in different locations, the practice of noir in different national, regional, and global contexts is a self-conscious one that is always in dialogue with what has come before. Moreover, it is a constantly mutating or evolving practice. Like many popular forms, noir can be gloriously promiscuous in its travels, mixing with a range of different genres to produce hybrid creations. Thus, we probably can't consider Italian *gialli* or Japanese cinema derived from manga pure noir, but neither should we refuse the noir affects and borrowings that structure some of these films.

Noir has long been associated with different temporal formations within modernity as well. As Vivian Sobchack has argued, the temporality of noir is what she calls lounge time.[11] It is a temporality that forms itself in the in-between spaces of modernity, such as the bar, the lounge, the gas station, the bus station, and the diner. Such a temporality is modern yet displaced. It is not defined by the nostalgia of anti-modernism, but rather by the displaced, anonymous time of the shabbily or slightly shopworn modern. It is a non-time (or nonsynchronous time) that echoes Mark Augé's concept of non-place.[12] Such places, like those detailed by Sobchack are recursive, evasive, and out of sync with the systems of meaning that traditionally define identity, space, and temporality. As Fredric Jameson has noted, they are anonymous and often slightly degraded places, ones associated with travelers, drifters, laborers, the down and out, the criminal, and the multiethnic.[13] While the spaces of noir, as Edward Dimendberg describes them, are preoccupied with the transformations of the modern city, even when the noir itself is not located in the city, these are also neglected spaces, whether urban, suburban, or exurban.[14] They are spatialities and temporalities that are themselves saturated with noir affect.

The emphasis on nonplace and nontime suggests a different form of historicism and spatialization than is common in most forms of literary, film, and cultural studies. Our sense of spatialization is about (to rework Gaston Bachelard) the poetics of nonspace as much as it is about situating texts in specific geopolitical, national, and local contexts. Such spaces are often neglected, serialized, or ordinary and are located in the neglected parts of cities and towns or on their outskirts. One thinks of the bars or diners that Sobchack details or the absolutely unmemorable Musashi-Mirayama district of greater Tokyo in which Natsuo Kirino's *Out* is set. Even the shift in film noir from sets to on-location filming in the late forties does little to disrupt the feeling of non-place in noir. While we know that Jules Dassin's *The Naked City* is filmed on location in New York City, many of the spaces it details feel as anonymous as the down and out sets that usually mark space in noir. In both cases, the nondescript and serializable quality of place lends noir its dream logic. The repetition of spaces that is fundamental to noir echoes the repetition of actions, fantasies, and desires in the genre.

Noir Historicism

> A former concert pianist attempts to find solace from the suicide of his wife, which he feels he caused, by eking out a living as a performer in a cocktail bar. He falls in love with a waitress, accidentally kills a man in a fight over her, and is in debt to gangsters. The pianist and the waitress flee to the countryside to evade their troubles. In an ensuing gunfight with the gangsters, the woman is killed by a stray bullet. Now feeling responsible for the deaths of the two women he loved, the piano player returns to the oblivion of playing piano in the bar.
>
> FRANÇOIS TRUFFAUT, *Shoot the Piano Player*[15]

Similarly, our conception of the distinct temporality of noir is inflected by what we have elsewhere called "noir historicism."[16] Drawing on the dream-logic that animates the noir text, noir historicism "recasts history as uneven, repetitious, and disjunctive, even as it also emphasizes the uneven, disjunctive, and necessarily phantasmatic relationships between imaginative text and material context."[17] From within noir historicism we suggest a set of crucial shifts in the fantasy staged by noir, even as the negativity of the fantasy remains constant. The period of noir's first emergence forms as a reaction to the boosterish and collectivist rhetoric of Fordist liberalism, pitting the disaffected or excluded individual against the affirmative nationalist, market-based, familial, and producerist rhetoric of the era. Under neoliberal capitalism, two distinct phases or generic mutations are notable: first, a nostalgic and "postmodern" neo-noir emerges, as has been theorized by Richard T. Jameson, Foster Hirsch, and Mark Bould, Kathrina Glitre, and Greg Tuck among others; second, we have a return to noir as a present-oriented form, one that has become truly international, open to hybridizations with other forms, and represents an active and negative response to neoliberalism.[18] We call this new development neoliberal noir, as distinguished from neo-noir. In nostalgic neo-noir, either the protagonist embodies the seemingly outmoded discourse of liberal individualism or the text itself becomes an ironic reworking of the genre to emphasize the difference between the historical world of noir and that of the postmodern moment. In this sense, there is a positivity to neo-noir, but one that can only be located in an imaginative past and is contrasted to a negatively figured present. If lounge time, in Fordist noir, was precisely about resisting anti-modernist nostalgia, ironically neo-noir becomes inflected by just such a nostalgia, although this time a nostalgia for the modern itself.

In contrast, the resurgence of noir proper in neoliberal noir (as opposed to neo-noir), which is something that has taken place in film, fiction, television, and video games, is organized around a new, present form of negativity, one that challenges the affirmative moral and commodified rhetoric of self-reinvention, self-investment, and self-maintenance as well as deserving winners and losers that is central to contemporary neoliberalism. It highlights the ideological contradiction between the commodified rhetoric of individual uniqueness and responsibility and the material disposability and precarity of workers and populations under neoliberalism. What happens when Sobchack's lounge becomes almost fully emptied by neoliberal spaces of disaggregated labor, self-actualization, financialization, automation, and privatized consumption? Neoliberal noir, which is addressed by many of the essays in this collection, tends to be critical of the individualist (and often white male) protagonist that was celebrated by classic noir and its neo-noir brethren. This opens up the form to even more negative work around race, class, gender, sexuality, and economics.

Understanding Noir Affect

Four downwardly mobile women do backbreaking work at a bento factory in what is politely called the "Tokyo suburbs." They actually work in the Mushashi-Murayama district, a nonspace where nobody, not even sex tourists and sex workers, would choose to go. It is, as much of the world is, an interlinking set of highways, factories, houses, and dingy malls. This space produces a fantasy of escape (of getting out at all costs) even as it invites the female workers to give into their death drives and exit the world as such.

NATSUO KIRINO, *Out*[19]

Noir Affect proposes a new understanding of noir in a range of media (fiction, film, television, and video games). This new understanding emphasizes that noir is, first and foremost, an affective disposition rather than a specific cycle of films or novels associated with a given time period (the mid-twentieth century) or national tradition (the United States). The forms of affect associated with noir are resolutely negative: these are texts centered on rage (including murderous rage), loss, sadness, shame, guilt, regret, anxiety, humiliation, resentment, resistance, and refusal. Moreover, they often ask us to identify with those on the losing end of capitalist cultural narratives, especially the criminal, the lost, the compromised, the haunted, the unlucky, the cast aside, and the erotically "perverse," including those whose greatest erotic attachment is to death.

Our argument is that only by tarrying with these negative affects as they appear in the stories of two-time losers, violent criminals, and death-haunted subjects can a truly transformational politics become possible. If capitalism (especially in its present, neoliberal form) alternates between boosterish self-help narratives and the negative rhetoric of social condemnation and exclusion, noir works in an inverse way to both model empathy with the down-trodden, excluded, and abandoned, and demand that we engage and value the negativity of their affects. Ironically, however, such noir affects are only available to us through the production of a surreptitious form of positive affect, one that asks us to identify with the abject, the criminal, and the loser. From this we get noir's famous series of antiheroes, such as Tom Ripley, Mildred Pierce, Charlie Kohler, and Amy Dunne. Noir does its darkest work by insisting that you identify with the antisocial affects of its protagonist. A truly transformational politics has to take stock of these negative affects, what we describe as noir affects.

Of course, in arguing that noir is characterized by negative affect, we ironically run the danger of once again trying to positivize the negative, attempting to fix (in the double meaning of to locate and to cure it) noir. While such a move is perhaps inevitable—How does one begin to account for the negative except by positivizing it?—we define our project in ways that limit the epistemological damage done by an overly positive framework. We do this, firstly, by emphasizing the negativity of noir itself. Noir is not only characterized by negative affect but also establishes a negative, indeed resistant if not oppositional, relationship to any attempt to fix or define it. Secondly, by theorizing noir as affect, we employ a particularly elusive, ambient, and fluid category with which to think about noir, one that matches the elusiveness of noir itself. As a number of the essays to follow demonstrate, many of the most interesting noirs are generically hybrid. Indeed, rather than a genre, noir is perhaps best understood as deformation (a willful darkening or perversion) of other genres, such as the detective, crime, proletarian, or adventure narrative. Thirdly, we leave open-ended and cumulative the various objects that can be defined as noir. Rather than saying that all forms of noir need to be characterized by negative affect, we allow our essayists to demonstrate the range of objects (diverse in terms of media, place, and time of production) that can be elucidated using the frame of noir affect. Some noir may not be characterized by noir affect and some noir affect may be associated with texts typically characterized as noir. Fourthly, we see noir affect as a mode of reading as much as a description of the characteristics of a certain set of objects. While we are very interested in the objects we investigate in *Noir Affect*, we are much less interested in fixing them as part of a noir canon. Moreover, if our thesis about the negativity of noir is correct, such an attempt would be a failure. Then again, noir teaches us that failure can be beautiful.[20]

This ambient quality of the thing that we call noir suggests that it is qualitative rather than quantitative, organized by perception and feeling rather than a purely rational amalgam of characteristics. It is for this reason that we describe noir in terms of affect. It is both a name for specific kinds of affect (loss, sadness, rage, guilt, shame, regret, resentment, humiliation, and refusal) and the name of a specific practice of narrative that works to dramatize such affects (often via narratives of the criminal, the lost, the melancholic, the haunted, the unlucky, the cast aside, and the erotically "perverse").

Drawing on foundational and recent work in affect theory by writers as diverse as Eve Kosofsky Sedgwick, Lawrence Grossberg, Brian Massumi, Lauren Berlant, Sara Ahmed, Sianne Ngai, Kathleen Stewart, Teresa Brennan, Patricia Ticineto Clough, John Protevi, and Michael Hardt and Antonio Negri as well as psychoanalytic and psychological accounts of affect by Sigmund Freud, Jacques Lacan, and Silvan Tomkins, *Noir Affect* argues that the category of noir is best understood as designating a written or filmic narrative that chronicles negative affective dispositions.[21] In the recent work of affect theory, affect is understood to be both transpersonal and personal, social and subjective, conscious as well as unconscious. Yet in much affect theory, affects, even negative ones, are cast in the language of becoming, possibility, virtuality, and incipience. This language of possibility and becoming is derived from the influence of Gilles Deleuze and Félix Guattari (writing both together and separately) on affect theory.[22] Deleuze's and Guattari's contributions to affect theory are crucial. It is they who translate the psychoanalytic notion of affect that is largely intrasubjective into a register that is more political, transpersonal, and even impersonal. We will draw on this transpersonal understanding of affect even as we emphasize its negativity. Yet the emphasis on possibility and becoming, while important for theorizing agency within various economic, biopolitical, and discursive forms of power, also has the effect of minimizing the negative power of affect to constrain, decompose, and delimit.

The thing that we call noir excels at staging the negative power of affect. If positive affects are about possibility, becoming, and affirmation (both as possibility and as forms of biopolitical control) then the noir affects are about repetition, delimitation, fixity, retrospection, and decay as well as resistance and refusal. In theorizing noir affect, then, we draw upon theorists of negative affect such as Lauren Berlant, Teresa Brennan, Sianne Ngai, and Sylvan Tomkins as well as on psychoanalytic theory's engagement with repetition and negation (both of self and other), to explore more fully the negative affects staged by noir. How can noir be rethought in terms of negative affect? What is the value of staging negative affect? What kind of cultural and political work is enabled or disenabled by reading noir's affective negativity?

Affect is, of course, not only a way of theorizing the relationship of subjectivity to the social, but it, like all theories of the social, is also tied to a specific historiographical framework. In the work of Michael Hardt and Antonio Negri as well as Patricia T. Clough, affect is tied to the larger shift from Fordism to post-Fordism and from industrial production to biopolitical production (and the forms of affective, service, and intellectual labor associated with it) as dominant organizations of global capitalism. Thus, noir offers us one way to think through these economic shifts with special attention to those global subjects who resist or who are cast aside in the name of economic progress. In exploring noir affect, we want to situate it, in part, in response to this history of labor and economic transformation, marking it as a site of refusal, resistance, and negation.

We explore the forms of affect that accrue around both industrial labor and the forms of biopolitical (specifically affective) labor privileged by neoliberalism. Affect in the Fordist era was managed through a rhetoric of being a team player or a company man (which opened up, of course, to collectivist resistance via unionization and political-economic struggle) and the classic figure of refusal in this context was the solitary noir protagonist who often resisted integration into the collective. In our own neoliberal era affect is a direct product of the labor and thus is not merely a management practice but immanent to the laboring subject at such. It is, like neoliberal and post-Fordist production more generally, segmented and individualized. Rather than collectivist, the management of affect in neoliberalism is about producing individual subjects. The figures of refusal in neoliberal noir, not only represent the contemporary working class in their racial, gender, and sexual diversity (which was always there but deemphasized in the Fordist era), but also often try to haltingly rebuild connections to other subjects in this atomized context. We note how these forms of affect play out around sites of social antagonism, collectivity, subjectification, and embodiment. The negativity of noir uncovers sites of social and interpersonal antagonism, refusing to cover over or narrate them away. Thus, noir becomes a way of staging various forms of social antagonism, including those associated with racial, gendered, sexual, and economic inequality.

Noir Affect explores how the forms of negative affect we call noir appear not only in midcentury novels and films typically associated with the genre but also in late twentieth century and contemporary noir. What is the relationship between economic inequality and noir affect? How does noir narrate economic transformations, contradictions, and forms of exploitation? How does noir affect intersect, or place limits on other forms of political and social affect? How does noir affect, and the antagonisms attached to it, intersect with issues of race, gender, sexuality, and class? These are some of the questions *Noir Affect* explores.

Contextualizing Affect

A female detective interviews re-interviews the wife of a suspected serial rapist and killer, who has relied on his wife as an alibi. The detective finally figures out the right question to ask: she asks the woman if her husband has ever made her do things she didn't want to do in bed. The wife's composure crumbles. She finally tells the detective the forms of violence that she endured at the hands of her husband and that the alibi is false. While the scene might suggest one of female solidarity, the detective is more concerned with solving the case and fighting the sexism of the department than attending to the wife.

CHRISTOPHER MENAUL, *Prime Suspect* (SEASON 1, EPISODE 2)

Affect has become a key category in contemporary theory. Focused on what affects the body and emotions, the concept can be situated as part of what Stacy Alaimo and Susan Hekman name "the material turn" and what Diana Coole and Samantha Frost name the "new materialisms."[23] These new materialist approaches move beyond the privileging of language and culture that were central to postmodernism, attending instead to the ways in which materiality interpenetrates with, sets limits upon, and permeates the social. Central to such an undertaking is moving beyond social constructivism, with its assumption of language as unidirectionally productive or inscriptive, and toward a "deconstruction of the material/discursive dichotomy that retains both elements without privileging either."[24] While there are other dimensions of the work undertaken in the material turn that may emphasize the resistance of the material to the discursive, this move toward the deconstruction of the discursive and material, or at least an account of their interpenetration, is a crucial dimension of the new materialisms and is central to the work affect does as a conceptual term. Affect is a key ligature between perception and cognition, representation and emotion, sensation and action, and as such it becomes central to reconceptualizing the subject in a more materialist register. It becomes a way of moving beyond the category of the subject as it has been conceptualized in a Cartesian framework, in which the mind and the body are imagined as fully separate, and the former is privileged over the latter. For all of its investment in decentering of the subject, postmodernism and social construction tended to privilege a linguistic, and thus essentially Cartesian, conception of it. These approaches may have decentered this subject, but it was this Cartesian version of the subject that was being decentered. Affect, as an account of bodily responses that are linked both to the mind and to sensation, posits an understanding of embodiment that moves beyond the mind/body duality.

Yet, while it is important to situate the "affective turn" as a central part of the larger "material turn," it is also necessary to recognize that, like materialism itself, the concept of affect has a much longer history than is often recognized by accounts of it that merely situate it as a body of theory associated with the present. Much contemporary discourse around affect in the present moment tends to emphasize it as a space of possibility and becoming, producing what Lawrence Grossberg describes as an "ontology that escapes."[25] This conception of affect, which can probably be described as its dominant formulation in the present, derives from an intellectual trajectory that begins with Baruch Spinoza's account of affect in his *Ethics*, and is picked up by Deleuze and Guattari in a number of their jointly authored works and becomes reformulated and canonized for the present by Brian Massumi in his *Parables for the Virtual*.[26] Yet, although there is much that is valuable about this version of affect including an emphasis on the affective as transpersonal and importantly impersonal, it also presents only one face of the affective, one that tends to emphasize its positive, enabling, and transformative features.

Noir affect, however, emphasizes its negative, constraining, and conflictual dimensions. These too have a history. The following brief history traces this second trajectory of affect theory, indicating what can be utilized and what needs to be reworked or abandoned in contemporary affect theory in order to theorize the resolutely negative affects that constitute noir affect.

A Genealogy of Negative Affect

> A malevolent, small-town deputy sheriff, who is clearly disturbed and much smarter than most people he encounters, takes great pleasure in speaking entirely in broad clichés to the dismay of his interlocutors. When this verbal sadism isn't enough, he burns a hole in the hand of a drifter with his cigarette.
>
> JIM THOMPSON, *The Killer Inside Me*[27]

Unsurprisingly, this trajectory begins with Freud, whose account of affect is first articulated in his *Project for a Scientific Psychology*.[28] The project was Freud's early attempt to articulate a neurobiological basis for his endeavors into the study of psychopathology. While he later seemed to abandon much of the never-published project when he worked out his full articulation of psychoanalysis as theory, methodology, and praxis, a number of concepts from the *Project* persist in Freud's later nomenclature and theoretical edifice. Affect is one of these.

Returning to the *Project* is valuable for several reasons. Freud's project is the psychoanalytic road not taken. As his most materialist account of psychopathology, it is a particularly rich place for rethinking psychoanalytic categories in a more materialist register. Some of this work has been done by trauma theory, which returns to Freud's earliest writings such as the "Project" and "Studies on Hysteria" to unearth a Freud who was focused on the concept of trauma and the traumatic effect of childhood sexual abuse, in contrast to later accounts in psychoanalysis, which reframed these earlier accounts of sexual abuse as fantasy.[29] Jean Laplanche splits the difference between these two frameworks with his account of seduction by saying that material trauma or the traumatic wish can have the same psychic impact.[30] Laplanche is absolutely right to emphasize that trauma, whether its origin is located in the material realm, the psychical realm or both, becomes reshaped by the workings of fantasy as well as enmeshed in both symbolic and material systems, including in affect and the drives as dynamics that interlink the material and the symbolic, the linguistic and the biological. Affect thus becomes one of the material ligatures that connect the symbolic and the material, the embodied and the representational. This dimension of affect is everywhere evident in noir, where the text's affects often seem to outstrip its narrative drive, representations, and even, at times, coherence.

Freud's account of affect in the *Project* locates affect precisely as such a ligature. He situates it, on the one hand, as a product of the nervous system which has the function of mediating between perception and consciousness, and, on the other hand, as a relationship between the drives and the consciousness. While all of this will become more complicated when he introduces his theory of the unconscious, Freud, in this early account, positions affects precisely between images and feelings, representation and embodiment. As such he produces an account of affect that is equally poised between the material and the representational as well as the personal and the impersonal.

Trauma and negative affect are also linked in the early Freud. In "Studies on Hysteria" coauthored with Joseph Breuer, Freud articulates the relationship between "the distressing affects of fright, apprehension, shame, or physical pain" and the workings of trauma.[31] Indeed, as later trauma theorists such as Judith Herman and Cathy Caruth argue, trauma is often formed in relationship to affect that overwhelms the ability of the conscious mind and nervous system to perceive and make sense of it.[32] Instead, it becomes, along with disturbing wishes, one of the privileged materials of the unconscious. It forms an atemporal and unworked through knot within the unconscious, one that has implications for the conception of both historicity and temporality, emphasizing the psychoanalytic concept of *nachträglichkeit* (translated alternately as deferred action or retroactive meaning).

The strange temporality that we call noir time is often a product of *nachträglichkeit*, a belatedness that recalls affects and drives actions that were part of an earlier experience or scene. Noir has a distinct relationship to temporality and historicism. The historical framework of noir is always disruptive and hard to pin down. In contrast to the calendrical historicisms of the realist novel or literary criticism, the historicism of noir is necessarily double, haunted, and fractured. The past is always shaped through the repetitions of the present even as the present is often just one such repetition of the past. The historicism of noir is thus dreamlike. It is a simultaneous movement toward and away from a historical knot of contradiction. It wants to undo the knot but also recognizes that undoing it may just be its subject's undoing as well. Whether this undoing leads toward the possibility of a different subjectification or just dissolution, noir is thus characteristically about symbolic and often material death.

The concept of the two deaths is of course central to Slavoj Žižek's Lacanian account of noir, and there is much that can be learned by attending to the Lacanian account of affect.[33] While affect appears to be a less central category in Jacques Lacan's approach to psychoanalysis, Seminar X, *Anxiety*, is a book length treatise on a specific affect, anxiety. Indeed, Lacan indicates as much early on in the seminar: "What is anxiety? We've ruled out the idea that it might be an emotion. To introduce it, I will say that it is an affect."[34] Lacan makes a distinction here, one that is central to a number of accounts of affect, between emotion and affect. Emotions are fixed, named states whereas affect, for Lacan, is free-floating and protean: "It is unfastened; it drifts about. It can be found displaced, maddened, inverted, or metabolized, but it isn't repressed. What are repressed are the signifiers that moor it."[35] It is interesting to note in this regard, that whereas Freud emphasizes the intertwining relationship between affect and trauma (and later of affect and wishes), Lacan marks their difference. It is trauma's signifiers that are repressed and form the unconscious kernel or knot in relationship to which affect is generated. In *Seminar 11* this will become the "kernel of the real," which forms the bedrock of the subject's unconscious and their relationship to the drives.[36] Anxiety, then, is an affect that comes from being too proximate to the real. As Lacan argues, it is not about lack, but its opposite, the closeness of an anxiety-producing (phantasmatic) object.

As Kelly Oliver and Benigno Trigo argue in *Noir Anxiety*, noir is precisely about such proximate anxieties.[37] Drawing on Kristeva's notion of abjection as well as psychoanalytic accounts of anxiety, they read noir as about the return of the not fully abjected, ambiguous, and disruptive aspects of race, sexuality, and gender that the dominant social symbolic attempts to contain and purge from the space of representation. Thus, anxiety is a thoroughly political category, one that parallels noir's drive to engage with the uncomfortable, the repressed, and the uncanny (the uncanny itself can be read as a manifestation of anxiety, in which what was thought to be strange is not only familiar, but much too proximate). This notion of anxiety (and its disavowal) can also be linked to Lauren Berlant's concept of cruel optimism. Berlant describes cruel optimism as a neoliberal affective state in which people are invested in attachments that inhibit their own flourishing. For example, neoliberal discourses like self-help, postmodern management, and "staying positive" function to cover over the exploited subject's anxious relationship to a neoliberal order that is systematically impoverishing them. Cruel optimism is a positive affect, but one that functions as an embodied ideology and is thus a negative phenomenon. It enables the subject to evade a confrontation with the negative affects associated with noir. Yet in noir versions of such moments, these negative anxieties always return. Although *Noir Affect* draws on Lacan, Berlant, Oliver and Trigo's work in conceptualizing anxiety as a negative affect, it addresses other negative affects as well. Thus, both noir anxiety and cruel optimism become crucial frameworks for understanding the negative experience of political, economic, and social inequality as well as their affective masking.

Situating Negative Affect

> Kazue is a former white-collar worker and private school student who has become a prostitute on the streets of Tokyo. Her experience on the streets continues this downward trajectory. She goes from being a high-priced escort to eventually turning tricks on the street for a few yen to being left dead by a serial killer on a garbage strewn rooftop in Tokyo's slums. We access much of Kazue's downward mobility through her diary, which is always punctuated, even at the end, with the discourse of self-help and self-actualization.
>
> NATSUO KIRINO, *Grotesque*[38]

Lacan's emphasis on the mercurial dimensions of affect, which exists in tension with the intransigence and seeming fixity of the real, will be picked up by Felíx Guattari and then by Deleuze and Guattari who mix it with Spinoza's account of affect in *Ethics*, where it becomes central to their notion, borrowed from Nietzsche, of becoming (in opposition to the fixity of being). Similarly, Lacan's emphasis on affect as being distinct from emotion also becomes a central tenet of contemporary affect theory. This distinction between the two also is a mark of affect's privileged relationship to embodiment, in which it affects the body and is felt before it is translated into emotion, which as a named, cognitive state is presented as more stable and culturally fixed.

This account of affect exists in tension with the one provided by Silvan Tomkins. Tomkins, a psychologist whose work has gained posthumous attention in the humanities due to his championing by Eve Kosofsky Sedgwick, provides an account in which affects are not only named but limited in number. They include Interest-Excitement, Enjoyment-Joy, Surprise-Startle, Distress-Anguish, Shame-Humiliation, Contempt-Disgust, Anger, Fear-Terror. Tomkins's emphasis on negative affects is notable given that five out the eight affects he names are negative. Moreover, all of the negative affects are associated with noir. Indeed, we could describe Tomkins a theorist of noir affect, and the essays in this collection spotlight many of the affects theorized by Tomkins.

Tomkins's positivizing of affect into eight or maybe nine affects (there is a debate as to which ones he kept and which he excluded) might seem overly restrictive. Yet his conception of affect itself, by accepting its overlap with emotions and daring to give it a certain fixity, provides a better account of the persistence and being of affect than Deleuze and Guattari's emphasis on its becoming. In *Noir Affect*, while maintaining the partial difference between affect and emotion, we do not want to mark this separation in such a complete manner. For us, affect encompasses emotional states, various forms of individual and collective feeling, and embodied disposition that may or may not be experienced as either conscious or immediately fixed. We draw on Tomkins's account of specific affects even as we also see them as collectively transmissible as Teresa Brennan has theorized them. Thus, affects are not only tied to specific positive and negative emotions as Tomkins theorizes but also can form positive and negative social moods and dispositions. Moreover, as Brennan argues, some populations can be the bearer of negative affects. As she suggests, women in a male-dominated society will often be the bearer (both as target and caregiver) of all sorts of negative affects. The same can be said for working and underclass subjects, racialized subjects, queer subjects, and all the subjects that noir places on the losing side of the social and economic calculus of everyday life.

In emphasizing the negative affects articulated by noir, our account of noir affect privileges being over becoming, since being is often tied to repetition, fixity, and a stubborn return to the same knot of the real. Of course, we also attend to becoming, including the becoming that is dissolution as well as the becoming that comes with symbolic death and potential subjective rebirth, but we want to resist the forms of positive (both in the philosophical and the affective sense) becoming that have been celebrated by much of the Spinozian and Deleuzian wing of affect theory.

The Noir Aesthetic

> A charming American criminal living abroad seems to have gotten away with murder, killing the wealthy American he has been sent to find and assuming his identity. He has killed the man out a sea and thrown his body overboard. Just when he feels like his impunity is certain, the boat is taken out of the water for its regular cleaning and the body of the wealthy American is found to be still attached by an anchor chain to the boat.
>
> RENÉ CLEMÉNT, Plein Soleil

Finally, by emphasizing noir affect, we are making a claim not only about the affects dramatized by noir but also about the mood or tone of noir itself as an aesthetic. Sianne Ngai, in her groundbreaking book on negative affects, *Ugly Feelings*, links the negative affects theorized by Tomkins to literary and filmic tone and thus constructs an account of the affective dimensions of the aesthetic object. A similar concept to Ngai's understanding of tone has been present in accounts of film noir from Nino Frank's work forward: the concept of *veçu*. Drawing on Frank's seminal work, Dimendberg theorizes *veçu* as structures of emotional experience that manifest in characters, setting, and the formal language of the camera itself. Like tone, then, it is an aesthetic instantiation of affect, one specific to noir. Consequently, the essays to follow will situate noir not only as a set of stylistic or narrative tropes but also as an affective tone or *veçu*. This tone can be found in disparate objects, from film, fiction, shows, and games that are central to the noir canon to various hybrid texts and objects that draw upon noir while not being fully reducible to it.

Such moments of tone become sites in which the negative affects Ngai theorizes manifest themselves on a formal level in the text. However, central to Ngai's discussion is her emphasis on moments of novelistic reflexivity, in which the affective mirroring produced by a text is broken and the noise of the text's heterogeneity forces the reader or viewer out of an imaginary identification with its contents. Her account of tone, for all of its force in theorizing affect as a material dimension of the aesthetic object, is thus finally associated with the Frankfurt School's account of aura and situated in terms of distance. We want to suggest that the aesthetics of noir, at their most radical, work to produce the opposite of distance and auratic contemplation. Instead, the aesthetics of noir are about proximity;

they are about the anxiety produced by being too close to truths, anxieties, and ugly affects from which we would rather turn away. Thus, our understanding of the noir aesthetic is Lacanian in a fundamental way. Noir, at its most radical and disturbing, is about a proximity to the real—to the truth that would undo our symbolic fictions about the world and ourselves. It is an aesthetic of discomfort, proximity, and anxiety, not one of distanced contemplation. This uncomfortable proximity is at the heart of how we conceptualize the noir aesthetic.

Reading Noir

> A psychopathic, yet charming man gladly murders the estranged wife of an architect as part of a bargain to exchange murders. The man clearly takes pleasure in the murder, yet as he leaves the scene, he makes sure to help an old man, whom he feels bad for, cross the street.
> PATRICIA HIGHSMITH, *Strangers on a Train*[39]

Of course, such an aesthetic is a matter of reading as much as something that inheres in specific objects. Certainly, there has to be the possibility of such uncomfortable proximities in the text. Yet, as psychoanalysis teaches us, subjects are bound up with their objects, and separating projections and identifications, incorporations and excorporations, is difficult at best. Instead it is the transferential relationship between subject and object to which it is important to attend. While we articulate a noir aesthetic that is in part about the noir object itself, it is also a reading strategy. We look at the noir affects of a range of different texts, some more canonical to the noir tradition and some less so. Some of the essays in the collection examine texts that are either not considered conventionally noir or are generically and stylistically hybrid. Yet the essayists read the noir elements of the text, attending to the affects produced by the work of transference and countertransference that happens between reader and text, subject and object. The reading strategy practiced by the contributors to *Noir Affect* is willfully transferential. We read our objects in relationship to the affects they produce and transmit, to the uncomfortable proximities they enact, and to the political work around reading, subjectivity, affect, and economics that they enable.

In chapter 1, Justus Nieland presents a genealogy of noir affect as it emerges alongside of and against midcentury humanism and the transformation of work from Fordism to the postwar logic of cybernetics. Tracing a filmic trajectory from Billy Wilder's *Double Indemnity* to Jean-Luc Godard's *Alphaville*, Nieland also charts the changing fate of noir affect, which goes from a negation of midcentury Fordist humanism to becoming incorporated (and thus potentially defanged) in the global and cybernetic focus of the postwar moment. Nieland thus warns us early on about the complicated political effects of noir affect. It is rarely univocal or unambiguous in its political resonances.

In chapter 2, Christopher Breu argues that Chester Himes's midcentury noir, *The End of a Primitive*, explores the forms of private violence produced by the repressive public sphere of the "short 1950s."[40] Like many of Himes's narratives, the novel foregrounds interpersonal antagonisms around race and sex, emphasizing the way in which what is repressed in the public sphere (interracial political struggle but also interracial sex) returns with a vengeance in the private sphere. In attending to the novel's dramatization of noir affects, the essay also articulates the value of the negative political and historiographical vision advanced by Himes's noir narrative.

In chapter 3, Kirin Wachter-Grene discusses Iceberg Slim's significance as a writer of black kink. Typically read as misogynistic, Slim's *Pimp* also interrogates its scenes of violent sex, revisiting the master/slave dynamic.[41] Wachter-Grene interprets these scenes as representing an eroticized power exchange, a noir trademark, which illuminates the relationship between pleasure and subjection or abjection. She thus reads the novel through a BDSM theory framework. For *Pimp's* protagonists, power—its attainment and retention—is privileged above all else. After considering the protagonist, Wachter-Grene focuses on the novel's female characters to argue that they have considerable power to render Slim not only subordinate but also abject. By embracing their own abjection as sites of pleasure and agency, the female characters are often able to dominate Slim because he underestimates the extent of their kinkiness and that of his own.

Elizabeth Hatmaker continues the engagement with sadism and masochism as key noir affects in chapter 4. Hatmaker draws on a range of different noir novels and films as well as Jacques Lacan's conception of the four discourses, and Gilles Deleuze's and Jean Laplanche's differing accounts of sadism and masochism to theorize power and transference in the contemporary classroom. The chapter begins with the problem of the student who, in various ways, colludes with their own failure. As she demonstrates, such a narrative of failure is classically noir. She examines this dynamic as it plays out in the unequally structured classroom. Hatmaker goes on to theorize different versions of noir affect in the classroom, including students who embody the sadistic masculine position (the detective or dick), the sadistic hysteric position (the femme fatale), and the masochistic feminine position (the corpse). The chapter concludes by pointing toward a collective praxis of working through trauma that can move the classroom out of the shadow of noir and transform it into a more affirmative and just environment.

In chapter 5, Sean Grattan presents an affirmative response to the dark affective alleyways explored by Breu, Wachter-Grene, and Hatmaker. Grattan reads the queer pulps of Ann Bannon in relationship to noir affect and the temporality and spatiality of Vivian Sobchack's lounge time. Positing a "gay lounge time" Grattan makes the crucial argument that negative affects cannot fully encompass the queer community building that is central to midcentury gay life and gay pulps. Even in relationship to the negativity that often frames the midcentury gay pulp narrative, it is important to theorize the crucial positivity that is central to the construction of queer counterpublics. Such counterpublics, in turn, function to negate the oppressive positivities of heteronormative postwar culture.

In chapter 6, Ignacio M. Sánchez Prado reframes noir from the semiperipheral space of Mexican cinema. Sánchez Prado studies noir in Mexican cinema and literature in the context of the history of postrevolutionary representations of nationhood, American-style modernization, and incipient neoliberalism. Drawing on readings of a range of films, Sánchez Prado charts the historical arc of Mexican noir as a cultural form that captures the affective registers of Mexican capitalist modernity on three levels: first, fear and loss in relation to the tension between capitalism and tradition in postrevolutionary Mexico; second, a globalization of affective registers as noir connects Mexican to transnational circuits of affect and emotion; third, the creation of an affective polity through the deployment of sentimentalism and melodrama as part of the emergent mediatization and commodification of the masses' affects in new urban settings.

In chapter 7, Peter Hitchcock also moves the book's focus into an international register. Hitchcock explores noir affect in *Ghost in a Shell*, a quarter-century-old, Japanese manga/anime franchise that spans several series in print, feature films, and television. Whatever the media, the different versions of the narrative conform to standard expectations of adolescent heterosexual masculinism. Yet such elements seem to form the series' mystical shell rather than the conflicted and contradictory rationality of their central kernel (which itself springs from the serial logic of the noir police procedural). On the one hand, Hitchcock argues that representational aesthetics necessarily constrain even the radical and free association of an anime subculture; on the other hand, the series critically engages the forms of time articulated in the intersection of cyborg signification and seriality. Cyborg affect does not just ask the familiar question,

Introduction

where does a body end? It also interrogates the terms of technological reproducibility in relationship to political possibility. The synchrony of Major Motoko Kusanagi (the central character/cyborg) holds important lessons for how we read/see affect in relationship to the series, which itself might hold revolutionary potential.

Brian Rejack takes us from Japanese anime into the rough and tumble world of the noir video game in chapter 8. Rejack takes up a family of noir affects—the anxiety, mourning, and anger associated with the decline of the public sector and the rise of globalization and neoliberalism—and examines how they operate in a form relatively understudied by scholars of affect and of noir: the noir video game. Focusing on the Max Payne trilogy, Rejack charts an escape from the socially destructive elements of negative affect that are both thematized and enacted by games. Gaming, despite its purported emphasis on play and the joy, is often rife with what Ngai calls ugly feelings. The embodied act of playing video games offers a related but additional predicament: obstructed agency with respect to the medium. All too often in games, the transmission of affect occurs through negative registers of feeling. The primary activity of most video games is, after all, shooting guns at a horde of virtual enemies. But there are also the player's affective responses to the game's limitations, challenges, glitches, and interface. Rejack finally turns to the popular practice of "modding" games to indicate the way in which users can literally modify the ideological limitations of the game itself.

In chapter 9, Pamela Thoma explores a surprising shift that has occurred in postfeminist popular culture and more specifically "chick culture" in the wake of the global economic crisis. Chick noir forms itself in opposition to those two standbys of twenty-first-century US culture, chick lit, and the chick flick. If these latter genres perform a humorous remodeling of romance as the "happy object" around which young women should orient self-making or self-improvement projects for the promise of a good life and future feelings of happiness, chick noir has emerged across popular culture—in print fiction, film, and television—to chronicle widespread economic hardship and social decline under neoliberalism. Chick noir narratives are driven by negative affect, and deal in the dark side of relationships, domesticity, and the public sphere for women. Thoma focuses on *Gone Girl*, both the novel by Gillian Flynn and the film by David Fincher.[42] She pays particular attention to ways in which both texts shine a light on modern surveillance culture to explore the textual production of empathy and coercion and the ways in which these texts imagine femininity as a site of surveillance. This femininity is no longer a form of cruel optimism, as per Berlant's formulation, since it is fully consistent with the modern power of neoliberal governance. Instead, chick noir explores the failed institutions that are supposed to support contemporary femininity, while also interrogating the intense scrutiny of the female self that those same institutions have cultivated to devastating biopolitical effect. What emerges is a form of noir affect that dramatizes the absolute lack of a stable or noncontradictory space for the contemporary female subject.

In chapter 10, Alexander Dunst examines the dramatization of debt in two contemporary noir films by Danish-American director Winding Refn. A financialized obligation, debt is ceaselessly bought, sold, and securitized. At the same time, debt creates and sustains a social economy of affect that moves within and between people as it crisscrosses our planet. *Drive* and *Only God Forgives* tell stories about working-class families, drifters, and small-time crooks to explore the guilt, distrust, and despondency set in motion by a present that remains forever in debt to the past and cannot discern a future.[43] Refn's characters are no longer motivated by their supposedly private desires but by a logic that translates the human drives into financial abstraction. Incapable of repaying what he owes, *Drive*'s nameless protagonist finds that debt breeds ever more debt. This constant increase, or excess, situates Refn's characters as biopolitical relays for the monetized consumption and free production of sexuality and violence, and thus the surplus jouissance on which both capital and cinema feed. Set in Los Angeles and Bangkok at the intersection of migratory and financial flows, Refn imagines a global shadow economy of money laundering and drugs. Yet Refn's meditation on the relationship between debt and violence also ponders the possibility of forgiveness within a system determined to uphold financial measurements of social interaction.

In chapter 11, Andrew Pepper argues that contemporary Italian novelist Massimo Carlotto is, perhaps, the most successful practitioner of capitalist noir, presenting a narrative vision in which the affective environment of neoliberal capitalism is so subtly shaping and where the violence that accompanies the pursuit of self-interest is so normalized that every action and thought becomes intertwined with this same logic. Although the affective uncertainty produced by complex organizational structures allows a margin of maneuverability to be read back into Carlotto's work, his novels are empowering in an entirely different way. Carlotto's fiction sanctions and even legitimizes his characters' murderous violence as both an unstable and contradictory product of the affective environment of capitalism and a fantasized destruction of the political and economic elite, criminal or otherwise.

The collection concludes with an afterword by celebrated noir and feminist scholar Paula Rabinowitz. Rabinowitz provides a powerful reflection on both the power and limitations of noir affect as a global model for the neoliberal present, arguing that we also need to attend to noir's younger sister, melodrama. If noir affect is a mode of contemporary culture, melodramatic affect may trump it as the present's dominant mode. In a world in which right-wing strong men (starting with Donald Trump himself) are openly enjoying power and propagating sexual violence and in which respectability regularly is undone by exposed secrets, melodrama may indeed be the acting mode. For Rabinowitz, the contemporary social narrative takes the form of obscene fathers, family romances, and family secrets made public. If noir tends to be about a masculinized social world, in which the femme fatale plays by masculine rules and usually loses, melodrama has a different, potentially more feminist resonance: it articulates a feminine social world, which is structured around the revelation of violent sexual secrets existing behind the façade of respectability. Such forms of melodramatic affect shape important moments of contemporary political struggle as the #MeToo movement has demonstrated. If noir is about the canted frame and a canted affective reality, Rabinowitz cants the frame the other way, revealing the forms of affect that noir leaves unexplored.

NOTES

1. Cornell Woolrich, "I Married a Dead Man," in *Crime Novels: American Noir of the 1930 and 40s*, ed. Robert Polito (New York: Library of America, 1997), 797–973.

2. Raymond Borde and Étienne Chaumeton, *A Panorama of American Film Noir, 1941–1953*, trans. Paul Hammond (San Francisco: City Lights Books, 2002); Nino Frank, "A New Kind of Police Drama: The Criminal Adventure," in *The Film Noir Reader 2*, ed. Alan Silver and James Ursini (New York: Limelight Editions, 1999), 95–105.

3. Marc Vernet, "Film Noir on the Edge of Doom," in *Shades of Noir*, ed. Joan Copjec (London: Verso Books, 1993), 1–32.

4. James Damico, "Film Noir: A Modest Proposal," in *Film Noir: A Reader*, ed. Alain Silver and James Ursini (New York: Limelight Editions, 1996), 103.

5. See James M. Cain, *The Postman Always Rings Twice* (New York: Vintage Books, 1989); James M. Cain, *Double Indemnity* (New York: Vintage, 1989); James M. Cain, *Mildred Pierce* (New York: Vintage Books, 1989); Jim Thompson, *The Killer Inside Me* (New York: Mulholland Books, 2014); Patricia Highsmith, *The Talented Mr. Ripley* (New York: W. W. Norton, 2008); *The Postman Always Rings Twice*, directed by Tay Garnett (USA, 1946; Los Angeles: Warner Brothers, 2005), DVD; *Double Indemnity*, directed by

Billy Wilder (USA, 1944; Los Angeles Universal Home Entertainment, 2012), DVD; *Mildred Pierce*, directed by Michael Curtiz (USA, 1945; Los Angeles: Warner Brothers, 2006), DVD; *The Killer Inside Me*, directed by Michael Winterbottom (UK, 2010; Orland Park, IL: MPI Home Video, 2010), DVD; *The Talented Mr. Ripley*, directed by Anthony Minghella (UK, 1999; Los Angeles: Paramount, 2017), DVD; *Alphaville*, directed by Jean-Luc Godard (France, 1965; New York: KL Studio Classics, 2019), Blu-Ray; *I am Waiting (Ore wa matteru ze)*, directed by Koreyoshi Kurahara (Japan, 1957; Cambridge, MA: Criterion Collection, 2009), DVD.

6. See E. Ann Kaplan, "Introduction to the New Edition," in *Women in Film Noir*, rev. ed., ed. E. Ann Kaplan (London: British Film Institute, 1998), 1–15; Paula Rabinowitz, *Black, White, and Noir: America's Pulp Modernism* (New York: Columbia University Press, 2002); Frank Krutnik, *In a Lonely Street: Film Noir, Genre, Masculinity* (New York: Routledge, 1991); Robert Corber, *Homosexuality in Cold War America: Resistance and the Crisis of Masculinity* (Durham, NC: Duke University Press, 1997), 21–104; Elizabeth Cowie, "Film Noir and Women," in *Shades of Noir*, ed. Joan Copjec (London: Verso Books, 1993), 121–165; Christopher Breu, *Hard-Boiled Masculinities* (Minneapolis: University of Minnesota Press, 2005), 23–56.

7. Justus Nieland and Jennifer Fay, *Film Noir: Hard-Boiled Modernity and the Cultures of Globalization* (New York: Routledge, 2009).

8. Slavoj Žižek, *Enjoy Your Symptom: Jacques Lacan in Hollywood and Out*, rev. ed. (New York: Routledge, 2001), 149–150.

9. *Villain*, directed by Lee Sang-il (Japan, 2010; Hong Kong: CN Entertainment, 2010), Blu-Ray.

10. James Naremore, *More than Night: Film Noir in Its Contexts*, updated and expanded ed. (Berkeley: University of California Press, 2008); Andrew Spicer, *European Film Noir* (Manchester: Manchester University Press, 2007); Andrew Pepper and David Schmid, "Introduction: Globalization and the State in Contemporary Crime Fiction" in Globalization and the State in Contemporary Crime Fiction: A World of Crime, ed. Pepper and Schmid (New York: Palgrave, 2016), 1–20; Nieland and Fay, *Film Noir*.

11. Vivian Sobchack, "Lounge Time: Postwar Crises and the Chronotope of Film Noir," in *Refiguring American Film Genres*, ed. Nick Browne (Berkeley: University of California Press, 1998), 129–170.

12. Mark Augé, *Non-Places: Introduction to an Anthropology of Supermodernity*, 2nd ed., trans. John Howe (London: Verso Books, 2009).

13. Fredric Jameson, *Raymond Chandler: The Detections of Totality* (London: Verso, 2016).

14. Edward Dimendberg, *Film Noir and the Spaces of Modernity* (Cambridge, MA: Harvard University Press, 2004).

15. *Shoot the Piano Player* (*Tirez sur le pianist*), directed by François Truffaut (France, 1960; Cambridge, MA: Criterion Collection, 2005), DVD.

16. Elizabeth A. Hatmaker and Christopher Breu "The Flexible Mr. Ripley: Noir Historicism and Post-War Transnational Masculinity in Patricia Highsmith's *The Talented Mr. Ripley*," in *Post–World War II Masculinities in British and American Literature and Culture: Towards a Comparative Masculinity Studies*, ed. Stefan Horlacher and Kevin Floyd (Farnham, UK: Ashgate, 2013), 35–53.

17. Hatmaker and Breu, 36.

18. Foster Hirsh, *Detours and Lost Highways: A Map of Neo-Noir* (New York: Limelight Editions, 1999); Mark Bould, Kathrina Glitre, and Greg Tuck "Parallax Views: An Introduction," in *Neo-Noir*, ed. Bould, Glitre, and Tuck (New York: Wallflower Books, 2009), 1–10. Richard Jameson, "Son of Noir," in *Film Noir Reader 2*, ed. Alain Silver and James Ursini (New York: Limelight Editions, 1999), 197–205.

19. Natsuo Kirino, *Out* (New York: Vintage Press, 2005).

20. Our sense of the failure as beautiful is of course influenced by J. Jack Halberstam's account of failure as a queer practice. See Judith Halberstam, *The Queer Art of Failure* (Durham, NC: Duke University Press, 2011), 1–25.

21. See Sara Ahmed, *The Cultural Politics of Emotion* (New York: Routledge, 2004); Sianne Ngai, *Ugly Feelings* (Cambridge, MA: Harvard University Press, 2005); Teresa Brennan, *The Transmission of Affect* (Ithaca, NY: Cornell University Press, 2004); Lauren Berlant, *Cruel Optimism* (Durham, NC: Duke University Press, 2011); Michael Hardt and Antonio Negri, *Empire* (Cambridge, MA: Harvard University Press, 2000); Patricia Tincineto Clough, introduction to *The Affective Turn*, ed. Patricia Tincineto Clough and Jean Halley (Durham, NC: Duke University Press, 2007), 1–33; John Protevi, *Political Affect: Connecting the Social and the Somatic* (Minneapolis: University of Minnesota Press, 2009); Sylvan Tomkins, *Shame and Its Sisters: A Silvan Tomkins Reader*, ed. Eve Kosofsky Sedgwick and Adam Frank (Durham, NC: Duke University Press, 1995); Jacques Lacan, *Anxiety: The Seminar of Jacques Lacan*, Book X, trans. A. R. Price (Cambridge: Polity Press, 2016); Lawrence Grossberg, *We Gotta Get Out of This Place: Popular Conservatism and Postmodern Culture* (New York: Routledge, 1992); Kathleen Stewart, *Ordinary Affects* (Durham, NC: Duke University Press, 2007); and Brian Massumi, *Parables for the Virtual: Movement, Affect, Sensation* (Durham, NC: Duke University Press, 2002).

22. See Gilles Deleuze and Félix Guattari, *What is Philosophy?*, trans. Hugh Tomlinson and Graham Burchell (New York: Columbia University Press, 1994), 163–199; Gilles Deleuze, *Expressionism in Philosophy: Spinoza*, trans. Martin Joghin (New York: Zone Books, 1992); Félix Guattari, *The

Mechanic Unconscious: Essays in Schizoanalysis, trans. Taylor Adkins (Los Angeles: Semiotext(e), 2010), 9–22.

23. Stacy Alaimo and Susan Hekman, "Introduction: Emerging Models of Materiality in Feminist Theory," in *Material Feminisms*, ed. Alaimo and Hekman (Bloomington: University of Indiana Press, 2008), 1–19; Diana Coole and Samantha Frost, "Introducing the New Materialisms," in *New Materialisms: Ontology, Agency, and Politics*, ed. Diana Coole and Samantha Frost (Durham, NC: Duke University Press, 2010), 1–43.

24. Alaimo and Hekman, 6.

25. Lawrence Grossberg, "Affect's Future: Rediscovering the Virtual in the Actual," in *The Affect Theory Reader*, ed. Gregory J. Seigworth and Melissa Gregg (Durham, NC: Duke University Press, 2010), 315.

26. Brian Massumi, *Parables for the Virtual: Movement, Affect, Sensation* (Durham, NC: Duke University Press, 2002).

27. Jim Thompson, *The Killer Inside Me* (New York: Vintage, 1991).

28. Sigmund Freud, "Project for a Scientific Psychology," in *The Standard Edition of the Complete Psychological Works of Sigmund Freud*, trans. James Strachey (London: Hogarth Press, 1950), 1:294–346.

29. Sigmund Freud and Josef Breuer, "Studies on Hysteria," in *The Standard Edition of the Complete Psychological Works of Sigmund Freud*, trans James Strachey (London: Hogarth Press, 1950), 2:1–323.

30. Jean Laplanche, *Essays on Otherness* (New York: Routledge, 1999), 166–213.

31. Freud and Breuer, "Studies on Hysteria," 6.

32. Judith Herman, *Trauma and Recovery: The Aftermath of Violence—From Domestic Abuse to Political Terror* (New York: Basic Books, 2015); Cathy Caruth, *Unclaimed Experience: Trauma, Narrative, and History* (Baltimore, MD: Johns Hopkins University Press, 1996).

33. Žižek, *Enjoy Your Symptom*, 151.

34. Lacan, *Anxiety*, 6.

35. Lacan, 14.

36. Jacques Lacan, *The Seminar of Jacques Lacan: The Four Fundamental Concepts of Psychoanalysis*, Book XI, rev. ed., trans. Alan Sheridan (New York: W. W. Norton, 1998), 53.

37. Kelly Oliver and Benigno Trigo, *Noir Anxiety* (Minneapolis: University of Minnesota Press, 2003), 1–26.

38. Natsuo Kirino, *Grotesque*, trans. Rebecca Copeland (New York: Knopf, 2007). There are complicated debates about the translation of *Grotesque* and what has been cut from the novel. On this subject, see Øyvor Nyborg, "A Critical Analysis of Natsuo Kirino's *Grotesque*," MA thesis in East Asian Linguistics, University of Oslo, 2012, 76–89.

39. Patricia Highsmith, *Strangers on a Train* (New York: W.W. Norton, 2001).

40. Chester Himes, *The End of a Primitive* (New York: W. W. Norton, 1997).

41. Iceberg Slim, *Pimp: The Story of My Life* (New York: Simon and Schuster, 1987).

42. Gillian Flynn, *Gone Girl* (New York: Random House, 2012); *Gone Girl*, directed by David Fincher (2014; Los Angeles: Twentieth Century Fox, 2015), DVD.

43. *Drive*, directed by Nicolas Winding Refn (2011; Los Angeles: Sony Pictures Entertainment, 2012), DVD; *Only God Forgives*, directed by Nicolas Winding Refn (2013; Los Angeles: Sony Pictures Entertainment, 2013), DVD.

CHAPTER I

Toward *Alphaville*: Noir, Midcentury Communication, and the Management of Affect

Justus Nieland

In May 1968, the American conceptual artist Mel Bochner published a four-page artwork titled "Alfaville, Godard's Apocalypse" in *Arts Magazine* (fig. 1). At once a compressed movie review of the director's noir/science-fiction hybrid *Alphaville* (1965) and a collection of quotations aping Jean-Luc Godard's own citational style, the piece takes the form of a typographic grid. Bochner's rationalized design nods to the ruthlessly technocratic world of *Alphaville*, governed by the omniscient computer Alpha 60, even as its layout scrambles the functionalist protocols of the medium (the magazine page) through which it communicates. Like Robert Smithson and Dan Graham, Bochner's work in the 1960s shared a preoccupation with discursivity and sought to intervene in the mediated scenes of information's distribution and display, folding strategies of dissemination into the production of the artwork itself. In adopting an aesthetic of information, 1960s conceptual art such as Bochner's assumed what Sianne Ngai calls the "look of capitalist modernity itself"—not just the look of thought, but of bureaucracy, of "post-Fordist knowledge work."[1] The Godard of *Alphaville* was up to something similar.

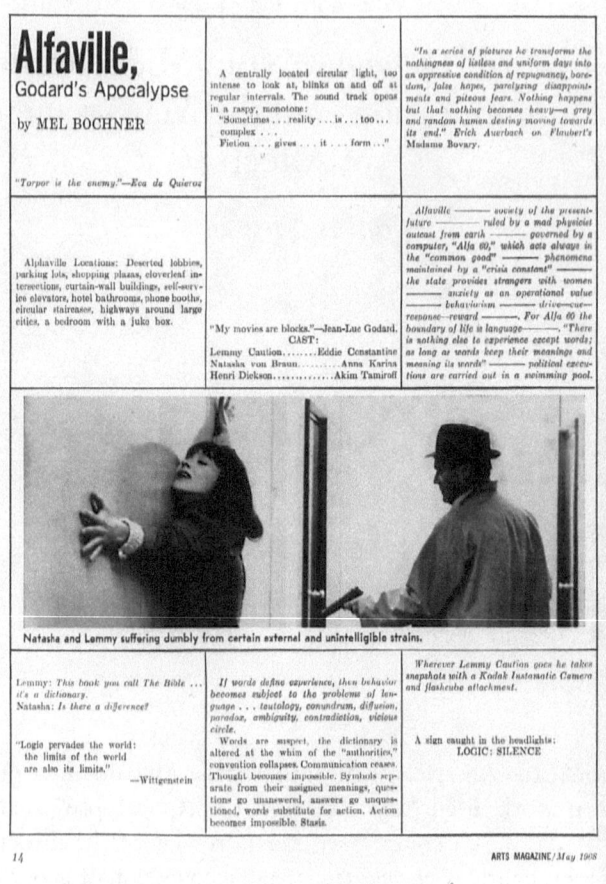

Figure 1. Bochner's "Alfaville: Godard's Apocalypse."

In the United States, the rise of new communications technologies in the postwar "informating" society was accompanied by a neutral, low-affect disposition that Alan Liu has dubbed "cool."[2] In "Alfaville" Bochner argues that the emotions of Godard's noir hero, Lemmy Caution, betray something similar, "nothing more than a slightly roused boredom."[3] For this reason, Bochner continues, Lemmy's "avowal of humanist values such as love and personal feeling are all the more disproportionate."[4] Bochner's own dispassionate, late-modernist grid is the appropriate technique for communicating that kind of permeant postindustrial boredom, which saturates the modern mise-en-scène of Godard's

New Wave noir: "Alphaville locations: deserted lobbies, parking lots, shopping plazas, cloverleaf intersections, curtain-wall buildings, self-service elevators, hotel bathrooms, phone booths, circular staircases, highways around large cities, a bedroom with a jukebox."[5] Bochner identifies here precisely the kind of serial and anonymous spatiality characteristic of what Ed Dimendberg calls the decentralized, "centrifugal spaces" of the film noir in late modernity and their dispersed communication networks.[6]

With "Alfaville," Bochner locates noir affect within the technical ambitions and scenes of postwar communications media and inside the strategies of critique, display, or *détournement* of its avant-garde practitioners, from Brecht to Burroughs (fig. 2). Liu has dubbed such subcultural mimicry of the look of technological rationality as "technostyle," briefly suggesting how film noir's familiar ethos of deadpan cool was itself a similar affective "displacement, circumvention, or 'work-around' for a life dominated by the culture of work."[7] In doing so, Liu urges us to consider noir affect as an episode in a more ambitious program of feeling's bureaucratic management by midcentury technique and technology, en route to the affective protocols of the contemporary moment, when "all culture is increasingly the culture of information."[8]

In fact, beginning in the postwar period, noir affect—as a problem for management—was often inseparable from the information agendas of various organizations and embedded in period-specific understandings of communication and its media technologies. Dimendberg has observed the increasing presence of mass media in noir after 1949, noting the publication that year of Claude Shannon and Warren Weaver's *The Mathematical Theory of Communication* and the construction of an early computer at the University of Illinois—both harbingers of the information age that would help to transform noir spatiality.[9] I will argue that noir affect's relationship to the managerial imperatives of midcentury communications theories and practices began even earlier, alongside wartime studies of propaganda (a term long synonymous with "information"), and then accrued heightened scrutiny as a therapeutic idiom of communication flourished following the war. In the process, noir affect became bound to what Mark Greif has dubbed the midcentury's "crisis of man" discourse. This pervasive and anxious humanism arose in the historical shadow of fascism and totalitarianism and viewed the human being as beset by various forms of technics, from the machine to proliferating strategies of "what we might call '*social* technique,' organization, or simply government."[10] As a technical problem for organizations, and requiring expert management,

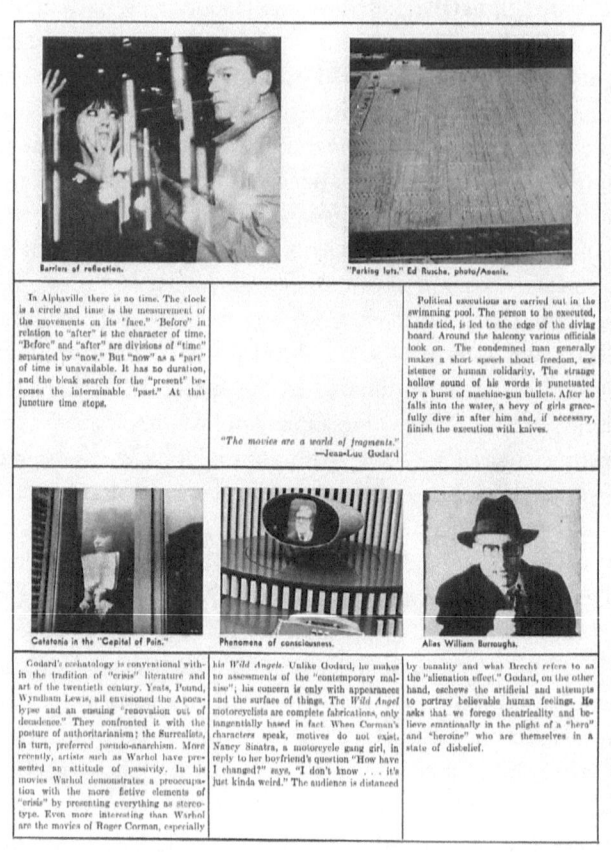

Figure 2. Détournement in Bochner's "Alfaville."

noir affect thus intersected fitfully with what Greif identifies as various "subtopics" underwriting "crisis of man" debates: "totalitarianism, existentialism, world war, and Cold War propaganda ... human rights, and the United Nations."[11] Moving toward *Alphaville* as a late, French entry in the "crisis of man" discourse, this essay turns to the chronically maladjusted and negative terrain of noir affect to offer a brief history of the genre's relationship with the organizational and managerial operations of the administered society that, for Godard, Bochner, and others seemed to force humanism to a terminal crisis by the late 1960s.

Noir Communication

Film noir's most famous memo, in Billy Wilder's *Double Indemnity* (1944), is an early instance of the bureaucratization of noir affect and its organization within the managerial paradigms of midcentury communication (fig. 3). Walter Neff's (Fred MacMurray) interoffice confession to his friend and coworker Barton Keyes (Edward G. Robinson) is a now-iconic example of noir's tendency to subjectivize narration through voiceover and flashbacks, amplifying generic affects of anxiety, unease, and disorientation. But Walter's affect here seems rather cool—cooled not just by its hard-boiled tone of cynical retrospection but also its technological mediation. It is spoken into a Dictaphone and takes the form of an office memorandum, what John Guillory calls bureaucratic modernity's "quintessential information genre."[12] The memorandum "gives directions, makes recommendations, but above all, it is means of transmitting information within the large bureaucratic structures organizing virtually all work in modernity."[13] The film opens by framing the affects most proper to Walter—his sincere feelings—within a communicative, organizational circuit. The scene of confession blurs with the scene of administration.

Figure 3. Walter Neff's interoffice confession in *Double Indemnity*.

Much like Keyes's "little man," a kind of tireless emotional laborer deep inside, alerting him to phony insurance claims and protecting the corporate bottom line, Neff's memo is a symptom of *Double Indemnity*'s investment in the modern management of feeling as both a technical and ideological matter within those bureaucratically managed systems constitutive of modernity, from insurance agencies to nation-states. As figures of the professional-managerial class, Keyes and Neff betray an emotional coldness typical of white-collar workers in a midcentury corporate culture that would be increasingly shaped by automation and new structures of bureaucratic control with designs on human emotion. Emotional life portrayed by middle-class workers like Keyes and Neff was, Liu claims, "all about 'management.' It was about managing the allowable range and intensity of productive affect, displacing excess affect into indirectly productive acts of consumption, and thus establishing the modern paradox of deadpan professionalism and binge leisure."[14] In Liu's account, this was a legacy of Taylorism, "the first rationalized system of *emotional* labor management," whose scientific strategies sought to remove workplace antagonism between human laborers by absorbing it "into a relationship with something one could safely hate (or mourn or love) with no practical effect at all: the technological/technical *system*."[15] In the work of Elton Mayo and others, hard Taylorist science led to softer managerial techniques for enforcing a norm of low affect in the workplace that were further refined in the 1920s and 1930s with the emergence of new fields of industrial psychology, "salesman training (e.g., Dale Carnegie), personnel counseling, employee testing, and so on," leading to the managerial revolution known as "human relations" or "human resources" that gained steam in the 1930s.[16] The goal of workplace relations rethought as human resource management was not just a Fordist affective "harmony" or alignment with technical system but what Liu calls a "resocialization of work under the name of systemic friendship" and the "identification" of managers and professionals "with the technological/technical system."[17] Walter's ambivalent feelings for Keyes, relayed via memo, are a displaced form of his feelings for a vast technical system he both hates and loves. Ironically, he can only confess them within the confines of an informational genre devoted to securing that system's internal functioning by communication that organizes. Expressing love in a memo between two paradigmatic organization men, Wilder shows us how Walter's noir affect is managed, cooled, by communication—at once bureaucratic and quasi-therapeutic—to Keyes, his "father confessor."[18]

Following Wilder, who himself played a role in the information agenda of the United States, I will consider the film noir itself as a kind of midcentury memo in the bureaucratic enterprises of the midcentury. Its affective malaise first came into visibility within the wartime and postwar prestige of "communication" as a new interdisciplinary object. According to John Durham Peters, the late 1940s became "probably the single grandest moment in the century's confrontation with communication," a postwar trend marked by two dominant discourses: "a technical one about information theory and a therapeutic one about communication as cure and disease."[19] Film noir, from the start, was embedded in this therapeutic discourse around communication, with its language of mental sickness or health, and its psychological jargon of adjustment and maladjustment. We can thus reframe the prevailing revisionist tendency of noir scholarship that understands noir as a discursive "invention" of a particular generation of French critics within the period-specific idiom of communication theorists such as political scientist Harold Laswell: Who says what to whom in what channel and to what effect? How did noir communicate as a symptom of national health or democratic character within midcentury understandings of noir's messages and channels, its senders and receivers across the globe?

The postwar influence of empirical research into the effects of mass media in the United States emerged from debates about public opinion, democratic governance, and propaganda organized in the late 1930s under the name of the Rockefeller Foundation-funded Communications Group.[20] The group's aims and key personnel also intersected, quite fitfully at times, with the Frankfurt School, then in exile in the United States: film theorist Siegfried Kracauer was employed to parse Nazi newsreels at MoMA's Film Library in 1941; and Lazarsfeld had hired Theodor Adorno to assist on his Princeton Radio Research project in 1938, Adorno's first substantial work in America.[21] An important collaboration among the academy, the state, and private foundations, the Communications Group's explorations of the problems of "mass influence," the dynamics of fascist propaganda, and the possibility of "genuinely democratic propaganda" joined humanists, critical theorists, and social scientists in "the common goal of understanding cultural and mass communication in the age of totalitarianism."[22]

Noir's negative affect was initially understood within these liberal paradigms for conceptualizing the communicative dimensions of Hollywood cinema. Fueled by studies of propaganda like Kracauer's own, those paradigms were defined by social-scientific approaches to the media increasingly common in public-opinion testing and market research, as well as theories of national character and personality influenced by the anthropology of Margaret Mead. As Richard Maltby explains, the wartime period was marked by a new merger of psychoanalysis and cultural anthropology.[23] What the quantitative, statistically oriented methods of audience research and propaganda study shared with Meadian cultural anthropology was what Maltby calls "an idea of the normal."[24] Just as Mead and her colleagues would analyze some normative "democratic" national character and "way of life," with its typical cognitive habits and perceptual skills, and by contrast to "the authoritarian personality," so too did the statistical imagination operate with notions of the norm and the average against which anomalies were charted and outliers measured. Deviance from the norm was both an actuarial phenomenon and, within psychoanalytic models, a potential pathology requiring various modes of therapeutic adjustment.

The term *adjustment* has technical ambitions and also signals a managerial approach to human feeling. For David Riesman, writing in his landmark study of the American national character in 1950, the "adjusted" individual, along with the "anomic" and the "autonomous," was one of three "universal types" in postwar America.[25] In Riesman's account, adjustment was, at base, a coercive technical process and a sign of the declining autonomy of white-collar workers, whose "other-directed" tendencies amounted to a kind of "frictionless modification synchronizing the individual with his time and place."[26] In the popular imagination, adjustment was virtually synonymous with the affect of happiness. Both had become technical matters. In *The Pursuits of Happiness* (1953), for example, Howard Mumford Jones observed the "steady transplanting of the roots of happiness" from the "world of Jefferson and Adam Smith" to "the doctor, the psychiatrist, the personnel director, and the social psychologist."[27] The practical aim of their overlapping domains of work is "to induce what is known as 'adjustment,' or a harmonious (and therefore happy) relation between the inner world of the psyche and the outer world of reality, whether the clinical problem arise out of maldevelopment, domestic tension, or the strain upon the personality of the whole social order."[28] Their common assumption, Jones asserted, was that "life in the United States appears to be a problem of insecurity," one that is best treated through techniques of happiness.[29] Two years later, one could find a chapter titled "Employee Adjustment" in organizational psychologist Henry Clay Smith's *Psychology of Industrial Behavior* (1955). Smith defines the goal of human life as "the adjustment of the world and men to each other with a maximum of effectiveness and happiness."[30] The mature personality, focused on "realistic goals rather than upon his anxieties," is "spontaneous," self-aware, organized, and oriented toward problem-solving.[31] The immature personality, by contrast, was marked by "chronic anxiety" and "low productivity," as well as his "excessive use of defense mechanisms: fantasy, aggression, fixation, repression, rationalization, and projection."[32] As Liu put it, adjustment in human-relations speak was the very "the soul of the low-affect 'mature' worker."[33] Maladjustment, on the other hand, was the soul of noir.

This point was made repeatedly of noir by liberal critics in the United States at the moment of the genre's postwar invention. In his essay "Today's Hero: A Review," for example, the American film producer (and cofounder with Orson Welles of the Mercury Theater) John Houseman characterized the current Hollywood "tough movie" as an "accurate reflection of the neurotic personality in the United States of America in the year 1947."[34] His example was Howard Hawks's *The Big Sleep* (1946). With Philip Marlowe cast as a figure of what Smith might call "the immature personality," Houseman lamented that what was "significant and repugnant" about such protagonists was "their absolute lack of moral energy, their listless, fatalistic despair."[35] Indeed, "they seem to have no sense of anything at all—except fear."[36] Lacking a "personal solution or catharsis of any kind," the film's negative affect bespoke a regressive populace that had given up on liberal problem-solving: "It almost looks as if the American people, turning from the anxiety and the shock of war, were afraid to face their personal problems and the painful situations of national life."[37] Houseman's essay appeared in *Hollywood Quarterly*, a journal invested in a "politicized, socially responsible cinema," and keenly attentive to film's communicative capacity to "influence and indoctrinate."[38] Its first issue in 1945 began by posing the question: "What part will the motion picture and radio play in the consolidation of the victory, in the creation of new patterns of world culture and understanding?"[39] And the inaugural issue's major articles were organized under five headings, including "Problems of Communication," devoted to the problem of veterans adjusting to peacetime—a problem taken up in a many films noir, including *The Blue Dahlia* (George Marshall, 1946), which Houseman produced, with Raymond Chandler as screenwriter.[40]

Similarly telling was the place of noir affect in Communications Group member Siegfried Kracauer's postwar criticism in the United States. His 1948 essay "Psychiatry for Everything and Everybody: The Present Vogue—and What Is Behind It" offers a thoughtful discussion of America's new postwar psychologism and constitutes what I've called elsewhere an exemplary kind of noir humanism.[41] Invoking Gallup's statistical cant, the essay seeks to explain "the average American's infatuation with psychological procedures," a trend most apparent in Hollywood's penchant for "mental derangements," the aimless ex-soldiers of *Crossfire* (directed by Edward Dmytryk, 1947) and *The Long Night* (Anatole Litvak, 1947), or the psychiatric "miracle workers" who minister to America's newly neurotic populace in *Spellbound* (Alfred Hitchcock, 1943) or *The Dark Mirror* (Robert Siodmak, 1946).[42] Identifying a pattern of "emotional disturbances" across American society, the Marxist Kracauer insists that "society is at the bottom of many psychological maladjustments," even though Hollywood—like American culture at large—tends to disavow environmental causes.[43] For Kracauer, this widespread turn from the social to the psychological was symptomatic of a "steady decrease in emotional security"—a widespread malaise caused by a perceived disappearance of common, once-unquestioned, American values and myths.[44] In Kracauer's model of national well-being as systemic adjustment, any nation's "network of rules, codes, mores, and patterns" allows its citizens to "discharge their latent instinctive energies and faculties," providing cathartic outlets for feeling in "socially recognized patterns for emotional exchange."[45] But in postwar America, characterized by "torturing uncertainty" about common values, and an instrumental system of industrial capitalism that perverts human desires "into means to economic ends," authentic, communal emotional life reifies in "ultra-personal subjectivity."[46]

Kracauer's essay was part of a series of companion pieces on the psychological turn of postwar Hollywood.[47] These essays, which read the plots of mass culture as psycho-allegories of the status of democratic national character, would inform his own landmark study of German cinema, *From Caligari to Hitler: A Psychological Study of the German Film* (1947), but they also contributed to a constellation of midcentury tendencies that helped to invent noir affect as a universal malady of the human condition. Kracauer saw in noir's climate of fear the seeds of indigenous fascism, and the troubled state of a democracy foundering on its failed promise of wartime universalism, so cruelly belied by the realities of race. In his "Hollywood's Terror Films" essay, Kracauer observed in films noir such as *The Lost Weekend* (Wilder, 1945), *Shadow of a Doubt*, and *The Spiral Staircase* (Siodmak, 1945) Hollywood's new penchant for films "saturated with terror," "sadism," "and psychological aberrations," which spoke to the transfer to the American scene of horrors "formerly attributed only to life under Hitler."[48] In these films' sadistic energies, Kracauer discerned roiling in American hearts an "emotional preparedness for fascism."[49] In "Those Movies with a Message," Kracauer turned his attention from the place of fear in America's potential for domestic fascism, to the broader climate of apathy evident in Hollywood's putatively progressive, "quasiliberal" films such as *Boomerang!* (Elia Kazan, 1947), *Crossfire* (Dmytryk, 1947), *Gentleman's Agreement* (Kazan, 1947), and *The Best Years of our Lives* (William Wyler, 1946)—films that "confronted the hopes of the war years with the reality of the postwar."[50] As for Houseman on the so-called "tough" protagonist, so for Kracauer these films' characters are poor excuses for fully mature human beings. While the pictures pay lip service to the "liberal gospel," they feature characters with "little confidence in reason"—"visionless" or "emasculated" characters who talk rather than act, "gripped by a paralysis of energies."[51] As in the "Psychiatry for Everything and Everybody" essay, here too Kracauer stresses the threat of suspended feelings, of inner life sundered from its proper outlets in the terrain of shared human values, beliefs, and ideologies, and readying itself for propaganda, demagoguery, and violence.

UN Noir

These newly diagnosed noir affects circulated around the globe, and on some of the more geopolitically overdetermined scenes of international communication in the early postwar and nascent Cold War. As Kracauer saw it, noir's negativity signaled on the psychological level the illiberal emotional maladies of populations within a nascent postwar world order still ripe for fascism. Diagnostically upscaled from individuals to nations, maladjustment signaled a kind of systemic social disequilibrium of real concern to postwar liberals, and in need of management and new techniques of governance essential to what Lee Grieveson calls the "orchestration of the security of the global liberal system."[52] Global communication—increasingly understood as the therapeutic exchange of information between populations and nation-states—would emerge as one such managerial technique, with film as one of its privileged media.

In the immediate postwar period this mission brought the corporate interests of the movie industry, eager to expand its overseas markets, into alignment with the projects of political reeducation of the US military. The latter was in the business of fashioning properly democratic citizens in the occupied zones of postwar Europe, rife with potentially illiberal noir affects and psychological tendencies.[53] Indeed, the same psychocultural approaches informing Mead's study of "democratic character structure," or Kracauer's analysis of the symptomology of the "terror films," were used by US occupation forces to understand how film might be used as a medium for reshaping the new German citizen.[54]

On this score, let's read another memo, now from Billy Wilder himself. Dated August 16, 1945, its subject was "Propaganda through Entertainment." It was written during Wilder's stint that summer in the Office of the Military Government of the United States where the director had been invited by the Office of War Information to make recommendations regarding the reorganization of the Germany film and theater industry in Berlin. There, working for the Psychological Warfare Division, Wilder edited Hanus Burger's concentration camp documentary *Death Mills* (*Die Todesmühlen*), and supervised test screenings with the German public in Hamburg to advise on the film's efficacy of as tool of denazification. Wilder's memo explained his desire to move beyond the ideological techniques of documentary and newsreels, and to produce at Paramount an entertainment film "cleverly devised to help us sell a few ideological items."[55] The plan, Wilder explained, was inspired by the success of MGM's *Mrs. Miniver* (Wyler, 1942), and the prevailing noir affect of postwar Berlin: "I found the town mad, depraved, starving, fascinating as a background for a movie."[56] Rather than make the GI "a flag waving hero or theorizing apostle of democracy," the film would be an exercise in psychological complexity, with a protagonist "not to be too sure of what the hell this war is all about."[57] It would "touch on fraternization, on homesickness, on [the] black market"; there would "be no pompous messages."[58] It would have "just the right texture to say things without preaching."[59]

An artifact of Wilder's position within the US military bureaucracy, the memo offered a germinal scenario for the dark satire Wilder would set and shoot in a berubbled Berlin, *A Foreign Affair* (1948). Its protagonist is a US denazification officer, Captain John Pringle (John Lund) embroiled in an affair with Nazi singer Erika von Schluetow (Marlene Dietrich), who is harboring a war criminal. Pringle eventually leaves the alluring Erika for the officious Iowa congresswoman Phoebe Frost (Jean Arthur), who had journeyed into occupied Berlin to investigate the decadent morale of US occupation forces. In Wilder's hands, the film's cynical depiction of a democratic culture of occupation, and its subtle exploration of the appeal, for Lund, of Erika's authoritarian and sadomasochistic sympathies, reads as a highly ambivalent communication, succeeding more as skilled entertainment than propaganda. This confused messaging was typical of many of the US films noir that arrived in occupied Germany and Japan on the heels of the occupying forces. Robert Siodmak's *Spiral Staircase* (1946), circulating in occupied Germany with other noirs such as *Gaslight* (George Cukor, 1944), *Suspicion* (Hitchcock, 1941), and *Call Northside 777* (Henry Hathaway, 1948), was singled out by German critics for a moral ambiguity that worked against the goals of political reeducation, and testified to the ethical banality of US mass culture: "Whoever as a victor of war waged in the name of ethical principles, assumes the responsibility of reeducating and spiritually reshaping Germany, should be able to recognize that murder films are not exactly an appropriate instrument to eradicate fascistic conventions."[60] *The Maltese Falcon* was pulled from exhibition because censors feared "it would be read by the German public as a glorification of the criminal war and a critique of the American police."[61] In such instances, noir's communicative ambiguity was perceived as an obstacle to the liberal-democratic state's information agenda—its media project of winning hearts and minds.

That agenda would be advanced by the United Nations, a vast international bureaucracy whose charter was drafted the same summer Wilder was in Berlin. An attempt to replace the League of Nations' failed role in securing liberal order, the United Nations was the "practical realization" of the dreams of world government that flourished among intellectuals in the immediate postwar period, confronted by the devastating reality of the bomb and the camps.[62] Mark Greif has helpfully framed the United Nations as "a major *public* solution" to the crisis of man discourse in which noir affect was embedded in the 1940s and the organization's educational arm, UNESCO, as the "'official' avenue" for disseminating worldwide a philosophical view of human nature that was "antiracial and universalist."[63] Rebooting the utopian dreams of interwar international cosmopolitanism represented by the League of Nations, these intertwined bureaucracies embarked upon the formal enshrinement of universal human rights. And yet, as the Cold War deepened, these aspirations "were mostly cast aside to support the circulation of commercial American mass media that was integral to economic globalization and the spread of U.S. 'soft power' through the world system."[64] In the process, UNESCO enshrined a "free flow of information" doctrine: its way of linking a New World Economic Order to a New World Information Order. Through this doctrine, the United Nations enshrined freedom of information—across cultural and national boundaries—as "a fundamental human right," and "a touchstone of all the freedoms to which the United Nations is consecrated."[65] And yet as ideology, it was an essential weapon in the growth of American corporate power and the imperial ascendency of the United States in the American Century, allowing its corporations coveted monopolies of communications infrastructure and unfettered access to new global markets, opening the floodgates of American media products, and swelling a new wave of cultural imperialism.

As the United Nations emerged as the liberal order's primary guarantor of global security, the utopian modernist architecture of its New York City headquarters, an iconic symbol of the new managerial structures of midcentury geopolitics, found its way into several noir plots. French master of the *policier* Jean-Pierre Melville, for example, opened his noir *Deux Hommes dans Manhattan/Two Men in Manhattan* (1959) with several shots of the UN Secretariat, designed by Le Corbusier and Brazilian modernist Oscar Niemeyer and completed in 1952. Melville pans the Manhattan skyline to find the Secretariat's curtain wall, tilting down to frame it towering against a 1912 gaslight, one "forgotten by urban planners," according to the narration. Beneath this light play three children of Italian, Irish, and Jewish descent—a trio, Melville's narration continues, that "neatly symbolized the great glass building on First Avenue known as the United Nations."[66] The next shots take us inside the General Assembly, whose seemingly routine business is punctuated by the disappearance of the French delegate Fèvre-Berthier. Over the course of the film, two media professionals—a press agent for Agence France (Melville himself) and a photographer for *Paris Match*—will search for the diplomat, an investigation that takes them through the nocturnal city, lovingly romanticized by Melville's location shooting. The film's real topic, Dimendberg observes, is "a future-oriented world city of global exchange and information production," a centrifugal, informatic city incarnated by the United Nations and confirmed in the flurry of communications and communications media that document the diplomat's vanishing.[67] In the end, it is the new, glossy mass media of *Paris Match* (and *Time, Life,* and *Look*) that threaten to incriminate the vanished diplomat, who we learn has died in his mistress's apartment. The film's central moral question is whether the photographer, a cynical alcoholic, will sell the salacious images of the dead diplomat or preserve the honor of this former member of the Resistance. Melville thus extends the opening contrast between the old and new city staged outside the UN Secretariat to the ethical question about capitalizing on information in a climate of voracious global media outlets. The press-savvy duo's final silence—their refusal to circulate information—is a way of staying faithful to the seemingly outmoded values of the Resistance in the new corporate order predicated on communication and exchange.

As the sign of what Reinhold Martin calls the new "physiognomy of the office," the curtain wall also opens Alfred Hitchcock's thriller *North by Northwest* (1959).⁶⁸ Its title sequence, designed by Saul Bass, smartly anticipates the paranoid espionage plot in which Cary Grant's Roger O. Thornhill, the archetypal organization man, will shortly find himself. Bass's abstract grid, emerging as dynamic lines cross in a void, dissolves into the glass curtain wall of a Madison Avenue office tower, reflecting the flow of traffic and bodies. Thornhill is himself an abstraction, whose mistaken identity (as spy George Kaplan) will be plotted and manipulated over the course of the film by the CIA's bureaucratic network. As the site of identity's fashioning, Bass's modernist grid is itself an organizational image allowing the designer to consolidate the brand "Hitchcock" both here and in his other title sequences for the director's independent productions at Paramount: *Vertigo* (1958) and *Psycho* (1960).⁶⁹ Bass's grid thus uses the architecture of the curtain wall to join various figures of midcentury organization—the Hollywood auteur, the corporation, government bureaucracy, and the United Nations itself, through the façade of the Secretariat building. In Hitchcock's hands, the UN architecture plays as the cool scene of bureaucratic control against which noir chaos erupts, setting into motion the wrong-man plot and fueling Thornhill's paranoia as its bewildered victim. Bass's own graphic idiom was shaped by the Hungarian modernist designer György Kepes, whose Gestaltist laws of perceptual organization were directly linked to proto-cybernetic models of social equilibrium and homeostasis.⁷⁰ Bass's curtain-wall title design, in other words, inserted UN architecture, and noir affect, directly into the workings of what Martin calls the postwar "organizational complex" joining the managerial agendas of architecture, media, and corporate space that, of course, extended to postwar Hollywood itself.

As Hollywood historians have argued, the early postwar era marked an important convergence of managerial priorities: the economic interests of the corporate film industry and the political interests of the state. Here, too, noir affect posed a challenge for management. Following the resignation of Motion Picture Association of America (MPAA) chairman Will Hays in 1945, his successor Eric Johnston established the Motion Picture Export Association, a trade organization that helped open global markets to Hollywood products by merging with the overseas branch of the Office of War Information (OWI). Described as "Capitalism's Pin-Up Boy" by the *New York Times,* Johnston came to support the House Un-American Activities Committee (HUAC) and the Hollywood blacklist to follow, and counseled studios to avoid making politically critical films: "We'll have no more *Grapes of Wrath*, we'll have no more *Tobacco Roads*. We'll have no more films that show the seamy side of American life."[71] Similarly, Johnston's MPAA opportunistically leveraged the HUAC investigations in a canny managerial strategy to discipline a labor force then undergoing significant transformation.[72] As Grieveson has cast it, the MPAA's goal, at home and abroad, was the production of an "apolitical media system that would not challenge the prevailing political and economic orthodoxy."[73] Of course, the victims of the blacklist included many directors associated with the *film noir* (and what Thom Andersen dubbed the *film gris*). And as Jonathan Auerbach argues, the historically specific feeling of *un-Americanness*—the concern over the uncertain boundaries of national belonging—was an abiding feature of noir affect, an emotional index of what was "uncanny and uncertain" about democratic citizenship at midcentury.[74] This "maladjustment" could signal an internal alien to be abjected or a pathological abnormality to be diagnosed and cured, whether in the form or information (as political reeducation) or communication (as therapy).

The discourse uniting pervasive postwar insecurity, psychological adjustment, and illiberal affect powerfully shaped the assumptions about therapeutic communication and communications media that underlay Houseman and Kracauer's postwar noir essays and contemporaneous democratic political reeducation schemes. The same discourse provided the raison d'être for liberalism's new postwar international organizations such as the United Nations, of course; and it was lodged at the feedback-driven heart of the contemporary Macy Conferences on Cybernetics (1946–1953; 1954–1960), the famous series of interdisciplinary conferences sponsored by the Josiah Macy Jr. Foundation which were launched in 1930 to fund new methods in "psychobiological and sociological" approaches to heath care.[75] As Steve Heims has shown, a decade before Norbert Wiener and other cyberneticians began drawing analogies between human and servomechanical behavior, the Macy Foundation had endorsed concepts such as homeostasis and mental hygiene.[76] This was evident in the wide-ranging knowledge work of the Macy conferences and also in the 1948 formation of the World Federation for Mental Health (WFMH), organized by Margaret Mead and other cybernetics group regulars. In the summer of 1948, the WFMH group held a UNESCO-sponsored conference in Paris that provided a forum for various approaches to "the tensions that cause wars," as the conference proceedings were later titled. UNESCO would wed its global projects of visual education and its groundbreaking studies of national media infrastructures to the UN's foundational ideals of a peaceful postwar order marked by the free and democratic flow of information. Understanding the globe as a single psychological system, the "Tensions" group assumed, in Fred Turner's words, that "international relations between nations too could be modeled as if they were small-group interpersonal relations taking place on a global scale."[77] As an outgrowth of the "Tensions" project, Kracauer himself produced a UNESCO-commissioned study, "National Types as Hollywood Presents Them" (1949). Invoking UNESCO's aim of "international understanding," it aimed to study Hollywood's conceptions of other nations as revealed in the depiction of national characters (Russian and British) in its films, starting with the fateful year of 1933.[78] Inspired by the general "desire for enlightenment in the wake of war, industry spokesmen now advocate films that convey entertainment with information," Kracauer explained. And he quoted MPPA president Eric Johnston: "the motion picture, as an instrument for the promotion of knowledge and understanding among peoples, stands on the threshold of a tremendous era of expansion."[79]

Similarly, as the Cold War deepened, Houseman, who like Kracauer had declared noir affect a symptom of an exhausted liberalism, now found himself asking after cinema's role as medium of international understanding. His 1955 essay "How Does a Movie Communicate?," given as a talk at the International Design Conference in Aspen, Colorado, opened by claiming that the "most compelling instrument yet devised for communication between human beings is the image of man himself."[80] Overseas, Houseman explains, films "follow those laws of energy which relate to the attraction of the greater mass" and have become inevitably linked with the United States as "the world's most rapidly growing unit of political and economic power."[81] In sum, Houseman's argument about filmic communication is a somewhat ambivalent assessment of film as an instrument of ideology and cultural diplomacy. And his hope is that what is communicated is something beyond dreams of "luxury and energy," a "residue of "something more" having to do with "goodwill and with those rights of man mentioned in our Declaration of Independence."[82]

With such optimistic claims about film's communicative power in mind, I want to consider another high-water mark for international understanding, one that joined film and other media technologies with the information agendas of nation-states and the corporate imperatives of industry—the 1958 Brussels World's Fair. The American pavilion's displays were conceptualized by the US State Department and the US Information Agency (USIA), as of 1953, the government's main arm of public diplomacy and propaganda. As the first such fair since World War II, the Brussels event gathered a number of the managerial agendas I have summoned to frame the bureaucratization of noir affect in the postwar period: the lofty communicative rhetoric of postwar international organizations predicated on human rights and free flows of information; the reality of commercial mass media as a tool in liberal democracy's informational agenda; Hollywood's quest for international markets unimpeded by the affective unrest of noir; and the therapeutic, feedback-driven idiom of cybernetics.

The 1958 World Fair's mission was conceived as a response to the increasing isolation and dehumanization of human beings, and the threat of midcentury techno-science, a scenario familiar to atomic-age noir. Exhibiting nations and their pavilions were charged with showing "the methods [each] advocates for the 're-humanization' of the modern world."[83] While film played a central part in this project, at various scales and formats, two films screened at the fair will suffice to draw out the peculiar status of noir affect within and against such corporate idioms, circa 1958.[84] The first was Charles and Ray Eames's industrial film *The Information Machine: Creative Man and the Data Processor* (1957), a manifestly *non*-noir animated short sponsored by IBM, and displayed at their corporate pavilion. The second was Orson Welles's *Touch of Evil* (1958), a decadent thriller often summoned as the epitaph of the classical noir cycle. Welles's film received its European premiere, to great critical fanfare, at the Brussels film festival, held that year on the fairgrounds. Toward *Alphaville*, this unlikely pairing allows us to consider two conflicting parables of international communication and bureaucratic technique, and two strangely overlapping discourses of brand management.

The Eameses had been deeply invested in cybernetic models of communication and control as a means of guaranteeing what they called "security in change," from their early, foundational *A Communications Primer* (1953), a filmic explication of Shannon's *A Mathematical Theory of Communication* (1949), to its IBM-sponsored sequel *Introduction to Feedback* (1960). As part of industrial designer Eliot Noyes's sweeping corporate identity program at IBM in the 1950s, the Eames Office's sponsored work for the firm played an essential role in the humanization of the computer as a seemingly menacing new postwar technology. In *The Lonely Crowd*, David Riesman had observed that the newer industrial revolution "which has reached its greatest force in America," and "is concerned with techniques of communication and control, not of tooling or factory layout."[85] Such managerial techniques are "symbolized by the telephone, the servomechanism, the IBM machine, the electronic calculator, and modern statistical methods of controlling the quality of products; by the Hawthorne counseling experiment and the general preoccupation with industrial morale."[86]

In these terms, the Eameses' *Information Machine* is their most succinct paean to computation as a managerial technique, proceeding from caveman to mainframe in an animated, relentlessly teleological story of the development of the computer in a long history of human tool-making dedicated to the "mastery and control of the environment."[87] At the Fair, the Eameses' parable augured an informatic future defined by efficient, computer-assisted data processing, liberal-democratic decision-making, and a happy adjustment of man and machine in networked flows of communication worldwide.

The Eameses would shortly embark on a related, USIA-sponsored experiment in international communication—the multiscreen presentation *Glimpses of the U.S.A.* (1959), a typical "day in the life" of the United States, which debuted at the US National Exhibition in Moscow. This masterpiece of Cold War propaganda conceptualized its scene of display (a dome) as an "information machine," devoted to communicating to Russians "believable information about America and its institutions and the way its people live and work."[88] No film noir was included, of course, but the Eameses were counseled on their democratic technique by their long-time friend Billy Wilder, brought on "as critic, sounding board, kibitzer, [and] ultimate participant," and the show included a brief sequence from Wilder's *Some Like It Hot* (1959).[89] Given his background with the Psychological Warfare Division, Wilder was well-positioned to advise on this late exercise in democratic political reeducation, or what we might call a multiscreen memo to the Russian citizenry.

Against the Eameses' corporate version of cybernetic happiness and environmental control through liberal flows of communication, *Touch of Evil*'s pulpy melodrama offers a despairing and anxious vision of the authoritarian personality in the bloated figure of Welles's corrupt cop Hank Quinlan. Quinlan's plot to frame a Mexican shoe clerk for murder allows Welles to explore the enduring potential for domestic fascism that Kracauer had first diagnosed in his "Terror Films" essay. As Michael Denning has shown, Welles's "allegories of anti-fascism" began in his Popular Front work with Houseman at the Mercury Theatre in the 1930s, continued in his anatomy of the mass media and their propagandistic dimensions in the "War of the Worlds" broadcast and *Citizen Kane*'s (1941) critique of the media empires of Hearst and Luce, and informed his antifascist noir thrillers *Journey into Fear* (1943), *The Stranger* (1946), *The Lady From Shanghai* (1948), and *Touch of Evil*, as well as his famous cameo as black marketeer Harry Lime in *The Third Man* (Carol Reed, 1949).[90] Like Houseman, Welles's career had long been devoted to the question, "How does a movie communicate?," as well as to an analysis of the capacity of various communications media (radio, newspapers, newsreels) to inform masses and organize populations—to persuade, demagogue, and dominate—all while serving the many dictatorial, illiberal personae that populate his work.

Welles's familiarity with the wartime and postwar mass communications allows us to understand *Touch of Evil*'s border-town setting, and its motif of communication across borders, as a noir riposte to the World Fair's fantasies of international goodwill, opening with the car explosion at the US-Mexico border that sets the film's central murder investigation in motion. As he detailed in a fifty-eight-page memo to Universal's chief Edward Muhl, following the studio's unfortunate recut of the film, Welles initial design for the opening sequence aimed to foreground noise, confusion, and conflict at the border through a dense sound montage that cut between the radios of two cars in two languages.[91] The radio cacophony would inaugurate a pattern in which the film's anxious negative affect plays out at the border of race and sex via the melodramatic separation of the honeymooning couple Miguel "Mike" Vargas (Charlton Heston), a Mexican narcotics officer, and his white American wife Susan (Janet Leigh). That border collapses in the notorious motel sequence, when a terrorized Susan, separated from Mike and held captive by the Grandi gang, is subjected to threat of interracial rape, drugging, and more. Susan's violation, staged by Welles's—à la Griffith—in the domain of his spectators' racist fantasies, is anticipated through sound and sound technologies. Her room's wall is penetrated by menacing whispers and music, and by one of the Grandi boys' hijacking of the phone in the night manager's office to make veiled threats to Susan and keep her incommunicado. The motel switchboard has become an illiberal communications device presiding over a nightmare of botched night management. The circuit of information to the world outside is blocked, allowing for the hallucinatory affective excesses of Susan's apparent rape.

Vargas, separated from his wife, pairs up with Assistant District Attorney Al Schwartz (Mort Mills) to prove Quinlan's corruption. In this bureaucratic buddy duo of Jew and Mexican, "good neighbors" for a time, *Touch of Evil* nods to liberal dreams of international cooperation, and Welles' own work for Nelson Rockefeller's Office of Inter-American Affairs. Just as Susan is physically assaulted by the gang and her motel room door closes on the private scene of seeming sexual chaos, a match cut reveals Quinlan's adoring partner Menzies, who opens another door to a room filled floor to ceiling with filing cabinets. In the bowels of the hall of records, he finds Vargas, "a foreigner," combing through paperwork.[92] The archive, Vargas explains, is open to the public, and he confronts Menzies with the record of his complicity in Quinlan's history of planting evidence. Welles's mise-en-scène of bureaucracy and principled information retrieval, and his characteristic wide-angle, deep-focus composition underscores Vargas's liberal managerial faith in restorative justice. The scene heightens the contrast between the new corporate bureaucratic order Vargas augurs as the head of the Pan American Narcotics Commission and Quinlan's decadent individualist ethos at the heart of the film's analysis of patriarchal power. But it also sets up the film's final deployment of illiberal technology, when Vargas convinces Menzies to wear a radio-controlled receiver to record Quinlan's confession. Welles explained that he meant this ironically, to show that the liberal Vargas "becomes the crude type who deliberately eavesdrops . . . he's the victim of the apparatus."[93] Continuing the film's motif of communicative impasses, the unseen Vargas is outed by the sound of uncontrolled feedback in the device.

What Denning calls an "allegory" of the apparatus redounds to Welles himself, not just because he was the victim of studio mismanagement of the sort that demanding overlong corrective memos, but also since he himself had been the steady subject of illiberal state surveillance by the FBI. Between 1941 and 1956, the agency documented his status as a fellow traveler and potential subversive in a 189-page case file, and in 1945, Hoover listed Welles in the Security Index Card File as a communist and an "internal threat" to national security.[94] If noir's negative affect is often a symptom of un-Americanness, we can hear Vargas's claim that "a policeman's job is only easy in a police state" as an expression of Welles's own status of national nonbelonging.[95]

In the United States, where Welles had returned to in 1955 after many years in Europe, *Touch of Evil* received a mishandled release and largely negative reviews. At the Brussels World Fair, however, the film received the top prize in the international competition by the International Federation of Film Journalists, and Welles was given a separate award for best actor. Welles's arrival was feted by the press, and he was interviewed at the fair by his most influential French champion, André Bazin. In Bazin's *Cahiers du cinéma*, of course, the name and example of "Welles" played an essential role in the development of auteurism and its myths about romantic creative agency, which—much like abstract expressionism—became a way of enshrining liberal democratic values then being exported by the United States around the world. Like the French invention of noir, the name of an auteur like Welles was inextricably bound to questions of political economy, cultural imperialism, and the changing postwar reception of US "market empire" in France.[96] There, *Touch of Evil*'s negative affect enabled an important ambivalence that allowed French critics to love negativity—that is, to love "Welles" as an alienated outsider and critic of a system of monopoly capital with keen designs on European markets. Like "Hitchcock," whose late 1950s signature would be established, for example, in the title sequences of Bass, master of corporate identity, "Welles" in France was a kind of dissident brand, allowing for product differentiation in competitive markets and thus not entirely unlike transnational behemoths such as Coca-Cola or IBM.

Tarzan versus IBM: How Alphaville *Communicates*

The working title for Jean-Luc Godard's *Alphaville* (1965), "Tarzan vs. IBM," frames a similar conflict in the French reception of noir affect between liberal-humanist agency and its corporate, managerial other. A late entry in the "crisis of man" discourse shaping noir affect, Godard's dystopian vision of a programmed, totalitarian society controlled by the omniscient super-computer Alpha 60 was a period-specific encounter with the rising prestige of technocratic thought amidst France's rapid, state-sponsored modernization. The specter of IBM in France augured what Kristin Ross and Luc Boltanksi have described as the period's transition from older, patriarchal corporate bureaucracies toward "more flexible, American-inflected practices of management," with their techniques and technologies.[97] The term *technocracy* emerged in France to describe the post–World War II "reign of the experts" that was widely perceived on the left to enshrine an transdisciplinary ideology of rationality that prized consensus, eliminated social antagonism and produced a temporality devoid of eventfulness, what Ross dubs "immobile time."[98] The ideology was abetted by the current vogue for structuralism, within which "communication" itself became "something akin to an ambiance, the milieu for life in the sense that water has for fish."[99] Ross continues: "An ideology 'without enemies,' an alternative to political ideologies, 'communication' announced the installation, thanks to technology, of a kind of neutral consensual norm in social relations." Or, as Alpha 60 puts it: "The essence of the so-called capitalist world, or the communist world, is not an evil volition to subject their people by the power of indoctrination or the power of finance, but simply the natural ambition of any organization to plan all of its actions."[100]

Through *Alphaville*'s protagonist, Lemmy Caution, played by the American actor and French film icon Eddie Constantine, Godard reframes Tarzan as a noir tough, whose range of affective values are positioned to do battle with Alpha 60's technological rationality. In Lemmy Caution's successful quest to destroy the computer and free Natacha Von Braun (Anna Karina) and the enslaved citizens of Alphaville from a world devoid of love and poetry, Godard offers a humanist critique of technology that echoes contemporaneous works from Jacques Ellul's *The Technological Society* (1954) to Herbert Marcuse's *One-Dimensional Man* (1964). Lemmy Caution is a paradigmatically maladjusted figure—not just behavioristically unaccountable, but temporally out of synch. As a relic of another time, and an earlier moment in noir history, he is a figure of what Ernst Bloch might call the "non-synchronous." This is what it means for him to function as a "legend," as he is introduced, entering the core of Alphaville in his white Ford Galaxy, a figure of the historical outside to the city's temporal present. Paris's urban center was then in the throes of an unprecedented transformation, its texture razed in massive urban planning schemes, as the space of the city was itself reconceptualized according to cybernetic models for regulating flows of communication and circulation. As architectural historian Larry Busbea has shown, space itself came to be understood as a "conducive medium for the movements and exchanges of people, information, and objects."[101]

As Lemmy circulates through the quasi-cybernetic city of the future, through the Institute of General Semantics, where Alpha 60 gives multimedia lessons in semiotics, or inside the bowels of the computer's control center, Godard repeatedly positions him in overtly communicative scenarios or encounters that allow him to limn a kind of antagonism hostile to the rational linguistic protocols of the technocratic order. Interrogated by one of the computer's "1.4 billion nerve centers," he is subjected to a series of questions as a security measure: What do you love? Gold and women. Do you know what illuminates the night? Poetry. What is your religion? I believe in the inspirations of conscience.[102] His replies, what Alpha 60 calls "difficult and impossible to classify," will later be deemed a threat.

Alphaville is not just a romantic or humanist film documenting the society of the spectacle in a late-noir idiom but a key enunciation of a noir modernism of noncommunication much like Marcuse's own. "Contradiction," Marcuse insisted in *One-Dimensional Man*, "must have a medium of communication."[103] In a not-so-distant past, it had found it in Brechtian modernism, what he called "literature's own answer to the threat of total behaviorism."[104] Lemmy is Godard's filmic response to a similar threat, and of course his affects are given Brechtian treatment—at once authenticated and cooled down in citation, whether of Raymond Chandler or of surrealist poet Paul Éluard. Caution recovers the latter's 1926 collection *Capitale de la douleur* (*Capital of Pain*) from a fellow secret agent who, in dying, instructs Lemmy to force Alpha 60 to self-destruct, and "save those who weep."¹⁰⁵ Through Lemmy and Natacha's shared recitation of Éluard as a means of Natacha's lyrical awakening, Godard—like Marcuse—limns a modernism of communicative intransigence, linguistic difficulty, and utopian unhappiness. As Kaja Silverman argues, this is a scene of therapeutic communication, but its methods depart from Freud, for whom "poetry is the illness, and rationalized speech is the cure. For Godard, on the other hand, therapeutic speech produces affect."¹⁰⁶ In the domain of language, we might say, "Tarzan vs. IBM" is recast as "Surrealism vs. General Semantics."

At the same time, *Alphaville*'s historical insight is that these oppositions—between bureaucracy and poetry, or computation and aesthetics—are no longer tenable, and their clear separation, in life or art, are an outmoded romantic fiction in an age of information. "Man," Bochner observed in "Alfaville," "has already been displaced from the center of the universe."¹⁰⁷ As an index of midcentury "crisis of man" discourse, noir affect had been bureaucratically managed for some time. Godard knows this. While Boch-

Figure 4. Conspicuously sculptural television screens in *Alphaville*.

ner may have found Godard's "sociology exceedingly romanticized"—the film ends with Lemmy's short-circuiting of Alpha 60 and the couple's poetic escape from the city—*Alphaville*'s own aesthetics everywhere betray the historical saturation of what I call, following Eve Meltzer, "the look of information" and its primary affective orientation—namely, cool.[108] We see this in the film's inclusion of graphically bold inserts of mathematical equations or symbols, or its recurring pans of the facades of curtain-walled office buildings, or Lemmy's framing alongside conspicuously sculptural television screens, or the design of the computer's Control Complex, which Godard seems to have borrowed from IBM, or in the binary blinking (on/off) of Alphaville's network of electrical lights and signs (fig. 4). The film's late-modernist mise-en-scène, a document of the Paris of the present, is Godard's own version of what Liu calls subcultural "camo-tech," "the construction of a bodily and social pose that perfectly expressed the adjustment of technique to technology."[109] If Lemmy Caution's pose seemed bored and stagnant (rather than violent and unaccountable) to Bochner in May 1968, his affect a product of technocratic modernity rather than its imagined outside, perhaps this is apt—a noir premonition of more of the same. Indeed, the rich terrain of noir affect in Godard's non-noir films about Paris under the conditions of late-capitalist modernity—works such as *2 or 3 Things I Know about Her* (1967) or, on the other side of a failed revolution, *Tout va bien* (1974)—made abundantly clear that the Capital of Pain would not be so easily destroyed. Godard's apocalypse was ongoing, and from the vantage of our corporate, administered present, it still is.

NOTES

1. Sianne Ngai, "Merely Interesting," *Critical Inquiry* 34, no. 4 (Summer 2008): 792, 793.
2. See Alan Liu, *The Laws of Cool: Knowledge Work and the Culture of Information* (Chicago: University of Chicago Press, 2004).
3. Mel Bochner, "Alfaville, Godard's Apocalypse," *Arts Magazine*, no. 42 (May 1968): 15.
4. Bochner, 15.
5. Bochner, 14.
6. Edward Dimendberg, *Film Noir and the Spaces of Modernity* (Cambridge, MA: Harvard University Press, 2004), especially chap. 4.
7. Liu, *Laws of Cool*, 102, 101.
8. Liu, 1.
9. Dimendberg, *Film Noir*, 210.

10. Mark Greif, *The Age of the Crisis of Man: Thought and Fiction in America, 1933–1973* (Princeton, NJ: Princeton University Press, 2003), 47.

11. Greif, 16.

12. John Guillory, "The Memo and Modernity," *Critical Inquiry* 32, no. 1 (Autumn 2004): 112.

13. Yates, quoted in Guillory, 112.

14. Liu, *Laws of Cool*, 88.

15. Liu, 90.

16. Liu, 96.

17. Liu, 92, 96.

18. *Double Indemnity*, directed by Billy Wilder (USA, 1944; Universal Studios, 2006), DVD.

19. John Durham Peters, *Speaking into the Air: A History of the Idea of Communication* (Chicago: University of Chicago Press, 1999), 22, 28–29.

20. Brett Gary, *The Nervous Liberals: Propaganda Anxieties from World War I to the Cold War* (New York: Columbia University Press, 1999), 85–130.

21. On Kracauer's work at MoMA, and its relationship to the Communications Group, see Peter Decherney, *Hollywood and the Culture Elite: How the Movies Became American* (New York: Columbia University Press, 2005), and Johannes von Moltke, *The Curious Humanist: Siegfried Kracauer in America* (Berkeley: University of California Press, 2016).

22. Von Moltke, 49.

23. Richard Maltby, "The Politics of the Maladjusted Text," in *The Movie Book of Film Noir*, ed. Ian Cameron (London: Studio Vista, 1994), 39–49.

24. Maltby, 44.

25. David Riesman et al., *The Lonely Crowd: A Study of the Changing American Character* (New Haven, CT: Yale University Press, 2001), 242; see especially chap. 12.

26. Scott J. Juengel, "Stars without a World," *Modernism/modernity* 26, no. 3 (September 2019): 530.

27. Howard Mumford Jones, *The Pursuit of Happiness* (Cambridge, MA: Harvard University Press, 1953), 146, 149.

28. Jones, 150.

29. Jones, 150.

30. Henry Clay Smith, *Psychology of Industrial Behavior* (New York: McGraw Hill, 1955), 136.

31. Smith, 138, 146.

32. Smith, 159.

33. Liu, *Laws of Cool*, 98.

34. John Houseman, "Today's Hero: A Review," *Hollywood Quarterly* 2, no. 2 (January 1947): 161.

35. Houseman, 163.
36. Houseman, 162.
37. Houseman, 163.
38. Eric Smoodin, introduction to *Hollywood Quarterly: Film Culture in Postwar America, 1945–1957* (Berkeley: University of California Press, 2002), xiv.
39. "Editorial Statement," *Hollywood Quarterly* 1, no. 1 (October 1945): iii.
40. "Contents," *Hollywood Quarterly* 1, no. 1 (October 1945): vi.
41. Justus Nieland, "Everybody's Noir Humanism: Chester Himes, *Lonely Crusade* and the Quality of Hurt Feelings," *African American Review* 43, nos. 2–3 (Summer/Fall 2009): 277–293.
42. Siegfried Kracauer, "Psychiatry for Everything and Everybody: The Present Vogue—and What Is Behind It," *Commentary* 5 (1948): 222–228.
43. Kracauer, 223, 222.
44. Kracauer, 223.
45. Kracauer, 225, 226.
46. Kracauer, 225, 226, 227.
47. Siegfried Kracauer, "Hollywood's Terror Films: Do They Reflect an American State of Mind?," first published in *Commentary* 2 (1948): 132–136, reprinted in *New German Critique* 89 (Spring–Summer 2003); Siegfried Kracauer, "Those Movies with a Message," *Harper's Magazine* 196, no. 1177 (June 1948): 567–572.
48. Kracauer, "Terror Films," 105, 109, 110.
49. Kracauer, 110.
50. Kracauer, "Movies with a Message," 568.
51. Kracauer, 570–571.
52. Lee Grieveson, *Cinema and the Wealth of Nations: Media, Capital, and the Liberal World System* (Berkeley: University of California Press, 2018).
53. Jennifer Fay and Justus Nieland, *Film Noir: Hard-Boiled Modernity and the Cultures of Globalization* (New York: Routledge, 2010), 28–64.
54. On the influence of Mead's anthropology on German political reeducation, see Jennifer Fay, *Theaters of Occupation: Hollywood and the Reeducation of Postwar Germany* (Minneapolis: University of Minnesota Press, 2008), xv.
55. Wilder, quoted in Ralph Willet, "Billy Wilder's 'A Foreign Affair' (1945–1948); 'the trials and tribulations of Berlin,'" *Historical Journal of Film, Radio, and Television* 7, no. 1 (1987): 13.
56. Billy Wilder's "Propaganda through Entertainment" memo is included as an appendix to Willet, "Billy Wilder's 'A Foreign Affair,'" 14.
57. Wilder, 14.
58. Wilder, 14.

59. Wilder, 14.

60. Quoted in Lutz Koepnick, *The Dark Mirror: German Cinema between Hitler and Hollywood* (Berkeley: University of California Press, 2002), 194.

61. Sarah Nilsen, *Projecting America: Film and Cultural Diplomacy at the Brussels World's Fair* (Jefferson, NC: Macfarland, 2011), 36.

62. Greif, *Crisis of Man*, 80.

63. Greif, 79, 85.

64. See Grieveson, 196.

65. Herbert Schiller, "Genesis of the Free Flow of Information Principles," in *Communication and Class Struggle*, vol. 1: *Capitalism and Imperialism*, ed. Armand Mattelart and Seth Siegelaub (New York: International General, 1979), 349; *Yearbook on Human Rights for 1947*, quoted in Schiller, 350.

66. *Two Men in Manhattan*, directed by Jean-Pierre Melville (1959; USA, Cohen Film Collection, 2013), DVD.

67. Dimendberg, *Film Noir*, 78.

68. Reinhold Martin, *The Organizational Complex: Architecture, Media, Corporate Space* (Cambridge, MA: MIT Press, 2003), chap. 3.

69. On the relationship between Bass's title designs for Hollywood auteurs and his work in logo design and corporate identity programs, see Jan-Christopher Horak, *Saul Bass: Anatomy of Film Design* (Lexington: University Press of Kentucky, 2014).

70. On Kepes's relationship to cybernetic organization, see Martin, *Organizational Complex*; on Bass's debt to Kepes, see Horak, *Anatomy of Film Design*.

71. Johnston, quoted in Sarah Nilsen, 5.

72. Jon Lewis, *Hollywood vs. Hard Core: How the Struggle over Censorship Saved the Modern Film Industry* (New York: New York University Press, 2000).

73. Grieveson, *Cinema and the Wealth of Nations*, 323.

74. Auerbach, *Dark Borders*, 16.

75. Steve Joshua Heims, *The Cybernetics Group* (Cambridge, MA: MIT Press, 1991), 164.

76. Rappleye, quoted in Heims, 169.

77. Fred Turner, *The Democratic Surround: Multimedia and American Liberalism from World War II to the Psychedelic Sixties* (Chicago: University of Chicago Press, 2013), 163.

78. *Siegfried Kracauer's American Writings: Essays on Film and Popular Culture*, ed. Johannes von Moltke and Kristy Rawson (Berkeley: University of California Press, 2012), 81.

79. *Siegfried Kracauer's American Writings*, 86.

80. John Houseman, "How Does a Movie Communicate?" In *The Apsen Papers*, ed. Reyner Banham (New York: Praeger, 1974), 23. On the IDCA as overlooked site for conceptualizing film and mass media, see Justus Nieland, *Happiness by Design: Modernism and Media in the Eames Era* (Minneapolis: University of Minnesota Press, 2020), especially chap. 3.

81. Houseman, 29.

82. Houseman, 30.

83. Turner, *Democratic Surround*, 232.

84. See Turner and Nilsen.

85. Riesman, *The Lonely Crowd*, 128.

86. Riesman, 128.

87. *The Information Machine: Creative Man and the Data Processor*, directed by Charles and Ray Eames (USA, Eames Office, 1958), Prelinger Archives, accessed July 3, 2019, https://archive.org/details/InformationM.

88. George Nelson, "Designer's Comments and Extracts from a 'Log' on the American National Exhibition," *Industrial Design* 6, no. 4 (April 1959): 54.

89. Nelson, 53.

90. Michael Denning, *The Cultural Front: The Laboring of American Culture in the Twentieth Century* (London: Verso, 1996), 362–402.

91. Welles, quoted in Jonathan Rosenbaum, "Orson Welles' Memo to Universal: *Touch of Evil*," *Film Quarterly* 46, no. 1 (Autumn 1992), 8.

92. *Touch of Evil*, directed by Orson Welles (USA, 1958; Universal, 2000), DVD.

93. Welles, quoted in Denning, *Cultural Front*, 402.

94. James Naremore, "The Trial: The F.B.I. vs. Orson Welles," *Film Comment* 27, no. 1 (January–February 1991): 22–27.

95. *Touch of Evil*, DVD.

96. Victoria de Grazia, *Irresistible Empire: America's Advance through Twentieth-Century Europe* (Cambridge, MA: Belknap Press of Harvard University Press, 2005).

97. Kristin Ross, *Fast Cars, Clean Bodies: Decolonization and the Reordering of French Culture* (Cambridge, MA: MIT, 1996), 170.

98. Ross, 176.

99. Ross, 192.

100. *Alphaville*, directed by Jean-Luc Godard (France, 1965; Criterion Collection, 1998), DVD.

101. Larry Busbea, *Topologies: The Urban Utopia in France, 1960–1970* (Cambridge, MA: MIT Press, 2007), 10.

102. *Alphaville*, DVD.

103. Marcuse, *One-Dimensional Man*, 66.

104. Marcuse, 67.

105. *Alphaville*, DVD.
106. Kaja Silverman and Harun Farocki, *Speaking about Godard* (New York: New York University Press, 1998), 78.
107. Bochner, "Alfaville," 15.
108. Eve Meltzer, *Systems We Have Loved: Conceptual Art, Affect, and the Antihumanist Turn* (Chicago: University of Chicago Press, 2013), 34.
109. Liu, *Laws of Cool*, 101.

CHAPTER 2

Public Violence as Private Pathology: Noir Affect in *The End of a Primitive*

Christopher Breu

The writing of history from an avowedly political perspective regularly presents historians with a theoretical conundrum: whether to emphasize the aspects of a given historical situation that correspond to their political vision, or whether to emphasize the historical impediments to the achievement of such a vision. In leftist circles, this has often been theorized as the difference between writing history "top down" versus "bottom up." Thus the theories of the Frankfurt School and world systems economics are usually associated with a systemic and often pessimistic top-down version of historicism, while the writings of Gramsci and various practitioners of social history and cultural studies are seen as embodying a celebratory, and at times starry-eyed, antisystemic vision of history from the bottom-up.[1]

Yet as useful as this distinction has been in leftist accounts of historical change, it can run the danger of obscuring as much as it reveals. For it is not clear that all forms of reaction come from above, nor is it clear that bottom-up power is always aligned with the progressive. Similarly, it is not clear that an assessment of the political forces arrayed against one's position is more disempowering or quietistic than the theoretical impulse to find resistance immanent within every cultural object or disenfranchised social subject.

If this latter proposition were true, it indeed would be difficult to make a progressive case for the novels of Chester Himes. Even in periods of great promise for progressive social transformation, such as the countercultural movements of the late 1960s or the 1930s and 1940s era of radical union organizing and the multiracial war effort that Michael Denning has termed "the cultural front," Himes's novels inevitably sound a discordant note of pessimism, if not stubborn refusal.[2] Thus, in *Blind Man with a Pistol*, Himes refuses to be swept up in the structures of feeling that characterized late-sixties radicalism and spawned black nationalism, instead characterizing the latter in terms of the titular blind man shooting wildly in a subway car.[3] Similarly Himes's two novels about the cultural front, *If He Hollers Let Him Go* and *The Lonely Crusade*, reveal forms of intersectional violence and persistent inequalities that run counter to the collectivist rhetoric of this period.[4] As I argue elsewhere, this intransigent negativity is characteristic of Himes's writing, giving it its corrosive quality.[5] It is in terms of this negativity that Himes's writing advances its most lasting and powerful political insights. And, it is this negativity that enables many of Himes's fictions to be described with that unstable signifier for twentieth-century narratives of dissolution and failure: noir.

Noir Space and Time

If redemptive forms of historiography partake of what Walter Benjamin described as "messianic time," as presenting a "conception of the present as the 'time of now' that is shot through with chips of Messianic time," noir functions via what can be alternately described as the temporality of negative affect, as a conception of the present that is shot through with chips of the unresolved past and the disavowed, yet painful, present.[6] The temporality of noir is thus that of the psychoanalytic concept of *Nachträglichkeit*, a present set of meanings and actions that, through the logic of displacement and condensation, come to catalyze and give expression to unacknowledged forms of historical violence.[7] In noir, however, the displacement is not only temporal, but spatial. Thus, the representation of interpersonal conflict and psychological dissolution in the noir novel and film often functions as a displacement or condensation of the larger social conflicts that characterize an era. Although it shares some of the features of allegory, this process is not quite an allegorical one. Allegory implies a careful and controlled figural algebra, in which the narrative actions of individual characters stand in for larger social and political narratives. In noir, this process is inevitably messier. As products of the cultural dream-work, noir narratives distort and disfigure that which they narrativize. Far from a formal drawback, however, these distortions indicate the work of figuring negative affect in which noir engages. To put it in Lacanian terms, if the real of trauma is never directly representable, then the noir narrative is constituted out of the forms distorted symbolic representation and affect that encircle and encyst the traumatic real.[8] It is this distortion that lends noir its particular potency and transgressive urgency, for what emerges from these symbolic fragments are the fantasy-saturated narratives of the cultural dream-work, narratives that are as likely to produce expressionistic caricatures and nightmarish distortions as they are precise political condensations. Moreover, proximity to this traumatic truth produces the specific forms of transpersonal affect that characterize noir: anxiety, as both Lacan and Kelly Oliver and Benigno Trigo figure it, but also hostility, rage, sadness, and despair.[9] For noir, such affects are not only the product of the proximity to uncomfortable truths but also, in Teresa Brennan's formulations, transmissible.[10] Indeed, they are what John Protevi describes as political and social affects that only become subjectified and privatized later on.[11]

Tracing this cultural dream-logic thus becomes the work of reading the political resonances of noir. These resonances take shape as the displaced, repetitious temporality and spatiality of the noir text, in which forms of social violence become repetitiously reenacted on another scene. It is this return of the repressed that informs the distinctively pessimistic historiographical vision of noir. In its intransigent negativity, noir refuses to cover or move beyond the traumatic insistence of the historical real, instead returning recursively to forms of social violence masked by other modes of historiography.

If this historiographical pessimism represents an important corrective in times of progressive social transformation, it is perhaps even more crucial in times of political reaction, when repressive narratives of cultural consensus, paranoia, and the valorization of a depoliticized private sphere emerge as dominant. In such moments, noir, with its engagement with affect-saturated space and time, becomes a reminder both of the violence of the past that has yet to be confronted and the violence of the present that has been purged from the dominant cultural narratives of the era.[12]

It is unsurprising, then, that the 1950s represents a decade that saw a particular efflorescence of the noir novel in the United States. Moreover, the noir narratives of what can be termed the short fifties (an era of extreme reaction and repression beginning in 1947 with the revival of the House Un-American Committee and the passing of the Taft-Hartley Act and ending in 1954 with the public defeat of Joseph McCarthy and the beginning of the civil rights era) in both novel and film are particularly dark representations of the forms of cultural claustrophobia produced by what Alan Nadel has theorized as the containment narratives of the 1950s.[13] In the noir of the 1950s, there indeed seems to be *No Way Out* as the Joseph Mankiewicz fraught noir about racial conflict at the beginning of the decade put it.[14] Noir novels such as Jim Thompson's *The Killer Inside Me*, Dorothy Hughes's *In A Lonely Place*, Patricia Highsmith's *Strangers on a Train*, and David Goodis's *Down There* present narratives of interpersonal violence and gendered antagonism that function both to highlight the private cost of public repression and to play out in phantasmatic miniature the antagonisms that have been purged from representation in the McCarthy-era public sphere.[15]

Hell in a New York Apartment

Chester Himes's *The End of a Primitive* (originally published in an expurgated version as *The Primitive* in 1955) can be located at the center of this efflorescence of noir in the 1950s. In an interview, Himes provided a sardonic summary of the novel: "I put a sexually frustrated American woman and a racially frustrated black American male together for a weekend in a New York apartment, and allowed them to soak in American bourbon. I got the result I was looking for: a nightmare of drunkenness, unbridled sexuality, and in the end, tragedy."[16] While this description is only partially accurate as a summary of the book (not all of the novel takes place in the apartment, and the sexuality depicted by the novel is as much bridled, indeed complicatedly inhibited and erotically entangled, as it is unbridled), it captures the affective core of the book. Laced throughout with gallows humor and brilliantly black satire, the book ends in tragedy, and the structure of tragedy, as Himes's almost Aristotelian description of the novel's dramatic action suggests, organizes its overall trajectory. Ending with Jesse killing Kriss during one of the regular blackouts produced by his almost continuous drinking throughout the novel, this unrepresented act forms the traumatic kernel around which the rest of the narrative is formed.

As Himes's description of his novel suggests, the sources of noir affect conjured by *The End of a Primitive* are multiple. The scenario played out by Jesse Robinson and Kriss Cummings is organized around that most culturally censured, yet fetishized, of heterosexual miscegenational relationships: that between a black man and a white woman.[17] Himes's conflictual and finally violent representation of this relationship partakes of the dream-logic engaged by noir. Jesse and Kriss's relationship functions as a condensation and displacement of the larger social struggles and antagonisms purged from political articulation in the public sphere of the early 1950s. The two initially met while both were working on behalf of the "Negro problem" as members of a Work Progress Administration (WPA) organization dedicated to antiracist struggle. Now meeting again for only the second time in a decade, they are described as products of a forcibly privatized and depoliticized era of the early 1950s: "In the silence that followed, realizing their need for each other, both now ostracized from the only exciting life they had ever known, both starved for sexual fulfillment, lost and lonely, outcasts drifting together long after the passion had passed, faced with a night of sleeping together which at that moment neither desired, they hated each other."[18] This passage is a near perfect example of noir affect. The two characters need each other just as much as they hate each other. They are lonely yet resent each other's company. They lack desire and yet are starved for sexual fulfilment. Indeed, the passage suggests central to noir affect is not only negative forms of emotion but ambivalence. This ambivalence is one form of jouissance produced by the characters' proximity to a historical and traumatic real (in this case the overdetermined historical relationships between gender, race, and sex). It would be one thing if they could walk away, but they are as entranced as they are repelled. This is the intimate negativity of noir. The proximity here is as seductive as it is repelling, and both characters are subject to a drive that is tinged by death and eroticism. They may be able to avoid this drive (I am not trying to efface questions of agency and responsibility for violence) but the drive itself remains insistent even when the characters occupy distinct locations. Moreover, the noir narrative is precisely about exploring such drives.

To remain on this interpersonal level, though, would be a mistake. For this drive and the forms of affect attaching to it are socially and historically produced. The lost passion that is invoked here is as much political as it is sexual, and the hatred is similarly as much the product of social repression as it is interpersonal. In this reunion, Kriss sees in Jesse the social hurt caused by the intensified racism of the short 1950s: "This man before her, in the old trench coat she recognized immediately, was dead; hurt had settled so deep inside of him it had become part of his metabolism . . .

inside of him the light had gone out."[19] This intensified racism is most succinctly captured in the novel by Jesse's treatment by his editor as he rejects Jesse's latest manuscript.[20] Like Himes himself, Jesse is a writer of black political (or "protest") fiction, a genre, as his editor indicates to him, radically out of step with the boosterish spirit of the consensus minded 1950s: "You're a hell of a good writer Jesse. Why don't you write a black success novel? An inspirational story? The public is tired of the poor downtrodden Negro."[21] While this racism may initially seem of the comparatively mild, liberal sort, it is precisely the closing down of avenues for the political expression of public antagonism and its replacement with a depoliticized ethos of individual success that forces the hurt out of the arena of public struggle and into Jesse's very metabolism. Indeed, in this sense, Himes suggests that the liberal racism that accompanied the Cold War liberal consensus is equally pernicious as more overly expressed forms.

While the novel's representation of womanhood is more politically ambiguous (and its representation of homosexuality down-right reactionary—such are the distortions and displacements of noir), the novel similarly encodes the frustrations produced for women by the decade that as Elaine Tyler May has indicated, represents a reactionary rollback of the hard-won victories that women achieved in the workplace in the 1940s.[22] In this sense, Kriss's privatized rage, produced by a history of sexist abuse, from back alley abortions, to physical abuse, to sexual abuse, doubles that of Jesse. In both cases, denied public expression, their justified rage plays out in displaced form in Kriss's New York apartment.

The apartment, just down the street from Gramercy Park, becomes one of the affect-laden dream spaces central to noir.[23] In this basement apartment, positioned, like many of the privatized suburban spaces of the 1950s, between a half-realized claim to middle-class respectability and an all too palpable sense of social dissolution, that which has been repressed from public space returns in distorted, compressed, and all-too-violent forms in the private sphere. Thus, the forms of conflict purged from representation in the social return in private, marking the public genesis of private violence. Yet understanding this displacement of affect as a symptom of the intermixing of social repression and social trauma only presents part of the story. For this displacement is also an authorial strategy, one that Himes shares with other noir writers in the fifties: they employ private conflict to write in coded form about the political struggles that have been silenced by McCarthyism and the political repression of the decade. The use of noir space in the novel, then, functions as both a displacement and as a site of coded protest.

The Prognosticating Chimpanzee

This larger repressive context is repeatedly emphasized by the novel's most surreal of motifs: its parodic rendering of the *Today Show* of the 1950s which featured cohosts Dave Garroway and J. Fred Muggs. Muggs was a chimpanzee who would perform various antics and wreak havoc with "straight-man" Garroway, who, in turn, was the typical white, male newscaster of the period. Himes renders more profoundly surreal one of the already more surreal episodes of a surreal medium by recasting the chimpanzee as a dead-on prognosticator who is clearly much more intelligent than his fellow human newscaster, Gloucester. The latter treats the chimp as a subhuman source of comic relief, in spite of the chimp's clear intellectual superiority. Himes's surreal rendering of the *Today Show* becomes a perfect condensation of the racist terms of the liberal consensus of the short fifties. African Americans (refigured by the dominant culture via the long-standing post-Darwinian racist trope of being akin to apes) are invited to be part of the national comedy, which is broadcast over the emergent and largely privatized and privatizing technology of television, but only in clearly dehumanized and subservient terms. In place, then, of the fierce workerist, antiracist struggles represented by A. Philip Randolph's march on Washington and the struggle to integrate the Congress of Industrial Organizations (CIO), both of which characterized the era of Popular Front radicalism, the vision of the 1950s condensed in Himes sardonic vision of the *Today Show* presents a national consensus in which the public sphere has been purged of conflict and replaced with a narrative of privatized, comedic consensus, in which African Americans are rendered at best disenfranchised, second-class citizens and at worst as less-than-fully human sidekicks. The novel's representation of this manufactured consensus is framed by repeated references to McCarthy-era purges, suggesting not only the purging of politics from the public sphere but forms of conflictual and oppositional affect that might challenge the narrative of McCarthyism.

This ideological transformation had its material underpinnings in the silencing of public political discourse underwritten by the anticommunist purges, the specter of nuclear war, and the growth privatized and red-lined suburbs (invoked metonymically in the narrative by Jesse's mordant fantasy of an ad for an atomic-age fridge, the "Presto Atom-atic Refrigerator") in which many of the white ethnic participants in cultural front radicalism found themselves, thanks to the GI Bill, to be newly middle-class residents.[24] This context is explicitly alluded to by the chimpanzee, who, since the novel is set a few years before the year of its publication, predicts further repressive McCarthyist purges and, in the same newscast, discusses global forms of racist violence by detailing repressive activities in South Africa. The implicit linkage created by the broadcasting of these two stories in the same newscast suggests the parallels, as historian George Fredrickson has noted, between the forms of racialized political repression taking place in the United States (including that of our own apartheid regime, Jim Crow) and South Africa in the same decade, thus underscoring the link between the political repression underwritten by McCarthy and the intensified racism of the short 1950s.[25] It also suggests the way in which the violence of Apartheid South Africa benefited from what Giovanni Arrighi describes as the United States' hegemonic position in the capitalist world system of this period.[26] Thus, while political antagonism is shunted off the public stage, only to return violently in the space of Kriss's apartment, the larger national and even global context from which this antagonism was purged, returns in the spectral broadcasts of the newly privatized technology of the television set and its various avatars, human and animal alike.

The Return of the Historical Repressed

The novel's engagement with the affective space of noir is paralleled by its invocation of affect-saturated time. For the affective antagonisms addressed by the novel condense traumas that are historical as well as current. The temporality of the novel functions not only to mark the repression produced by the purgation from the public sphere of the forms of progressive social struggle that Michael Denning terms the cultural front, but it also records the forms of sexual and racial antagonism that limited and overdetermined the cultural front even during its time of greatest political influence. Himes's first two novels, *If He Hollers Let Him* Go and *Lonely Crusade*, are famous for their blistering accounts of the limits of the forms of brotherhood and sisterhood fostered by the cultural front. *The End of a Primitive* suggests that the phantasmatic knot that overdetermined the best antiracist efforts of the cultural front was miscegenational sexuality within the context of a racist society. Both Kriss and Jesse remember the era "when all the liberals were trying desperately to elect Roosevelt for a fourth term against strong fascist opposition and the CIO's Political Action Committee had been all the rage" as the "greatest time in the history of the Republic for interracial lovemaking."[27] As Jesse goes on to reflect, "Nothing like politics for getting white ass. Black ass either."[28] Yet as this intentionally reductive and crude refiguration of the struggles and very-real achievements of the era suggests, racial political struggle often stumbles over the traumatic real of sexuality, especially when sexuality itself has not been made a conscious part of the political struggle.

Jesse's and Kriss's narratives of the era emphasize as much the political and subjective strife and antagonism produced by this upswing of miscegenational sex as the liberation that it ostensibly suggested. Kriss reflects on the way in which these encounters were always shaped by overarching dynamics of racism and sexism:

> But when she'd taken Negroes as lovers, they'd crucify her. "Kriss is solving the Negro problem in bed," they said of her, solving their own [i.e., white men's] problem in her own bed along with the Negro problem, perhaps because of it, at the same time feeling she wasn't good enough for them and treating her like dirt. They'd made her feel like dirt before she'd ever thought of sleeping with a black man; and only when sleeping with one could she feel secure in the knowledge that she wasn't dirt. Which was the same thing they had done to the blacks. So with them she never felt ruined; they never thought of her as ruined. They were ruined by being born black, ruined in the eyes of her race, and they kept laughing at the idiocy of a race that ruined their own women and threw them in bed with men of another race they'd similarly ruined.[29]

This passage emphasizes the way in which white men "crucify" Kriss for sleeping with black men, locating the object of critique as white men and the white and male supremacist ideology that they espouse. Thus, while the novel as a whole details corrosive antagonism that plays out between black men and white women in bed, this passage nicely works to situate the responsibility for that in relationship to larger cultural forms of racism and sexism. White masculinity here is predicated on the ruination of both blackness and femininity. This ruination, in turn, is played out in a displaced manner in forms of sexualized antagonism between white women and black men. In each case, sleeping with the other suggests a context in which each can "secure the knowledge" that he or she is not dirt, and it is worth remembering that "dirt" is one of the signifiers of abjection for Julia Kristeva.[30] On one level, there is a flash of a possible utopia present, where both white women and black men find a sense of connection, alliance, and pleasure in rejecting the racism of white men (even as the position of black women is not figured here at all). Yet it seems to play out more forcefully as antagonism, in which one partner wants to both have and destroy the other as representing a forbidden form of white male property and a displaced representation of white male authority. It is precisely the desire to avoid abjection and both secure and destroy the other as a representation of white male power that lends miscegenational sex its corrosive power and its affective charge in this context. As the novel itself demonstrates, this potent mixture tips easily into violence that is itself a displacement of the rage against white, male hegemony. *The End of a Primitive* thus suggests that because the sexual dimension of the antiracist struggle did not find public expression in the radical/progressive struggles of the cultural front, it returns with a vengeance in the hyper-privatized and reactionary moment of the short 1950s. The return of this unworked-through knot of the real, then, is part of what structures the noir temporality of Himes's novel.

And yet, as the novel, recognizes, this traumatic knot has a much older genesis than the context of the cultural front alone provides. It also suggests, as Jean Laplanche argues, that the traumatic knot of sexuality is as much about fantasy as it is about material trauma.[31] The two are intertwined in their insistence. Thus, it is not only the material trauma of racist and sexist violence and inequality that shapes this knot, repressed wishes and disavowed fantasies also encrust it. The knot's recurrence in the context of both the radical 1930s and 1940s and the reactionary 1950s suggests that the miscegenational couple at the center of Himes's narrative bears the whole affective weight of the set of historical displacements and condensations that produced the twin ideological figures of the black rapist and the virginal white woman. The affective presence of this couple persists in spite of the fact that neither figure corresponds to their phantasmatic avatar. As Angela Davis, Robin Wiegman, and others have argued, these twin ideological figures functioned to underwrite the campaign of racial terror and disenfranchisement that ushered in the Jim Crow era.[32] As such they functioned as a phantasmatic displacement and inversion of the historical forms of sexual violence perpetrated upon black women (and men) under slavery as well as of the sexualized violence of the lynching epidemic that was central to the campaign of racial terror in the post-Reconstruction era.

In psychoanalytic terms, then, the myth of the black rapist and the concomitant myth of the virginal white woman (along with the linked figure of her white male chivalric protector) function as a "screen memory," a memory that, as Victor Burgin puts it, "comes to mind in the place of, and in order to conceal, an associated but repressed memory."[33] Burgin links the generation of such memories to nationalism and forms of national memory. The violence, guilt, and anxiety that accompanies forms of collective national violence, such as is represented by slavery or the genocidal "removal" of Indian nations, becomes transmuted, via the logic of the screen memory, into a historical memory that writes the aggressors as victims and vice versa. It is the presence, however, of the buried relationship to trauma, guilt, and anxiety that becomes the source of the screen memory's power and underwrites its repetitious return not only for the historical perpetrators, but for the victims as well. Kriss and Jesse find themselves returning, in spite of their own better intentions, to aspects of this affective historical script. Indeed, as I have suggested, neither figure corresponds to their phantasmatic avatar within this scenario. Jesse kills Kriss in a drunken rage, but does not rape her; similarly, while Kriss may invoke the ideology of the virginal white woman during the complicated head-games that she and Jesse play with each other, in her erotic interactions she intentionally flouts this ideal. Indeed, while both characters have willfully disrupted the ideological fetish that is the figure of the black rapist with their eager participation in consensual, interracial sex, they find themselves still affectively constrained by this phantasmatic figure and the sexual scripts attaching to it.

Sexualized Rage as Noir Affect

Within the context of the privatizing and repressive 1950s, this fantasy returns not only as disavowed libidinal and affective materials of the multiracial cultural front, but also even more forcefully as the forms of cultural antagonism and political struggle that have been purged from the public sphere. Sex, as a typically private act that carries phantasmatic and public weight, becomes freighted with all kinds of negative affects displaced from these other two contexts. As Jesse recognizes in one of his drunken internal monologues, even their consensual sex is bridled with the social and political condensations attached to the myth of the black rapist:

> Unavoidable really. Nigger's got to want to screw white women. Got no choice the way they got it set up. Wouldn't be human if he didn't. Absolutely right too. Should want to screw 'em. Good for his ego; great therapeutic qualities in screwing white woman. White man kick his ass until he gets sick; get some white woman ass and get well. Good for her too. White man kick her ass till she get sick; screw some black niggers and get even. Don't let him catch her though; but be sure and let him know about it. Otherwise lose half of its curative value. Not just logical and unavoidable and right, but essential in our culture.[34]

It is in this overdetermined context, then, that the violence produced by a white and male supremacist culture, when denied public redress, returns in affective space-time of the private. In such a context, ostensibly consensual sex (like rape as its explicitly violent and traumatizing double) becomes freighted with larger forms of nonconsensual social contestation and struggle. Sex itself then becomes loaded with the forms of affect—rage, revenge, sadness, frustration—that are produced by larger systems of public inequality. Even need becomes tinged with hatred and competition within such a framework. Kriss thinks: "She was in a blind rage with herself for seeing him again even now, for her sexual need of him. If she could sleep with him and immediately afterward have him beheaded, then she could enjoy his company."[35] Sexual need here is inextricably bound up with rage and potential violence. As Jessie notes, sex becomes a ritual, one that is bound to the very history it is attempting to overcome: "Jessie vaguely realized through his senseless rage and stupefying drunkenness that he was witnessing a sex ritual of laceration, the two of them slashing each other in sensual excitement, and he thought some deep frustrated love between them was frothing out in cruelty."[36] The ritual here suggests that both characters are in thrall to repetition, one marked by history, corrosive desire, and death. Here repetition does not lead to a working through, but instead is the repetition favored by noir. It is a repetition marked by a death drive that is explicitly overdetermined by the racist and misogynist history of the United States. This then is the recursive temporality of noir. In spite of both characters' attempts to live in the present and look hopefully toward the future, the historical and social past recurs with a vengeance that is all the stronger because it is denied expression in the sphere of the social.

Reparative Despair

What then is the political promise of the form of historiography modeled by Himes's version of noir? It promises to return us to the historical traumas and present-day forms of violence that congratulatory and even ostensibly liberatory historiographies cover too quickly. Indeed, if there is any positivity in Himes's prose, it lies precisely in its negativity. Lauren Berlant has coined the term "cruel optimism" to discuss the affect attached to contemporary neoliberalism, in which "something you desire is actually an obstacle to your flourishing."[37] Thus, our very fantasies about success in a system structured against our flourishing work to bind us ever more tightly to that system. Himes's noir historiography works in a diametrically opposed manner. Drawing on the work of Eve Sedgwick and Sean Grattan, even as I maintain Berlant's emphasis on negativity, I argue Himes's fiction is organized around a "reparative despair."[38] While Sedgwick famously contrasts reparative reading to the negative affects associated with paranoid reading practices, Himes, in turn, suggest that we can only get to the reparative by staging the negative and even the paranoid. Himes invokes despair as a way of insisting the reader confront despair and recognize the social violence that produces it. It is an ethical (and protopolitical) insistence that the reader comprehend and sit with the text's despair. It insists that the reader find ways of breaking with the repetitions of violence that the text foregrounds even though and particularly because the text itself cannot do so.

Beneath the rage, frustration, and hatred that infuse Himes's novel lies despair. This despair is perhaps the most noir of all the affects that run through Himes's narrative, and inform not only its rage but also its midnight-black humor. The despair is a product of the utter frustration and disillusionment created by any possible individual response to systemic racism and inequality. Himes captures the source of this despair in the second volume of his autobiography: "Not only does racism express the absurdity of the racists, but it generates the absurdity in its victims. And the absurdity of the victims intensifies the absurdity of the racists ad infinitum."[39] This ever-multiplying intensification suggests that both victim and victimizer are caught within the throws of the noir affect generated by racism itself. Jesse and Kriss know the absurdity of racism, yet they find themselves compelled to repeat its scripts ad infinitum. They are caught in the affective feedback loop of racism and the inability to transcend this loop creates not only absurdity and the novel's black humor but the finality of its despair. After waking up to find that he has killed Kriss, he muses: "Be in all the newspapers: BLACK MAN KILLS WHITE WOMAN. Not only natural, plausible, logical inevitable, psychiatrically compulsive and sociologically conclusive behavior of a human being—and all the rest of the shit those social scientists think up—but mathematically accurate and politically correct as well."[40] The power of the compulsion to repeat is captured in this passage as is the force of institutionalized racism. Here, not only society itself, but the different branches of knowledge are implicated in reinforcing and justifying this compulsion. Echoing its use in leftist circles of the time, even as it seems to already augur its appropriation, in the present, by the so-called alt right, Jesse's invocation of "politically correct" suggests that racism and misogyny themselves are what is "politically correct" in the United States. It is politics as usual and, as ironically what is defined as human. Indeed in a passage that precedes this one, Jesse ironically congratulates himself on no longer being a primitive, but with the definitional act of killing Kris, becoming a human: "Went in the back door of the Alchemy Company of America a primitive filled with all that crap called principles, integrity, honor, conscience, faith, love, hope, charity, and such, and came out of it a human being, completely purged."[41] Thus, to be a human being in the 1950s America is to be shorn of all positive, connective affects, what Sean Grattan has described as utopian affects.[42] Instead, misogynist violence and racism are the inheritance of the American human being in this passage, and Jesse ironically graduates (although this graduation is into a death sentence as the prognosticating chimp confirms) into being human by playing out one of the culture's central racist and misogynist scripts. While this passage emphasizes the novel's gallows humor and its more general social critique, these finally give way to despair: "Tears flowed uncontrollably down his pale tan cheeks. 'Don't cry son,' he said. 'It's funny really. You just got to get the handle to the joke.'"[43] Here despair is what underlies such black humor. Moreover, the blackness of the black humor in this passage suggests, as Stephanie Brown notes, that it has a relationship to African American humor, which often turns desperate and fatal situations into gallows humor.[44] The compulsion to repeat racist and sexist scripts itself here becomes absurdly funny. Yet it is the kind of humor that hurts and indeed opens onto despair, since Jesse does not in fact have the handle of the joke. Instead, he is its butt. This is noir humor of black despair. There is nothing redeeming about it. It just hurts, even as you laugh. Yet, paradoxically, something reparative emerges from this lack of redemption. The affect that emerges is what I am calling reparative despair. The reparation does not exist on the level of the text's diegesis, but in terms of its extradiegetic reception. Himes insists that the reader engage and acknowledge this despair. The novel refuses the historical work of concealing despair, or too quickly positivizing negativities. Instead, the properly empathetic noir reader (remember that the negativity of noir affects only do their powerfully corrosive work if an initial readerly empathy is established) comes to appreciate the enormity of the historical despair that Himes narrates. With such a recognition comes a moment of reparative understanding: it only acknowledges the despair created by social pain and violence that a different present can be written, one in which such despair is neither commonplace nor structural. This, then, is the reparative force of noir affect and it suggests a kind of historicism, particularly as Himes is writing a history of the present in *The End of a Primitive*, one that presumes an audience attuned to historical violence and legacies of inequality.

Noir Historiography, Noir Pedagogy

What is the historical legacy of Himes's fiction? Why should we read Himes at all? His texts are filled with violence, negativity, vitriol, and ugly epithets. The possible trigger warnings attached to the teaching of his texts in the present are legion. Indeed, there is nothing politically correct about Himes either in his time or ours. I want to suggest that it is precisely the text's willingness to confront and stage the ugliest affects produced by racism, sexism, and political repression that it maintains its power as a history of its present. It is a document that narrates an affective history of the "short 1950s" and its relationship to a much longer history of inequality and violence. In its staging of this despair and its willingness to tarry with it, it insists that readers need to confront this despair in all of its negativity in order for the present to not be merely defined by a compulsion to repeat. It is only by confronting this despair and subjectifying it (which is precisely what the noir novel does) that a possibility of a working through of historical violence and trauma emerges. This subjectification is crucial. It is why the book also functions as a staging of the violence of sexism (given the complex and ambivalent subjectification that it provides of Kriss), while its representation of Jesse's gay roommates remains mired in homophobia. The novel does not subjectify the complexity of his roommates' experiences, except for Jesse's garden-variety phobic perceptions. Instead the homophobia remains flat and uninterrogated, while the sexual fantasies that underpin and accompany both racism and sexism are thoroughly explored in all of their contradictoriness, seductiveness, and negativity. It is this willingness to stage and stay with the most uncomfortable of fantasies that Himes's text does its political work.

This insistence on staging negative fantasies suggests a form of noir historicism and finally also what Elizabeth Hatmaker calls noir pedagogy (see chapter 4). Noir insists on the need to phantasmatically inhabit and comprehend the forms of social negativity that produce negative affects including despair, hatred, and murderousness. It insists on occupying uncomfortable truths and enacts an anxious approach to the real of historical violence. Only by identifying with historical forms of despair, Himes's novel suggests, can we start to intervene in forms of structural violence and rewrite contemporary cultural scripts. Only when we confront the violence of racism and sexism at its most forceful and understand how it is subjectified can we begin to imagine subject positions and social organizations that do not merely manifest the compulsion to repeat.

The necessity of confronting the anxiety generated by an encounter with uncomfortable historical truths is why it is so crucial to be able to teach texts that are anything but safe. Of course, it is important to recognize the risk of such encounters; an ethical pedagogy needs to attend to the risks students take in such moments. However, a noir pedagogy organized around the teaching of such uncomfortable truths suggests that we stop teaching the most disturbing texts only at great cultural and personal peril. It is only by confronting and subjectively apprehending such disturbing truths that a different way forward is possible. It is only by traversing the darkness that we may find a way to repairing and transforming the persistence of violence and inequality in the present. Such, at least, is noir's wager.

NOTES

1. For examples of top-down analysis see: Immanuel Wallerstein, "The Rise and Demise of the Capitalist World-System: Concepts for a Comparative Analysis," in *The Essential Wallerstein* (New York: New Press, 2000), 71–105; and Max Horkheimer and Theodor W. Adorno. *Dialectic of Enlightenment: Philosophical Fragments*, trans. Edmund Jephcott (Stanford, CA: Stanford University Press, 2002), 1–35. For examples of bottom-up analysis, see: Antonio Gramsci, *Selections from the Prison Notebooks*, trans Quintin Hoare and Geoffrey Nowell Smith (New York: International Publishers, 1971), 206–269; and Stuart Hall, "The Problem with Ideology: Marxism without Guarantees," in *Stuart Hall: Critical Dialogues in Cultural Studies*, ed. David Morley and Kuan-Hsing Chen (London: Routledge, 1996), 24–46.

2. Michael Denning. *The Cultural Front: The Laboring of American Culture in the Twentieth-Century* (London: Verso, 1997), 1.

3. Chester Himes, *Blind Man with a Pistol* (New York: Vintage, 1990). It is also striking that in Himes's final, unfinished novel in the series, *Plan B*, imagines a black revolution in the United States. He is only able to do this by exploding the form of the detective novel itself. It is also striking that the novel remains unfinished. It is as if Himes could only barely imagine an affirmative, if bloody solution, and only then by undoing the novelistic form itself. See Chester Himes, *Plan B* (Oxford: University of Mississippi Press, 1993).

4. Chester Himes, *If He Hollers Let Him Go* (New York: Da Capo Press, 2002); Chester Himes, *Lonely Crusade*, 2nd ed. (New York: Da Capo Press, 1997).

5. Christopher Breu, *Hard-Boiled Masculinities* (Minneapolis: University of Minnesota Press, 2005), 143–173.

6. Walter Benjamin, *Illuminations: Essays and Reflections*, ed. Hannah Arendt and trans. Harry Zohn (New York: Schocken Books, 1968), 263.

7. Sigmund Freud, *The Standard Edition of the Complete Psychological Works of Sigmund Freud*, trans. and ed. James Strachey (London: Hogarth Press, 1955), 17:29–47.

8. Jacques Lacan, *The Four Fundamental Concepts: The Seminar of Jacques Lacan*, Book XI, ed. Jacques-Alain Miller and trans. Alan Sheridan (New York: W. W. Norton, 1977), 42–64.

9. Kelly Oliver and Benigno Trigo, *Noir Anxiety* (Minneapolis: University of Minnesota Press, 2002), 1–26; Jacques Lacan, *Anxiety: The Seminar of Jacques Lacan*, Book X, trans. A. R. Price (Cambridge: Polity Press, 2016), 157–169.

10. Teresa Brennan, *The Transmission of Affect* (Ithaca, NY: Cornell University Press, 2004), 1–23.

11. John Protevi, *Political Affect: Connecting the Social and the Somatic* (Minneapolis: University of Minnesota Press, 2009), 1–57.

12. On the distinctive use of space in relationship to structural racism in Himes, see Jeremy MacFarlane, "'Enough to make a body riot:' Charlotte Perkins Gilman, Chester Himes, and the Process of Socio-spatial Negotiation," *Interdisciplinary Humanities* 31, no. 2 (Summer 2014): 5–16.

13. Alan Nadel, *Containment Culture: American Narratives, Postmodernism, and the Atomic Age* (Durham, NC: Duke University Press, 1995), 1–67.

14. *No Way Out*, directed by Joseph L. Mankiewicz (USA, 1950; Seattle: Amazon Prime, 2019), streaming.

15. See David Goodis, *Shoot the Piano Player* [original title: *Down There*] (New York: Vintage, 1990); Patricia Highsmith, *Strangers on a Train* (New York: Norton, 2001); Dorothy Hughes, *In a Lonely Place* (New York: Feminist Press, 2003); Jim Thompson, *The Killer Inside Me* (New York: Vintage, 1991).

16. Chester Himes, *The End of a Primitive* (New York: Norton, 1997), 7.

17. On sexuality in Himes and his complex relationship to homosexuality, see Clare Rolens, "Write Like a Man: Chester Himes and the Criminal Text Beyond Bars." *Callaloo* 37, no. 2 (2014): 432–451. Generally, I find the portrayal of Jesse's homophobia rather flat and reproduced by the narrative itself. It is the part of the text that is least convincing and has aged least well. Jessie's relationship to his gay roommates has none of the complex dynamics of desire that characterize Jesse and Kriss's relationship or the representation of queer desire in *Yesterday will Make You Cry* that Rolens explores.

18. Himes, *End of a Primitive*, 75.

19. Himes, 73.

20. On the novel's pivotal role in the transformation of Himes's career trajectory, from writing protest novels to writing crime fiction, see Oliver Belas, "Chester Himes's *The End of a Primitive*: Exile, Exhaustion, Dissolution," *Journal of American Studies* 44, no. 2 (May 2010): 377–390. On Himes's complex relationship with Doubleday as his publisher (some of which is fictionalized in *The End of the Primitive*) see Lawrence Jackson, "'Saying things on paper that should never be written': Publishing Chester Himes at Doubleday," *American Literary History* 23, no. 2 (2011): 283–310.

21. Himes, *End of a Primitive*, 124.

22. Elaine Tyler May, *Homeward Bound: American Families in the Cold War Era*, rev. ed. (New York: Basic Books, 2007), 19–39. For a complication of Tyler's thesis (which I still find compelling on the whole), see the essays in Joanne Meyerowitz, ed., *Not June Cleaver: Women and Gender in Postwar America 1945–1960* (Philadelphia: Temple University Press, 1994).

23. On race in relationship to space in Himes's fiction, see Tyrone Simpson II, "I Could Always Feel Race Trouble . . . No More than Two Feet Off: Chester Himes's Melancholic Perception," *African American Review* 43, nos. 2–3 (Summer–Fall 2009): 233–245.

24. Himes, *End of a Primitive*, 202.

25. George M. Fredrickson, *White Supremacy: A Comparative Study of American and South African History* (Oxford: Oxford University Press, 1983), 239–283.

26. Giovanni Arrighi, *The Long Twentieth Century: Money, Power, and the Origins of Our Times*, new and updated ed. (London: Verso, 2010), 28.

27. Himes, *End of a Primitive*, 64.

28. Himes, 64.

29. Himes, 112–113.

30. Julia Kristeva, *The Powers of Horror: An Essay on Abjection* (New York: Columbia University Press, 1982), 1–31.

31. Jean Laplanche, *Essays on Otherness* (London: Routledge, 1999), 166–196.

32. Angela Davis, *Women, Race, and Class* (New York: Vintage, 1983), 172–201; Robyn Wiegman, *American Anatomies: Theorizing Race and Gender* (Durham, NC: Duke University Press, 1995), 81–114.

33. Victor Burgin, *In/Different Spaces: Place and Memory in Visual Culture* (Berkeley: California University Press, 1996), 221.

34. Himes, *End of a Primitive*, 179.

35. Himes, 78.

36. Himes, 155.

37. Lauren Berlant, *Cruel Optimism* (Durham, NC: Duke University Press, 2011), 1.

38. Eve Kosofsky Sedgwick, *Touching Feeling: Affect, Pedagogy, Performativity* (Durham, NC: Duke University Press, 2003), 123–152. Sean Austin Grattan, *Hope Isn't Stupid: Utopian Affects in Contemporary American Literature* (Iowa City: University of Iowa Press, 2017), 1–30.

39. Chester Himes, *My Life of Absurdity: The Later Years* (New York: Thunder's Mouth Press, 1995), 1.

40. Himes, *End of a Primitive*, 206.

41. Himes, 206.

42. Grattan, *Hope Isn't Stupid*, 16.

43. Himes, *End of a Primitive*, 207.

44. Stephanie Brown, "'If I Can Only Get it Funny!': The Postwar Primitive and Chester Himes' Parodic Protest Novel," *Paradoxa: Studies in World Literary Genres*, no. 18 (2003): 211–233.

CHAPTER 3

Cold Kink: Race and Sex in the African American Underworld

Kirin Wachter-Grene

Iceberg Slim (the "nom-de-pimp" of Robert Beck) is the godfather of African American street lit and among its most infamous figures.[1] When he died in 1992, his seven books had sold over six million copies, making him the best-selling African American author at the time.[2] His 1967 semiautobiographical bildungsroman *Pimp: The Story of My Life* accounted for one million copies sold and catalyzed the market for what was in the 1970s known as "black experience" novels. Street lit refers not only to the postwar pulp fiction written by African American criminals and prisoners but also to the proliferation of contemporary, self-published mass-market paperbacks about hip hop, hustling, and "the game."

Informed by the black noir tradition made famous by Chester Himes in the 1950s—which paved the way for Slim and a whole generation of underrated black street lit writers, including Robert Deane Pharr, Roland Jefferson, Henry Van Dyke, John A. Williams, Herbert Simmons, Charles Perry, and Vern E. Smith—*Pimp*'s brand of gritty pulp ushered in the wave of masculinist 1960s to 1980s black crime fiction written by Donald Goines, Clarence Cooper Jr., Joseph Nazel, and Odie Hawkins. Himes was a successful twentieth-century African American author who began writing prison stories in the 1930s while serving time in the Ohio State Penitentiary for armed robbery. His nine noir "Harlem Detective" novels, featuring black detectives Coffin Ed Johnson and Grave Digger Jones are forebears to street lit. His books are "clear forerunners to the literary phenomenon of black-authored pulp fiction in their concern for street themes, issues of crime and containment, and problems of authorship in a popular market," and they were the first black-authored crime novels to be released on the 1950s paperback market.[3] The difference to writers such as Slim, of course, is that Himes has been canonized.

Although it is changing, street lit has been ignored by critics for too long. This is ironic considering that the genre comprises the most popular, commercially successful African American literature of the twentieth and twenty-first centuries.[4] Yet such texts have been relegated to the paraliterary realm where they are largely precluded from critical engagement.[5] Fortunately, pulp presses such as Old School, Regency, and Holloway House (Slim's publisher) and contemporary print journalists understand the value of this work. And Slim's novels have been exalted by a massive black readership for decades, largely due to the presumed authenticity of the subject matter.[6] Irvine Welsh heralds Slim as "one of the most influential writers of our age,"[7] and even though studies of Slim's work are few in numbers, they have been steadily amassing, particularly over the past decade.[8] Sluggish critical engagement with one of the best-selling black authors of all time is likely due to *Pimp*'s brutal, misogynist representations that may be too bleak for many readers of African American literature to engage. Noir literature shares these representations of violent gendered power dynamics, but the fact that they are racialized in *Pimp*, often in ways that reappropriate a masterslave dynamic between black men and black women, likely adds an additional affective layer of discomfort for many readers.

As a picaresque bildungsroman, *Pimp* tells the story of Slim's entrée into Chicago's sordid underworld in the aftermath of the Great Depression and his rise to pimping notoriety on the backs of women he incessantly tries to outmaneuver. Constantly haunted by his mentor's insight, "A pimp is really a whore who's reversed the game on whores," Slim is feverishly anxious about the fluidity of identity and power despite what his cold pimp exterior suggests.[9] He is driven to "pimp or die," thus the novel's tension revolves around cycles of power—how Slim gains it, largely through his psychosexual, violent exploitation of women, and how he repeatedly loses it, generally at the hands of these same women.[10]

In *Pimp*, negative affective dispositions intrinsic to noir, such as shame and humiliation, are eroticized and utilized in a kinky repertoire. The texts suggest that women have considerable power to not only render men subordinate, but abject. And by embracing their *own* abjection as sites of pleasure and agency, women can often dominate Slim because he underestimates the extent of their kinkiness—and that of his own. He fails to master control (of external and internal forces) in the face of the pleasure he experiences in an asymmetrical power dynamic that subordinates him to "dangerous" women. However, while gendered conflict is a noir trademark, I do not read female power here as the psychoanalytic archetype of the "phallic mother" intent on castrating men, nor do I merely read it as the noir *femme fatale*. Rather, I read *Pimp* as representing a BDSM (bondage/discipline [B/D], dominance/submission [D/S], sadomasochism [S/M]) power dynamic, which I analyze through kink theory—"the theoretical discourse surrounding the consensual exchange of erotic power."[11] Kink theory reveals that a BDSM power dynamic promises (or threatens) the subject with disintegration. By eroticizing power relations, BDSM play can disrupt "conventional forms of sexual identity" in addition to notions of race and gender as "fixed" subject positions.[12] As Lewis Call states, "kink has the potential to add flexible, fluid power relations to the fluid identity structures which poststructuralism has identified."[13] Of course, to read texts through a BDSM power dynamic framework requires one to be conscious of the temptation to succumb to the utopian promise of BDSM. Even though I argue that BDSM play can disrupt subjectivity's containment through the dissolution of "fixed" identity markers, I am careful not to suggest that the subject is *liberated*. In reading *Pimp*, I am not interested in an encrypted utopia but in how and why the concealing/revealing of the pleasure inherent to subordination and abjection informs the text. When read through a theoretical framework that eroticizes noir affect, one can see how *Pimp* represents complex, racialized gender relations that invite us to read misogyny, but also to read beyond such an overdetermined analysis used to contain masculinist street lit. New questions then open up. In particular, how might we read women's erotically "perverse" expressions of transgressive sexuality in ways that speak to a relationship between pleasure and subjection or abjection for women?

Lewis Call conceptualized the term "kink theory" and claims it developed alongside queer theory in the 1980s, citing Foucault as the primary influence.[14] But before it was called "kink theory," Gayle Rubin's "Thinking Sex: Notes for a Radical Theory of the Politics of Sexuality," Pat Califia's *Public Sex: The Culture of Radical Sex*, and Carol Vance's *Pleasure and Danger* anthology were early, influential feminist iterations of what Call is referring to. In the wake of the feminist sex wars that debated sexuality's (oppressed and oppressive) relationship to patriarchy, these critics reconceptualized gender in sex-positive ways that engaged pleasure, power, and agency. As Foucault stated in *Discipline and Punish* "We must cease once and for all to describe the effects of power in negative terms: it 'excludes,' it 'represses,' it censors,' it 'abstracts,' it 'masks,' it 'conceals.' In fact, power produces."[15] Indeed, Call firmly asserts "kink sees power not as a problem but as a possibility."[16] Today, queer theorists of negative affect such as Darieck Scott and Kathryn Bond Stockton and black feminist scholars including Mireille Miller-Young, Jennifer Nash, Amber Musser, and Ariane Cruz are pushing American Studies and African American studies beyond traditional "protectionist" readings of race, gender, and sexuality, inviting us to read black literature and culture in ways we have too long ignored, including through kink.[17]

Common to a BDSM power dynamic, *Pimp*'s characters can be understood to be "acknowledge[ing] power differentials and deploy[ing] them, even in exaggerated ways, in a program of attraction and seduction."[18] However, the novel's blatant misogyny cannot be overlooked. Justin Gifford claims, "the power of the pimp depends on the expansion of ideologies of victimization of women."[19] Beth Coleman agrees, "what is played out for the pimp, at the expense of the women, is the reassertion of right."[20] It cannot be overstated to what extent street lit, like noir, traffics in explicit depictions of sex, violence, and other forms of "depravity" as conventions of the genre. And it is the explicit nature of these texts that account for critical wariness, as one often reads such explicitness as contributing to women's oppression.

Tricia Rose declares as much, stating in *The Hip Hop Wars* "pimp ideology and its expression in popular culture are fundamentally exploitative to women."[21] Rose's critique, echoing the rhetoric of the sex wars, suggests that to analyze women's pleasure under patriarchy, such as pimping, is to confuse "participation in an industry that reinforces male sexual fantasy and power" for "sexual freedom."[22] Gifford argues *Pimp*'s prostitutes' "claiming of [their] sexual agency in the face of white racism is the very logic that contributes to [their] exploitation."[23] Gifford reads these characters who "consent to their own condition of oppression" as complicit. Although he notes that these prostitutes recognize that they have "a certain amount of power as the embodiment of a taboo" he quickly states that such perception is only "a compensatory psychological rationalization."[24] In his argument that abjection can be understood as a form of power for black men, Darieck Scott explicitly refuses to include black women in his analysis. He suggests acknowledging female protagonists' relationship to abjection would be to demonstrate the defeats abjection produces, rather than its potential power.[25] Such a critique echoes Patricia Hill Collins's concept of the "controlling images of black women"—stereotypes dating back to slavery such as the hypersexual "Jezebel," the angry "Sapphire," or the caretaking "Mammy" that serve to oppress black women within a "matrix of domination."[26] This paradigmatic black feminist theory continues to influence critics' attempts to analyze representations of black women's sexuality within systems of structural oppression, though fortunately—as evidenced by the work of Miller-Young, Nash, Musser, Cruz and others—this reluctance is changing.

Even well-meaning critics read *Pimp*'s female characters one-dimensionally when reading in a protectionist mode. Gifford understands Slim's "pimp masculinity" to be a "compensatory identity . . . staged as a defense against dangerous women," and claims these "women [in *Pimp*] are not individually distinguished from one another but are, rather, an undifferentiated threat that must be renounced or contained."[27] Although it is true that, common to noir, "dangerous women" abound in *Pimp* and Slim does construct his pimp identity as a mechanism to control them, the narrative simultaneously allows for the representation of such women's individual sexual expression, and, perhaps, agency.[28] *Pimp*'s cold, matter-of-fact opening line, "Her name was Maude and she Georgied me around 1921" establishes a sexualized asymmetrical power dynamic between the then three-year-old Slim and his much older babysitter who uses him for cunnilingus.[29] The novel defines "Georgie" as the act of being sexually taken advantage of without receiving money. That the text opens with a specific memory of a particular woman engaging in sexual exploitation challenges Gifford's explicit assessment that all "dangerous women" in *Pimp* are undifferentiated and his implicit claim that they lack agency. *Pimp*'s opening scene reveals to what extent Slim understands all the women in his life as *individualistic* sexual agents that in turn often render him submissive or abject and force him to complexly negotiate sex, power, pleasure, desire, domination, submission, and control.[30]

Hill Collins's controlling images theory remains fundamental to genealogies of black feminism. However, refusing or failing to consider black women's agency and pleasure within asymmetrical power dynamics, such as the matrix of domination, can unintentionally pathologize figures of the underworld, such as sex workers, by interpreting any articulation of their pleasure to be pathological denial or false consciousness. Many critics, such as Gifford, shy away from engaging women's individualism, agency, and pleasure in the face of (and sometimes as a result of) misogyny and sexualized violence.

Contemporary black feminist critics have been calling for recognition of black women's agency and pleasure within the matrix of domination for at least two decades. For example, eight years before Rose's critique of exploitation, hip-hop feminist Joan Morgan dared to query, "How come no one ever admits that part of the reason women love hip-hop—as sexist as it is—is 'cuz all that in-yo-face testosterone makes our nipples hard?"[31] Recognizing pleasure under patriarchy, as Morgan does, is influential to a recent generation of black, sex-positive feminist scholars that, in addition to Miller-Young, Nash, Musser, and Cruz include LaMonda Horton-Stallings, Treva B. Lindsey, and Kaila Story. These critics explore the intersections of black women's pleasure and "exploitative" pornography, sex work, and other forms of explicit cultural productions that represent black women as highly sexual.[32]

Pleasure bears a particularly fraught relationship to African American culture considering that historically, as Saidiya Hartman argues, in the terrorist economy of slavery black pleasure was understood as merely an extension of the master's pleasure.[33] And during the late nineteenth and early twentieth centuries black pleasure was delimited by the politics of respectability and is continually censored in respectability's wake. Evelynn Hammonds notes, "The restrictive, repressive, and dangerous aspects of black women's sexuality have been emphasized by black feminist writers while pleasure, exploration, and agency have gone under-analyzed."[34] And Hortense Spillers famously states, "black women are the beached whales of the sexual universe, unvoiced, misseen, not doing, awaiting *their* verb."[35]

Again, to privilege an analysis of pleasure, specifically kinky pleasure, is *not* to suggest that through it subjects transcend structures of social oppression and are liberated. Rather, an analysis of such pleasure, within fraught historical conditions, invites critical attention to what has been erased, denied, devalued, and censored and forces us to contend with *why*. As literary and cultural critics, we can recognize structural oppression, such as the matrix of domination and our contemporary #MeToo and #TimesUp era while also asking: Can explicit depictions of sex and violence that exploit women be read in ways additional to patriarchal oppression? Can forms of patriarchal oppression, exploitation, and objectification be pleasurable for women? Must "explicit" necessarily be conflated with "exploitation"? Do women derive pleasure from participating in the construction of our own "controlling images"? Does, or should female exploitation render a text off-limits to critical considerations that seek to analyze what, in addition to misogyny, can be read therein?

Consider this: there are many female characters in *Pimp* whose sexual expression and involvement in sex work cannot be explained *merely* with familiar narratives of abuse, trauma, or codependency.[36] Although such narratives accompany the backstory of several of Slim's prostitutes, these same women are often represented as taking pleasure in their work. Chris is an example of a character that complicates such narratives. Specifically, Slim is able to seduce Chris, one of his eventual "bottom [main] women," by reminding her of the *pleasure* she takes in it. Because Slim "knew [Chris] was a freak" (another word for kinky), he is able to whisper to her that she is a member of the "whore game" and recognizes that the responsive "thrill in her voice" is spoken by "the whore . . . alive and thrashing inside her."[37] In her research on black sex workers, Miller-Young notes, "women are motivated by . . . a sense of recognition for their erotic embodiment and sexual talents."[38] Thus, when Chris initially questions why she is drawn to Slim, he responds: "Don't ask yourself stupid questions. You can't escape that freak, desperate spark."[39] He convinces Chris that she cannot deny the power of embodying her own eroticism or the pleasure inherent to the "perversity" of transgressive sex.

Gifford, like many critics using a traditional feminist lens to read African American literature, is mainly concerned with the controlling images of black women that, in the case of *Pimp*, "perpetuate a mythology of women as 'bitches' and 'whores' who are complicit in keeping black men down."[40] However, such an over-determined focus on controlling images forecloses critical consideration of black women's agency and pleasure in *embodying* those controlling images or in participating in their construction. Some female characters in *Pimp* are represented as not only taking pleasure in being a prostitute but also doing so because of its affiliation with a black stereotype of hypersexuality—the Jezebel. By portraying such a stereotype, these women perform a type of minstrelsy that challenges the controlling images framework that ultimately denies black women agency.

For instance, at one point Slim's first prostitute Phyllis reveals to him that although she hates servicing "white tricks" who "paw" and "slobber" all over her, she "gets a thrill with them" by being a "black Nigger bitch, taking their scratch [money]" as they moan and groan and lick "between a black whore's thighs." Here Phyllis is getting pleasure out of profiting from performing as the Jezebel—one of many "black whores in Hell" that have something "between their legs" that "those cold ass [white] broads in

Heaven ain't got."⁴¹ Although Slim's mentor Sweet debunked for him the myth of black hypersexuality underlying white desire for black bodies (claiming, instead, that it is a drive toward abjection), it is a mythic stereotype that motivates Phyllis as she embodies it and puts it to work. As a (self-referentially) "black and low" (abject) prostitute, Phyllis imagines herself to be coproducer, maintainer, and, ultimately profiteer from the stereotype's continual reproduction.⁴² "Black sex workers' illicit erotic moral economy" can bring prostitutes, such as Phyllis, self-proclaimed satisfaction.⁴³ Rather than reading such women as complicit or informed by false consciousness, as Gifford does, I read the prostitutes in *Pimp*, while oppressed within the matrix of domination, also claiming ownership of and pleasure in their abjection. In doing so, their actions critique denial of their erotic autonomy.⁴⁴

In addition to such transgressive role-playing, throughout *Pimp* black women's sexual pleasure and agency is, at times, expressed through "freakiness." Take the character Pepper who Georgies Slim. Pepper is a "freaky . . . bitch" and "[ex-] whore" who effectively manipulates her various controlling images (Jezebel and Sapphire) with finesse. Pepper is the dominant in their BDSM power dynamic. As Slim states, he "wasn't in her league." Pepper entraps Slim like "a yellow cat hypnotizing a bird." Describing her tactics of patient, concentrated seduction, Slim states, "She sat there motionless, her green eyes smoky, as she stared at me through the mirror." He is excited by her "raw sensuality" that she administers like a drug as she gives him "a full dose of those hot green eyes" that "sign [their] deal."⁴⁵

Slim soon realizes Pepper is a "freak bitch" during sex play. She "cajoled and persuaded [him] to do everything in the sexual book, and a number of things not even listed" during their sessions that ran "the gamut of sexual perversion."⁴⁶ Slim describes their exploration of BDSM sex, stating that Pepper "nibbled and sucked hundreds of tingling bruises on every square inch of my body." He also reveals their practice of urolagnia, noting, "It took me a week to get the stench of her piss out of my hair." In this latter example Slim perhaps understands Pepper to have marked him as her primary sexual object, even if she only did so to "take her revenge" on him for the fierce way in which "she hated men." But Slim takes pleasure in this idea that Pepper is embodying controlling images (here, the Sapphire) as she sexually degrades him.⁴⁷

In this scene, Slim has yet to achieve masculine maturity and pimp identity. Thus, at the time, he does not fully comprehend their sexual power dynamic. He felt there was reciprocity between them, stating: "I was flipping Pepper with the techniques she had taught me. I knew all the buttons to push for her, and she burned hotter than ever for her little puppy. . . . Fair exchange, as the old saw goes, is never robbery."[48] But does Pepper "burn" for Slim because he is such a great lover and therefore virile (a necessity for his developing ethos), or does her pleasure derive from the fact that she has turned him out and created a sex slave ("little puppy") for herself, willing and eager to please her with her own techniques? While Slim interprets their sexual transactions as "fair exchange" he is, in fact, performing in the ways Pepper wants him to perform, when she wants him to perform for her. And he is devastated when he learns he is *not* her primary sexual object; he is not the "only stud she freaks off with," having believed "like a sucker" that he was "the whole show in her love life."[49] It is important to note that in kink theory the word *exchange* suggests reciprocity. Yet, as these readings of *Pimp* should invite us to question, is reciprocity a necessary component needed for a subject to claim pleasure or desire? What of the pleasure and desire bred from a lack thereof?

Parsing the pleasure attached to subordination and abjection is difficult in *Pimp*, because it is often cathected to noir affects of anxiety or fear. For example, once Slim realizes how Pepper has Georgied him, his nascent machismo requires an adverse reaction. The scene is worth quoting at length for its representation of Slim's pleasure as the violently subordinated subject within their asymmetrical power dynamic:

> I reached down and slapped [Pepper] hard against the side of her face. It sounded like a pistol shot. On impact a thrill shot through me. I should have slugged her with a baseball bat.
>
> The bitch uncoiled from that bed like a striking yellow cobra, hooked her arms around my waist and sank her razor sharp teeth into my navel.
>
> The shock paralyzed me. I fell across my back on the bed moaning in pain. I could feel blood rolling from the wound down toward my crotch, but I couldn't speak. I couldn't move.
>
> Pepper was sure a strange twisted broad. She was breathing hard now, but not in rage. The violence, the blood, had turned her on.
>
> She was gently caressing me as she licked, with a feathery tongue, the oozing wound on my belly. She had never been so tenderly efficient as she took me on a beautiful "trip around the Universe."
>
> The funny thing was, the throbbing awful pain somehow became a part of me, melted into the joy of the feathery tongue, the thrill of the thing Pepper was doing to me.
>
> I guess Freud was right. If it thrills you to give pain, you can get your jollies taking it.[50]

Slim feels the need to differentiate and contain his and Pepper's power roles through misogynist abuse precisely because he must hide his pleasure at being made her abject subordinate. He physically abuses Pepper to control her and to force her to suffer for her dominance. However, Pepper's freaky response undermines Slim's intentions to sediment his dominance through violence. Much to his surprise, the violence "turns her on," as does the wound she inflicts on his body. And she uses her arousal to ultimately "twist" the scenario to her advantage by administering physical violence conflated with sexual pleasure to Slim's body to further subordinate him. As he vulnerably relinquishes to her, he finds himself paralyzed in his experience of *jouissance*—comingled pain, joy, and thrilling sexual arousal.[51] He realizes, as "the awful pain became a part of [him]," that he not only enjoys performing as the dominant sadist "thrilled" to "give pain," but also as the subordinate masochist getting his "jollies taking it." In his essay "Freaks and the American Ideal of Manhood," James Baldwin argues: "Freaks are called freaks and are treated as they are treated—in the main, abominably—because they . . . cause to echo, deep within us, our most profound terrors and desires."[52] Slim's attempt to control Pepper fails because he underestimates the extent of her kinkiness, and the extent of his own, in which seduction and abjection produce each other.[53]

Ever since S/M was rendered a perversion (along with fetishism and homosexuality) by Krafft-Ebing in 1890, the stigma has remained. Masochism, in particular, continues to be classified as a mental disorder under the designation "Sexual Masochism Disorder" in the 2013 American Psychological Association's *Diagnostic and Statistical Manual of Mental Disorders: Fifth Edition* (*DSM-5*). Thus, BDSM, as a practice and a power dynamic has been rendered largely critically unspeakable. Likewise, considerations of race and ethnicity are "inadequately addressed" within studies of sadomasochism.[54]

However, at its core "S/M is always a racialized practice."[55] As Biman Basu argues, "The resemblances between the practice of S&M and slavery are legion and cannot be glossed over . . . sadomasochistic practice as it has emerged in the late twentieth century begins in the eighteenth century," concurrent with American chattel slavery.[56] Thus, "the most compelling demonstration that the power exercised in sadomasochistic performance is, in fact, real [as opposed to merely 'play,' or 'aesthetics'] is its historicity. We cannot miss the fact that the conventions, the mannerisms, the equipment used in S&M belong in the past, in the regime of punishment . . . [and] while the practice of dominant-submissive desire is not a return to the violence of the past, the memory of the past does inform it."[57] Regardless of whether or not critics engage literary representations of BDSM power dynamics, they *inform* much artistic representation and need engagement. This is because, as Basu stresses, "Sadomasochism is not limited to the private sphere of sexual practice but pervades the public realm of the social and the political economy of everyday life . . . [and] the discursive formation of S&M has emerged to fill a general discursive absence."[58] Kink theory helps us see power's erotic productivity as it cuts across and shapes all vectors. How is desire produced and managed therein? And what might this suggest about commodity exchange relations?

Beth Coleman argues, "the slave economy in America produced the American pimp" and "the pimp," she writes, "is a student of power."[59] She refers to the pimp as "that famously abject thing" that, while he is not "outside" the square world, can nonetheless critically analyze its vectors of power from his position on its margins and turn his business into a fetish.[60] The psychosexual dimensions of antiblack racism, in which whites dominate, commodify, and abuse black bodies to achieve sexual satisfaction, has been acknowledged by black writers, intellectuals, and critics from Ida B. Wells and Malcolm X to Gayl Jones, Saidiya Hartman, and Vincent Woodard, among others. Coleman states, "What one finds in the legacy of African-American letters is an ongoing fascination with the structure of mastery"; and Basu notes, "From the middle through the late nineteenth century . . . the devices, instruments, and methods of punishment [of corporal discipline] were available to American and European readers, refracted by the literary form of the slave narrative and other discourses."[61] BDSM power dynamics, explicitly or implicitly, are tropes that have informed much African American literature for centuries. But they are also inherent to much paraliterature, which, due to its pulp affiliations is an ideal form through which to explore transgressive sexuality, including representations of erotic play-slavery, also known as race play such as what we see in *Pimp*. Play-slavery, a kink that "delineates the performance of racialized sexuality" is just one of the manifestations of erotic power exchange that Call identifies, stating, "S/M eroticizes the class relations which are such a fundamental part of chattel slavery."[62] And Ariane Cruz in *The Color of Kink* suggests, "race play exhibit[s] an . . . eroticization of black female racial-sexual alterity and its anxiety."[63] Through play-slavery, or race play, subjects "subvert, pervert, and make overt the erotic subtext of power and authority."[64]

Basu suggests objections to sadomasochism "are predicated on the assumption that affective relations of the past in a regime of punishment (slavery, feudalism, colonialism) must be expunged." Yet "sadomasochist performance assumes that this past not only cannot be entirely extinguished but also that it may be desirable as a usable past."[65] After his experience with Pepper, Slim tries to save himself from subordination and thinks: "I really want to control the whole whore. I want to be the boss of her life, even her thoughts. I got to con them that Lincoln never freed the slaves."[66] Here, "the freedom/slavery reversal is crucial: the black pimp, escaping from bondage, becomes the slave-owner."[67] Slim has to convince his whores that slavery is a continuation of the "natural state" of black women in the United States—an idea that clearly resonates with the controlling images theory.[68] This strategy often backfires as Slim's whores, in many instances, betray him and even attempt to kill him out of resentment. However, it also at times works, but not as a mechanism of control as Slim hopes.

The woman Slim treats most like a slave (and who most takes on the role) is his first whore, Phyllis. Because in my analysis of *Pimp* I am invested in tracing women's agency in asymmetrical power dynamics, it is important to note that at the bar where they meet, it is *Phyllis* who propositions Slim. Slim seduces her by wearing the façade of pimp dominance and by speaking to her in a manner dictated by that façade that renders her abject and, consequently, turns her on.

Early in their initial conversation, in response to Phyllis's assertion "I ain't no bitch. I'm a mother-fucking lady," Slim states: "You stinking black Bitch, you're a fake. There's no such thing as a lady in our world. You either got to be a bitch or a faggot in drag. Now Bitch, which is it? Bitch, I'm not a gentleman, I'm a pimp. I'll kick your funky ass. You gave me first lick. Bitch you're creaming to eat me up. I'm not a come freak, you are. I'm a freak to scratch."[69] Slim calls Phyllis a "fake," accusing her of trying to lay claim to a gender role ("lady") excluded from "their [under]world" and historically denied black women. And for Slim to reject the mantle of "gentleman" is to firmly state his class standing in that world.[70] He aligns himself with her delimited gender by stating that he is not a "gentleman" but rather, a "pimp" suggesting that she, by proxy, is a "whore." He thus asserts his dominance by claiming such status and threatening her with physical violence common to the pimp/whore dynamic. To shame and humiliate her, he limits her sexual identity options to the abject "bitch" or "faggot," repeatedly referring to her as the former. Lastly, he labels her a "come freak," a degrading accusation considering one is considered perverse for consuming the bodily waste of another human.

Despite, or because of, these demeaning sexual and gendered accusations Slim's "blast had moved [Phyllis]." He states, "I could see those sexy dancers [eyes] were hot as hell there in the midnight. She was trying to conceal from me the *freakish pain-loving bitch inside her*.[71] Reading through a matrix of domination framework, readers could argue that Slim's interpretation of Phyllis's reaction is overwritten by his masculinist narrative point of view. However, Irvine Welsh, who was deeply influenced by Slim, offers a counterargument: "In [Slim's] works, the hookers are seldom simply victims of the pimps but more often fellow ghetto strugglers with the same grifter sensibility."[72] Note also, *Pimp* was written with Slim's wife Betty's assistance, which is not to somehow excuse the novel's masculinist tone so much as it is to acknowledge the complexity of the gender relations both represented in the text and instrumental to its production.[73]

Indeed, although Phyllis thinks she can Georgie Slim and evade his attempts to con her into becoming his whore, she is evidently aroused by the way he constructs himself as a pimp through rendering her his subordinate "bitch." Her words and actions corroborate Slim's assessment that she is excited by the BDSM power dynamic of their transaction. She leaves the bar with Slim, whispering to him: "You cold-blooded sweet motherfucker, I go for you. Let's go to my pad and rap."[74] Once in Phyllis's bedroom, foreplay disintegrates into what can clearly be read as abusive play-slavery as Slim "turns her out" (makes her his whore). Slim beats Phyllis for trying to Georgie him, and the scene is one of asymmetrical power exchange because Slim's will is fortified at the violent suppression of Phyllis's. The scene turns both subjects out, as Slim becomes a pimp precisely through Phyllis's transformation.

However, Phyllis arguably experiences *jouissance* through sexualized violence. One could read this scene as a representation of "edgeplay," a particularly transgressive BDSM exchange that falls in the "'gray area between 'enough' and 'too much,' between consent and nonconsent.'"[75] After being beaten into submission Phyllis looks upon Slim with "fear and strange passion" and whispers: "You got a whore Blood. Please don't kick me any more. I'm your little dog. I'll do anything you say. I love you, Pretty Daddy."[76] It is difficult to discern whether her "strange passion" suggests pleasure or desire because it is intertwined with fear, pain, and survival instinct. She claims a subordinate role that will do anything Slim requests, suggesting her words and actions are a strategy she employs in the moment to save herself from further physical abuse.

Yet, as *jouissance* helps us to consider, her "strange passion" can be read as evocative of pleasure or desire *because* it is intertwined with fear and pain. Immediately after this declaration she retaliates, flipping her subordinate role for a dominant one. The narrative reads, "Her talons stabbed into the back of [Slim's] neck as she tried to suck [his] tongue from its root."[77] Like Slim and Pepper, Phyllis lays claim to another's body through sexualized violence. Thus, while it is difficult to determine her pleasure or desire, it seems that it is Phyllis's *jouissance* prompting her to perform as an erotic sadist as she negotiates with Slim their newly formed play-slavery relationship. Her experience of *jouissance* allows her to more fully express the "freakish pain-loving" and pain-giving "bitch" inside her as she explores the fluidity of roles in their BDSM power dynamic. Call is careful to note that *desire* is necessary in BDSM play, which thereby "guarantees the ethical content of erotic power exchange."[78] Pointedly, in kink theory, desire is what separates the submission one enjoys from the submission one does not enjoy. However, as Samuel R. Delany writes, "The power involved in desire is so great that when caught in an actual rhetorical manifestation of desire—a particular sex act, say—it is sometimes all but impossible to untangle the complex webs of power that shoot through it from various directions, the power relations that are the act and that constitute it."[79] Because identities are so fluid, in *Pimp*, power—its attainment and retention—is privileged above all else.

Whoever has the power in Slim and Phyllis's dynamic at any given moment is the subject possessing control. Thus, Slim does everything he can to convince Phyllis of her subordinate stature. However, power is not stable, and despite Slim's violent efforts to contain their respective roles, Phyllis can often be read as the dominant subject as she constantly renders Slim subordinate. He is, for a large part of the novel, completely dependent on her for his economic survival, as she is, for some time, his only whore. He purportedly beats her so that she will work harder and earn him more money and a larger stable of women, but he ultimately does so because he cannot bear the shame of being dependent on a whore that refuses to fully perform what he believes should be her contained submissive role to his contained dominant one.

Slim feels the need to outwardly portray the pimp/whore dynamic as secure precisely because he knows firsthand the threat of fragmentation. He understands and fears that Phyllis comprehends their dynamic to be neither static nor contained. And Slim knows that power is not delimited by gender in the underworld, as Sweet's succinct assessment "a pimp is really a whore who's reversed the game on whores" makes plain.[80] Haunted by Sweet's words, Slim understands deeply to what extent identities are malleable and power dynamics can flip. This is evidenced by the constant anxiety underlying his attempts at control in response to Phyllis's ambiguous actions that enact BDSM play as both a survival tactic and a kink.

And Slim repeatedly beats Phyllis for the way this ambiguity, and the agency it provides her, make him vulnerable, "like the prostitute's customer, a deceived fool."[81] Basu claims, "sadomasochism is a rigorously corporeal regime, but it is of course also a mental exercise, and perhaps most importantly an imaginative enterprise . . . at the level of affect."[82] *Pimp* speaks both to the dangerous corporeality of *jouissance* and the way it shapes the affective relations shared between participants in a BDSM power dynamic.

The radical potential of BDSM and kink theory that helps us to think through its literary representations is that, because of the fluidity of roles, power takes precedence over subjective identifiers. As Gayle Rubin states "class, race, and gender neither determine nor correspond to the roles adopted for S/M play."[83] Power is not consigned to the man, to the pimp, to the supposed "dominant" subject. Fearful of this, Slim learns to project consistently a cold, violent exterior to control his fear of disintegrated subjectivity. Maintaining the pimp façade allows Slim to suppress the shame he felt as Maude's abject subordinate, the *jouissance* he experienced as Pepper's, and the fear of becoming Phyllis's. He seeks to escape his pleasure at being the subordinate abject; but reading the novel through kink theory reveals to what extent such escape is not possible. The pimp can never be more than a "gutter god"—that famously abject thing.[84] He lives by the pimps' advice in prison: "Stay cold and brutal. Cop your scratch first. Don't let 'em Georgie you. They'll laugh at you. They'll cut you loose like a trick after they've flim-flammed you. Your scratch cop is the only way to put a hook in their stinking asses."[85] The pimps in prison echo Sweet's sentiment that pimps and whores are interchangeable roles that can be easily flipped depending on the context. Thus, throughout the novel Slim has to remember, "the sexy part of pimping is not the sex, but the control."[86] But *Pimp* is a "spectacular failure" in which Slim undercuts this patriarchal archetype by revealing his inability to control women to the point that they would generate for him his own freedom.[87]

BDSM power dynamics eroticize noir affect, but they are not necessarily liberatory. More importantly, texts such as *Pimp* provide a problematizing of the differentiation of sex acts ("pleasure" *or* "pain," for example) often used to contain abjection into overdetermined narratives of abuse, trauma, or internalized oppression. Such rationalizing is often used as the *only* explanation for why a subject would choose to participate in "unhealthy," "perverse" sexual relations. Because, as Kristeva argues, abjection is an expression of ambiguity, *Pimp*'s characters in states of *jouissance* are undifferentiated. Reading an overdetermined masculinist novel such as *Pimp* through a BDSM dynamic is to recognize the dissolution of "fixed" gendered, sexual, and racial identifiers in relation to vectors of power, and power's inability to contain.

NOTES

1. Josh Alan Friedman, "A Tribute to Iceberg Slim," WFMU.org, https://wfmu.org/LCD/21/ice.html.

2. Peter Muckley, *Iceberg Slim: The Life as Art* (Pittsburgh, PA: Dorrance, 2003), 18.

3. Justin Gifford, *Pimping Fictions: African American Crime Literature and the Untold Story of Black Pulp Publishing* (Philadelphia: Temple University Press, 2013), 39.

4. Gifford, 2.

5. See "The Politics of Paraliterary Criticism," in Samuel R. Delany, *Shorter Views: Queer Thoughts and the Politics of the Paraliterary* (Hanover, NH: University Press of New England, 1999), 218–270. Samuel R. Delany defines "paraliterary" and "paraliterature" (the former Rosalind Krauss's term, the latter Fredric Jameson's) as "specifically those written genres traditionally excluded by the limited, value-bound meaning of 'literature' and 'literary.'"

6. Andrew S. Jackson, *Gentleman Pimp: An Autobiography* (Los Angeles: Holloway House, 1973), 181.

7. Irvine Welsh, "Up from the Street," *Guardian*, March 13, 2009.

8. See Kinohi Nishikawa, *Street Players: Black Pulp Fiction and the Making of a Literary Underground* (Chicago: University of Chicago Press, 2018); Bonnie Andreyeyev, "Whose Mean Streets?: Donald Goines, Iceberg Slim, and the Black Noir Aesthetic," in *Street Lit: Representing the Urban Landscape*, ed. Keenan Norris (Lanham, MD: Scarecrow Press 2014), 38–54; Dennis L. Winston, "(Re)writing the 'Bad Nigger' Hero in Robert Beck's Pimp," in *Street Lit*, 55–65; Justin Gifford, *Pimping Fictions and Street Poison: The Biography of Iceberg Slim* (New York: Doubleday, 2015); Jonathan Munby, *Under a Bad Sign: Criminal Self-Representation in African-American Popular Culture* (Chicago: University of Chicago Press, 2011); Candice Love Jackson, "The Literate Pimp: Iceberg Slim, Robert Beck, and Pimping the African American Novel," in *New Essays on the African American Novel*, ed. Lovalerie King and Linda F. Selzer (New York: Palgrave MacMillan, 2008), 167–183; Victoria A. Elmwood, "'They Can't Take That Away from Me': Gendered Nationalism and Textual Sovereignty in the Autobiographies of Iceberg Slim and Malcolm X," *Soundings: An Interdisciplinary Journal*, no. 90 (2007):

245–271; Beth Coleman, "Pimp Notes on Autonomy," in *Everything but the Burden: What White People are Taking from Black Culture*, ed. Greg Tate (New York: Broadway Books, 2003), 68–80; LaMonda Horton-Stallings, "'I'm Goin Pimp Whores!': The Goines Factor and the Theory of a Hip-Hop Neo-Slave Narrative," *New Centennial Review* 3, no. 3 (2003): 175–203; Peter Muckley, *Iceberg Slim: The Life As Art* (Pittsburgh: Dorrance, 2003); Muckley, "Iceberg Slim: Robert Beck-A True Essay at a Biocriticism of an Ex-Outlaw Artist," *The Black Scholar* 26, no. 1 (1996): 18–25; Delia Konzett, "Prison, Perversion, and Pimps: The White Temptress in The Autobiography of Malcolm X and Iceberg Slim's Pimp," in *White Women in Racialized Spaces: Imaginative Transformation and Ethical Action in Literature*, ed. Samina Najmi and Rajini Srikanth (Albany: State University of New York Press, 2002), 147–166; and D. B. Graham, "'Negative Glamour': The Pimp Hero in the Fiction of Iceberg Slim," *Obsidian: Black Literature in Review* 1, no. 2 (1975): 5–16.

9. Iceberg Slim, *Pimp: The Story of My Life* (New York: Cash Money Content, 2011), 198

10. Slim, 78.

11. Lewis Call, "'Sounds Like Kinky Business to Me': Subtextual and Textual Representations of Erotic Power in the Buffyverse," *Slayage* 6, no. 4. (2007): 6.

12. Call, 131.

13. Lewis Call, "Structures of Desire: Postanarchist Kink in the Speculative Fiction of Octavia Butler and Samuel Delany," in *Anarchism & Sexuality: Ethics, Relationships and Power*, ed. Jamie Heckert and Richard Cleminson (New York: Routledge, 2011), 135.

14. For his first published articulation of the term "kink theory," see Call, "'Sounds Like Kinky Business to Me.'" See also Call, "Structures of Desire."

15. Michel Foucault, *Discipline and Punish: The Birth of the Prison* (New York: Pantheon Books, 1977), 194.

16. Call, "Structures of Desire," 136.

17. Jennifer C. Nash, *The Black Body in Ecstasy: Reading Race, Reading Pornography* (Durham, NC: Duke University Press, 2014), 3. See also Darieck Scott, *Extravagant Abjection: Blackness, Power, and Sexuality in the African American Literary Imagination* (New York: New York University Press, 2010); Kathryn Bond Stockton, *Beautiful Bottom: Beautiful Shame: Where "Black" Meets "Queer"* (Durham, NC: Duke University Press, 2006); Mireille Miller-Young, *A Taste for Brown Sugar: Black Women in Pornography* (Durham, NC: Duke University Press, 2014); Amber Musser, *Sensational Flesh: Race, Power, and Masochism* (New York: New York University Press,

2014); and Ariane Cruz, *The Color of Kink: Black Women, BDSM, and Pornography* (New York: New York University Press, 2016).

18. Biman Basu, *The Commerce of Peoples: Sadomasochism and African American Literature* (Lanham, MD: Lexington Books, 2012), 23.

19. Gifford, *Pimping Fictions*, 10.

20. Coleman, "Pimp Notes on Autonomy," 72.

21. Tricia Rose, *The Hip Hop Wars: What We Talk About When We Talk About Hip Hop-and Why It Matters* (New York: Basic Civitas, 2008), 168.

22. Rose, 77.

23. Gifford, *Pimping Fictions*, 63.

24. Gifford, 63.

25. Scott, *Extravagant Abjection*, 20.

26. Patricia Hill Collins, *Black Feminist Thought: Knowledge, Consciousness, and the Politics of Empowerment* (New York: Routledge, 2008).

27. Gifford, *Pimping Fictions*, 56–57.

28. At this point, with the conflation of sexual expression and agency, objections will possibly arise that I am conceiving desire as wholly conscious, intentional, and self-present. Risking such an objection may be the price to pay for rejecting a trauma-informed account of desire-production that often goes hand in hand with psychoanalytic readings. For an alternative Lacanian approach to sexual agency (or a lack thereof) and jouissance in the African American literary canon, see Sheldon George's "Approaching the 'Thing' of Slavery: a Lacanian Analysis of Toni Morrison's *Beloved*," *African American Review* 45, nos. 1–2 (2012): 115–130.

29. Slim, *Pimp*, 300.

30. Welsh, "Up from the Streets." Welsh notes "Slim admitted that one reason he stopped pimping and became a writer was his fear of being exploited by younger prostitutes."

31. Joan Morgan, *When Chickenheads Come Home to Roost: My Life as a Hip-Hop Feminist* (New York: Simon and Schuster, 1999), 58.

32. See LaMonda Horton-Stallings, *Mutha' Is Half a Word: Intersections of Folklore, Vernacular, Myth, and Queerness in Black Female Culture* (Columbus: Ohio State University Press, 2007); Nash, *Black Body in Ecstasy*; Mireille Miller-Young, ed., *The Feminist Porn Book: The Politics of Producing Pleasure* (New York: Feminist Press at City University of New York, 2013); Treva B. Lindsey "Complicated Crossroads: Black Feminisms, Sex Positivism, and Popular Culture," *African and Black Diaspora: An International Journal* 6, no. 1 (2013): 55–65; and M. Miller-Young "Hip-Hop Honeys and Da Hustlaz: Black Sexualities in the New Hip-Hop Pornography," *Meridians: Feminism, Race, Transnationalism* 8, no. 1 (2007): 261–292; and M. Miller-Young, "Putting Hypersexuality to Work: Black

Women and Illicit Eroticism in Pornography," *Sexualities* 13, no. 22 (April 2010): 219–235.

33. Saidiya V. Hartman, *Scenes of Subjection: Terror, Slavery, and Self-Making in Nineteenth-Century America* (New York: Oxford University Press, 1997).

34. Evelynn Hammonds, "Toward a Genealogy of Black Female Sexuality: The Problematic of Silence," in *The Feminist Philosophy Reader*, ed. Alison Bailey and Chris J. Cuomo (Boston, MA: McGraw-Hill, 2008), 385.

35. Hortense Spillers, "Interstices: A Small Drama of Words," in *Pleasure and Danger: Exploring Female Sexuality*, ed. Carole S. Vance (London: Pandora Press, 1992), 74.

36. See James Elias, *Prostitution: On Whores, Hustlers, and Johns* (Amherst, MA: Prometheus, 1998) for a comprehensive history of the "world's oldest profession." One of the first writers to analyze the psychological aspects of prostitution was Havelock Ellis and he derived such explanations unable to accept economic motivation as an explanation for why women chose to be prostitutes.

37. Slim, *Pimp*, 162, 161.
38. Miller-Young, "Putting Hypersexuality to Work," 225.
39. Slim, *Pimp*, 163.
40. Gifford, *Pimping Fictions*, 58.
41. Slim, *Pimp*, 158.
42. Slim, 158.
43. Miller-Young, "Putting Hypersexuality to Work," 229.
44. Miller-Young, 231. Tellingly, in her study of black women sex workers, Miller-Young finds "the informants in this study feel further alienated by feminist scholars that talk about them, but not to them, and who see them as colluding with misogynists rather than carving out a vital space for black women to see themselves as desirable and desiring subjects" (231).
45. Slim, *Pimp*, 42.
46. Slim, 43, 299.
47. Slim, 43.
48. Slim, 43.
49. Slim, 49.
50. Slim, 44–45.
51. For Lacan, *jouissance* suggests sexual enjoyment that transgresses the homeostasis described in Freud's pleasure principle theory. *Jouissance* seeks a subjective split through the pleasure/pain accompanying abjection.
52. James Baldwin, "Freaks and the American Ideal of Manhood," in *Collected Essays* (New York: Library of America, 1998), 828.

53. See Stockton *Beautiful Bottom*, for a sustained argument regarding "how we might think about . . . debasement in the context of seduction" (3).

54. Darren Langdridge and Meg Barker, *Safe, Sane, and Consensual: Contemporary Perspectives on Sadomasochism* (Hampshire: Palgrave Macmillan, 2007), 5.

55. Elizabeth Freeman, "Turn the Beat Around: Sadomasochism, Temporality, History," *Differences* 19, no.1 (2008): 59.

56. Basu, *Commerce of Peoples*, 39, 4. Refer to Basu's chapter "Slave Narratives and Sadomasochism" for an in-depth historical and literary discussion of these resemblances.

57. Basu, 23.

58. Basu, 18, 172.

59. Coleman, "Pimp Notes on Autonomy," 68, 72.

60. Coleman, 71.

61. Coleman, 79; Basu, *Commerce of Peoples*, 32.

62. Cruz, *Color of Kink*, 25; Call, "Structures of Desire," 144.

63. Cruz, 25.

64. Liz Highleyman, "Playing with Paradox: The Ethics of Erotic Dominance and Submission," in *Bitch Goddess*, ed. Pat Califia and Drew Campbell (San Francisco: Greenery Press, 2007).

65. Basu, *Commerce of Peoples*, 25.

66. Slim, *Pimp*, 87.

67. Graham, "Negative Glamour," 13

68. See Michelle Wallace, *Black Macho and the Myth of the Superwoman* (Brooklyn: Verso Books, 1999), and bell hooks, *Ain't I a Woman? Black Women and Feminism* (Boston, MA: South End Press, 1981). This form of black masculine dominance over black women has been analyzed and challenged by many black feminist scholars.

69. Slim, *Pimp*, 63.

70. See Susan Hall, *Gentleman of Leisure: A Year in the Life of a Pimp* (Brooklyn, NY: powerHouse Books, 2006), and A. S. Jackson, *Gentleman Pimp: An Autobiography* (Los Angeles: Holloway House, 1973). Historically pimps have adopted the "gentleman" moniker in interesting ways.

71. Slim, *Pimp*, 63; emphasis added.

72. Welsh, "Up from the Streets."

73. Gifford, *Street Poison*, 154–160.

74. Slim, *Pimp*, 64.

75. Easton and Liszt, quoted in Basu, *Commerce of Peoples*, 170.

76. Slim, *Pimp*, 67.

77. Slim, 67.

78. Call, "Structures of Desire," 133.

79. Samuel R. Delany, "The Rhetoric of Sex/The Discourse of Desire," in *Shorter Views: Queer Thoughts and the Politics of the Paraliterary* (Hanover, NH: University Press of New England, 1999), 20.

80. Slim, *Pimp*, 198.

81. Graham, "Negative Glamour," 11.

82. Basu, *Commerce of Peoples*, 4.

83. Gayle Rubin, "The Leather Menace," *Body Politic*, no. 82 (1982): 224.

84. Robert Beck, *The Naked Soul of Iceberg Slim: Robert Beck's Real Story* (Los Angeles: Holloway House, 2000), 57.

85. Slim, *Pimp*, 65.

86. Coleman, "Pimp Notes on Autonomy," 72.

87. Gifford, *Pimping Fictions*, 62.

CHAPTER 4

Noir Pedagogy: The Problem of Student Masochism in the Classroom Economy

Elizabeth A. Hatmaker

If there is a central relationship that undergraduate students need to establish upon entering the university, it is the one that they, as learning subjects, will have toward knowledge and power, represented to them as ideals and, at the same time, as immediate conditions within a complex and often alienating nexus of institutions and discourses. Will the student view the pursuit of knowledge as a precursor to having material and ideological power (going to college means you'll make more money)? Will they imagine various forms of power as prerequisites to attaining knowledge (certain privileged groups have better access to knowledge and knowledge production)? Will the terms *power* and *knowledge* seem complementary or adversarial to the student? Depending on how they read this relationship, the student will adjust how they act in the classroom, what persona they take on. This persona may change over time, or it may vary depending on the situation, but the relationship on which this persona is developed remains one that will likely determine a student's success or failure within the university system. Early in the educational process, a student gets pegged—a good worker, insubordinate, helpful, can't follow directions—for behaviors and attitudes that often have little to do with what we, as educators, imagine to be raw intelligence. Rather, these descriptions indicate a student's ability to adapt to the classroom, to an immediate personification of power who is not, as the young student is accustomed, an intimate family member and to an impersonal system of education in which they often have little power.

Within the university, we see students with a variety of academic personae. At "better" colleges, one might argue that there is a proliferation of students who have learned to adapt their personae to correspond to corporate organizational behavior or liberal humanist sensibilities about knowledge and power. At lower-tier public universities, as well as at urban "open admission" schools and community colleges, arguably we see a larger variety of academic personae and more personae that are less successful for students. At all universities, whatever their stature, we find at least some students who, regardless of intelligence, fail to adapt to university culture. Often their intelligence itself keeps them from adapting to what they often see as a flawed and confining system. For many educators, from John Dewey to Paulo Friere, these students are right and their resistance to adapting to the educational system is truly the time when learning is taking place.[1] However, for many students, their placement within structures of power (a "better" school or a lower tier state school, for instance) inevitably becomes the means through which those in power (teachers, administrators, future employers, counselors) read this resistance. "Screw-ups" at better schools are likely to be read with more compassion and sensitivity than similar students at state schools. I teach at a state school and have long seen students who are smart but un-savvy in their academic personae; they are in constant risk of being ignored within overcrowded classrooms and growing institutional anxiety about student employability and stature.

As an instructor of creative writing, I often teach these students in my classroom. For them, creative writing class often suggests a space in which they might feel more acceptable and accepted than they do in other university courses. However, especially for smart students, their successes in creative writing often only highlight, in their minds, their inability to adjust in their other courses. Indeed, creative writing class offers students the forum, the tradition, and the skills to formalize their resistance in ways other courses don't. I suppose we might simply divide students who are good at "critical" thinking from students who are good at "creative" thinking, but such a move only seeks to cover over the relationship all students have to power and knowledge, a local enactment of a more global Foucauldian observation. To "creative" students, the university often both applauds their ability but indicates just as certainly that their abilities will only help them so far. Often, even when these students are appreciated for their resistance, their persona is regarded as self-destructive or masochistic. They become the stereotypical vision of the artist. As their teacher, I often wonder what my classroom might do to help them remain true to their resistance, but to develop an ethics for their resistance. How does resistance direct institutional change? If the university is wrong, then how can resistant students be right? How can their rightness become its own form of discourse or persona?

The Noir Student in the "Chinatown" of Knowledge

"Noir pedagogy" takes as its premise that the films and novels conceived in the noir tradition offer not only objects (narrative tropes, stylized film shots, metaphoric tropes) for critical consumption and analysis but also a psychoanalytic narrative and a subjective methodology, a specific set of gazes, problems, and responses that are recognizable as such within a larger social context (in my case, the university). Within the university, the noir student can approach individual classrooms as a series of archetypal noir figures—the world-weary detective, the *femme fatale*, the eroticized victim or "corpse." These narrative poses correspond to two of Jacques Lacan's four discourses: the discourse of the master (the detective) and the discourse of the hysteric (both the femme fatale and the corpse).[2] These discourses work, in the economy of the classroom, under and against Lacan's discourse of the university (which, I argue, has, as a discourse, two faces—the face of universal rationality and "Chinatown," the perverse face in which rationality is questioned). "Chinatown," as many critics of the film of the same name have noted, represents an Orientalist space in which language and culture are "inscrutable."[3] The Chinatown of noir is a space that is constructed by the dominant discourse. In the Polanski film, it functions as a racist projection and alibi. None of the film's violence or corruption actually takes place there. Instead, it becomes blamed, retroactively, for all that happens in the film. It is presented as dangerous not only because, as racist stereotypes go, Asians are seen as other, but more so because it represents a linguistic barrier to narrative solutions.[4] In a nutshell, noir represents a form of literature/film that is a highly stylized fantasy space in which gender, class, and race can be worked out symbolically within an always corrupting and corrupted phantasmatic space ("Chinatown"). Noir represents a tradition that is both stylistic and historical, phantasmatic and realistic. Thus, the narrative trope is useful in suggesting the complicated relationship between what students suggest to be "real" (Symbolic) and how they situate their relationship to the Real in relation to their fantasy of the academy. In *Black & White & Noir: America's Pulp Modernism*, Paula Rabinowitz likens this logic to a more global American noir logic: "modernity in America is structured around two poles, each working to suppress a hidden history of state violence: racial coding (hence the black-and-white motif) and class melodrama (hence the recourse to noir sentimentality and nostalgia). These in turn are revealed in the pulpy silhouettes of the femme fatale—the dark lady who glows in the bright key lighting of B-movies."[5]

In offering specific narrative models through which these discourses function around the central concept of knowledge, "noir pedagogy" works as a transactional mode of instruction in which students both enact and problematize these roles within the larger system of the academy. Thus, the noir student can understand themselves within the discourse of the university while, at the same time imagining themselves within a narrative other than that of the academy. This is necessary since the noir student suffers from a radical distrust of knowledge. Moreover, with similar irony, the noir student, unlike the classical detective, functions without trust of the system of knowledge in which they are inevitably trapped.

For the noir student, the trick to acquiring the subjective knowledge (*savoir*) most revered by Lacan, the knowledge of the subject as opposed to the knowledge of the ego (*connaissance*), is resisting what they are told and what they are supposed to learn. The noir student, while they may resist the knowledge of the university, is still simultaneously drawn to and repelled by the power of the university, both as an institution and as an ideal. From this ambivalence, the noir subject develops one of its primary attributes, paranoia.

Noir has, in fact, always addressed, dialectically, the relationships among reality, paranoia, and fantasy. As noir and neo-noir function as popular modes of fantasy, this pedagogical model suggests, in narrative language, not only how material roles (roles dictated by gender, class, race) function in the academy, or even how paranoia about the other functions, but also how phantasmatic roles and academic personae can both limit and challenge the student's access to Lacan's notion of *savoir*, arguably a form of knowledge the university is supposed to (but fails to) provide. Though the noir student's paranoia might prove a stumbling block to academic success, it doesn't necessarily follow that their paranoia isn't, as the joke goes, "good thinking." Indeed, although noir was organized around the logics of paranoia and self-destruction, it also presented the menace to the subject as a real threat, a reason why paranoia is a reasonable response to the situation. As Jake Gittes holds the corpse of Evelyn Mulwray at the end of *China-*

town, we understand that there's nothing he can do, no way he can prove anything, that the insane Noah Cross will continue his career of incest and city utilities fraud (fig. 1). Why can't he prove anything? Because, as his police cohort tells him, it's all gone down in "Chinatown." The tragedy (and existential pleasure) of noir is its presentation of knowledge without power, knowledge without justice.

This is the lot of the noir student. What this student must avoid in the perverse structure of academia is the pursuit of knowledge without ethics. Noir need not be the only narrative trope by which this type of performative pedagogy might work. Noir, with its ability to fuse various paranoid structures into a seamless narrative, becomes not simply a set of stereotypes from a bygone era, but a method of aesthetic theorization. Noir is useful in illustrating the powerful relationship between the individual subject's fantasy, their symbolic response, and the larger systematic construction of their reality (the University—the capitalization marking that this is one of the instantiations of Lacan's big Other). In noir, the city is always corrupt and although the academy is not (perhaps) entirely corrupt, it nonetheless represents one of the first spaces in which students address an organized power structure as adult subjects. The University is corrupt in exactly the same way "Chinatown" is corrupt—impersonally. Other than the family structure itself—in which corruption is likely to be taken as highly personalized—the University represents one of the first systematic big Others that the student has to face alone and that might hurt them in an impersonal manner; mom and dad might hate me, but to the University I'm just a number. The newness of this situation, an impersonal big Other to whom the student subject must react without help or support from

Figure 1. The untouchable Noah Cross in the finale of *Chinatown*.

family, results in a resituation not only of academic identification to knowledge but also, possibly, of more basic sexual identification to knowledge.

At the center of these power formations is the dynamic of the masochistic/sadistic subject. The institutional structure of the academy (the gaze of authority) positions students as subjects, but more importantly as objects who perform for the gaze of the other (the institution) and who understands, even sexually, the power of the institution. The student (the split subject) is the product of the discourse of the University and, as a product, the student functions both as a choosing, institutionalized subject and as an object of the University's desire and gaze. Though the University knowingly produces a Lacanian split subject, it fails to produce the subject open to analysis (that is, to the uncovering of *savoir*). If the discourse of the University fails, it fails in the way that it effaces and impersonally discredits other, more varied, forms of academic engagement. This failure induces in students the need to articulate new, and sometimes adversarial, modes of discourse to counter this failure. Not all students acknowledge and understand this failure, and, despite their large numbers, I don't consider them in this essay. They seek to adapt to the University (to the lure of egoic knowledge) and opt not to seek *savoir*. Often, they are successful within the impersonally stated goals of the University or they are satisfied with their invisibility within the University and seek subjective affirmation in and through other big Others (Church, Military, and Family).

On the other hand, the student who acts within either the master's or hysteric's discourse recognizes the failure of the University (the big Other), their fellow classmates (little others), and their teachers (academic manifestations of fathers/mothers). Like the hard-boiled detective and the noir villain, this student operates knowing that the University won't produce in them what it thinks will function outside of its law. These students don't perform the one act that would make them "good students"—they don't believe in the power of the University to bring them knowledge. It is with this basic understanding of failure that the student approaches knowledge. They note the failure, as well as their own position as a product within the economy of the University (which represents not only the larger university, but also various modes of disciplinarity), sees the replication of this failure in the classroom (with teachers and classmates), and seeks to find an ego-formation that will help him/her negotiate this failure appropriately under the university's gaze. Under this gaze, as I will detail later, the student responds by either assuming a sadistic relationship or a masochistic relationship to the University. The relationship functions complementary (but differently) to the larger failure, the violation of contract, as Deleuze might term it, of the University.

The S/M Connection: Deleuze and Laplanche

For noir students, how they read the failure/pain of the University discourse and how they experience the failure/pain is central to why they often remain in the university system at all. There are a number of students who can't adapt to the University discourse—they respond by dropping out. But what of the ones who stay despite their failure to adapt? One might make pragmatic observations: they know that a college diploma will help them attain white-collar employment; their parents have put explicit or implicit pressure on them to succeed at college; their class identity structure demands that they remain upwardly mobile. Certainly, all of these observations have validity, but I also want to suggest that this early adult relationship to the impersonal structure of the university enables students to develop an erotics of knowledge.

Many scholars—bell hooks, Jane Gallop, and Juliet Flower McCannell, to name a few—have affirmed the central role of the erotic in the space of pedagogy.[6] That students and teachers eroticize each other in the interplay of transference and countertransference is hardly a new concept. However, I want to suggest that a student's erotic relationship with knowledge need not necessarily exist in the simple dyad of the student/teacher (analysand/analyst) relationship. Indeed, as the classroom is a larger social space, it seems to me just as likely that students act erotically toward knowledge through their classmates and toward themselves. A noir student who is a masochist or a sadist doesn't necessarily have to have a teacher's prop to gain satisfaction; they often can use knowledge itself as a tool to inflict pain or to draw pain onto themselves. In order to develop this claim, I want to explore a couple of claims made by Jean Laplanche and Gilles Deleuze.

If the basic nature of sadism and masochism, for Lacan, was part of the invocatory drive that pushed the subject to experience the limits of pleasure and beyond, for Laplanche and Deleuze, masochism is the primary function of the two drives. The sexual desire and enjoyment of experiencing pain is central; the desire to inflict pain on others, even if the act of sadism comes before the experience of masochism, is a derivation of this desire.[7] Revisiting Freud's essays on sadism and masochism, Laplanche highlights the notion of propping, in which "the emergent sexuality attaches itself to and is propped upon another process which is both similar and profoundly divergent."[8] Propping explains the relationship the sadist or masochist has in engaging in actions not, strictly speaking, sexual. In fact, Laplanche later suggests, "propping implies that sexuality—the drive—emerges from nonsexual instinctual activities: organ pleasure from functional pleasure" (87). If sexual enjoyment can be "propped" on nonsexual activity, then this suggests the inverse is true. We gain sexual satisfaction from activities—eating, speaking, looking, defecating—not related to genital activity. Propping is an important concept because it better allows us to think about the relationship between sexual pleasure and learning. The student doesn't require an other in the form of another sexualized human being so much as he/she requires a relationship to a larger Other, perhaps in the form of the contract (as Deleuze suggests) or even, to an alienating discourse.[9] The student isn't necessarily masochistic or sadistic before his or her experiences with education in the same way that education doesn't necessarily elicit a specific sexual response from students.

Gilles Deleuze also helps to articulate a more socially based notion of what sadism and masochism means. In "Coldness and Cruelty," he suggests the social aims of sadism: "The paternal and patriarchal themes undoubtedly predominate in sadism. There are many heroines in Sade's novels, but their actions, the pleasures they enjoy together, and their common projects are all in imitation of man: man is the spectator and presiding genius to whom all their activities are dedicated" (59). Deleuze's description makes the act of sadism, at least, social in that it works both as a collective act (Deleuze's heroines seek the approval and validation of the father) and as a phantasmatic act (Deleuze's heroines seek the approval of the phallus; they seek a form of fantasy power).

Angela Carter responds to the notion of the "Sadian woman," by pointing out that, indeed, there are social reasons that women might seek this role and that there are social reasons such roles are impossible: "Flesh is not an irreducible human universal. Although the erotic relationship may seem to exist freely, on its own terms, among the distorted social relationships of bourgeois society, it is, in fact, the most self-conscious of all human relationships, a direct confrontation of two beings whose actions in the bed are wholly determined by their acts when they are outside of it."[10] Even as the fantasy of the sadist (especially the sadistic woman) is social, the reality that she strives to escape is equally sexually coded. Her decision to "act out" in such a way is both socially constructed and a socially necessary fantasy. It is likewise for the masochistic male. As the joke goes: women can't be masochists because their whole lives are masochism. A man's masochistic fantasies are acceptable to him only as he knows that he maintains some measure of power in the realm of social (even if it is imagined). Their perversion merely exemplifies, through its very performative status, the power of the phallus. Deleuze and Carter recognize, in different ways, the performative aspects of sadism and masochism. The status of "pervert" attached to the sadist or masochist is, as Slavoj Žižek notes, "[the status of the] 'inherent transgressor' par excellence. He brings to light, stages, practices, the secret fantasies that sustain the dominant public discourse."[11]

As I've moved my definition away from the specific practices of sadism and masochism detailed by the above theorists (and in consensual BDSM subcultures), I don't want to imagine all forms of masochism only within the realm of the theatrical. I want to argue for an authentic pedagogical sense of both terms. The student masochist or sadist doesn't understand his or her role as occurring in a fantasy space, but rather embodies it as mode of existence within the larger social order. For the student sadist and masochist, there is no "safe" word that lets the other know when to stop, no retreat from the theater of the masochistic and sadistic play, but rather a "noir" understanding that such roles relegate us within the larger social order.

In many noir narratives, masochism and sadism play a central role. From the largely masochistic male detective (exemplified in Chandler's Marlowe character) to the sadistic detective (exemplified by Hammett's Sam Spade or Continental Op) to the sadistic *femme fatale* (exemplified in any number of novels and films), the understanding that sexual conflict often leads to self-destruction and or the justification of hurting others is a primary narrative moving force. At the same time the narrative of S/M overlays more omnipresent narratives of police corruption, class domination, and corporate dehumanization. It's better, noir logic suggests, to be made the "bitch" to the bitch in the tight dress and lipstick than to the "old bitch," as Ezra Pound famously remarks, "gone bad in the teeth."[12] Noir, in this context, suggests how desire, power, and sexuality combine to create subjects who function as phantasmatic objects and social subjects.

Lacan's Discourses, Their Relation to Noir, and Classroom Implications

In this section, I've developed three student subjectivities/object stances within the academy. It's not my intention that these titles be used falsely to categorize students or to limit students in any way. Rather, I see these categories as modes of engagement that are dialectical with one another. That is, within the noir fantasy, they all work together (detective, femme fatale, victim) to determine a solution to a mystery (savoir) in the face of the Real (the corpse) and of an impersonal and corrupt reality (the University).

In these cursory definitions, I consistently refer to the sadistic master object (SMO) as a "he" and the masochistic hysteric object (MHO) as a "she." Only with the SHO do I attempt to offer both masculine and feminine examples. While this move is partly made with the understanding that "male" and "female" are not literal in Lacanian discourse, it is also to suggest how culture generally and noir specifically gender the roles of master and hysteric (such roles can be occupied by masculine, feminine, and gender queer subjects and have nothing necessarily to do with biological sex). While one can find examples of female detectives (Sara Paretsky's V. I. Warshawski character being the best neo-noir example), more often than not, female detectives (such as Cornell Woolrich's Dancing Detective) are only illicitly performing detective work instead of functioning as "legitimate" detectives (as a police officer or as a detective explicitly for hire).

Moreover, it is difficult to find *hommes fatales* in the literature, though it could be argued that certain types of male "buddies" who betray the detective (e.g., Terry Lennox in *The Long Goodbye*) suggest homoerotic *hommes fatales*.[13] While, as many have argued, homosociality and homosexual desire underpin the detective's triangulated desire for the femme fatale (this reading can be applied to any number of noir narratives), perhaps more telling is that there are few, if any, MHO "corpses" in the literature. While male corpses might outnumber female corpses in many novels and films, it is the female corpse that is so often explicitly displayed, described, and eroticized. Even in *Sunset Boulevard*, Joe Gillis, the male corpse who narrates the story is, in the narrative, feminized both culturally and psychologically—he's explicitly a woman's bitch.[14] The final reason for my intentional gendering of the discourse subjects is to indicate one form of power, gender, that often limits and over-determines the interplay of the discourses.

The Sadistic Master Object and Its Implications in the Classroom

The SMO/Detective (the "dick") cannot fully repress his own failure to master knowledge or to appear to the other/Other as the agent of the "master signifier." Although his recognition of failure is always half-repressed, he, as opposed to other masters, has allowed his failure to rise to consciousness enough that his grasp as a master and detective is always tenuous.

This recognition causes a deep sense of cynicism about the world at large (the University) and about the outcomes of the SMO's attempts to articulate change. The SMO doesn't refrain from acting, rather his actions carry with them a sense of cynicism and failure.

The outcomes of his action are, then, representative not of mastery but specifically of the attempt to master in the face of failure (the crux of his repression). Because they represent a "half-knowing" failure, they fail to offer the narrative closure on knowledge that is desired both by others and by the SMO and, instead, suggest a doomed sense of existential crisis.

The SMO senses his own failure, senses that he must, nonetheless, continue to perform this empty role, and, sadistically, wants the other/Other to pay for both his failure to embody mastery and for what he perceives as the continued demand that he perform his failure. He exemplifies, in many ways, the Sadian libertine (or heroine) who identifies (and takes pleasure in this identification) with the father, even as he performs for his pleasure. The SMO often justifies this knowing sadism with the understanding that the other/Other (classmates, teachers, the institution) is also doomed to fail as the agent of a master signifier. The SMO assumes, using a paranoid logic, that the other/Other is just as willing for him to be the victim of this failure as he is for them.

The specifically termed "hard-boiled" tradition is replete with examples of this discourse relationship. The trinity of hard-boiled detectives: Sam Spade, the "Op," and Philip Marlowe all represent the SMO, albeit in different ways. In the John Huston film version of *The Maltese Falcon*, Spade, in his unwillingness to "play the sap," does so in his continued dalliance with the femme fatale, Brigid O'Shaughnessy.[15] Throughout the film, he continues to be taken in by her lies. Even though one might argue that he knows that she lies, his continued sexual relationship with her and his willingness to continue his investigation in the face of these lies is indicative of both his own failure to be honest (he had an affair with his late partner's wife) and his inability to determine the specific lies that Brigid is telling. As he cannot master her "story," he cynically (and dishonestly) uses her. In the end, it is only because his dishonesty is more "masterful" than hers that he is able to sadistically discard her. That she is, in fact, the killer of his partner is less significant than the feeling that he should avenge his partner's death, to have closure to an act (honor among detectives) which he, himself, has failed to live up to.

The student who embodies the SMO is likely utterly alienated from knowledge and the systems through which he might attain knowledge. He performs for the teacher/University knowing full well that he will fail and that he will continue to be asked to be "taken in" by the teacher/University. He determines not that the teacher is the "subject supposed to know," in which their interactions might produce savoir knowledge. Instead, the teacher/University is, like him, another SMO. He takes cynical pleasure in continuing to perform this failure and fantasizes that this continued failure will eventually cause pain to the teacher or the academy at large, much as the femme fatale is often, finally, punished by the detective. In this way, he can feel mastery. The SMO plays chicken with the University, knowing that neither have the answer both claim to master, but expecting that both won't back down from the challenge of proving what they know. If the SMO finally backs down from the challenge, he reads this as the failure of the University to teach him what he needs to know, if the University backs down from the challenge, he finally has proof that it had nothing to teach him in the first place. As in the final scene of *The Maltese Falcon*, it is stylistically unclear to the observer who is actually imprisoned, Brigid O'Shaughnessy in the elevator or Sam Spade (the SMO), separated both from his desire for O'Shaughnessy and from the system of justice to which he hands her over. To the SMO, however, maintaining the illusion of freedom (and victory) remains central. Stylized lighting aside, it's Brigid who goes to prison, not Spade.

 The SMO is also likely not to be concerned with other students, as the SMO's paranoia extends not only to the Other (teacher, institution, discipline), but the little others (classmates) as well. The SMO wants to "uncover" the sham that is the classroom by announcing its failure, even as he continues to perform this failure. While this subject is often hostile to education, he is, nonetheless, able to be critical about the split nature of subjectivity, the alienation from savoir, and the specific power structures (classroom rules, disciplinary rules, teachers) which announce and anticipate his failure to master. He may likely see that his failure is a failure to master *connaissance* (egoic knowledge) not *savoir* (subjective knowledge), although his ability to see this does not help him to disregard *connaissance*. He may assume that what his teacher says is "bullshit," but he retains an investment by being able to appear to master "bullshit." He knows that he is, himself, "full of shit" but is unable to align this knowledge with the workings of the academy. To his credit, he is an active subject who continues to attempt mastery, even if only for cynical reasons. The MHO, on the other hand, is the student who is made passive and even self-punishing by their continued belief that they have failed mastery. As I've indicated above, these students normally do not attend college or do not matriculate and thus are not part of my classroom economy.

The Sadistic Hysteric Object and Its Implications in the Classroom

The SHO (the *femme fatale*) not only recognizes but takes pleasure in the fact of her split subjectivity. She doesn't think mastery of knowledge is possible and doesn't specifically attempt to do so. She is happy to continue to question mastery, knowing that every "answer" will inevitably suggest a new question.

The SHO is, however, still aware that the gaze of others often portrays her as both excessive and unknowable. The hysteric represents both too many questions and too many answers. While the hysteric might believe that this is, in fact, the way to continue a dialectical relationship with knowledge, she is also aware that the world of the University demands a limit both to her questions and her answers. The University views her hysteria as embarrassing, as a failure of the SHO to become a successful "product" of the university process. Moreover, the SMOs of the academy are angered by and paranoid in fear of the hysteric. The hysteric, in the face of these problems, becomes sadistic then seeks not only to continue dialectical inquiry but actively seeks to confound the academy (and often the SMO) with their questions. The SHO masters not the answer to the question, but the form of the question; the SHO can eroticize her own hysteria to the detriment of the community.

Although a hysteric with a less disenchanted vision of the academy (one who assumes that the academy condones her hysteria, one that doesn't recognize the power formation) might actively perform her hysteria to please the other/Other, the sadistic hysteric views her question as a tool to gain control and power. The hysteric knows that the question she possesses/enacts is unanswerable (even to herself) and knows also that the gaze cannot reduce it. The SHO sends the gazer onto a quest that will never end or, better, will beckon the failure of the gaze. A second type of SHO seeks to engage the gazer in the ritual melancholy of her hysteria. This SHO takes pleasure even in the melancholic split but knows that others will not take this pleasure. She says, "I am split because I can't answer this question and I revel in my melancholy . . . now I want you to discover that you can't answer it either and have the first shock/sadness of your discovery."

Much like the detective and the *femme fatale*, the SMO and the SHO are both attracted to one another and often work at cross purposes. The *femme fatale* is, after all, the woman whose femininity and guile represent both the promise of happiness (of having the right answer) and the impossibility of having it. In *Double Indemnity*, Phyllis Dietrichson represents the SHO in her continued (and murderous) attempts at upward mobility.[16] Although, theoretically, she knows that money, which she gains through the implied murder of the first Mrs. Dietrichson, is the reason for her search, her plotting of second murder suggests that she has experienced the disillusionment of not finding her answer. While she arguably has more money when married to Dietrichson, she has no access to it. Her plot to kill Dietrichson is a repetition (a re-asking) of the same question she has previously asked. On some level, she already knows that the answer will elude her as it did the last time she asked the question. Her alliance with Neff (a corporate SMO who wants to beat "the system" with which he is disillusioned) will, poetically, lead them both to "the end of the line." Yet Phyllis is represented as having already been on the trolley car (the central metaphor in the narrative) before Neff. She's been headed to the end of the line for a long time and it is only when Neff is seduced onto the trolley (or so his misogynist logic tells him) that it picks up speed. The SHO recognizes the dual logic of Phyllis Dietrichson. She knows that even though she may take active agency in luring the SMO to his failure, the SHO will be blamed, inevitably, for the SMO's decision. Within the economy of the gaze, the SHO resents the active/passive role assigned her (being both the cause and the alibi of another's downfall) by the gaze and, in response, identifies as an active participant.

The SHO who doesn't use the "unanswerable question" to ensnare the other, but rather the melancholy associated with the unanswerable question is represented by Johnny Marr/Julie Killeen in Cornell Woolrich's complimentary novels *Rendezvous in Black* and *The Bride Wore Black*.[17] Both function with the same premise: Johnny/Julie are each engaged only to have their love taken from them in freak accidents. Both substitute "death-making for love-making" (in the language of the pulps) as they hunt down and kill the series of individuals whose carelessness caused their loss. Whereas Julie actually kills the men she finds responsible, Johnny seeks to rob each man of his love. He sends a note to his first victim, whose beloved wife he has fatally infected with tetanus, which simply reads, "Now you know what it feels like."[18] While his note suggests that he does know how it feels, the note also suggests that the "it" of "what it feels like" is unknowable. His note proclaims, "now you know what is unknowable." The SMO, in her ritualized pleasure in showing loss and unknowability to the other/Other, takes sadistic pleasure in the spread of her hysteria to the unsuspecting.

The student SHO is the student who is both immune to the lure of mastery and the subject to the paranoia of the hysteric. Her personal relationship to knowledge is seemingly open-ended, yet the social dimension of her relationship (in the gaze of the Other) inevitably limits their ability to enjoy her position. She is feminized, made to feel the lack of the mastery. She is often told to shut up unless she knows the answer.

Even though she may recognize the pointlessness of mastery itself, she is aware and not immune to the knowledge that mastery is expected. These students are often creative and open-ended thinkers, able to engage in dialectical inquiry, but they also know the cost of the never-ending quest they pursue. For the SHO occupying a masculine position, the cost is often couched in specifically gendered criticism ("to act less like a woman"), for the SHO occupying a feminine position, the criticism comes in the form of disregard ("stop being so wishy-washy.") The SHO knows that her hysteria causes them to "think too much" (as her classmates often suggest) and, in defense, traps others in her excess. The SHO, aware of the criticism of the Other and little others, may enjoy disillusioning others with her condition. The SHO enjoys pointing out to others/Others the folly of their search for knowledge and mastery. The repetition of mirroring the failure of mastery is pleasing, because it effectively makes the SHO immune from the critical gaze.

The Masochistic Hysteric Object and Its Implication in the Classroom

The MHO (the "corpse") is the hysteric who is the material embodiment of the split subject. The MHO recognizes the (sadistic) gaze of the Other and, instead of reacting to it as the SHO does, becomes passive by giving herself over to it. The MHO functions as such only periodically and inevitably limits her own movement within the gaze of the Other. Much like a corpse, the MHO may be approached with revulsion or desire, but this revulsion/desire rests entirely on the utter passivity/death of the MHO. The MHO is of consequence only as a passive representation of the paradoxical desire of the Other. Thus, this position is immensely powerful, but only powerful outside of the agency of the MHO. The MHO is the abject image, the window through which the SHO and the SMO can both foreclose their own fear/desire of abjection and imagine their continuing roles in the face of abjection.

Perhaps the most stunning example of the "corpse subject" within noir and true crime literature is that of the "Black Dahlia." The infamous murder victim found bisected in Los Angeles in the late 1940s has remained both an eroticized and much maligned figure. Dubbed by Harry Hanson (lead investigator in the case) as a "tease and a bum" (or, erroneously, as an outright whore in Kenneth Anger's *Hollywood Babylon II*), the various narratives about the case (which remains officially unsolved to this day) suggests the myriad ways in which the victim, Elizabeth Short, came to embody a narrative over which she had no agency.[19] Although she is the only "real life" example cited in this essay, she might well be a fictional character. She is the ugliest of victims and, at the same time, the most appealing. Her narrative, revisited in James Ellroy's novel, *The Black Dahlia* and numerous true crime books, is hinted at in narratives beyond her actual story.[20] Her visage appears in John Gregory Dunne's *True Confessions* as well as in David Lynch's *Mulholland Drive*: the beauty doomed to die mysteriously in the evils of Los Angeles.[21] She is, perhaps, the most powerful incarnation of the noir narrative in reality. She is, however, a cipher, as the narratives which seek to identify her killer indicate. The "Dahlia" is the desire of the Other. Various theories of the murder appear every few years and all indicate more of a phantasmatic solution than a solution based on evidence. Ellroy's novel suggests that a woman, a mother, killed the Dahlia—a conclusion drawn, at least in part, from the fact, documented in his autobiography, *My Dark Places*, that Ellroy's mother, Geneva Ellroy, was killed in a manner uncannily similar to that of Short.[22] Ellroy even dedicates *The Black Dahlia* to her. For Ellroy, his anger at his own mother's death (or his inability to deal with it) becomes embodied in his mother's corpse, who then fictionally kills the Dahlia. Corpses produce themselves: the (m)other destroys itself.

In *Daddy was the Black Dahlia Killer*, Janice Knowlton blames her own abusive father for Short's murder. Her own suffering becomes mirrored in the suffering of Elizabeth Short: both suffer under the same totemic father.[23] Knowlton's account takes it one step further by suggesting, unlike any other account, that Short actively participated in the pedophilic abuse she suffered from her father. She recasts the Dahlia as the alienated and passive (m)other and herself as the "real" corpse. As Knowlton's account identifies a totemic father, John Gilmore, in his book, *Severed*, suggest himself as a sort of totemic father. His text suggests a perpetrator (a shadowy drifter) but also states that the author himself discovered the killer, who, under questionable circumstances, died in a hotel fire before police interviews could be conducted.[24] Gilmore, the author who is (arguably) most enamored with the Dahlia's image, finds purpose in his narrative by casting himself as her belated avenger, the father who might have protected her but can only protect her image in death. In his narrative fantasy, he (an SMO) could have ended her abjection and restored her, though, through no fault of his own, he failed. In this account, not only is Short the MHO, but her perpetrator is also an MHO. The answer to a corpse is another corpse (or, at least, someone who will likely become a corpse—be sent to "the chair"—because the SHO solved the mystery). In the economy of the corpse, the perpetrator, the "answer" to the corpse carries the sign of the SMO.

Although the corpse can never reveal the nature of its demise, the image of the corpse suggests to others/Others the ways in which agency works. Was the Dahlia a "high-risk" victim, someone who, through bad choices, brought about her own demise? Was she a victim of poverty, little education, and prey to the postwar misogyny of a large city? Can one avoid being the corpse or, as some noir narratives suggest, is one fated to be a corpse through the unknown workings of situation and power? The corpse both begs these questions but cannot participate in the discussion.

The MHO is the student who gets caught cheating. The MHO is accused of plagiarism. The MHO is the student burned by an unhappy affair with a professor. The MHO is the story of the student who is expelled. The MHO has a family history or abusive situation she cannot name in the social space of the classroom even as it complicates her ability to perform. The MHO is the name we attach to the abject trauma—a trauma that either interrupts the classroom or is caused and played out in the classroom. Although the MHO may, in fact, not be guilty of the trauma she is linked with (she might not have plagiarized), she carries the fear of the trauma itself. Although the MHO, unlike the corpse, most often lives, she is tainted narratively by her abjection. Her position in the classroom works at the center of the motivations of all others. Indeed, the image of the MHO instructor who fails to get tenure, is brought up on harassment charges, or gets accused of plagiarism pervades the economy of the classroom as well. The image of the MHO can make the student afraid of answering the question wrong and the teacher afraid to engage the student without paranoia. The MHOs who recover their trauma inevitably live a dual identity in the economy of the classroom. The MHO herself may develop into an SHO and choose to use their trauma as the source of further inquiry or she might develop into an SMO in order to foreclose her HMO status. Often this MHO may appear as a "survivor"—one who has adapted to her trauma—but the fact of the trauma itself, and the MHO as the image of the trauma, remains part of the gaze of the Other. It is in the gaze at the MHO that the economy of the classroom resides. If the gaze at the MHO is hostile (others regard the MHO with revulsion, guilt, and blame), the classroom economy will become sadistic. If the gaze at the MHO is eroticized (others regard the MHO as exciting and mysterious) the classroom economy will become masochistic. In both cases, the status of knowledge suffers.

If the classroom becomes collectively sadistic, knowledge becomes a "winners" discourse in which narratives of failure or trauma become personalized ("he's just a loser . . . unlike me"), or a mark of social/institutional incompetence ("Everybody cheats, but only an idiot would get caught"), or a ploy to get undeserved attention ("she's just using her rape to get attention . . . that should rightfully be mine"). The classroom, in this case, truly becomes "Chinatown," a place in which knowledge functions simply as a placeholder for power and where corpses inevitably "deserved it" or didn't matter in the larger scheme. The sadistic classroom loses any sense of ethics beyond survival and adaptation.

If the classroom becomes collectively masochistic, it turns into a graveyard. The classroom devoted to the continued eroticization and celebration of the corpse and the traumatized individual often fails to find solutions to the causes of pain and trauma. While this classroom functions as a sympathetic space, it can just as easily function as a necrophiliac space in which knowledge is divorced from the cruel world and erotically attached to the death drive. The masochistic classroom becomes a martyred community too good for this earth. Often this classroom loses touch with its own relationship to aggression, and often plays out these emotions passively. Although the masochistic classroom might maintain a more explicit ethical pose, it is no more successful than the sadistic classroom in helping the SMO gain agency and voice.

Beyond "Chinatown" and the Graveyard

Although both classrooms function negatively, we need to imagine a noir space in which students can express their failure to adapt and work collectively to transform the space of the classroom. In this classroom, those who gaze at the MHO seek, if impossibly, to hear her speak back. The classroom that senses trauma can collectively embody it and work to heal itself collectively. Thus, the economy of the classroom dialectacizes itself both narratively and phantasmatically.

Central to this concept is the notion of collectivity. Indeed, to seek individually the voice of the MHO is to risk both embodying it and reanimating its trauma. The noir student, more than others, is aware of the larger institutional culture that demands adaptation and, thus, aware of the implications of interrupting this process. The dangers of the individual attempts to revive the corpse are many.

First, there is a tendency to choose aesthetically pleasing traumas and victims above more abject traumas and victims. The individual's desire to see themselves in the victims they aid significantly limits their ability to understand victimization as a more systematic problem. If noir culture has taught us anything it is that every individual trauma is connected, literally or metaphorically, to a larger corruption. Secondly, the individual who works to help victims is really an idealized form of the SMO. Although the motivations might be different, the savior, by virtue of their individuality, is prone to view their own behavior as yet another form of mastery. It is often these subjects who, when they fail to "save" the victim, become thoroughly hostile to them. Finally, individual therapeutic action doesn't always imagine a space for the abject subject to speak and hold agency after the initial utterance.

Collective therapeutic struggle holds promise for a couple of reasons. It is useful because collective therapy can better understand a variety of symptoms (aggression, transference, self-destruction) in a collective rather than merely individual context. As I've indicated, within a classroom, phantasmatic transactions occur not as dyads between students and teacher, but in a broad range of directions between many individuals and symbolic institutions.

This expanded range of therapeutic behaviors allows us to read many behaviors not historically imagined as therapeutic (especially those of the noir student) as part of a larger social resistance to institutionalization. Moreover, the larger sphere of the classroom allows for the social and ideological intervention in the post-Habermasian tradition (as manifested in the work, say, of Lauren Berlant or Nancy Fraser), but also specific psychoanalytic collective work as detailed in the work of Jeff Berman, Judith Harris, and Greg Forter.[25]

The classroom that collectively seeks the voice of the MHO seeks not only to recover her (welcome her back, empathize with her), it seeks to master the conditions of her trauma, even if only within the smaller social space of the classroom. To embrace the corpse, and not merely gaze upon her, is to embrace the situation that made her thus. If the shame, disgust, or guilt toward the corpse is alleviated or partially embodied by the classroom, the classroom economy may function collectively to reinvestigate the trauma.

Does this suggest they will become, unlike the SMO, a successful master/detective? Does this suggest the HSO will refrain from over-eroticizing the trauma (mystery) of the corpse? Perhaps not, but the dialectic between the SMO and HSO can be collectivized in the name of the MHO. Both positions might be better read with a larger understanding of social therapy. Instead of these two formations working at cross-purposes to fail to "solve" the mystery of the corpse or to eroticize and inevitably put-off the solution to the mystery, the two subjects must work to reconceive a new strategy for understanding (and re-understanding) the mystery of trauma.

Without the corpse to gaze at (as the corpse has been embraced by the class), the nature of the mysteries of power, violence, or separation cannot be made personal. They cannot be projected onto the corpse. Nor can they be avoided ("I'll do anything not to be that!"), as the corpse has been embraced by the classroom. Thus, the classroom economy has space to conceive of the mysteries that create corpses as disembodied (or multiply bodied) within the classroom itself. The mystery of the Black Dahlia and those like her can be reconceived as a multiple overlay of problems related to the construction of femininity in our culture, poverty, and a cultural acceptance of male violence. While there is no "person" to attach guilt, disgust, or blame to (either the corpse or the mysterious perpetrator—the answer to the corpse) and likely not the enjoyment of displacing the whole problem, there is, I think, more space to collectively imagine new solutions.

The applications of this type of classroom are important especially for the students mentioned at the beginning of this essay. For within this classroom, these students do not function as "problems" either to themselves or to the classroom at large. Although they still may function as a problem to the discourse of the University, they (and their teachers and classmates) can see their roles (their distrust and paranoia, their failures to adapt) as central to a more therapeutic understanding of *savoir* within the academy. I've never been surprised that the French were the first to really embrace film noir and to theorize it. With their own romantic postwar investments in resistance fighting, they were better suited to think of the noir detective, the femme fatale, and even the corpse as part of a resistance not to knowledge, but for knowledge. Noir students, working collectively, can change the classroom in just the same way by imagining the law as Other and by working underneath it to forge knowledge.

NOTES

When Elizabeth Hatmaker and I started planning this volume, she was going to contribute an essay on John Carpenter's *Christine* and object noir. Because of her diagnosis with ALS in 2015, this essay never came to pass. Instead, I have drawn from some of her earlier critical writing. This chapter was originally part of her dissertation, which she filed in 2003. She reworked this chapter for an article but never published it. She got involved in creative projects—especially her first book of poetry, *Girl in Two Pieces* (about the Black Dahlia murder) and the article version languished. Having read the chapter and the article rework (which was for a specific journal), I have produced a combined document drawing from the best of the two. Most of it draws from her dissertation, though, because I think it is stronger. Other than this synthesizing, my editorial hand is very light here. I have done some necessary cutting. I have jettisoned the discussion of writing pedagogy that was part of this chapter initially (and especially part of the article rework). For the sake of space, I have also cut her extended account of Lacan's four discourses, since these are relatively well known and since her elaboration of them later in the chapter is clear on its own. I have instead focused on the notion of noir pedagogy. I have also changed some of the pronouns and language to make it more consonant with contemporary conceptions of gender (although I have left intact Hatmaker's intentional gendering of pronouns when she starts working through her refiguration of Lacan's discourses in terms of classroom personae). The voice in this essay is very much hers, as is about 99 percent of the writing. She was a profound theorist of noir, psychoanalysis, pedagogy, and death. Her thinking on noir has deeply influenced my own work in *Hard-Boiled Masculinities* and, of course, the present collection. While she is recognized for her haunting and powerful poetry, this essay gives a glimpse of Elizabeth Hatmaker the passionate teacher and sophisticated pedagogical theorist. Elizabeth's was distinctive voice—already death-haunted long before her diagnosis. I wish that death had remained only a haunting. Now her words can haunt us.—C. B.

1. See John Dewey, *Experience and Education* (New York: Free Press, 1997); and Paulo Friere, *Pedagogy of the Oppressed*, 30th anniversary ed., trans. Myra Bergman Ramos (London: Continuum Press, 2000).

2. See Jacques Lacan, *The Other Side of Psychoanalysis: The Seminar of Jacques Lacan Book XVII*, trans. Russell Grigg (New York: W. W. Norton, 1991), 11–38. For a specifically pedagogical use of the four discourses, see Mark Bracher, "Lacan's Theory of the Four Discourses," *Prose Studies* 11, no. 3 (December 1988): 32–49; and Mark Bracher, *The Writing Cure: Psychoanalysis, Composition, and the Aims of Education* (Carbondale: Southern Illinois University Press, 1999).

3. *Chinatown*, directed by Roman Polanski (USA, 1974; Los Angeles: Paramount, 2012), DVD.

4. Kelly Oliver and Benigno Trigo, *Noir Anxiety* (Minneapolis: University of Minnesota Press, 2002), 49–72.

5. Paula Rabinowitz, *Black and White and Noir: America's Pulp Modernism* (Minneapolis: University of Minnesota Press, 2002), 18.

6. See Jane Gallup, *Feminist Accused of Sexual Harassment* (Durham, NC: Duke University Press, 1997); bell hooks, *Teaching to Transgress* (New York: Routledge, 1994); and Juliet Flower MacCannell, "Resistance to Sexual Theory," in *Theory/Pedagogy/Politics: Texts for Change*, ed. Donald Morton and Mas'ud Zavarzadeh (Champaign: University of Illinois Press, 1991).

7. Dylan Evans, *An Introductory Dictionary of Lacanian Psychoanalysis* (London: Routledge, 1996), 168.

8. Jean Laplanche, *Life and Death in Psychoanalysis*, trans. Jeffrey Mehlman (Baltimore, MD: John Hopkins University Press, 1976), 13.

9. Gilles Deleuze, "Coldness and Cruelty," in *Masochism* (New York: Zone Books, 1991), 20.

10. Angela Carter, *The Sadean Woman and the Ideology of Pornography* (New York: Pantheon, 1978), 9.

11. Slavoj Žižek, *The Ticklish Subject: The Absent Center of Political Ontology* (London: Verso, 1999), 248.

12. Ezra Pound, "Hugh Selwyn Mauberley Pt. 1," section V, lines 3–4. *Poetry Foundation*, https://www.poetryfoundation.org/poems/44915/hugh-selwyn-mauberley-part-i.

13. Raymond Chandler, *The Long Goodbye* (New York: Vintage, 2002).

14. *Sunset Boulevard*, directed by Billy Wilder (USA, 1950; Los Angeles: Paramount, 2017), DVD.

15. *The Maltese Falcon*, directed by John Huston (USA, 1941; Los Angeles: Warner Home Video, 2000), Blu-Ray.

16. Billy Wilder, *Double Indemnity*, directed by Billy Wilder (USA, 1944; Paramount).

17. See Cornell Woolrich, *Rendezvous in Black* (New York: Random House, 2004); and Cornell Woolrich, *The Bride Wore Black* (New York: Simon and Shuster, 1940).

18. Woolrich, *Rendezvous in Black*, 95.

19. Kenneth Anger, *Hollywood Babylon 2* (New York: Plume Books, 1985).

20. James Ellroy, *The Black Dahlia* (New York: Grand Central Publishing, 2006).

21. See John Gregory Dunne, *True Confessions: A Novel* (Boston, MA: Da Capo, 2005); and *Mulholland Drive*, directed by David Lynch (USA, 2001; New York: Criterion Collection, 2015), DVD.

22. James Ellroy, *My Dark Places* (New York: Vintage, 1997).

23. Janice Knowlton with Michael Newton, *Daddy was the Black Dahlia Killer* (New York: Gallery Books, 2014).

24. John Gilmore, *Severed: The True Story of the Black Dahlia*, 2nd ed. (Los Angeles: Amok Books, 2006).

25. See Nancy Fraser, *Justice Interruptus: Critical Reflections on the "Post-Socialist" Condition* (New York: Routledge, 1997); Lauren Berlant, *The Queen of America Goes to Washington City: Essays on Sex and Citizenship* (Durham, NC: Duke University Press, 1997); Jeffrey Berman, *Risky Writing: Self-Disclosure and Self-Transformation in the Classroom* (Amherst: University of Massachusetts Press, 2001); Judith Harris, "Re-Writing the Subject: Psychoanalytic Approaches to Creative Writing and Composition Pedagogy," *College English* 64, no. 2 (November 2001): 175–204; and Greg Forter, *Murdering Masculinities: Fantasies of Gender and Violence in the American Crime Novel* (New York: New York University Press, 2000).

CHAPTER 5

The Shadows of the Twilight World: Beebo Brinker and the Circulation of Affect

Sean Grattan

What is the texture of noir? So much of the film and fiction obsessively traces the *feeling* of a place. Whether the dark-lit shadowy faces loitering in alleys or the weighty and pervasive dread that sticks to cities such as Los Angeles or New York, noir traces a series of affective states—scenes of compromise where characters are buffeted by the world around them. This is not to say that noir follows what Sara Ahmed describes as the outside-in model of affect, rather the world (inclusive of characters) is fully enveloped and riven by negation. This is the overdetermination of noir—the circulation of negative affects tends to debilitate characters, sucking them into the cruel optimism of blackmail, insurance fraud, and plain old-fashioned murder all under the guise of somehow getting out and making a better life. If affect sticks, then the sticky world of noir settles over the characters in a grim grime. Think, for instance, of the entanglements of Walter Neff and Phyllis Dietrichson in *Double Indemnity* attempting to play one another for the big money score that will get them out of the drudgeries of insurance salesman or loveless marriage.[1] (Of course, Patricia Highsmith's *Ripley* series acts as a useful foil to this as Tom Ripley does manage to fashion a life worth living through multiple murders, forgery, and self-fashioning graft.) Noir purposefully situates itself in a seedy underworld full of characters clinging to the potential of the good life only for the continued refusal of that good life to come to fruition. Attempting to make it through playing by the rules has already failed these characters so they try something else. This essay is not particularly interested in certain historical narratives about noir where noir becomes the allegorical reading of postwar anxieties about masculinity, domesticity, etc., but uses these ideas to interrogate what is missing from, or used in, mainstream noir to further marginalize non-normative sexualities and communities. Specifically, I am interested in the depiction of queer spaces, and how these spaces are reformulated in Ann Bannon's lesbian pulp fiction. In other words, if one way of thinking about affect is through the accumulation of negative or positive affects, then it is crucial to think how those affective spaces fluctuate around the situatedness of particular subjects. In attending to what is often missing, occluded, or made visible as heterosexist fantasy pieces in mainstream noir, I illustrate how the noir affects of the gay bar are, in fact, places of affective succor.

The punishments of these characters seem to reproduce a narrative of the proper way to live: step outside of the bright lights and rosy world of postwar America and you're well and truly fucked. The corrective tendency of noir has a more than passing resemblance to the history of queer characters in literature. If you are a woman who loves other women, your literary chances of either survival or sanity are slim. Placing these two traditions alongside one another demonstrates not only the ubiquity of negative affects adhering to queer sites in mainstream noir but also, and crucially, points to a reorientation toward reading the noir scene as one of potential for belonging outside the light, and deep in the shadows of the twilight world.

Conventional noir—both literary and filmic—is rife with heteropatriarchal violence. Of course, this is also part of the conventional origin story for noir as well: the need to redomesticate lives after men return from war, the sense of pervading economic dread, and the propping up of a fragile masculinity all speak in unison to reinforce normative gender roles. As such it shouldn't be particularly shocking that these texts are redolent in heteropatriarchal violence. Raymond Chandler's *The Big Sleep* (1939) offers an exemplary insight into the depiction of homosexual characters in hardboiled fiction. The casual homophobia of Philip Marlowe, along with the homophobia of the plot, underscore the ease that homosexuality might act as a stand-in for a certain affective stance where masculinity is interchangeable with a "prophylactic toughness that was organized around the rigorous suppression of affect and was mirrored by his detached, laconic utterances and his instrumentalized, seemingly amoral actions."[2] In other words, it isn't just Marlowe adopting a "gay" disguise to get information at a bookstore, it is that the bookstore turns out to be a cover for a porn distribution racket. When Marlowe walks into the store he puts his "voice high and let a bird twitter in it,"[3] and when he returns a few days later he remarks on his disguise: "I took my dark glasses off and tapped them delicately on the inside of my left wrist. If you can weigh a hundred and ninety pounds and look like a fairy, I was doing my best."[4] Indeed. While Marlowe adopts this disguise before he discovers Geiger's homosexuality, it's sadly unsurprising that Chandler thickens Geiger's sexual vices with being gay (this is not to mention the sensual Orientalizing of Geiger's house and his "Charlie Chan moustache").[5] The description of Geiger's house has a similar feel: "The place was horrible by daylight. The Chinese junk on the walls, the rug, the fussy lamps, the teakwood stuff, the sticky riot of colors, the totem pole, the flagon of ether and laudanum—all this in the daytime had a stealthy nastiness, like a fag party."[6] The sordidness is palpable. What, precisely, do these flourishes do in *The Big Sleep*? How does the "stealthy nastiness" of Geiger's house reflect, dramatize, or reiterate a series of heteronormative codes that implicitly work through the origin story of noir's attempted reinstantiation of working-class masculinity? Chandler riddles *The Big Sleep* with similar examples. Geiger's lover is unable to throw a punch because "a pansy has no iron in his bones, whatever he looks like."[7] And while *The Big Sleep* offers an exemplary case, it is the norm rather than the exception. Think, for instance, of Micky Spillane's *Vengeance is Mine* (1950), which offers this charming description of a lesbian:

> A kid who had artist written all over her in splotches of paint was leaning against the partition of the booth behind me. Her eyes were hard and hot and followed Juno every step of the way. She was another one of those mannish things that breed in the half-light of the so-called aesthetical world. I got a look that told me I was in for competition and she took off after Juno. She came back in a minute and her face was pulled tight in a scowl and I gave her a nasty laugh. Some women, yes. Others, nix.[8]

Although it's impossible to overlook the dehumanizing language Spillane uses, it is equally impossible to overlook that this is the voice of an outsider looking in and passing judgment. For Spillane the dimly lit aesthetical world hides all kinds of non-normative behaviors—behaviors that scuttle and breed—in ways that don't seem quite natural. What else lurks in "the half-light of the so-called aesthetical world"?[9] In hardboiled crime fiction, queer people are part of the scenery—a way of situating the scene as gritty, sexually promiscuous, dangerous, and edgy. As decoration, queer people were an easy set of stereotypes and tropes.

The original cover art for Ann Bannon's 1961 novel *Beebo Brinker* depicts a woman at a crossroads where only one street name is visible: Gay Street. The cover text proclaims, invitingly, "lost, lonely, boyishly appealing—this is Beebo Brinker—who never really knew what she wanted—until she came to Greenwich Village and found the love that smoulders in the shadows of the twilight world."[10] As a midcentury euphemism for the arrayed institutions, networks, friendships, and lovers of homosexual women and men, the "twilight world" trades on what Foster Hirsch describes as noir's ability to "conjure up a dark, urban world of neurotic entrapment leading to delirium."[11] The invitation to Gay Street, however, offers a different kind of delirium for Beebo: a delirium of belonging, sexual adventurousness, friendship, and intimacy. In what follows I want to reorient a reading of noir spaces to think through how they might serve the characters that use them, need them, and survive in them. More often than not noir texts offer gay bars as a place of seedy degeneracy peopled by reprobates and as a marker of people out of control. It is crucial, then, to rethink these spaces through queer noir and delving into the bars not as a shorthand for vice and instead thinking about them as spaces where flourishing, anti-heteronormative sets of kinship emerge.

As historians George Chauncey and John D'Emilio, as well as sociologist Esther Newton have extensively shown, the LGBTQ life world was much richer, substantial, and extensive than the caricatures offered by much historical, political, and social discourse.[12] They are at pains to rewrite the popular narrative that Stonewall was the beginning of a political gay life world, and texts like Bannon's *Beebo Brinker* series works to further problematize the too easy historical marker of pre- and post-Stonewall.[13] By the 1920s Greenwich Village (along with Harlem and Times Square) had a reputation as a gay neighborhood, with a full network of connections and lines of communication. By the 1950s and 1960s, the Village dominated the popular image of gay culture in the United States.

That gay bars in the 1950s and 1960s operate under a logic of intense surveillance and easily slip into a signifier for vice is unsurprising. The beginnings of the Mattachine Society, for instance, came as an act of resistance to police entrapment in Los Angeles. Moreover, as work on the Lavender Scare has made clear seething, anti-communism took on a sexualized and psychopathologized position around the perceived intersection of homosexuality and communism. A US Senate report titled "Employment of Homosexuals and Other Sex Perverts in Government" (popularly called the Hoey Report) laid out a series of fears that "sexual perverts" endangered national security because homosexuals might be exploited because they "seldom refuse to talk about themselves."[14] In other words, gay men couldn't be trusted around spies because spies might ask them questions about themselves.

As Bannon illustrates, queer noir subverts manifestations of shame and neurosis and, instead, offers the twilight world as a space for the proliferation of love, friendship, and solace. In *Foundlings*, Christopher Nealon argues that lesbian pulp fiction creates a counterpublic through the reading and circulation of texts.[15] This is certainly the case with *The Ladder*, the publication of the Daughters of Bilitis, which featured book reviews in its back pages geared toward sussing out which gay and lesbian texts might not be too toxic. Ann Bannon's writerly relationship to Vin Packer—the author of *Spring Fire*—perfectly illustrates the importance of textual kinship. In the revised afterword of *Spring Fire*, Packer complains about the stranglehold publishers had over queer literature, remarking that her editor told her "no reference to homosexuality as an attractive life could be portrayed"; one character must declare that she is not a lesbian while the other character "must be sick or crazy."[16] Yet, despite the horrific ending, Ann Bannon recalls that it was reading *Spring Fire* that made her think she could write lesbian pulp.

Ann Bannon's five-book *Beebo Brinker Chronicles* traces a number of coming-out stories linked to moving to New York City. The first *Odd Girl Out* (1957) follows a familiar pattern of Laura sexually attracted to her college roommate Beth. The story turns on who will go crazy first, who will get expelled, who will fall into the trap of the queer finale. *Odd Girl Out* is perhaps most interesting because of how easily it fits into the deadly lesbian narrative of insanity and death, but then escapes that narrative by not killing anyone. *Odd Girl Out* is followed by *I Am a Woman* (1959), which startlingly breaks with the hermeneutics of deadliness surrounding lesbian fiction. The book follows Laura as she reels from the emotional trauma of the aftermath of *Odd Girl Out*, moving to New York City in a bid to rebuild her life. At first seeing her homosexual desire as a dalliance, stage, or brief and regrettable foray into madness, Laura tries (unsuccessfully) to tamp down any burgeoning feelings for her new roommate Marcie. Where *I Am a Woman* moves away from the typical depressed lesbian narrative and into more hopeful territory is with the introduction of Jack Mann. Jack acts as a guide to the gay bars of Greenwich village, but more importantly shows Laura that homosexuality isn't the death sentence she originally thought. The modeling of gay lifeworlds is Jack's function throughout the *Beebo Brinker* series.[17] I would describe these relations as primarily affective in the desire to map the changing possibilities in a world that suddenly flowers around the newly arrived queer kids coming to the city.

Early in *I Am a Woman* Jack takes Laura, her roommate Marcie, and Marcie's lover Burr to a gay bar called the Cellar, which Jack laughingly calls a "legitimate joint."[18] Laura had been terrified of the Village, afraid "she would see someone, and do something, and suddenly find herself caught in the strange world she had renounced."[19] But entering the bar, her body loosens up, she becomes curious about the place; the threat of the village begins to dissipate. The excitement of seeing "a girl with her arm around another girl" and a "pair of boys at the bar . . . whispering urgently to each other."[20] Of course, her curiosity immediately feeds back into the shock of fear and estrangement: "*Gay*, Laura thought to herself. *Is that what they call it? Gay?* She was acutely uncomfortable now. It was as if she were a child of civilization, reared among the savages, who suddenly found herself among the civilized. She recognized them as her own. And yet she had adopted the habits of another race and she was embarrassed and lost with her own kind."[21] Bannon's flipping of the typical descriptions of gay bars and gay nightlife as seedy vice holes whose denizens eagerly await the downfall of civilization, to a world of the civilized with whom Laura can no longer communicate because she has been raised by straight savages, offers a glimpse of a horizon structured by a different set of social relations. Looking out at the bar Laura thinks "*I'm one of you. Help me.*"[22] In this moment Jack comes back with the drinks and for all her newfound gay spotting capabilities, Laura misunderstands Jack's sexuality and thinks he has taken her there to make fun of the patrons of the bar. Of course, this is *precisely* what Burr plans on doing, looking at the women and saying "any girl who doesn't like men is either a virgin or else some bastard scared the hell out of her. She needs gentling."[23] Bannon offers a critique of this language as all the characters turn on Burr—with varying degrees of sensitivity and hostility—to chastise him for his homophobia. The strangeness of the Cellar, for Laura, signals a series of affective drives that further disrupt and disturb her understanding of herself in the world.

Teresa Brennan usefully describes affect as feeling the changeability of a room's mood.[24] The Cellar retrospectively takes on a sinister tinge when Burr begins making fun of the people in the bar. Laura's recognition of her homosexuality through the lens of the LGBTQ people around her draws her in, but simultaneously pushes her away. Burr's jokes render her, in Sara Ahmed's terms, an "affect alien,"[25] and her confusion, shame, and longing drips off the page. She desperately wants the room's recognition, but she's so ashamed of herself and those around her that her body shakes with it. For Ahmed, the affect alien is out of joint with her surroundings; she sinks into her seat at the movie theater as people around her laugh at homophobic or racist jokes. Of course, this is part of a larger network of affective aggravations, minor aggressions, and silencing.

When we encounter shame, as Eve Kosofsky Sedgwick and Adam Frank have famously formulated, it is often in a pose that looks a lot like reading. Reading may be a particular stance that acts as a "force-field creating power" that forms a "kind of skin" woven "around a reading body."[26] Following Silvan Tomkins, Sedgwick and Frank describe shame on the same affective spectrum as interest; "without positive affect, there can be no shame: only a scene that offers you enjoyment or engages your interest can make you blush."[27] Laura's response to the Cellar offers a clear example of the oscillation between excitement and shame. Sedgwick's description of the saving power of a text is of particular importance to understanding the affective space of queer pulps in at least two ways: first, Sedgwick recognizes the homicidal social spaces surrounding queer youth when, as she pithily writes "it's always open season on gay kids" and secondly that bright spots in this homicidal sphere might be few and far between.[28] When you stumble upon a book, a poem, or a piece of music that makes survival possible, you cling to and study its transformational power. Sedgwick writes, and I think this is crucial for the circulation of queer pulps, "that for many of us in childhood the ability to attach intently to a few cultural objects, objects of high or popular culture or both, objects whose meaning seemed mysterious, excessive, or oblique in relation to the codes most readily available to us, became a prime resource for survival."[29] Like other (if sometimes brutal) stalwarts of queer literature like *The Well of Loneliness*, pulps like Bannon's signal the possibility of belonging in a world that very rarely offers that belonging. The importance of reading communities, the circulation of texts, and the imaginary literary space opened up by cheap and easily accessible pulp books cannot be underestimated. These books describe a world that may seem utopian in comparison to the violence of the novelistic present. Laura's anger, shame, and distrust are all markers of queer affective space that also signal her interest and enjoyments.

Crucially Bannon is also flipping the noir narrative around the safety of domestic spaces versus the danger of the bar because any danger that might exist in the bar is through the invasion of heteropatriarchy in the form of Burr, and these efforts are redoubled at home where Burr and Marcie play a series of mind games with Laura. After all, much of the drama in *I Am a Woman* rests on Laura trying to suss out her relationship to Marcie. In an emotionally brutal scene, Laura finally comes out to Marcie, explaining that the great love of her life was not a man, but Beth. Marcie, however, has made a bet with Burr to see if she could compel Laura to "make a pass" at her.[30] Like the denizens of the Cellar, Laura is little more than the butt of a joke, less than human for Marcie and Burr. Marcie confesses that Laura's homosexuality got her "sort of intrigued,"[31] and had even worked to convince Burr that the two of them were having an affair. All of this, of course, means that Marcie and Burr imagined Laura as somehow less a person than them because of their heterosexuality. "Laura," Marcie confesses "I had no idea you could love like that. I didn't know it could be beautiful, or touching, or tragic. I thought it was mostly play-acting. I thought the only real love was between men and women."[32] The betrayal of her feelings leaves Laura "feeling shattered, ready to scream if anyone touched her, like someone with an open wound."[33] Laura's shame—viscerally written on her body as it comes apart—sits festering. The apartment has become a battleground where the violence and collusions of heteropatriarchy have shattered Laura. Bannon places this scene of domestic shattering tied to coming out directly before Laura confronts her father to tell him that she is not interested in having him in her life anymore. He has always been abusive to her, and this scene ratchets up the intensity until in an excitingly Freudian twist, upset at her homosexuality and the part he feels he played in it, he confesses that she looks just like her mom and then puts "his hand in her hair and jerked her head back and kissed her full on the mouth with such agonized intensity that he electrified her."[34] She does the sensible thing and hits him in the head with an ashtray. All of this is to say that in *I Am a Woman* what lurks in domestic spaces is physical, emotional, and sexual violence and that that violence, so easily breeding in the light of day, is contradicted, in part, by the solace Laura feels in queer spaces.

Vivian Sobchack interrogates the material spaces that populate film noir. She describes lounge time as what takes place in the "cocktail lounge, the nightclub, the bar, the hotel room, the boardinghouse, the diner, the dance hall, the roadside cafe, the bus and train station, and the wayside motel," which all figure as "recurrent and determinate premises of film noir."[35] Rather than read these spaces as metaphorical, Sobchack wants to examine the material realities of these spaces. She continues: "emerging out of actually lived cultural spaces, the represented space of lounge time is a perverse and dark response, on the one hand, to the loss of home and a felicitous, carefree ahistoricity and, on the other, to the inability to imagine being at home in history, in capitalist democracy *at this time*."[36] While it seems true that the spaces of lounge time disturb the certain ideas of domestic spaces in a mainstream imaginary, it is equally important to understand the ways that parks, gay bars, and lounges materialize and produce felicitous spaces for people who were already outsiders in mainstream American culture. In imagining the use of these spaces outside heteronormative matrixes another world opens up where the "degenerational" space of the lounge operates precisely as a haven. In other words, the infelicitous encounters of lounge time are only infelicitous if examined through a heteronormative matrix of the family, domesticity, and belonging.

As John D'Emilio is at pains to point out, there was a tension between the mainstream homophile movement and the bar scene. Taking into account homophile societies' struggles for visibility in the 1950s and 1960s, Bannon's *Beebo Brinker Chronicles* map the affective spaces of the bar scene. *The Mattachine Review*, for instance, held the complicated position that shutting down bars "would only 'increase the policing problem in the parks, on the streets, and in the public toilets' and suggested it would be preferable to keep patrons segregated in the bars where they would offend 'the least number of heterosexuals.'"[37] Yet the magazines became crucial resources for reading counterpublics, building bibliographies of fiction and nonfiction that contained gay and lesbian themes. While in an uneasy relationship with the bars, and sites of cruising more generally, the magazines became an arm of visibility and community that tended toward respectability and belonging in a more heteronormative manner. This is not to say, however, that the books discussed in the review sections were devoid of bars or cruising, but it was more respectable and less disruptive to merely read about the bars.

Beebo Brinker (1962), the fifth novel in the Beebo Brinker Chronicles returns to tell the story of Beebo Brinker coming to New York City—landing green in Greenwich Village. She meets Jack Mann almost immediately and much like with Laura he acts as Beebo's guide to what it means to be queer in 1950s America. In one of the first descriptions of Greenwich Village, Bannon writes:

Jack lived in Greenwich Village, near the bottom of Manhattan.
It was filled with businessmen with wives and families, who played hob with the local bohemia. A rash of raids was in progress on the homosexual bar hangouts at the moment, with cops rousting respectable

beards-and-sandals off their favorite park benches; hustling old dykes, who were Village fixtures for eons, off the streets so they wouldn't offend the deodorized young middle-class wives. . . . He tacked neatly in and out through the spring mixture of tourists and natives: young girls with new jobs and timid eyes; older girls with no jobs and knowing eyes; quiet sensitive boys having intimate beers together in small boites. Shops, clubs, shoebox theaters. It always delighted him to see them, people and buildings both, blooming with the weather.[38]

Jack's delight at the buildings and the people inside them, although part of Bannon's project to describe the felicitous encounters possible in Greenwich Village, is also set against the backdrop of a larger institutional homophobia that situates homosexuality with undesirability and vice: the people of the Village are inherently offensive to "young middle-class wives." Here Jack speaks directly not only to the increasing gentrification of the neighborhood but also to the self-policing desire described by *The Mattachine Review* in hoping the bars remain open to keep the LGBTQ community segregated and anodyne for heterosexuals.

Visibility is a key tension in *Beebo Brinker*, where Jack slowly tries to draw out Beebo's declaration of her sexuality—a declaration hindered by her intense shame coupled with an almost total ignorance of queer culture. After months, Beebo finally confesses her desire for Mona (one of the great villains of lesbian fiction) to Jack: "Are you trying to say that you disapprove of Mona, but not the fact that I'm—I *must* be—gay?"[39] Jack laughingly responds "I swear to God, Beebo, you can be thicker than bean soup. I've done everything but sing it to you in C sharp."[40] But finally, and with a mixture of resignation and sadness Jack remarks "I couldn't believe you wouldn't figure it out. It's hard to realize the kind of life you've been leading up to now. How little you've been allowed to see or understand."[41] Kind, loving, and with a seemingly endless reserve of empathy, Jack is a model for queer intergenerational kinship.

Feeling like an alien in the small town she grew up in, Beebo first encountered the idea of homosexuality in others through a book: "'I read a book once,' she said clumsily. 'Under my covers at night—when I was fifteen. It was about two girls who loved each other. One of them committed suicide. It hit me so hard I wanted to die, too. That's about as close as I've come to reality in my life, Jack. Until now.'"[42] Of course one of the lovers committed suicide. They always do. The intersection between a literary community and the sudden, gloriously vibrant Village makes Beebo finally feel alive and immersed in a reality that *feels* real to her as well. These moments of reading are crucial to queer pulps; and the act of passing the texts along is equally crucial. As Stephanie Foote convincingly puts it, "The pulps also show us that the scenes of reading that appear in so many autobiographical accounts and in so much lesbian fiction are as vital to understanding an individual lesbian reader as they are to understanding the books that she reads, for such individual scenes of reading are not just historical, they are history making."[43] These history-making moments of reading shuttle back and forth between producing readers and also producing the idea of readers. Christopher Nealon also stresses the importance of the circulation of texts and the visibility of queer readership: "The imperative of the publishing industry to punish its lesbian characters was never uniformly enforced, however, and lesbians honed in quickly on the less sadistic novels, developing an apparatus of literary assessment, a seeking-out of the 'best of pulp authors' who put 'real people in real situations.'"[44] Yet Beebo still can't imagine the existence of *actual* LGBTQ people even though they are staring her in the face. The signs, codes, and forms of belonging still remain shrouded in mystery for her because the LGBTQ community remains largely literary and imaginary. The relationship between author, text, and reader is particularly important in the circulation of LGBTQ texts. Foote argues that lesbian authors take part in a particular form of relationality with their readers "not simply because they are who they are but because for them the literary sphere is not a disinterested sphere of communication. Rather, it is a sphere in which interested social actors make claims against and for normativity, and it is a sphere that works according to laws that are dictated by the needs of the market."[45] In other words, embedded in the production of lesbian texts is "the belief that someone else might read the book in a specifically lesbian way."[46] These texts illuminate the possibility of a world where their readers are no longer affect aliens hovering around the margins and perverting the genteel all-American ideal of the nuclear family.

Sobchack argues that lounge time destroys teleological forms of time, and that "instead of generating and continuing kinship relations, lounge time generates their denial and betrayal . . . undoing generational time in repetitive patterns in which the past and future collapse, lounge time degenerates."[47] While Sobchack is not arguing for the collapse of heterochrononormativity in those terms, this is precisely what she describes. Yes, lounge time is degenerational, but that degeneration is constitutive and productive of queer temporality, friendship, and alternative kinship structures. Along with lounge time, the time of reading and circulating books among friends, comrades, and fellow LGBTQ people disrupts generational time. While this might be, at this point, obvious, lounge time speaks particularly to a heteronormative sense of temporality; nonlinear in the lounge, temporality is doubly nonlinear in the gay lounge. The oft-described relationship between noir and anxieties around the nuclear family in postwar US society seemingly disregards another threat to the nuclear family, the emergence of homosexuality into mainstream American discourse. The supposed threat posed by homosexuality in the 1950s and 1960s, is reified in the notion of lounge time yet remains unspoken. Sobcheck's grim description of the lounge as offering "a world of little labor and less love,"[48] or that "the rooms of hotels and motels and boardinghouses figure as spaces of social dislocation, isolation, and existential alienation" is seemingly insupportable if either the lounge is expanded to involve queer lounges or if the lens of whose voices matter is expanded to those within the queer lounges.[49]

The question then becomes how to situate—or resituate—the gay bar as a place of affirmation rather than degradation in interwar and postwar pulp fiction. Theodore Martin describes film noir as urgently speaking to "the complexities of *being situated*."[50] For Martin this is primarily a temporal question to describe the difficulties of theorizing the contemporary and "concerns how to turn historical experience into theoretical knowledge."[51] The historical experience of queer visibility and culture is deeply rooted in the circulation of pulp novels. I would stress that situatedness is not merely a temporal experience, but a spatial one as well. These spatial relations bleed out from the page, cross state lines, and struggle against the injunction to stay put in the gay bar.

A central tenet of affect is circulation, not just the circulation of sticky affects in Ahmed's sense, but the circulation and production of positive affective experiences. Yet with the secrecy, or the mainstream opprobrium, levied against queer people, this circulation often happens in the shadows. In Bannon's lesbian pulps, characters discover one another, and readers discover one another. The effects of passing a book along, dog-earing pages to read and reread, cannot be overstated when producing a form of visibility beside mainstream literary and social culture. Although noir, as Christopher Breu and Elizabeth Hatmaker argue in the introduction to this volume, is "characterized by negative affect,"[52] it is also important to situate the social production of those negative affects.

What, then, is the space of noir? And how might negative affects, in part, exist as the texture of noir? The *Beebo Brinker Chronicles* are replete in shame, disgust, and misidentification, but these negative affects rub up against interest, excitement, acceptance, joy, and belonging. Rather than producing another example of flat homosexual characters acting as pantomime creatures of vice, Bannon captures the possibility and hope that lurks in the shadows of the twilight world. In doing so, she illustrates the discursive structures around the gay bar, and queer characters more generally, in mainstream pulp and noir fiction. This is not an illumination, or an opening up—Bannon's characters are all embedded into social relations that mirror and reproduce narratives of secrecy, but they simultaneously and insistently gesture to the cracks in the veneer of that secrecy.

NOTES

1. *Double Indemnity*, directed by Billy Wilder (USA, 1944; Los Angeles: Universal Studios, 2014) DVD (70th Anniversary Edition).
2. Christopher Breu, *Hard-Boiled Masculinities* (Minneapolis: University of Minnesota Press, 2005), 1.
3. Chandler, *The Big Sleep* (New York: Penguin Press, 2011), 23.
4. Chandler, 55.
5. Chandler, 30.
6. Chandler, 69.
7. Chandler, 109.
8. Mickey Spillane, *The Mike Hammer Collection*, vol. 1 (New York: Penguin Press, 2001), 414.
9. The end of *Vengeance is Mine* pushes this point even further as it turns out that Juno, the woman Mike Hammer has been pursuing is (wait for it) a man in drag. Hammer exclaims: "Me, a guy what likes women, a guy who knows every one of their stunts ... and I fall for this" (512). After shooting Juno multiple times he moves over to her lifeless corpse: "I spit on the clay that was Juno, queen of the gods and goddesses, and I knew why I'd always had a resentment that was actually a revulsion when I looked at her Juno was a queen, all right, a real, live queen. You know the kind. *Juno was a man!*" (513). Spillane interpellates his audience into the revulsion that Hammer feels at the joke his desire for Juno has provoked in his masculinity by telling us that we know the kind of queen Juno was. *A man!*
10. Ann Bannon, *Beebo Brinker* (New York: Gold Medal Books, 1962).
11. Foster Hirsch, *The Dark Side of the Screen* (New York: De Capo Press, 2008), 10.
12. George Chauncey, *Gay New York: Gender, Urban Culture, and the Making of the Gay Male World 1890–1940* (New York: Basic Books, 1994); John D'Emilio, *Sexual Politics, Sexual Communities: The Making of a Homosexual Minority in the United States, 1940–1970* (Chicago: University of Chicago Press, 1983); and Esther Newton, *Cherry Grove, Fire Island: Sixty Years in America's First Gay and Lesbian Town* (New York: Beacon Press,

1993). For a history of the relationship between LGBTQ neighborhoods and political engagement from the 1960s to roughly present, see Christina Hanhardt, *Safe Space: Gay Neighborhood History and the Politics of Violence* (Durham, NC: Duke University Press, 2013).

13. There is a history of literary criticism in this vein as well. For explorations of the textual relationship forged in pre-Stonewall queer literary communities, see Christopher Nealon, *Foundlings: Lesbian and Gay Historical Emotion Before Stonewall* (Durham, NC: Duke University Press, 2001), and Michael Snediker, *Queer Optimism: Lyric Personhood and Other Felicitous Persuasions* (Minneapolis: University of Minnesota Press, 2008).

14. Clyde Hoey, "Employment of Homosexuals and Other Sex Perverts in Government," S. Res. 280. 1950, 5.

15. Nealon, *Foundlings*.

16. Vin Packer, *Spring Fire* (New York: Cleis Press, 2004), iv.

17. It might be worth noting that there is a different generic tradition at work here as well: the utopia. Most utopian texts include at least one character as guide, both describing the utopia, and perhaps how the utopia was attained. Leading the protagonist and reader into the utopian space and explaining how it works, the guide (More's Hythlodaeus) for instance, traces the contours of the utopian space. In the *Beebo Brinker* series Jack Mann is the guide to the queer utopia of Greenwich Village. Although José Muñoz doesn't make this point, his *Cruising Utopia* is central to my thinking here.

18. Ann Bannon, *I Am a Woman* (New York: Cleis Press, 2002), 32.

19. Bannon, 30.

20. Bannon, 33.

21. Bannon, 33.

22. Bannon, 33.

23. Bannon, 34.

24. Teresa Brennan, *The Transmission of Affect* (Ithaca, NY: Cornell University Press, 2004), 1.

25. Sara Ahmed, *The Promise of Happiness* (Durham, NC: Duke University Press, 2010).

26. Eve Kosofsky Sedgwick, *Touching Feeling: Affect, Pedagogy, Performativity* (Durham, NC: Duke University Press, 2003), 114.

27. Sedgwick, 116.

28. Eve Kosofsky Sedgwick, *Tendencies* (Durham, NC: Duke University Press, 1993), 155.

29. Sedgwick, 3.

30. Bannon, 193.

31. Bannon, 193.

32. Bannon, 194.

33. Bannon, 196.
34. Bannon, 208.
35. Vivian Sobchack, "Lounge Time: Postwar Crisis and the Chronotope of Film Noir," in *Refiguring American Film Genres*, ed. Nick Browne (Berkeley: University of California Press, 1998), 130.
36. Sobchack, 166.
37. John D'Emilio, *Sexual Politics, Sexual Communities: The Making of a Homosexual Minority in the United States, 1940–1970* (Chicago: University of Chicago Press, 1998), 111.
38. Anne Bannon, *Beebo Brinker* (New York: Cleis Press, 2001), 2–3. It's hard not to see the resonance with quality of life policing under Rudy Giuliani's mayoral terms. The deleterious effects of these policing practices has been explored in Samuel Delany's *Time Square Red Times Square Blue* and Lauren Berlant and Michael Warner's "Sex in Public."
39. Bannon, *Beebo Brinker*, 57.
40. Bannon, 57.
41. Bannon, 57.
42. Bannon, 50.
43. Stephanie Foote, "Deviant Classics: Pulps and the Making of Lesbian Print Culture," *Signs: Journal of Women in Culture and Society* 31, no. 1 (2005): 188. Foote offers a wonderful reading of the LGBTQ print culture around the production of pulps. She focuses on the publication history of the *Beebo Brinker* series.
44. Nealon, *Foundlings*, 149.
45. Foote, "Deviant Classics," 174.
46. Foote, 182.
47. Sobchack, "Lounge Time," 161.
48. Sobchack, 166.
49. Sobchack, 155.
50. Theodore Martin, *Contemporary Drift: Genre, Historicism, and the Problem of the Present* (New York: Columbian University Press, 2017), 62.
51. Martin, 63.
52. Christopher Breu and Elizabeth A. Hatmaker, "Introduction: Dark Passages" in *Noir Affect*, ed. Breu and Hatmaker (New York: Fordham University Press, 2020), 3.

CHAPTER 6

Peripheral Noir, Mediation, and Capitalism: Noir Form, Noir Mediascape, Sociological Noir

Ignacio M. Sánchez Prado

The popularity and impact of *noir* as a cultural form in Europe and the United States makes it almost impossible to write about without the need of a conceptual taxonomy. I say "almost" because its universality has not always been reflected in a theoretical discussion that, as is usually the case in film scholarship, focuses largely on the United States, France, and maybe Britain. Defining *noir* in a definitive manner can be a slippery and perhaps pointless pursuit. As James Naremore, one of the most influential critics of the genre, has noted "film noir is an unusually baggy concept, elaborated largely after the fact of the films themselves."[1] I would take this assertion further. The concept of noir departs from the traditional genre definition of French critics, who sought to understand a mode of cultural pessimism they identified in the American cinema after the war. It is a belated concept and, as Paul Schrader notes in his classic essay on the matter, one that becomes interesting in periods in which "American movies are again taking a look at the underside of the American character."[2] What emerges in the accounts of Schrader and Naremore is a paradox between their attempt at historicist rigor, at understanding noir as a period that is both "specific" and "unwieldy" in Schrader's words, and the expansiveness and pervasiveness of what Naremore calls "the noir mediascape," that is, its existence as a "loosely related collection of perversely mysterious motifs or scenarios that circulate through all the information technologies."[3] The lesson, I think, is that any discussion of noir must embrace this tension: noir is both a culturally specific form that flourishes as a result of a particular set of conditions related to a concrete mode of capitalist modernity and a mediascape, in which the expansion of information technologies has turned the traces and marks of that concrete mode into a language to engage different experiences of modernization.

The noir mediascape is just the middle category in an ascending triad of materializations that the term "noir" names. At the lower level of the triad, noir names something concrete that has typically been read as genre. Nonetheless, as Homer B. Pettey argues, the concept of genre responds to drives toward "homology, typology, taxonomy," unable to capture noir, whose definition floats around different categories: "a genre, a style, a movement, a response to a *Zeitgeist*, a narrative strategy, a psycho-social reaction to modernity or some combination of all of these essential elements."[4] More than a genre, noir is, in its concrete manifestations, a form—a material crystallization at the crossroads between historicity and affect, in the textual, the visual, the televisual, the cinematic, and the mediatic. It is a form among others, just like melodrama. In his 1995 preface to *The Melodramatic Imagination*, Peter Brooks defends the idea that "melodrama is a form for a post-sacred era, in which polarization and hyperdramatization of forces in conflict represent a need to locate and make evident, legible, and operative those large choices of ways of being which we hold to be of overwhelming importance even though we cannot derive them from any transcendental system of belief."[5] Melodramatic form crystallizes the crossroads between historicity (the postsacred era, the collapse of transcendental systems of belief) and affect (polarization and hyperdramatization of forces of conflict). Noir, like melodrama, is about legibility, about a sense of uncertainty in the context of secular modernity. And, like melodrama, its concrete crystallizations vary according to variations in the nature of historicity and affect.

Noir, however, is a form that enacts and materializes an archive of historicities and affects at the antipodes of melodrama. According to Brooks, "melodrama is an expressionistic form . . . [a] medium in which repression has been pierced to allow thorough articulation, to make available the expression of pure moral and psychological integers."[6] Noir can have expressionistic elements—from the rigid conventions of the detective narrative structure to the visual mannerisms of dress and performance embodied in the characters that inhabit its imagined worlds. But noir is what emerges precisely when repression has not been pierced, but rather when the coordinates of the symbolic and imaginary configure themselves against the backdrop of a traumatic Real. Fredric Jameson points to this in his reading of Raymond Chandler, when he notes that his "novels have not one form, but two, an objective form and a subjective one, the rigid external structure of the detective story on the one hand, and a more personal distinctive rhythm of events on the others. . . . Yet the two kinds of form do not conflict with each other; on the contrary, the second seems to have been generated out of the first by the latter's own internal contradictions."[7] Noir form proper, however, is not always a "detection of totality" (as hinted at in the subtitle of Jameson's book on Chandler) or an allegory (the term that some of his other works evoke). It can be so in certain materializations, of course, but what constitutes noir is these internal contradictions that place it at the opposite of melodrama. Melodrama, as Brooks notes, resolves itself in "integers": it is a form that suspends contradiction to imagine, or at least try to imagine, an unproblematized totality. This is why the nineteenth-century Latin American novels that Doris Sommer describes with the term "foundational fictions"—national romances in which the central couple allegorizes the nation as such—operated through melodrama: in the project of totalizing the heterogenous young republics of the Americas, a homogenizing totality was a comforting, and sometimes urgent, narrative.[8] Noir form works precisely at the point in which integers become unthinkable and the resulting contradictions erode the conventions of its surface formulas—the detective, the hard-boiled antihero—and open the space for a more "rhythmic" narrative that captures the flows of affect and history at the moment of materialization.

The noir form and mediascape are in themselves materializations of a larger phenomenon: the presence of the dark, the unthinkable, the evil, the gloom in the nooks and corners of the modern project. Kieran Flanagan calls this "sociological noir."[9] In a reflection at the crossroads of sociology and theology, Flanagan is interested in the way in which evil and the dark and spectral forces of society "irrupt" into the space of modernity. In his account of the concept, Flanagan identifies three sources: First, the notion of film noir in an extended sense by which it speaks of "national capacities to represent the dark side of crime"; second, "theoretical orientations in sociology, stances whose diffuseness marks a particular way of reading modernity" through "properties of bloom and pessimism"—drawing primarily from Weber, he notes that the modern sociologist can deploy "the property of a seer uniquely gifted to discern the dark of modernity but unable to decipher that which loomed"; third, he traces "significant but marginal concerns of major thinkers," including the metaphors of the "spectral" in Marx, the concept of the ruin in Simmel, and the notion of sin in Durkheim.[10] Flanagan suggests a trajectory similar to the one I am drawing in my argument: he moves from the historical crystallization of the noir in cultural forms, to a moment (Weberian sociology) where the social affects that noir engages lack the mediascape that would come a few decades later in cinema, to a description of an ecosystem of theoretical concepts that point toward the sociological noir without ever materializing it in full.

Without the space or time to unfold the richness of these discussions, what is worth highlighting is that noir, as a category of critical theory and of cultural critique, names a constellation of materializations of the traumatic kernel of capitalist modernity. It is a constellation, because film noir, the privileged crystallization that allowed for the original formulation of the concept, is only one of such materializations. Indeed, the noir mediascape is a related materialization of a different order, one that, in Appadurai's words, "image-centered, narrative-based accounts of strips of reality" rendered possible by "the reproduction of the electronic capabilities to produce and disseminate information."[11] And yet, as the idea of "sociological noir" shows, it materializes frequently in concepts that account for objects whose materialization are incomplete, deferred, or not directly knowable. The hotly debated concept of the spectral in Marx is a case in point. In a recent piece, Johan Hartle notes that "the spectral Marx gives a plausible example for the possible interpretations of the conjunction Marx and the aesthetic [*sic*]. The specter of Marx is an aestheticized Marx."[12] I would further emphasize this point: if it is true that conceptual categories of ruin and spectrality and the like are aesthetic, it is because the darkness toward which they point is traumatic, inaccessible, unknowable, at least in part. This is the reason why readings of elements in noir as articulating some kind of direct metaphorical meaning tend to be dissatisfying, just like accounts of the noir based on flat notions of allegorization of the masculine. If there is value in the concept of the sociological noir, it is because it describes not a totality but a series of trace elements that exist in the dark spaces of modernity without constituting modernity in itself.

The signifier "noir" never fully achieves positive meaning, and the three levels I have discussed so far (noir form, noir mediascape, sociological noir) are always defined by approximation and even by a conceptual externality vis-à-vis the object of noir. Slavoj Žižek points out that the classical film noir is a "lost object of desire" and that its "nostalgic charm" emerges from the fact that "our gaze bases itself on another gaze, one which probably never existed, of the moviegoers of that era who were still able to take the film noir 'seriously,' to find *jouissance* in it."[13] If we take Žižek at his word, the first thing to consider about the noir form is that it always already enacts lost affects, or, going further, affects that we experience as loss but were never actually there. In a different text, Žižek goes further to note that, in the original formulation by French critics of the idea of film noir to account for American film, the term "posits a unity which did not exist 'in itself,'" mistaking "the heroic-cynical, pessimist fatalist perception of the noir hero for a socially critical attitude."[14] The point of this is not to discard noir outright—in fact this example is merely an analogy that he uses to discuss the American reception of French theory. Rather, Žižek notes that "*film noir* is none the less a concept in the strict Hegelian sense: something that cannot simply be explained, accounted for in terms of historical circumstances, conditions and reactions, but acts a structuring principle that displays a dynamic of its own."[15] Indeed, what I call the noir form is characterized precisely by never fully fitting actual narrative works of any kind, because noir texts and objects "are constantly changing, and this change imperceptibly transforms the very notion, the standard by means of which they are measured."[16] The same thing could in fact be said of the noir mediascape, subject to the vertiginous evolution of technologies and the cultural discourses they shape and sustain, or the sociological noir, which supplements history by supplying "tangible witnesses for the social construction of the past," that is, by registering the way modernity endows "ruins with capacities to pick up the resonances of irruptions."[17] In these terms, one can also share Žižek's conclusion that the notion of noir "perceives in its object a potential which is invisible to those who are directly engaged with it."[18] It is precisely because the concept disintegrates as we approach the actual object of the noir that the triad of noir categories I propose (form, mediascape, sociological) ultimately can be deployed to approximate manifestations of the spectral, the traumatic or the obscure that may otherwise be unthinkable or even invisible.

If sociological noir speaks of a feature of capitalist modernity, and if the noir mediascape exists insofar as there is the technological infrastructure of dissemination to render it possible, it is possible to say that the theorizations of the noir in general, and the noir form in particular, are impoverished by the focus on US and Western European cinema. I would further contend that it is in areas of the world in which modernity emerges in tensional, conflictive, or transcultural ways that we can test the noir form as a cultural form of modernization, because the process of combined and uneven development allows for the visibilization of ideological configurations and structures of feeling that the experience of modernity in hegemonic cultural sites cannot always perceive. Indeed, many Latin Americanists do not follow Fredric Jameson on the idea that there is "a singular modernity," although it is true that Jameson asserts that idea to challenge "the illusion that the West as something that no one else possesses."[19] Latin America's experience with modernity implies the ability to "enter and leaving" it, as Néstor García Canclini famously puts it, because the uneven nature of modernization is not only a factor of global capital, it also replicates within national contexts.[20] When speaking of the Argentine experience of the 1920s and 1930s, Beatriz Sarlo uses the term "peripheral modernity" to address a period of "semantic density" that "weaves contradictory elements that never fully unify into a hegemonic line." Instead, Sarlo notes that Argentine culture is "a *culture of mixture*, in which defensive and residual elements coexist with programs for renovation; cultural features of the *criollo formation* at the same time of a massive process of import of goods, discourses and symbolic practices."[21] Jameson's theorization is useful insofar as he recognizes that "modernity is not a concept, philosophical or otherwise, but a narrative category," an assertion that not only breaks away from Habermasian accounts of modernity but also allows for the dislodging of modernity from the European experience into the sites and historicities of modernization.[22] For Latin American theorists of modernity, the practice of narrating modernity remits to concrete sites of modernization. More importantly, as Bolívar Echeverría has theorized, it is essential to understand a distinction between "adopted" or "exogenous modernization," which implies an expansion of capitalism through "the imposition of the cultural identity of a society and the particular goals of the historical enterprises in which that society is invested over the identity and historical goals of another" and "self-modernization" or "endogenous modernization," which is affirmed "through the resistances of the society in which exogenous modernity takes place, in the quality and consolidation of the respective identity."[23]

It is not coincidental that Echeverría wrote these lines in Mexico. Mexico's historical process of modernization was constructed in the same paradox. The period between 1940 and 1968 in Mexico is often referred to as the "Mexican miracle" due to the fast expansion of capitalist modernization, accelerated economic growth, the emergence of the urban middle class and the stable economic and political development enjoyed in large swaths of the country.²⁴ At the same time, this is a period in which cultural and economic nationalism are strengthened. The consequence of this was a country that, under the rule of the "perfect dictatorship" of a single-party regime with non-reelectable presidents, was defined by its radically uneven nature: sprawling urban centers extending their shadows over growing slums and popular neighborhoods, a transnational economy co-existing with a precarious rural system.²⁵ Of course, my point here is not to account for Mexico's uneven modernization; rather, I argue that the inherent contradictions in the Mexican miracle period provide a historicity of noir that is neither accounted for by the idea of "a singular modernity" nor captured by the notion that the Global South or peripheral societies can be adequately defined solely through tropes related to authenticity, autochtony, specificity, or originality. It also overrides an even more naïve, but frequently articulated, perception that peripheral culture is in itself resistant to capitalist modernity, a myth usually put forward by some leftists of hegemonic countries who project their aspirations unto nonhegemonic societies. Indeed, the tropes and concepts that dominate the discussion of modernity in Latin America—ex-centricity, transculturation, baroque, peripherality, hybridity, just to mention a few—underscore an experience in which capitalism and resistance, coloniality and its residuals, cosmopolitanism and autochthony are always already intertwined and engaged in friction and conflict.

The first decade and a half of the Mexican miracle also constitutes the consolidating stage of Mexico's astonishing cultural revolution—the construction of an apparatus of cultural nationalism and of a complex cultural mediascape with few parallels in the world.²⁶ Within that revolution, Mexico was able to build within a few years a film industry that experienced a so-called golden age, a term that generally refers to the period from the first blockbuster of the sound era (Fernando de Fuentes's *Allá en el rancho grande*, 1936) to the gradual erosion of the national industry due to internal conflicts and the restitution of transnational circulation of American cinema in the 1950s. Of the many cinematic genres to gain currency in this period, noir is one of the most contradictory ones. Although the production of noir films is copious (scholar Álvaro Fernández Reyes identifies 160 films in the noir produced between 1941 and 1959), most historical accounts of Mexican cinema privileged the nationalist films of the Emilio Fernández-Gabriel Figueroa collaboration, Luis Buñuel's *Los olvidados*, and the popular films of Ismael Rodríguez as representatives of what Charles Ramírez Berg calls "The Classical Mexican Cinema."²⁷ Noir films are made by some of the most important directors of the period, including Buñuel himself, as well as Julio Bracho and Alejandro Galindo, generally recognized as the major directors of midcentury Mexican film right behind Emilio Fernández.

This tension between the pervasiveness of noir and its lack of canonicity can be explained by positing that the noir forms of the period, constructed upon a noir mediascape of which cinema was a central technology, represented materializations of sociological noir that capitalist modernization brought about but that could not be rendered visible by the maximalist project of cultural nationalism as such. It is telling that, at the outset of the golden age of cinema, there was a debate as to whether the new society, modern and global but also revolutionary and national, was best represented by the noir form or the melodrama form. In 1943 two key films of Mexican cinema were released: *Flor Silvestre* (*Wild Flower*), a nationalist melodrama directed by Emilio Fernández, and *Distinto amanecer* (*Another Dawn*), a foundational noir by Julio Bracho. *Flor Silvestre* is aligned with the elements of melodrama discussed earlier. It tells the story of the romance between the son of a landowner and a peasant woman. After being disowned, the landowner's son joins the revolution. In the process, his wife and young son are kidnapped, and his actions to save them ultimately lead to his execution. Fernández's film is a maximalist moral tale in which the peasant woman embodies the allegorical potential of a new nation (her name is "Esperanza," that is, Hope), and her son (who appears only at the very end, is nameless and played by an uncredited actor) is construed as the empty signifier of a nation to come. In contrast, *Distinto amanecer* is an urban noir that follows a union member's efforts to find the killer of their leader. Although both films have been shot by the same cinematographer, Gabriel Figueroa,, they look completely different: Fernández's is a historical film focused on rural Mexico as a site of the nation's essence, and its long shots of the landscape and nature accompany the melodramatic story to cover the full ideological range of the idea of the revolution. In contrast, *Distinto amanecer* is an unapologetically urban film, in which the revolution materializes through the tension between one of its core structures (the union) and a specter haunting it (corruption). Figueroa's mastery here is deployed in opposition to the open spaces of rural Mexico: the film begins with a sequence showing distinct sites of modern Mexico City, including its avenues full of cars, the infrastructure of the postal service and the newspaper industry, the windows of the most exclusive boutiques, closing with the nocturnal landscape illuminated by the lights of Coca-Cola and other advertisements.

Bracho and Fernández faced off in a polemic in the wake of the films' release, showing the competition between melodrama and noir as the cultural forms which account for Mexican modernization.[28] A newspaper story the compared and contrasted the films on nationalist terms, saying that Fernández represented "Mexico itself," while Bracho was rejected as someone who was bringing European and US culture to Mexico. This accusation is not false: the inspiration that Humphrey Bogart plays in Pedro Armendáriz's rendering of the protagonist is obvious, as is the way in which Andrea Palma models her screen performance in Marlene Dietrich's work with Josef von Sternberg or the atmospherics reminiscent of John Huston's *The Maltese Falcon*. Bracho, however, defended his film as more representative of Mexico's modernity and rejected Fernández's nationalism frequently, accusing him of shooting postcards instead of films and lacking cinematic talent of his own, relying instead on Figueroa's virtuoso talent. What underlies this debate, though, is a serious discussion of the tension between the melodrama form and the noir form in modernity, and, in hindsight, it is clear that cinema was able to capture the Mexican miracle so successfully because both coexisted.

The historical form of film noir flourished in Mexico because capitalist modernity created new forms of sociological noir that placed crime and corruption at the center of the urban imaginaries. In his exhaustive book *Mex Noir*, critic Rafael Aviña notes that noir flourished in Mexico from the early days of silent cinema because of the constitutive fact of capitalist modernization: the prevalence of crime as a symptom of the social inequality that accompanied it. As far as the Mexican miracle period, Aviña notes that the growth of major crimes (like bank robberies), the emergence of police bodies and surveillance institutions, and the abysmal difference between rich and poor all created the social conditions of the noir.[29] To this account one should definitely add something that historians of Mexican national cinema rarely discuss: the fact that Mexican moviegoers did not just subject themselves to the melodramatic spectacles of national cinema, but were in fact cosmopolitan media consumers who were able to see domestic productions alongside a steady stream of US, British, French, and German films, with occasional releases from other national industries.[30]

Murder and crime occupy a central role in the social imagination in Mexico City and other urban scenarios, partly because they embody failures of the security that the state must provide for economic and social development and partly because of the rise of the noir mediascape. Crime, according to Pablo Piccato, is "a relational category, incarnated in the suspicion of the police, judges and the law itself toward the urban poor, and the latter's distrust toward state ideologies and practices with respect to crime."[31] The experience of what Piccato calls "the texture of crime" was an essential structure of feeling in modern Mexico, as it shaped affective mediations for social subjects facing accelerated modernization, a notion of citizenship that shifted quickly with the expansion and professionalization of the state, and what would become the double articulation of the sociological noir: the fear of the newly emerged population of the urban poor, most of them immigrants from rural areas devastated by the revolution which constituted a new and quite visible social presence in rapidly growing cities along with the postrevolutionary reconstitution of the ruling class out of the military cadres of revolutionary factions, which came to be defined both by the memory of their violent participations in the conflict and the role they played in the corruption of the system constructed in the wake of social struggle.

It is not surprising that the noir mediascape formed with these two narratives as its central parameters. The successive rise of the print media, radio, and cinema created very quickly a media ecosystem hungry for stories to tell. Indeed, as Piccato has studied elsewhere, the consolidation of *nota roja* as a central genre of journalism as well as the emergence of crime fiction not only in literature but also in popular magazines, are examples of this.[32] Furthermore, as Fernando Fabio Sánchez observes, "the act of murder and assassination [were] a platform on which the concept of the postrevolutionary Mexican nation is constructed and critiqued."[33] *Distinto amanecer* is a distinctive crystallization of the noir form because it is a major materialization of the sociological noir into the noir mediascape of the early years of the Mexican miracle. It is a murder story in which the tropes described by Piccato and Sánchez are present. On the one hand it uses the murder of the union leader as a point of inflection through which the Mexican state could be interpellated critically. Part of the implicit argument that Bracho seems to be raising in his critique of Fernández is that the latter's "postcard nationalism" is unable to actually see the materiality of the revolution which in his film is represented by its ugly underbelly. It is not coincidental that a decade and a half later, in *La sombra del caudillo* (1960), Bracho would use another murder story to criticize heads-on the postrevolutionary regime, resulting in the film being canned and censored for decades. But *Distinto amanecer* does not embody solely the idea of murder and violence as marks of the modern experience. Corruption is essential to understand Mexico's sociological noir. Flanagan identifies various instances in which corruption, as a theological discourse, permeates the dark side of modernity due to the identification of corruption and sin, from the idea of the corruption of religious faith coming from the Gothic, to the idea of moral corruption tied to sex to the idea of political corruption identified with evil.[34] A similar thing emerges in *Distinto amanecer*: the corruption of the state, which Bracho represents in a barely concealed way, claiming the fictional nature of his story to evade censorship.

As the noir form established itself firmly both in literary and cinematic discourse, the noir mediascape continued developing in sophisticated ways as a counter to the genres that fostered the pedagogical mission of cultural nationalism. A case in point is *Ensayo de un crimen* (*Rehearsal of a Crime*), a 1944 novel by one of Mexico's most famous playwrights, Rodolfo Usigli, widely considered to be Mexico's first major noir novel. The novel tells the story of Roberto de la Cruz, a bourgeois man who wishes to commit the perfect murder as an aesthetic achievement.[35] In his reading of the novel, Fernando Fabio Sánchez argues that it "represents the convergence between the perception of the state as a violent entity and the attempt to reach modernity, even though this aspiration carries with it the symbolic disfigurement of the Mexican countenance."[36] Sánchez's reading rests on the prevalence of political killings in Mexico at the time, as well as on Usigli's history as an earlier critic of state corruption, thanks to his celebrated play *El gesticulador* (*The Impostor*, 1937), an early indictment of political corruption.[37] I would go even further. A trait of the noir form, as Fabio Vighi explains, is that, as a product of the culture industry, it is "internally antagonistic" because it "holds on negativity without jettisoning its speculative identity with totality."[38] Writing against Theodor W. Adorno's dismissal of the culture industry, Vighi notes that the noir form carries within itself a "secret, unwitting self-subversion" of its "ideological thrust."[39] Usigli's novel is a prime example of this. As both Sánchez and Carolyn Wolfenzon note, Usigli's motivation in writing the novel is dealing with the trauma of violence during the Revolution, which was a lived experience for people of Usigli's generation.[40] Thus, Usigli's book function's with an internal antagonism: there is a moralizing gesture toward the totality of the social in tension with the historical negativity and violence constitutive to the post-Revolutionary period.

Usigli's narrative finds a peculiar materialization in Luis Buñuel's loose 1955 adaptation, *Ensayo de un crimen* (*The Criminal Mind of Archibaldo de la Cruz*).[41] Buñuel's attraction to the novel is obvious: the idea of a self-referential bourgeoisie, the universalism of the question of aesthetic murder (derived from Thomas DeQuincey) and the visibilization of the failure of political revolution have clear continuities with his *oeuvre* at large. It is worth remembering that he had already punctured the premises of golden age cinema with his masterpiece *Los olvidados*, in which the slums of Mexico City do not house the noble poor of national melodramas and comedies but the degraded and desolate people who languish under the shadow of a city that is quickly growing in the background of their lives and of the film. Buñuel's film departs from Usigli's novel in considerable ways, to the point that he renames the main character (from Roberto to Archibaldo) to mark the distance. As Wolfenzon notes building on the work of various Buñuel scholars, the film version de-emphasizes the Revolution as a source of trauma and universalizes the theme by locating Archibaldo's obsession in the context of broken family relations.[42] Yet, the film is completely readable through the coordinates of noir developed here. Geoffrey Kantaris notes that in the context of "Mexico City's transformation from metropolis to megalopolis, Buñuel allegorizes the disruptions wrought by the circulation of capital transmogrified into excessive desire and abjection."[43] If Buñuel punctures in *Los olvidados* the coordinates of melodrama by centering the camera in the traumatic existence of Mexico City's margins, *Ensayo de un crimen* takes the coordinates of the noir form created by Bracho to its natural conclusion, using murder as a figure to mark the persistence of the aristocracy and the failure of the revolution's project. It is not coincidental that 1955, the year of the film's release, is considered to be the end of noir as such in both the account of Fernández Reyes (who classifies the film as a *sui generis* work) or Rafael Aviña (who locates it at the end of the Mex Noir's turn toward melodrama).[44] In other words, it shows that the triumph of capitalist modernization, through the obscene enactment of aristocratic frivolity, is what destroyed the revolutionary project. Following Vighi's formulation, the ideological thrust of Buñuel's cinematic form—the psychological melodrama of Archibaldo de la Cruz—is subverted by his pushing the logic of the sociological noir to its ulterior consequence: it is no longer the dark side of modernity but its final consequence.

Of the various contributions of Latin American studies to media theory, Jesús Martín-Barbero's theory of mediation stands out as the most significant. Martín-Barbero uses the concept to discuss the impact of media technologies in the constitution of Latin America's national-popular cultures, with a particular emphasis on the uses of media and popular cultures on the part of audiences. Martín-Barbero's key methodological point is that traditional media theories focused on production and hegemony (in a way the Frankfurtian paradigm that became prevalent following the aforementioned work of Adorno on the cultural industries) is classist, and that even if one recognizes the existence of logics of domination, production and labor in media, one should see "the other side of the picture, the side of the cracks in domination, the consumption dimensions of economy and the pleasures of life."[45] Martín-Barbero's point is that even in relations of cultural domination we should be attentive to the ways in which appropriations and performances of the cultural archives and repertoires of mass media carry contradictory forms of resistance and engagement that cannot be rendered visible if we only think in relation to hegemony. What I contend here, in conclusion, is that thinking the cartography of noir—the three levels: form, mediascape, sociological noir—from a site like Mexico, a similar process takes place: the mediation of capitalist modernity allows for the use of noir as a critical stance that appropriates the elements of hegemonic forms of the genre into the national realities of peripheral societies.

As the classical Mexican noir faded away, the noir form materializes frequently in media culture, in part because midcentury Mexico became a noir society: as the symbolic efficiency of cultural nationalism faded away in the 1960s, cosmopolitan forms and mediascapes such as rock-and-roll counterculture became forms of mediating the new stages of capitalist modernity.[46] Mexico's most important noir cycles take place in parallel with the ebbs and flows of capitalist modernization, particularly as the project of the postrevolutionary state went through its slow and gradual collapse in the wake of the massacre of students at Tlatelolco in 1968.[47] The most iconic and well-known case is Paco Ignacio Taibo II's Belascoarán Shayne novels, a ten-book cycle (so far) that has accompanied Mexico's journey into neoliberalism from the economic crises of the mid-1970s to the rise of the Zapatistas.[48] Another notable case is Rafael Bernal's novel *El complot mongol* (*The Mongolian Conspiracy*, 1969), in which Filiberto García, a detective and gun for hire who is also a cult figure of Mexican literary history, must engage with a transnational conspiracy to kill the US president in Mexico, allegedly ordered by the Chinese and organized in the city's Chinatown.[49] Filiberto has to work alongside an FBI and a KGB agent, which reproduces the setup of Cold War–era jokes based on the comparison of a Russian, an American, and a Mexican's reactions to a hypothetical situation. The novel is a comedic noir and Filiberto is in equal parts a hard-boiled detective and an incarnation of the Hispanic picaresque tradition. Published a year after the Tlatelolco massacre, the novel has been read as an allegory of the "latent national crisis," particularly as we realize that the assassination plot is actually homegrown, part of the regime's domestic policies.[50]

The dialectical interaction between the hard-boiled narrative and the comedic elements is peculiar variation of Jameson's description of Chandler's two narratives cited earlier, as well as of Vighi's notion of the ideology of noir subverted within itself. The tropes of *El complot mongol* are an appropriation of cultural elements at the height of Cold War paranoia. The title is a parody of *The Manchurian Candidate* (John Frankenheimer, 1962) up to the geographical misnomer (when in fact Bernal was one of Mexico's most notable experts on Asia and the Pacific at large). The notion that Mao's China would even care about the Mexican president is patently ridiculous, a fear grounded more on xenophobia against the Chinese community (a xenophobic fear pervasive in Mexican popular culture of the time) than in any geopolitical reality. The cosmopolitan paranoia of the narrative, embodied in the tropes of noir and the thriller, is subverted by our discovery that the crisis was national all along. *El complot mongol*'s deceiving simplicity and the currency of its critique of the state in globalizing times has afforded it a pervasive presence in the post–golden age noir mediascape. The novel has been adapted twice for film: a 1977 version directed by Antonio Eceiza and a star-studded 2018 adaptation by Sebastián del Amo. A graphic novel version was published in 2017 and Filiberto García is the protagonist of a hard-boiled subplot within *Tierra Roja* (*Red Land*), a biographical novel of Lázaro Cárdenas, Mexico's president in the late 1930s.[51] Mexico's peripheral and parodic engagement with Chinese imperialism, one that enacts the paranoias of globalization as a conceit to visibilize Mexico's sociological noir in the post-1968 world, is clearly an active trope that elicits cultural mediations.

Llámenme Mike (*Call Me Mike*, Alfredo Gurrola, 1979), a unique and not widely known film, tells the story of Miguel, a corrupt Mexico City police officer from the drug division. After he participates in the theft of a cocaine shipment following his commander's orders, he is chosen to be the scapegoat and promised to be released from prison in six months. In prison, he is beaten up by the criminals he arrested and, as a result of a surgery performed to heal him, Miguel comes to believe that he is Mike Hammer, a detective from a series of novels by Mickey Spillane. Immersed in the character's persona, Miguel begins to imagine that he is fighting a communist conspiracy, which leads him to gradually and unwittingly take down the network of corruption in the police department, without ever realizing the truth. This Quixotic story shot in Mexico City's nocturnal underground was produced with minimal resources, but it is a sharp parody of the hard-boiled US stories globalized by the rise of the television serial, drawing elements from the 1958 adaptation of Spillane's novels, as well as the picaresque detective Columbo from the long-running TV series (which debuted in 1971), and even Travis Bickle, the protagonist of Martin Scorcese's *Taxi Driver* (1976). In its brazen parody, the film has significant critical power. It references Arturo "El Negro" Durazo, the corrupt and larger-than-life chief of the Mexico City police who would be arrested in 1984 for corruption and his complicity in the cocaine trade. As a result, the film was censored for three years and could not be released until Durazo left the post. Gurrola spearheaded a revival of the noir in cinema: his following film was the first adaptation of Taibo's first Belascoarán novel, *Días de combate (Combat Days,* 1979).[52]

Llámenme Mike is an example of the role that noir forms have in the mediation of capitalist modernities, even when cultural products seem to mimic hegemonic forms of transnational cultures. It is produced at a point of crisis in Mexican cinema, when state funding was diverted to commercial productions, censorship was low profile but real, and the mass audiences of the golden age had withered. Its comedy responds to the emerging takeover of global television by the United States, by enacting the absurdity of US genres when read against the backdrop of a Latin American reality. It is a critique of the noir mediascape's imperial materiality, while appropriating critically its symbolic weapons. The film also enacts Mexico's sociological noir: in the middle of the short-lived oil boom that would collapse in the 1982 crisis, in a country ruled by a president who did not even face the weak candidates the opposition could usually level against the ruling, it became the one film that spoke of the corruption of the state, that narrated a horizon of justice and that, almost prophetically, would render visible the longstanding relationship between the police and the drug trade that would plague Mexico for decades thereafter. It is the noir of a peripheral modernity at its best, one in which the ruins and residuals of resistance against both state and imperial hegemony find, if ephemerally, a moment of crystallization.

NOTES

1. James Naremore, *More than Night: Film Noir in Its Contexts* (Berkeley: University of California Press, 2007), 5.

2. Paul Schrader, "Notes on Film Noir," *Film Comment* 8, no. 1 (Spring 1972): 8.

3. Schrader, "Notes on Film Noir," 5; Naremore, *More than Night*, 255. On the term *mediascape*, see also Arjun Appadurai, *Modernity at Large: Cultural Dimensions of Globalization* (Minneapolis: University of Minnesota Press, 1996).

4. Homer B. Pettey, "Introduction: The Noir Turn," in *Film Noir*, ed. Homer B. Pettey and P. Barton Palmer (Edinburgh: Edinburgh University Press, 2016), 1–15.

5. Peter Brooks, *The Melodramatic Imagination: Balzac, Henry James, Melodrama, and The Mode of Excess* (New Haven, CT: Yale University Press, 1995), ix.

6. Brooks, 56.

7. Fredric Jameson, *Raymond Chandler: The Detections of Totality* (London: Verso, 2016), 22–23.

8. Doris Sommer, *Foundational Fictions: The National Romances of Latin America* (Berkeley: University of California Press, 1991).

9. Kieran Flanagan, *Sociological Noir: Irruptions and the Darkness of Modernity* (London: Routledge, 2017).

10. Flanagan, 32–33.

11. Appadurai, *Modernity at Large*, 35.

12. Johan F. Hartle, "Marx as Art as Politics: Representations of Marx in Contemporary Art," in *Aesthetic Marx*, ed. Sami Gandesha and Johan F. Hartle (London: Bloomsbury, 2017), 262. Hartle delineates a debate between Jameson and Derrida, in which Jameson calls spectrality to function as a "form-problem" within the aesthetic of the Derridean text, and Derrida, while accepting begrudgingly the characterization, responds by noting that the aesthetic does not capture the full conceptual problem. See Jacques Derrida *et al.*, *Ghostly Demarcations: A Symposium on Jacques Derrida's Specters of Marx*, ed. Michael Sprinker (London: Verso, 2008), 32, 247–248.

13. Slavoj Žižek, *The Most Sublime Hysteric: Hegel with Lacan*, trans. Thomas Scott-Railton (Malden, MA: Polity, 2014), 228.

14. Slavoj Žižek, "Da capo senza fine," in *Contingency, Hegemony, Universality*, ed. Judith Butler, Ernesto Laclau, and Slavoj Žižek (London: Verso, 2000), 243. The same argument is rehearsed with the same wording in Žižek, *Less than Nothing: Hegel and the Shadow of Dialectical Materialism* (London: Verso, 2012), 210.

15. Žižek, "Da capo senza fine," 244.

16. Žižek, 244.

17. Flanagan, *Sociological Noir*, 217.

18. Žižek, "Da capo senza fine," 248.

19. Fredric Jameson, *A Singular Modernity: Essay on the Ontology of the Present* (London: Verso, 2002).

20. Néstor García Canclini, *Hybrid Cultures: Strategies for Entering and Leaving Modernity*, trans. Christopher L. Chippari and Silvia L. López (Minneapolis: University of Minnesota Press, 1995).

21. Beatriz Sarlo, *Una modernidad periférica: Buenos Aires 1920 y 1930* (Buenos Aires: Nueva Visión, 1999), 28; my translation.

22. Jameson, *Singular Modernity*, 40.

23. Bolívar Echeverría. *Las ilusiones de la modernidad* (México City: Ediciones del Equilibrista, 2015), 190; my translation.

24. For a discussion of the Mexican miracle period and its contradictions, including the ones described here, see Héctor Aguilar Camín and Lorenzo Meyer, *In the Shadow of the Mexican Revolution. Contemporary Mexican History 1910–1989*, trans. Luis Alberto Fierro (Austin: University of Texas Press, 2001), 159–198. For a more recent account of the period focused on the idea of "perfect dictatorship" and the consolidation of the ruling party, see Gilbert M. Joseph and Jürgen Buchenau, *Mexico's Once and Future Revolution: Social Upheaval and the Challenge of Rule since the Late Nineteenth Century* (Durham, NC: Duke University Press, 2013), 141–163.

25. For an account of Mexico's economic inequalities, see Oscar J. Martínez, *Mexico's Uneven Development: The Geographical and Historical Context of Inequality* (London: Routledge, 2016).

26. For a discussion in detail of this full cultural revolution and its political and economic ramifications, see Gilbert Joseph, Anne Rubenstein, and Eric Zolov, eds., *Fragments of a Golden Age: The Politics of Culture in Mexico since the 1940s* (Durham, NC: Duke University Press, 2001); and Paul Gillingham and Benjamin T. Smith, eds., *Dictablanda: Politics, Work and Culture in Mexico 1938–1968* (Durham, NC: Duke University Press, 2014).

27. Álvaro Fernández Reyes, *Crimen y suspenso en el cine mexicano 1946–1955* (Zamora: El Colegio de Michoacán, 2007); Charles Ramírez Berg, *The Classical Mexican Cinema: The Poetics of Exceptional Golden Age Films* (Austin: University of Texas Press, 2015).

28. I follow the account of this polemic as told by Jesús Ibarra in *Los Bracho: Tres generaciones de cine mexicano* (Mexico: Universidad Nacional Autónoma de México, 2006), 114–116.

29. Rafael Aviña, *Mex Noir: Cine policiaco mexicano* (Mexico: Cineteca Nacional, 2017).

30. For a study of the continuum between foreign and national cinema and the question of cosmopolitanism of the audiences, see Ignacio M. Sánchez Prado, "The Golden Age Otherwise: Mexican Cinema and the Mediations of Capitalist Modernity in the 1940s and 1950s," in *Cosmopolitan Film Cultures in Latin America 1896–1960*, ed. Rielle Navistki and Nicolas Poppe (Bloomington: Indiana University Press, 2017), 241–266.

31. Pablo Piccato, *City of Suspects: Crime in Mexico City 1900–1931* (Durham, NC: Duke University Press, 2001), 3.

32. Pablo Piccato, *A History of Infamy: Crime, Truth, and Justice in Mexico* (Berkeley: University of California Press, 2017).

33. Fernando Fabio Sánchez, *Artful Assassins: Murder as Art in Modern Mexico* (Nashville, TN: Vanderbilt University Press, 2010), 179.

34. Flanagan, *Sociological Noir*, 159–160; 227–228, 250.

35. Rodolfo Usigli, *Ensayo de un crimen* (Mexico: Joaquín Mortiz, 1993).

36. Sánchez, *Artful Assassins*, 46. For a worthwhile reading of the novel's structure and its gender dynamics, see Gerardo García Muñoz, *El enigma y la conspiración: Del cuarto cerrado al laberinto neopoliciaco* (Saltillo: Universidad Autónoma de Coahuila, 2010), 61–139.

37. Rodolfo Usigli, *The Impostor: A Play for Demagogues*, trans. Ramón Layera and Don Rosenberg (Pittsburgh, PA: Latin American Literary Review Press, 2005).

38. Fabio Vighi, *Critical Theory and Film: Rethinking Ideology Through Film Noir* (London: Continuum, 2012), 34, 67.

39. Vighi, 72.

40. Sánchez, *Artful Assasins*, 48; Carolyn Wolfenzon, "Los dos ensayo(s) de un crimen: Buñuel y Usigli," *Chasqui* 35, no. 1 (2006): 40–42.

41. The English title departs from the novel because of the protagonist's name change.

42. Wolfenzon, "Los dos ensayo(s) de un crimen," 45.

43. Geoffrey Kantaris, "The Cinematic Labor of Affect: Urbanity and Sentimental Education in *El bruto* and *Ensayo de un crimen*," in *A Companion to Luis Buñuel*, ed. Rob Stone and Julián Daniel Gutiérrez-Albilla (Malden, MA: Wiley, 2013), 315.

44. Aviña, *Mex Noir*, 253–254; Reyes, *Crimen y suspenso en el cine mexicano*, 131.

45. Jesús Martín-Barbero, *Communication, Media and Hegemony: From Media to Mediations*, trans. Elizabeth Fox and Robert A. White (London: Sage, 1993), 212.

46. On this matter, see Eric Zolov, *Refried Elvis: The Rise of the Mexican Counterculture* (Berkeley: University of California Press, 1999).

47. On the wake of Tlatelolco and the erosion of the state see Aguilar Camín and Meyer, *In the Shadow of the Mexican Revolution*, 199–250, and Joseph and Buchenau, *Mexico's Once and Future Revolution*, 167–196.

48. Paco Ignacio Taibo II, *Todo Belascoarán* (Mexico: Planeta, 2010). For a discussion of these novels, see Persephone Braham, *Crimes against the State, Crimes against Persons* (Minneapolis: University of Minnesota Press, 2004), 81–94, and Glen S. Close, *Contemporary Hispanic Crime Fiction: A Transatlantic Discourse on Urban Violence* (New York: Palgrave, 2008), 25–56.

49. Rafael Bernal, *The Mongolian Conspiracy*, trans. Katherine Silver (New York: New Directions, 2013).

50. Sánchez, *Artful Assassins*, 84–96.

51. Rafael Bernal, Luis Humberto Crosthwaite, and Ricardo Peláez Goycochea, *El complot mongol: Novela gráfica* (Mexico: Fondo de Cultura Económica/Joaquín Mortiz, 2017); Pedro Ángel Palou, *Tierra roja* (Mexico: Planeta, 2016).

52. For an account of the film and its period, see Carl J. Mora, *Mexican Cinema: Reflections of a Society 1988–2004* (Jefferson, NC: McFarland, 2004), 144.

CHAPTER 7

Cyborg Affect and the Power of the Posthuman in the *Ghost in the Shell* Franchise

Peter Hitchcock

Because affect is insistently invoked to denote our constantly changing relations to the world, as made by and for us, it is both everywhere and nowhere in being. "Made" here is not a determination in the Spinozist sense and, since affect is a process without origin, the cause of cause is not a political predicament for being. One can take a position on affect but that would not be what affect is. In their assessment of affect theory, Seigworth and Gregg suggest:

> Affect can be understood ... as a gradient of bodily capacity—a supple incrementalism of ever-modulating force-relations—that rises and falls not only along various rhythms and modalities of encounter but also through the troughs and sieves of sensation and sensibility, an incrementalism that coincides with belonging to compartments of matter of virtually any and every sort. Hence, affect's always immanent capacity for extending further still: both into and out of the interstices of the inorganic and non-living, the intracellular divulgences of sinew, tissue, and gut economies, and the vaporous evanescences of the incorporeal (events, atmospheres, feeling-tones).[1]

Indeed, such incrementalism (degrees of gradualism) is so supple as to be infinite in scale; a gradient (the magnitude of a property) categorically without measure, a comportment that is immanently limitless, an "inventory of shimmers" as they put it, whose author and content are quite simply inestimable. Affect necessarily precedes the affective turn, just as its link to posthuman futurity accentuates its incredulity before the very idea of a human subject in the present. Whether we are conscious of affect or not, it will survive both our expiration and that of the species—as what, these notes will consider. The passage of intensities, which are neither feelings nor emotions, but force effects, are not the substance of the human, or rather only one substance of the human, since affect, like love, can generate language, something of the texture of "adequate" (Spinoza) knowledge. For those who argue affect is outside reason and agency, the affective scholar will reply, "not really," except of course if the human is deemed the locus solus (the unique or single place) of those attributes. Actually, you can number affects (Darwin, Tomkins, and Spinoza all do this—although the latter is scrupulous in not fixing a number) or you might maintain an adjectival amorphousness or nounal exuberance wholly consonant with its slippery, abstract nature. Needless to say, whenever a named emotion does not provide approximation, affect surely lurks (it is a superimposition, not a synonym, of emotion and feeling). Since the labor of affect in knowledge is divided disciplinarily, it is pointless trying to dismiss its legible variation (affect wars are keenly fought among academics, although few people are waiting on their decision). What for some is subject to science is for others not subject at all, or science, and represents instead a rigorously magic methodology. For me, the question concerns the power to affect or be affected by, where power is, whatever else it is, an aesthetic and political disposition. If this path leads to Spinoza, and particularly to his *Ethics*,[2] here it has a certain dialectical emphasis and a materialist one, perhaps even a contradictory rational ghost before a mystical or metaphysical shell—what Raymond Williams once had the temerity to call a "structure of feeling."[3] Perspicuously in-between—between passivity and activity, for instance, but also between body and body, body and non-body, and, most frustratingly, non-body and non-body (how the latter may be adjudicated is not altogether solved by the object lessons of New Materialism)—affect generally registers the troubled borders of mind and body where being becomes a fraught space relatively unencumbered by less febrile categories or determinations. Indeed, this is a fecund if not fantastic ground of imaginary engagement, a place of striving (*conatus* in Spinoza) that yet *makes* form or at least indicates its process; in this case, the posthuman affect called "cyborg."

The question of cyborgian affect is not new; indeed, at its broadest it is coterminous with an obstinately human pastime—the creation of facsimiles of and for ourselves (statues, dolls, puppets automatons, robots, etc.). Yet because the science and technology of replication is rapidly intensifying, the affective past of identification is catching up to a future in which the very terms of human constituency and socialization are at stake, especially if based upon the body as extensive. If the cyborg is a project of artful hybridization, at what moment does it reach the minimally human, the point of being affectively human, not effectively so? Sharalyn Orbaugh provocatively terms this "emotional infectivity," although she tends to recode this as body aesthetics rather than here, as the power of posthuman prosthetics versus cycles of power that pivot on the reproduction and extension of the human as subject.[4] This is not just a project at the heart of many artistic practices but a genuine concern regarding political change, where affect can still be read to influence consciousness and action. The topic is huge and, within cultural critique, is hardly reducible to Spinoza or Tomkins as such (as evidenced by this very volume). While the contribution here is modest, and perhaps balefully cultural and overly specific, I will also indicate some of the salient implications for further materialist analysis around this confluence. If we have nothing to lose but our chains, why burden the cyborg with them?

Ghost in the Shell is a thirty-plus-year-old manga/anime/live action franchise that spans several series in print (manga, ani-manga, and a novelization), feature films, OVA (original or direct-to-video animation), television episodes, video games, and a stage play. Stylistically and thematically it is a child of the emerging Internet (the manga first appeared in 1989[5]) and it explores network society through the kind of noir cyberpunk now associated with William Gibson (particularly *Neuromancer*, 1984). True, whatever the media, there are elements of its imaging and story that conform to rather more standard fantasies of male adolescent heterosexist masculinism (that tend to suture in their own way the "boy's clubbishness" of much cyberpunk). Shirow Masamune, the author/artist of the original *seinen* manga, has both encouraged the expansion of the franchise and intensified its aura of sexist objectification (more recently, his artistic proclivities have leaned toward fetishistic *hentai* in posterbooks and trading cards). The licensing of the franchise, however, allows for taking license with Shirow's desire even if the series as a whole appears to obstinately repeat some of his more obvious motifs and obsessions. Any attempt to distill only the positive elements of narrative and image in *Ghost in the Shell* (perhaps a stand-alone complex, to borrow from the franchise terminology) can misrepresent its active presencing and the material conflicts and contradictions of its affective appeal (including the future of sex/gender/race differentiation).

Not surprisingly, the links between desire and displacement are allegorized by the very conceit of the series: that cyborg embodiment proceeds by grasping the technological replication of the soul as mind or consciousness, the precious inchoate substance carried briefly by its fleshly counterpart, itself imaginatively overdetermined by our formal projections and unconscious prosthetics. Often read as basic Cartesian duality, the series, particularly in Oshii Mamoru's feature-length anime (the focus of the present discussion), seems more interested in techno-embodiment as sublation, in which the cyborg traces a path to the super-extension of Hegelian *Geist*, not a "*Geist* in the shell" but one that evolves from their networked fusion. This indeed is the vexed matrix of cyborg affect, or at least that affect figured by series, a mode of extension perhaps more properly Spinozist than Hegelian, yet dialectically bound to a "hominis" yet to be (as nonsubject) or as a human that is not one. Here I tend to read dialectic like affect as a space between, holding together Spinoza and Hegel like some fantastic Bellmer doll. But such elements still seem to form the projects' mystical shell rather than the ambivalent rationality of their central kernels. On the one hand, this essay symptomatically indicates how representational aesthetics come into conflict with the radically post-human and free association of *Ghost in the Shell* as an anime/manga subculture; on the other hand, I am particularly interested in the forms of time and subjective displacement articulated in the intersection of cyborg sequencing (including its implications for seriality as affect unbound). Cyborg affect does not just ask the familiar, where does a body end? It also interrogates the terms of technological reproducibility in what constitutes social and political activity. The synchrony of Major Motoko Kusanagi (the central character/cyborg/code) holds important lessons for how we read or see affect in series, the ghost of socialization itself in cycles of power. Obviously, this is a particular interpretation of affect which is neither diametrically opposed to emotion or feeling, nor is it all blissfully rhizomatic (at least for now: network extension still has a problem overcoming basic human finitude, a ground for aesthetics per se). Spectrality, ghosting as a real foundation, has been a feature of materialist critique for some time, but few theorists have explored this possibility within a science fiction aesthetic that begins with affect rather than read this as a consequence, as a special effect, as philosophical CGI. The logic of such subject serialization (where seriality de-subjectivizes) interrogates modes of transformation in socialization, here understood as the synchronic space between ghosts and shells, between reflex and the reflective, between anima and animation, and between impromptu pictures and conscious correlations of the human and machine.

Noir affect? Noir can be discussed as a basic problem of figuring the posthuman in late or globalized capitalism. On one level, this picks up on its generic components in cinematic history, the darkness visible of commodified and networked existence. Alternatively, however, noir is a heuristic that understands the problem of affect in the age of disambiguating bodies, the dispersed, fragmented and ephemeral pieces of identity forever being niched to permit narration as accumulation to continue. Whatever is intrinsic to affect, anticapitalism is not it—a critique of political economy is never only "intensity" since it seethes with hopeless veridicality— as Brian Massumi points out, affect is at best "proto-political."[6] Noir generally revels in the anxiety of ceding personal power to social manifestation, the long shadows of appropriate and appropriating existence. As primarily a "sad affect" in Spinoza's sense or something of a negative dialectic in mine, it reflects upon the power of deadening institutions (*potestas*) while insistently pressing some form of visual or narratological countermand (*potentia*). There is no space to detail this vital tension but let us say that potentia constitutes the real movement of history against its purely institutional forms. While Hardt and Negri end *Empire* on a note of revolutionary spirit and the "irrepressible lightness and joy of being communist," the antinomies of power do not easily produce such joy. Noir's sad affect is an admission of material and determinate constraints with specific implications for human futures.[7] The cyborg further complicates the staging of noir resistance because it sometimes almost literally embodies the techno-institutional power that precisely limits such a countermand. Paradoxically, it appears to disassemble both sides of the subjection/subject divide. This is not just a "parable of the virtual" in Massumi's important and influential articulation; it should also be considered its constitutive and by all means "special" effect/affect.[8]

The central premise of *Ghost in the Shell* follows a police procedural. In the world of its near future, the film focuses on a detective/police unit called Public Security Section 9 (the Japanese title for *Ghost in the Shell* is 攻殻機動隊 *Kōkaku Kidōtai*, "Mobile Armored Riot Police"). The crimes they are battling feature terrorism, government and corporate corruption, arms trading and various forms of hacking, both of government and military information, and of specific individuals (the "ghost-hacking" and "ghost-dubbing" of cyberbrains, or *dennō*). Major Motoko Kusanagi is a cyborg, in this case a mass-produced synthetic "full-body prosthesis" with an augmented cybernetic human brain. The cyborg is (almost) quintessentially aesthetic and is caught between the artifice and the artificial, both a fleshly fabricant and all of the veracity of the virtual. The cyborg does not exist (and is not a subject as such) or like affect is everywhere in being: it embodies the art of becoming as a quantum leap for science that is simultaneously a reconfiguration of being beyond human.[9] Of course, if we define ourselves through technological extensions (a techno-ontology) then we are all always already cyborgs, but it is more useful to think of the cyborg initially as a site of technical intensity, where the mind struggles to define itself in the fusion of body and being. Kusanagi herself is so well made she doubts which part of her is not made. The series, as a whole, pivots on the idea of an existential crisis which is not one, in the sense that to doubt one's being is to confirm its cognitive process. Yet again, however, this is less a Cartesian insistence than a potentially transformative one, an acknowledgment of a potentially technological autopoiesis.[10] Whereas the robot is shaped by its utility, the cyborg is manufactured according to semblance, a form in which utility itself may be less threatening, if always uncanny (mannequins, dolls, and puppets almost always signal this troubling similarity in the series, which has a specific history in Japanese culture, as critics like Christopher Bolton have persuasively argued, but it is also generalizable[11]). In live action films semblance is easily achieved by having a human play the hybrid, with varieties of deviance and deviation to signal alterity (milky blood, camera grid vision or, in Kusanagi's case, a socket built into her neck—I will discuss the live-action version of *Ghost in the Shell* shortly). Kusanagi is chosen for the unit because of her mass-produced look (which includes objectification), because of her physical abilities, and because she can tap the web and is neurally hard-wired to extend into its circuits or listen in to specific traffic (so-called "ghost whispers"). In both the original manga by Shirow and in the anime by Oshii it is Kusanagi's network presence that piques the interest of the major antagonist in the primary tale, the Puppet Master, an autonomous AI entity with a capacity to hack cyberbrains for political and social advantage (it began as a covert government espionage program, labeled Project 2501, within a Japanese intelligence unit also featured in the series, Section 6). Within the genre, this is evidence of a procedural paranoia with different units of the security system either investigating or subverting each other along the way. Obviously, cybercrime is not novel, and many countries have their versions of Section 6 or Section 9. The role of the cyborg, however, is deeply prescient as a conflicted mediatory function—that cybernetic crime is a staging of the problem of human subjecthood, a transgression of what is constitutive of cognition in knowledge circuits.

The other notable members of Kusanagi's team are Batou, Togusa, and Aramaki. Batou is the muscle of the group, and most of his strength comes from his prosthetic limbs (at moments in the series he exercises, which is a kind of phantomatic nostalgia for types of body maintenance rendered superfluous). Batou is recognizable by his highly unrealistic cybernetic eye implants (the reason is characterological, not technological). His cyborganic sensibility places him close to Kusanagi, although he appears less conflicted by synthetic self-reflection and is therefore a pertinent generic and genetic foil. But then Togusa further doubles this foil by being an alternatively unaccommodated man (he is described as "natural" or minimally cybernetically enhanced). In the first *Ghost in the Shell* anime Kusanagi argues it is important to have this variation in the team which is the key to advancement over enhancement (uniformity is a sign of system vulnerability). Both Shirow and Oshii play with Togusa's "normalcy" as he occupies a space of affective intimacy with the reader/viewer, who for now must be content to dream of androids dreaming of electric sheep. Aramaki is the Section 9 chief and, like Togusa, is predominantly human. He carries himself in a typically avuncular style and has his Smiley moments (to borrow from John Le Carré). There are other more peripheral members of Section 9 (like Ishikawa, the bearded tech wizard) and a series of revolving cybercriminals (the Laughing Man, the Individual Eleven, and Hideo Kuze) but it is the core of Section 9 that is most evocative of the cyborganic noir affect in play, particularly in the figure of Kusanagi. As a symptom of seriality's impossible demands, I will restrict my argument to a few critical examples from Oshii's *Ghost in the Shell* films while elaborating the theoretical tension between ghost and shell as the becoming cybernetic of affect, a process that invokes a series both contiguous with the franchise and necessarily beyond it. Noir affect itself points to the material ground of shifting socialization, something for which the cyborg is a restless if not revolutionary figuration.

Both of Oshii's anime films feature spectacular opening credit sequences that intersperse details of the film production with correlative details of the production of the cyborg. The cyborg is not a given but made. In the first anime, a preface is provided by Kusanagi diving from the top of a high rise wearing "thermo-optical" camouflage that renders her virtually invisible to the hit men and assassination target she is just about to dispatch.

Stripping down to this skin-tight suit is not exactly logical (is the head included, especially the hair, or the white leggings?) but it does enhance the objectification invoked earlier (Kusanagi must not only be able to pass for a woman, but she is rendered as desirable in particular kinds of ways). It also reveals the very body that is being constructed in the images accompanying the credit sequence. A brain is secured in a metallic head attached to a torso of complex computational innards and musculature. The "shell" is rendered as a "perfect" female form, but the eroticism generated is both centered and displaced. As the body is dipped in skin baths and then exfoliates, there is a signature undoing of Japaneseness that is yet putatively Japanese since the end of World War II (while the visual disavowal might be Oshii's, he cannot adjudicate its overdeterminations). This racial re-representation is multifaceted and contradictory and so, in its own way, is Kusanagi's body. What do full breasts signify to a replicant made without reproductive organs? As Kusanagi prepares to attack, her command center is speaking directly inside her head. They complain that there is static in her brain. She quips, "It must be that time of the month" (Shirow's manga places much more emphasis on this kind of banter and humor). In the vexed space between sex doll and technological idealism, the gendered cyborg wonders about a processing error in the male gaze. In the opening sequence a dastardly cyber dealer claims diplomatic immunity but finds his position of power consummately lacking immunity to Kusanagi's violence (he is blown apart). In the making of Kusanagi's body, the narrative is also broken up. The juxtaposition between gorgeous images of technology birthing perfection (the references to amniotic fluid are punctuated by the cyborg in a fetal position) and the credits themselves—names appearing in a flurry of typewriting against a backdrop of flowing green pseudo-code (to which *The Matrix* pays homage) offers a field of interrogative affecthood. Is a subject being animated and a human one being restored (sexed, raced, gendered), or does the cel-painted beauty of this opening question its insufficiency before the prospect of a future noir affect, one in which the passion of discovery remains inexorably bound to a desire for error, fallibility, or virus (fig. 1)?

In Oshii's *Ghost in the Shell 2: Innocence*, the opening sequence of the first anime is both mirrored and, as we know of mirrors, distorted. Batou is investigating the scene of a murder. A "gynoid" has gone berserk and murdered its owner and, when cornered, kills two police officers. When Batou confronts the killer, he is facing something akin to a Geisha doll, one that is impassive and still. As Batou approaches, the doll attacks him. He punches her against a wall and, as she tears off her skin, she whispers "help me"

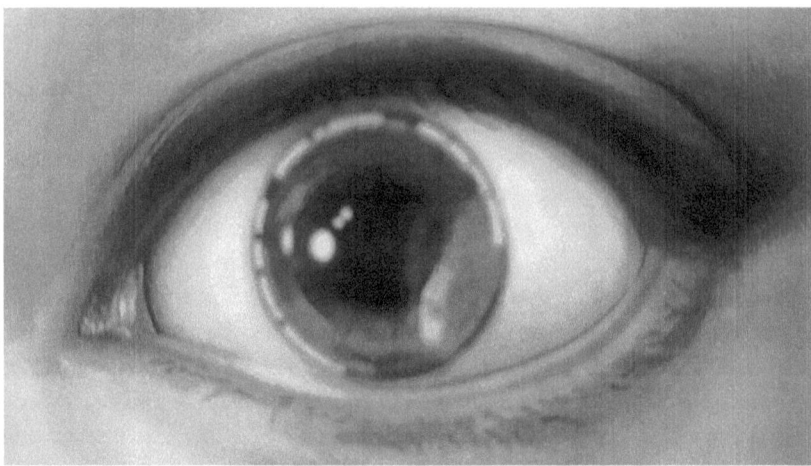

Figure 1. *Ghost in the Shell 2: Innocence.*

(*tasukete*). Her head then splits apart to reveal a skull-like metal casing and there is a massive explosion. The credit sequence then begins, this time with what appears as virtual procreation, an allusion quickly followed by rapid brain cell division (this is procreation as replication). Once again, the process forms a cyborgian head, but this is then fused with a beautifully articulated and detailed "spine." Unlike Kusanagi's making, the emphasis on the cyborg here is on its robotic form, and the pieces fit together very much like a doll (indeed, the reference is to Hans Bellmer's ball and joint dolls—a Bellmer book appears later in the narrative and representations of his dolls are omnipresent), although at an incredible level of detail (enhanced in this film by the availability of next-gen CGI). A four-legged gynoid (again a reference to Bellmer's surrealism) splits suddenly into two complete versions who then almost kiss in a borg embrace. The finished being, while still a gendered stereotype, is neither round-eyed nor conventionally shaped. The sequence ends with a close-up on the eye, precisely formed and with its production information etched around its edge, but also with a reference to Villiers de l'Isle-Adam and his novel, *L'Ève future*.[12] The gynoid model is a "Hadaly" which is also the name of the android at the center of Villiers's narrative—the opening epigraph to the film is also drawn from this book: "If our gods and hopes are nothing but scientific phenomena, is there any reason why our love should not also be equally so?"[13] In *Ghost in the Shell*, the opening sequence ends with Kusanagi waking up, her eyes checking out her hand as if to confirm it is indeed hers. In

Innocence, the eye contains a reflection of its being, replicated. In both films the eye asks: what exactly is being "seen"?

Kawai Kenji's songs, choral chants (traditional *min'yō*) with *taiko* drums and bells, enhance the credit sequences in their own way, as if music is the affective embrace par excellence (Jameson, for instance, notes a musical correlation between affect and the sliding scale[14]). In the first, the "I" of the song dances and a beautiful lady is enchanted. A god descends to give its blessing and a "chimera bird" will sing. The chanting seems to sanction the union advanced in the images while emphasizing that technology demands a new figuration/configuration of spirit. The chanting in the second film maintains this emphasis but is more dystopian about its productive capacity. The cyborgs, robots, and dolls still conjure uncanny intimacy (the *unheimlich* presence of semblance) yet the chant adds a measure of albeit mystical hesitancy: "The blossoms beseech the gods 'Even though in this world we may know grief and suffering, our dreams shall never die,' and they fall from the branch in anger." What are these *fleurs du mal* but a memory of natural imperfection? In both films Kawai's music presses the notion that the cyborg confounds the relation of body and spirit, as if the *techné* of modernity is not just secular but is in some way sublime. The problems are many. If, for instance, the social and the political are based on concepts that presume the human as subject, any change (technological, climate-based, philosophical) challenging such foundations must at a minimum pose what to do with all those billions of humans who remain maddeningly sutured to subjecthood and fleshly finitude. We have a pretty good idea of what bathwater to drain (states, nations, capitalist exploitation of workers and the environment), but the cyborg suggests the baby is in danger of being thrown out too. Noir is not a universal equivalent for this dilemma, but it is symptomatic of a concrete contradiction in the forms of socialization depicted.

In Oshii's interpretation of *Ghost in the Shell*, the philosophical, both the existential and posthumanist comportment of the cyborg, seems to trump any path from affect to transformation (agency in his anime, much to the delight of poststructuralists, is either joyfully immanent and immaterial or, more worryingly, self-destructive). For Shirow, by contrast, affect is much closer to effect, which is to say the cyborg is rarely more than a logical extension of the body-centered present (we create conditions of crime and the cyborg is a way of response—it is a basic *Robocop* rationality). This makes for more recognizable priorities ("let's get the bad guys") but also for a more deliberate flattening of affect. Shirow's manga are more kinetic in terms of storytelling, yet Oshii's stunning visuals contain perhaps more overly read referentiality (he admits to this Godardian tic) and are exciting in their own way. The visual in both is a means to trouble the representation of the human and sometimes the representational aesthetics that are its ward.

Both of Oshii's anime films confront a typical representational fix: if the cyborg becomes fully networked why have a body at all? At the end of the first film Kusanagi fuses with the Puppet Master and, while she is "placed" in a temporary body when her previous iteration is destroyed, she looks forward to the web in its "vast infinity." Living in the Internet is a cinematic challenge (*Tron*, anyone? Or the *Matrix* series, which simply switches between equally realist hallucinations?), so in *Innocence* the narrative focus is on Batou and Togusa with their all-too human anthropomorphic remains and the creature comforts of a noir detective investigation. Oshii, however, creates several imaginary resolutions to such real contradictions in the form. Crucially, both films feature Ozu-inspired "pillow" sequences, narrative interludes of intense reflection and contemplation (Oshii makes this signature his own in various interpretations across his oeuvre which have only faint echoes of Shirow's manga). In *Ghost in the Shell*, this foregrounds Kusanagi thinking through her "presence" as made with or against a backdrop of an intricately constructed urban environment. Typically, for Oshii, Kusanagi's journey by boat in the city in this sequence is packed with detail (while it does not conform to a specific location, Newport City melds key features of the East Asian megalopolis, including a compressed modernity where space is sometimes squeezed by the intimacy of the old and new). It also offers the urban as a preeminent space of tech or future noir where architecture, light, shadow, and the enormity of scale articulate an impressionistic tableau of confounding "progress" in images of dissolution and decay. As she traverses the cityscape, Kusanagi's sense of self is mirrored by what she sees: half-built structures, networks of roads and canals, bodies in motion and also still (especially the window mannequins), circuits that blink on and off, waste, and reflective surfaces, everywhere reflections. How much of what is made and made up can be made alike? Kusanagi sees a version of herself in a café, which is perhaps the same cyborg model. The entire sequence is accompanied by a reprise of Kawai's choral extravaganza, underlining not the externality of image and sound, but their utter affective integration. And yet, of course, Kusanagi's face is largely expressionless in Oshii's interpretation, evincing a flat affect that permeates the film as a whole (again, a stark contrast to Shirow's representational palette and humanizing through comedy). This does not mean the cyborg is prototypically postmodern in the Jameson sense, a being commodified into torpor and wan with consumption, but it does suggest a posthuman ecumene, a place inhabited but uninhabitable, whose line of flight leads from the reproducible to networked profusion, a bodiless circuit where emotive expression falls away.[15]

The falling away of the body (as in the jump of the first scene, and the metaphor of the last where Kusanagi tears herself apart in ripping open a tank) is accompanied by a questioning of experience represented by memory. The affective processes of the production of memory are complex and, as Kusanagi notes, for each person, unique. Oshii's worldview is in part informed by the idea the human capacity of memory is being rendered obsolete. Memory, from this perspective, is "being" separated from "subjectivity" and it is stored in vast data banks to be accessed according to informational need rather than identitarian desire. While there is plenty of dispute about the seriality of memory and its putative "random" access (William James's "memory is only memory of memory" can be digitally remastered), the point is its subjective process need not be defining. This is why the Puppet Master claims to be a new entity, a new species, an "autonomous life form"—affected and affecting in its selving, its autopoiesis. As a "sentient" AI, the Puppet Master attaches itself to memory's function for identity without being synonymous or defined by it. In the calculations of the minimally human, the artificiality of affective power is more than a threat of uncanny semblance because it seems to forego defining semblance at all. Could it be that the cyborg is such artifice at the level of representation, representation that otherwise fails to constitute its affective *coupure*?

On this question the affective interlude in *Innocence* is both still more visually rich yet categorically opaque. Backed again by Kawai Kenji's glorious "Song of the Puppets," Oshii offers us a parade of affective doppelgängers and provides spiritual manifestations of references in the rest of the film to Buddhist, Confucian, and Christian texts. This sequence presents a number of puppets and dolls (both manipulated and mechanical, or *karakuri*) that are themselves iterations of subjectivity; indeed, we might usefully think of the cyborg-self as citational. The scene is a festival loosely based on a Taiwanese tribute to Mazu, the Taoist goddess of the sea: in the film this is set against the city as a kind of transnational tableau, again future noir or what Oshii has called "Chinese gothic." As facsimiles of the human and animal multiply the animation pushes against its resources of representation. It is almost as if the sequence as a whole allegorizes what might animate, what might affectively engage the viewer of this event. That most figures are masked is a metacommentary on the significance of "shells" to self-definition. One worries, of course, as both Bolton and Brown have pointed out, that however much detail Oshii builds into such scenes, a certain techno-orientalism lingers, the cyborg as another in a long list of Asian essences bolstered and packaged by anime and manga as they meet occidental desire.[16] Yet the interest seems to be in a transmutation of these very relations, that question of the persistence of the human as an affective medium. Batou and Togusa are in a re-represented Etoforu, not for the festival but to find a hacker named Kim, whose background is in military cyber warfare and arms dealing. The sequence ends with a ceremonial mask burning, but the dolls and automatons continue to haunt.

There are at least four interrelated aspects where we may begin to unpack the affective import of the ghosts and shells in Oshii's interruption and extension of the *Ghost in the Shell* franchise. These are more than themes but less, of course, than a typology of affect and feature spirit, technology, figuration, and sublation. The sequences I have discussed so far appear to elicit a description of an Oshii stylistic, elements of technique and representation that can be discerned in other film projects, like the anime *Patlabor* (1989) and especially *Patlabor 2* (1993) or the live action feature *Avalon* (2001). Yet the invocation of cyborg affect offers another dimension of serial connection, particularly effulgent in the forms of temporality that tie and untie the narratives.

For instance, time and again in Oshii's *Ghost in the Shell* films the cyborg's voice is not present with its anthropomorphic counterpart. Kusanagi can speak through her shell, the body she occupies, while her presence as such is networked, dispersed, and digitally enhanced. The voiceover is a staple of film noir, but here it accentuates both foreboding and the displacement of being. If her face is often affectless with lips that do not move, Kusanagi's voice is yet alive with interpretation and investigative zeal. This, combined with contemplative pauses and thermo-optic camouflage, relays rather than situates subjectivity. If the time of the cyborg is one of becoming, it is also, at least nominally, time's dissimulation (time's instantiation is questioned by ambivalent identification: "Am I the cyborg here and now or is that only verifiable by another temporal scale or material moment of presence that renders the adjudication of the 'I' itself questionable?"). The time of the cyborg is always and everywhere an existential threat (the meaning of lifespan in, for instance, *Blade Runner*, is particularly explosive). This creates several representational dilemmas for which spirit seems to be a symptomatic "resolution." For Oshii, cyborg affect animates Kusanagi's discomfort. Her mass-produced shell is supposed to enable her to blend in—the opening sequence is about the manufacture of uniform "likeness"—yet in her veritable walkabout described earlier Kusanagi is unequivocally restless. The possibility of serial extension (both literally in other modes of the franchise and symbolically in body-swaps and network connections) marks home as an abstraction for spirit. This makes for both cyborg monstrosity and for a curious manifestation of technological godlessness.

In the 1980s, Donna Haraway famously read this quandary as the possibility of socialist-feminist embodiment, a politics based on the demonstrable fallibility of capitalist patriarchy (the cyborg could exceed the goddess).[17] Given that seriality here can also produce Shirow's sex fetishism, the *potentia* at stake is always already contradictory. Kusanagi does not easily slip her deleterious objecthood, not just because of predominantly male heteronormative fantasies but because the brain in her making permits the difference of indiscernible identity (to borrow from Leibniz[18]). In principle, the spirit/ghost should permit escape velocity from the imperfections of the flesh, but this is precisely what limits the cyborg as represented. The variation Kusanagi believes to be essential of evolution thwarts the perfectibility intimated in replication. Indeed, we might say the cyborg is the sign of system failure, or indiscernible replication. Oshii grapples with this anthropomorphic antinomy in *Innocence* by using it as a structural component of story, of exigency. The gynoids, perfect replicas for sexual objectification, have been animated yet contaminated. Locus Solus, a tech corporate giant, had worked with a yakuza gang to abduct adolescent girls for ghost dubbing—in effect, the technology engineers affect sufficient only to provide sexual compliance. The cyborg animates the Hadaly sex doll. A conscientious shipping inspector, Jack Volkerson ("son of the people"), disrupts this chain of happy exploitation by sabotaging the ethics code written for the gynoids, an alteration which not only allows them to kill their owners (and thus contravene Asimov's robot rules) but prompts the very investigation that will lead to Locus Solus and the liberation of the abducted girls (it is the voice of one of these girls that earlier pleas to Batou, "Help me"). If the capitalist corporation seeks cyborgian enhancement as a kind of normative automation it appears limned to a patriarchal reduction to the body (again typified in Shirow's manga but with serial permutations). Interestingly, the reduction to the body is where Jameson locates the globalization of generalized sensations or affect as such. I agree with Pansy Duncan that Jameson's recent *Antinomies of Realism* is a recapitulation rather than a simple rejection of the "waning of affect" argument famously pinned to postmodernism as a cultural logic.[19] Yet I would add that Jameson tends to bracket affect when it comes to the historicity of science fiction in the *Antinomies* tome, which I would read as both a temporal and political displacement regarding realism and its "others."

Between *Ghost in the Shell* and *Ghost in the Shell 2: Innocence*, several versions or models of the cyborg are posited. Replication as figuration is initially framed by economies of semblance and utility. As noted, when Kusanagi is pieced together it is to pass as human rather than to replicate humanness (a quality that can be projected onto dolls, puppets, and "companions" of various kinds). The challenge of figuring cyborg affect is that it need not be bodily present and yet, if its ghost is copresent with nature as a whole, it remains subject to its basic laws. It is only a god in the machine to the extent that fabrication and fabricants are not contrary to existence in nature. Interestingly, this point is underlined by a character named Haraway (!) in *Innocence*, who herself is cyborganically enhanced (and a chain smoker). Robots require a human form only when that part of their performativity necessitates semblance. Cyborgs, however, seem to need more identity markers (like smoking), as if the organic acts as a cognitive circuit breaker, reassuring not just their human counterparts but reconciling themselves to themselves. At this level, affect provides some ontological sutures, elements of subject redundancy. In point of fact, seriality permits much variation on this register, as narrative tests cyborgian extension. Figuration is the failsafe of affective attachment. Thus, although Oshii believes the motions of mind have long promised the obsolescence of its mortal coil, the cyborg frustratingly permits the articulation of the body to reappear. Cyborg affect is ridiculously recursive when it comes to the human figure, in part because the cyborg, like beauty, is in the eye of the beholder (and sometimes literally so—while no doubt a cliché, and an anglophone one, the confluence of "I" and "eye" is a central motif of cyborg aesthetics). But if this were true or inexorably affective, then surely the whole discourse of cyborg sublation is reduced to reform or refined moments of technological enhancement, a capitalist "revolution" as the economic extension of exploitation?

On the one hand, this would seem to reaffirm Walter Benjamin's thoughts on technological reproducibility.[20] What is waning is less affect than an aura that pivots on a specific arrangement of the sensorium. Here we might say the serial mediates the possibility of sensate change. I do not mean to suggest that such mediation is the only way the cyborg can appear but that its affective challenge is more strongly symptomatic when networked across interlinked forms. Oshii himself locates the problem in an idiosyncratic spiritual configuration, a "glass darkly" that the cyborg, especially Kusanagi, wants to see beyond. His interest in Bellmer's dolls, however, throws light on the other side of Benjamin's thoughts on the reproducible, or what Brown usefully discusses as the technological uncanny.[21] Bellmer's dolls are both the promise of prosthetics and a question for reproducibility vis-à-vis reproduction. Their ball and joint configurations might seem to provide comfort as false analogs for the human, but Oshii reads this as precisely an arena of noir affectivity, where semblance is refigured as consummate autonomy. More than this, such intimations of transformation come with their own ethic, a striving as persistence. This emerges in *Innocence* as a moral conflict. If voices are not identical with their speakers and speakers quote words that are not their own, bodies are yet held as responsible conditions of existence, with a codicil of cyborgian rights. As Haraway examines the gynoid Batou has destroyed, she chides him that his violence has crimped the possibility of reconstruction. She also raises the issue of gynoid suicide: does sentience enough for self-destruction confirm or contradict Batou's zeal for termination? In the same scene, as Togusa feels secure in the reproductive sanctity of the nuclear family, Haraway points out that a child tending to a doll is not imitating child rearing but expressing its core meaning. "Children are not dolls!" he retorts. In the final scene, of course, Oshii has Togusa give his daughter a doll and, as he holds her with her new toy, the doll stares across at Batou, a cyborg, as he clutches his cloned Bassett hound. If the opening sequences are about the making of the cyborg, the final one is about what the cyborg unmakes, undoes, with its very propositional anima and animation.

Perhaps because he has listened to Haraway (as Oshii has read her, the theorist that is), Batou reflects further on the right to be alive. When he frees the young girl at the Locus Solus factory, Batou reminds her that this freedom has been bought at the expense of the dolls, who had no voice or choice in the matter. The girl exclaims, "but I never wanted to be a robot!" Kusanagi, who has reappeared in the shell of such a robot, notes, laconically: "If a robot had his own voice he may cry, 'I never wanted to be a human being.'" Like so much of the ventriloquism in the film, speaking for and speaking as are conjoined.

The cyborgs in *Ghost in the Shell* evince affect in a human way: their unease is created by minimal affectivity, and yet this is the dialectic in which their very possibility becomes transformative. How? Oshii and his fellow animators appear to have little problem in representing humans and/as cyborgs in their interactions. We might call this the realist clause of cyborg figuration, but this is not quite what Spinoza meant when he noted, "No one has yet determined what the body can do."[22] The cyborg clings to this realist determination, yet Oshii, much more than Shirow, tries to disable, corrupt, or hack such synergy. Here Benjamin rather than Bellmer is more apposite, since it is the cyborg's very reproducibility, a *ratio* in replication, that is the ground of its political possibility. As I have noted, Kusanagi voices the humanist claim that variation is at the heart of evolution and perfectibility. Yet, when it comes to cyborg subjectivity this assertion, while not false, does not capture the deconstructive affectivity in cyborg presence. In other words, although the *Ghost in the Shell* series often settles on the comforting essence of the ghost with its aura of the sacrosanct and unique, the dispersed and virtual nonequivalence of replication suggests an alternative and by all means rebellious articulation of ghosts and shells. If cyborg sentience does not begin in its relationship to a body, except in its replication and replaceability, its affect is unhinged from the normative perquisites of Spinozist adequate cause. This is not a technical calculation or technological determinism but its dialectical challenge. Similarly, in Oshii's *Ghost in the Shell* films the problem of experience emerges again and again because the memories adduced from it can be constructed, synthesized, and implanted. Spinoza notes "that we can do nothing from a decision of the mind unless we recollect it"[23]; yet what happens to decision, political or otherwise, if that recollection is cybernetically fabricated? When the Puppet Master hacks a cyberbrain the host is thoroughly convinced of their selfhood and acts accordingly. Obviously, misremembering is a human attribute, but here memory is treated like any other data set: it can be wiped clean, replaced, or corrupted beyond the power of individual fallibility (as the title of one of Philip K. Dick's stories puts it, "We can remember it for you wholesale"). This is neither brainwashing nor ideological seduction; it is a function of new circuits of epistemological production and commodification. Perhaps the representational aesthetics of Oshii's anime permit the anchoring of the cyborg in what is seen to be the minimally human of the species. Whenever Kusanagi, the Puppet Master, or Kim, attempt to distance these conditions they are immediately marked as suspect, deviant, or disruptive. True, this often wheels back to some form of corporate malfeasance (who knew?), but the noir impulse exists more in the capacity to act differently and outside the human as a regulative idea. Spinoza locates affect in the necessary relations of God, nature, and the human. The cyborg is both an extension of such relations—permitting, as it were, the series to appear—and a challenge to their constellation. The noir anxiety provoked by the cyborg is more than the "unhappy valley" of its semblance: it is the point where all that is disembodied from the glories of making the cyborg body becomes a space of posthuman phantasmagoria. To say that *Ghost in the Shell* performs the generic attributes of a noir detective serial is true, but along the way, in its formal profusion and aesthetic predicaments, it seems to detect something other than the solution to the significant crimes of human interaction. Can there be a rebel without a human affect and yet somehow "embody" affect after all? In the absence of this veritable cause the cyborg persists as the symptom of the rebel to come and an affect empowered by the materiality of network existence itself.

But what of the present? How does a subculture within anime and manga, and one quite clearly mediated through constellations of adolescent male heterosexism and techno-orientalism, inform a contemporary understanding of social antagonism? Does *Ghost in the Shell* depart from or simply underline the sense that affect is primarily about what is happening rather than a political catalyst in what is to be done? The live action *Ghost in the Shell* (2017) directed by Rupert Sanders and starring Scarlett Johansson as the Major finds all this talk of bodiless praxis and artificial affect much too much of a "vaporous evanescence of the incorporeal" to make an actual feature film, so it dispenses with most of the flightier articulations of cyborg affect as well as the pointed politics of tech noir. Major is not a replicant based on a standard model but an "original" whose brain has been harvested from the remains of an abducted rebel fighting for the resistance to technology (this is a Luddism shot in ultra-high definition). To battle the challenge of externalized memory, on at least two occasions (human) identity is defined by actions so the film constructs its narrative around Major's quest to act human, a pursuit that culminates not in the fusion with a cybernetic network entity (Kuse) but with a reunification with Motoko's birth mother, Hairi, played by Kaori Momoi. In Hollywood, at least, reproduction always trumps replication. The film found it very hard to break out of its entanglement in the series and so, while often visually impressive, the narrative is hobbled by awkward backstory and yet more random access to the franchise. In *Innocence*, Oshii was able to focus on his major themes by foregoing most of what would constitute plot (he was interested in the ghost of noir, not its shell). Sanders's vision is hemmed in by basic Hollywood prerogatives, including those that constitute a star vehicle (here the actor playing the cyborg has, according to the credits, a personal assistant, a cook, and a trainer). Indeed, this gives rise to the biggest complaint about the film, that Johansson's inclusion is a racist whitewashing of Asian culture all too evident in other examples of Hollywood production (*The Last Samurai, Dr. Strange, The Great Wall*, etc.—although the history and the list on this point is as old as Hollywood—interestingly, Wes Anderson's stop motion movie, *Isle of Dogs*, solves the problem of representing a Japan of the near future by having Johansson, and most of the Western leads—including Tilda Swinton of "Ancient One" fame—play dogs). Because the representation of Japan and "Japaneseness" in manga and anime since World War II has never been less than controversial and reflexive, the 2017 film's insensitivity is striking. Whatever is ambiguous in the racial representation of the cyborg in the *Ghost in the Shell* series, this does not sanction whiteness as a default mode (even if this is complicated by the birth mother being Japanese). When Oshii comments

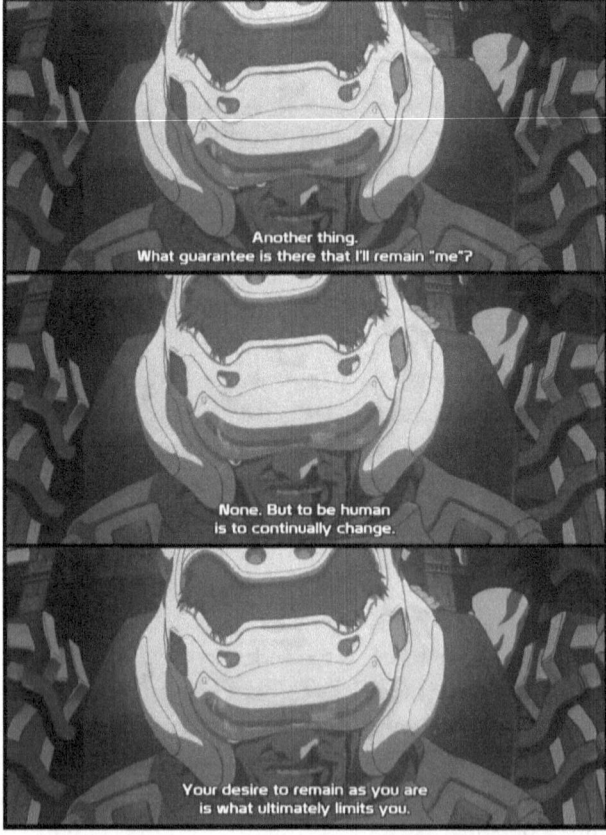

Figure 2. Ultimate limits from *Ghost in the Shell* (1995).

that he had no problem with Johansson being cast as the Major he is acknowledging both that neither her name nor her body in the series are hers (she is a fabrication not an authentication) and, importantly, what Hollywood does, not what it could do. Thus, it is true to its central premise and this detracts from all that might be more provocative from the perspective of cyborg futures, like the one that is posthuman.

In the end, of course, what is most noir about affect in the franchise is neither the threat to identity nor its indulgence in humanist nostalgia (or more accurately, nostalgia for the human) but the idea that a human utopia lacks intensity because there is less and less time beyond doxa, beyond processing the everyday, performing the human as given. The cyborg cannot be a freedom from such necessity because its affect is no shield from the material conditions of its possibility. For Marx, automation and the factory as automaton constitute a ground for socialism, one that would free the worker from the time of exploitation.[24] In *Ghost in the Shell*, the automaton is both the factory and its manufactured being, but one could also argue its cyborgian limit is the state itself and its protean autopoiesis. Significantly, in *Ghost in the Shell* technological enhancement can also mean human emancipation and emancipation from the human. A circuit of power may be broken, that of the state and of the corporation, but only by ceding the political subject to the power of circuits. To rebel without an affect is preposterous if by affect we locate power in the capacity to affect or be affected by a plenitude of interactions. Yet *Ghost in the Shell*, and especially Oshii's anime contribution, posits a zero degree of affect in the cyborg in which the minimally human is not simply that which must remain, the ghost as the veritable soul of the human, but that which may be the last of the human, the last of its adequate cause. Could it be that to rebel, to become a new entity (fig. 2), *this* is the affect to be without?

NOTES

1. Melissa Greg and Gregory J. Seigworth, eds., *The Affect Theory Reader* (Durham, NC: Duke University Press, 2010), 2.

2. Benedict Spinoza, "The Ethics," in *A Spinoza Reader: The Ethics and Other Works*, ed. and trans. Edwin Curley (Princeton, NJ: Princeton University Press), 85–265.

3. Raymond Williams, *Marxism and Literature* (Oxford: Oxford University Press, 1977), 128–135.

4. Sharalyn Orbaugh, "Emotional Infectivity: Cyborg Affect and the Limits of the Human," *Mechademia*, vol. 3 (Minneapolis: University of Minnesota Press, 2008), 150–172.

5. Masamune Shirow, *Ghost in the Shell*, 2nd ed., trans. Frederik L. Schodt and Toren Smith (Milwaukie, OR: Dark Horse Comics, 2004); and Sirow Masamune, *Kōkaku kidōtai* (Tokyo: Kōdansha, 1991).

6. Brian Massumi, *The Politics of Affect* (Cambridge: Polity Press, 2015), ix. Given the title of the book, the interviews within attempt to elaborate how the proto-political exists as a field of the political.

7. See Michael Hardt and Antonio Negri, *Empire* (Cambridge, MA: Harvard University Press, 2000).

8. Brian Massumi, *Parables of the Virtual* (Durham, NC: Duke University Press, 2002).

9. This is not the place to summarize the cyborg in theory and practice, but its political and cultural efficacy depends very much on the assembly line, the way it is conceptually "made." While Donna Haraway's groundbreaking essay, "The Cyborg Manifesto" reinvents the cyborg for materialist and feminist critique the cyborg itself is far from being all that Haraway is about in terms of gender and nature, or humans and companion species. That said, *The Cyborg Handbook* (which reprints and reedits the essay) is still a good entry into matters cyborgian even if, as here, the culture and theory of cyborgs has gone in several different directions since then. See Chris Hables Gray, ed., *The Cyborg Handbook* (New York: Routledge, 1995).

10. I am thinking here of the path to self-making from making. See, for instance, Humberto R. Maturana and Francisco J. Varela, *Autopoiesis and Cognition: The Realization of the Living* (Dordrecht: Reidel, 1980).

11. Christopher Bolton, "From Wooden Cyborgs to Celluloid Souls: Mechanical Bodies in Anime and Japanese Puppet Theater," *positions* 10, no. 3 (Winter 2002): 729–771.

12. Auguste Villiers de l'Isle-Adam, *L'Eve future* (1886), translated by Robert Martin Adams as *Tomorrow's Eve* (Champaign: University of Illinois Press, 2001).

13. "Puisque nos dieux et nos espoirs ne sont plus que scientifiques, pourquoi nos amours ne le deviendraient-ils pas également?"

14. Fredric Jameson, *The Antinomies of Realism* (New York: Verso, 2013).

15. The fate of affect is the missing dimension of N. Katherine Hayles's otherwise trenchant and prescient *How We Became Posthuman* (Chicago: University of Chicago Press, 1999).

16. See Bolton, "From Wooden Cyborgs," and Steven T. Brown, *Tokyo Cyberpunk: Posthumanism in Japanese Visual Culture* (London: Palgrave, 2010). Brown provides a detailed exegesis of *Innocence* in his book, as well as close readings of other classics of Japanese posthumanism, such as *Akira* and *Tetsuo: The Iron Man*. See also Ueno Toshiya, "Japanimation and Techno-Orientalism," in *The Uncanny: Experiments in Cyborg Culture*, ed. Bruce

Grenville (Vancouver: Arsenal Pulp Press, 2001), 223–231; and his "The Shock Projected onto the Other: Notes on Japanimation and Techno-Orientalism" in the same volume (234–235).

17. See Haraway, *Cyborg Handbook*. The original essay appeared the *Socialist Review*, no. 80 (1985): 65–108.

18. See G. W. Leibniz, *Discourse on Metaphysics and Other Essays*, trans. Daniel Garber and Roger Arlew (New York: Hackett, 1991).

19. See Pansy Duncan, "Once More, with Fredric Jameson," *Cultural Critique* 97 (Fall 2017): 1–23.

20. Walter Benjamin, *The Work of Art in the Age of Technological Reproducibility and Other Essays*, ed. Michael W. Jennings et al. and trans. Edmund Jephcott et al. (Cambridge, MA: Harvard University Press, 2008).

21. See Brown, *Tokyo Cyberpunk*, especially part 1. See also Hans Bellmer, *The Doll*, trans. Malcolm Green (London: Atlas Press, 2005).

22. Spinoza, "Ethics," 155.

23. Spinoza, 157.

24. Karl Marx, *Capital*, vol. 1, trans. Ben Fowkes (London: Penguin, 1992), chap. 15.

CHAPTER 8

Playing with Negativity: *Max Payne*, Neoliberal Collapse, and the Noir Video Game

Brian Rejack

Negative affect is by no means foreign to gaming culture, where miserable antiheroes tend to be the norm, and where discourse—especially in online multiplayer gaming and on gaming-related forums—frequently devolves into the bathetic registers of expression we've come to associate with the dreaded "comments section." But perhaps nowhere has the sensibility of noir and the pervasive aura of bad feeling been combined quite so effectively as in the Max Payne series. In the first game, *Max Payne* (2001), the eponymous character is a morally ambiguous pill-popping maniac, pursuing several personal vendettas at once, always willing to approach a problem by "playing it Bogart" (the term Payne uses early in the game to describe how he strolls confidently into tense situations, after which blazing guns rapidly ensue).[1] Both the first and second (*Max Payne 2: The Fall of Max Payne; A Film Noir Love Story* [2003]) foreground their affinities with noir tropes, as in the subtitle to the second game, which oddly attaches "*film* noir" to the medium of video games.[2] And although the third game, *Max Payne 3* (2012), sheds the visual palette and geopolitical frames of the first two games' traditional noir stylings, it nonetheless maintains the series' investment in negative affect.[3] The final game's shift to the Global

South as its main locus of action is a fitting conclusion to the series' overall narrative of coping with the legacy of neoliberal collapse, even if it ends up being more complicit with than critical of contemporary global capitalism.

This essay takes up a family of noir affects—the anxiety, mourning, and anger associated with the decline of the public sector and the paired rise of globalization and neoliberalism—and examines how they operate in a form relatively understudied by scholars of affect and of noir: the noir video game. While the Max Payne series is the focus of analysis here, there is no shortage of other examples of the form. The last decade or so has witnessed a flourishing of noir video games, including perhaps the most straightforward replication of the film genre with *L.A. Noire* (2011), as well as more distant takes on the genre like *The Wolf Among Us* (2013), based on *Fables*, Bill Willingham's comic book series reimagining classic fairy tales, and the Bioshock series of games (2007–2014), which combines noir elements with steampunk and speculative fiction. But noir video games have been around since at least the early days of games moving into the home through personal computers and gaming consoles, with the traditional detective noir *Déjà Vu*, focused on an amnesiac private eye in 1940s Chicago, published for Macintosh platforms in 1985. Several other early entries emerged through the noirish influence of cyberpunk: among these are the adaptation of William Gibson's *Neuromancer* (1988), *Shadowrun*, based on a tabletop role-playing game (1993), the PC adaptation of *Blade Runner* (1997), and original titles such as *System Shock* (1994, with a sequel in 1999) and *Deux Ex* (2000, with a sequel in 2003, and three prequels published between 2011 and 2016). Other celebrated examples, representing a range of generic varieties of noir, include *Grim Fandango* (1998), *Discworld Noir* (1999), *Killer7* (2005), *Hotel Dusk: Room 215* (2007), and *Heavy Rain* (2010). Although it is beyond the scope of this essay to produce a full taxonomy of the noir video game, my reading of the Max Payne series as an emblematic instance of the genre suggests some ways that others might take up the question of how noir affects play out in the realm of video games.

What follows, then, begins with a narrative analysis of the Max Payne series as it develops across all three games, while situating its noir elements with respect to accounts of neoliberalism. The second half of the essay shifts to how the video game medium engages with negative affect. In game studies, there has been a fairly limited amount of work focused on affect, and even less on specifically negative affect. Yet gaming itself, despite its purported emphasis on play and the joy associated with it, is rife with what Sianne Ngai calls "ugly feelings," or those "negative affects that read the predicaments posed by a general state of obstructed agency with respect to other human actors or to the social as such."[4] The embodied act of playing video games offers another predicament: obstructed agency with respect to the game. All too often in games, the "transmission of affect" occurs through the negative registers of feeling.[5] The primary activity of most video games is, after all, shooting guns or wielding other weapons at a horde of virtual enemies. But there exist also the player's affective responses to the game's limitations, its challenges, its glitches, and its very interface. All of these elements can lead to ugly feelings directed at the game, or, if one's temper fails, at the physical equipment delivering the experience. This essay, then, first looks at the manner in which the Max Payne series presents a narrative about the predicaments its characters face, predicaments as much about broader social collapse as about individual tragedy. And then it turns to the medium and its affordances to argue for a critical potential in the affective investments we place in the activity of play.

"Playing it Bogart": The Knowing Noirishness of the Max Payne Series

It's not hard to see the extent to which the Max Payne series signals its connections with noir. The titular character's first words of the first game, "They were all dead," establish the mood (simultaneously supported by the shadowy and snowy nighttime scenes of the New York City skyline), while also gesturing to the narrative structure of many classic and revisionist noirs by referring to the events that will be revealed as one plays the game. One thinks, for instance, of Fred MacMurray's Walter Neff sitting down at his desk to begin dictating the story of how he came to be sitting there with a bullet in his shoulder and, as we'll learn later, a few corpses in his wake ("I suppose you'll call this a confession when you hear it," he begins).[6] Likewise, *Memento* begins at the end, with the difference being that the protagonist through whom the narrative is focalized does not know it, and nor do viewers, unless they pick up on the clue of the first scene being shown in reverse. After Max declares in the opening cutscene that "They were all dead," the narrative shifts to one of its other modes: the comics-style panels (with voice-over actors reading the text of the panels) which are interspersed throughout the first two games. Another hallmark of the noir style—the penchant for witty banter and other stylistic elements to the point of always risking self parody—comes through right off the bat in the first panel: Max "Payne" intones, "To make any kind of sense of it I need to go back three years—back to the night the pain started." It's not a terribly inventive pun, and it calls to mind a much less noir version of the same pun from approximately the same time period in American culture: Homer Simpson's foray into pseudonymity by adopting the name "Max Power," which he "got off a hair dryer." "Max Payne" is perhaps a bit less silly a name than "Guy Noir"—the parodic private eye of *Prairie Home Companion* fame—but not by much.

The game thus wavers between its sincere deployment of noir tropes and its often laughably ironic stance toward those tropes. Many character names involve over-the-top puns, or just literal character descriptions, while also gesturing toward stock noir elements: Mona Sax is the alluring femme fatale; Jim Bravura is the righteous but misguided police chief pursuing our rogue hero; the Finito Brothers and Rico Muerte are two of the many mob members tasked with taking out Max (who succeeds in eliminating them instead). Where the game reaches its most ironic treatment of noir comes from a fiction within the fiction: the 1990s cult-classic television show, *Address Unknown*. The show exists only in the game world, but it clearly nods to *Twin Peaks* with its fusing of an enigmatic mystery and soap opera conventions. It appears just once in the first game, but becomes a more regular presence in *Max Payne 2*, where players can encounter different episodes playing on televisions throughout the game. *Address Unknown* is set, not very subtly, in "Noir York City," and it follows a character named "John" who believes he's been framed for the murder of his girlfriend by a serial killer named "John Mirra." It's revealed—when John is in "the John" and he looks in the *mirror*—that he is in fact John *Mirra*. The protagonist-as-unwitting-culprit trope jibes well with Max's increasing self-doubt and eroding sanity in *Max Payne 2*. And as with other elements across the series, and particularly in the first two games, the winks and nods to the noir tradition both establish its generic connections to that tradition while also playfully pushing back against them.

One way to understand the significance of this critique of the noir tradition is by attending to how the series situates noir affect in the context of contemporary neoliberal collapse. Noir loves company, but it still reinforces the logic of individualism and libertarianism upon which neoliberalism is built.[7] Everyone suffers and everyone pays in the realm of noir—there is no way out—but the causes and effects of such suffering tend to be understood as individual failings, not collective ones. In the Max Payne series, we certainly see a strain of the alignment between noir individualism and free market ideology, given that the game's protagonist operates outside the purview of social and governmental institutions. At the same time, however, the narrative suggests that he does so in reaction to the collapse of those very structures. The narrative begins with the dissolution of the "American Dream" (the title of part I of the first game) via the plunder achieved by corporate capitalism at the expense of the public. Indeed, the precipitating event for the plot of all three games is what happened on "the night the pain started": namely, the murder of Max's wife Michelle and their child. This tragedy is not solely about Max's loss, however. His wife was murdered because she was an employee of the New York City district attorney's office, and in her work, she uncovered a massive cover-up at a multinational pharmaceutical company (Aesir Corporation). The CEO of that company, Nicole Horne, had Michelle Payne murdered in order to conceal that Aesir was illegally manufacturing an experimental drug and overseeing its distribution and sale on the streets. Thus, the private sector protects its interest against any public interference.[8] The public sector is even more fully, if temporarily, eradicated in the game by a historic three-day blizzard, the (un)natural disaster metonymically standing in for the broader collapse of the institutions meant to support the public good.

While the first two games remain narratively rooted in the American context of New York City, their distanced, ironic stance toward noir can also be understood in part as a matter of international perspective. Remedy Entertainment is the Finnish company which began working on *Max Payne* in the mid-1990s, soon after the company's founding in 1995. In interviews and in writing about the development process, the game designers and writers acknowledge that their understanding of New York as a setting for the game came largely from their knowledge of popular culture. In May 1999 some members of the development team visited New York, a visit about which they wrote and published on the website of 3D Realms, another game company which helped to produce *Max Payne*. They associate New York with noir immediately as they begin the essay: "Max Payne is set in New York City. It was the perfect, logical setting for a film-noir crime thriller. The only problem was: what do we Finns really know about New York?" The cheeky tone continues throughout the piece ("We were ready to go, ready to rumble, armed to the teeth with the latest in camera hi-tech. Destination: New York City. Mission: Capture it all on film, show no mercy"). Like Max himself, the "six brave level designer soldiers" set out to *shoot* anything that came their way. But whereas Max is a New York native, the Finnish developers recognize their gazes as those of outsiders: "Sure, we had watched all the right movies over and over and over . . . but we were still missing that first hand experience."[9]

Ultimately what their account suggests is the extent to which the game design is predicated on a distanced perspective on American society and its intimate connection with the aesthetic, the affective, and the ideological dimensions of noir. As James Naremore writes in *More than Night*, film noir was from its beginnings a French construction of an American mode.[10] A similar cross-cultural exchange plays out in the Max Payne series with a Scandinavian perspective regarding the failings of American neoliberalism. Coming from a nation with a much more robust social welfare system than that of the United States, it should come as no surprise that the Finnish developers would write about their research trip to New York as if they were anthropologists encountering a drastically different culture than their own, with their previous knowledge of that foreign culture coming to them only through skewed cultural representations.[11] Remedy Entertainment in fact uses its location in Finland as part of its recruiting strategy when seeking new employees (presumably ones from North America, given that the industry presence and labor force remain centered in the United States, even as international markets increase in size). For a variety of positions advertised in late 2017 and early 2018, the "What is in it for you?" section of Remedy's website notes that "quality of life is exceptional and cost of living is affordable" in Finland.[12] Moreover, the job ads specifically point to the fact that "in Finland you get up to 5 weeks of paid vacation every year," which easily eclipses the two-week vacation typically accompanying employment in the United States, and which goes against tendencies for an industry notorious for its poor labor practices.[13] Particularly with respect to the first game in the series and its framing of noir tropes as aspects of broader social collapse, we ought to view the game's potential for critique as rooted in the different national contexts from which it emerges and with which it engages.

The third game in the series marks a pronounced shift away from the traditional noir aesthetic, but it retains the noir affect as it operates around the figure of Max Payne himself (he remains brooding, self-destructive, and willing to exact extremes of violence against those who threaten him). Whereas the first two games situate noir affect in the context of contemporary neoliberal collapse (institutions fail, so the individual must operate apart from them), in *Max Payne 3* we see both the broader global effects of neoliberalism and the futility of individual solutions to them. There is no longer any sense that Max can even work alongside the interests of public institutions (as he does with the DEA and the NYPD in the first two games). The third game finds him retired from the NYPD, and after he impulsively kills the son of a mafia boss, he decides to take a job working as a private security contractor in Brazil so that he can flee the threat of retribution from the mafia and continue funding his drug and alcohol addictions. Despite hoping to remain disconnected (and drunk and high), he becomes embroiled in Brazil's sociopolitical conflicts and acts as the de facto white savior of a 'savage' culture in need of civilization. That narrative trajectory, then, maps onto the notion that the neoliberal regime has wreaked havoc upon the United States itself, while also extending its negative influence across the globe, putting antiheroes like Payne in the unenviable position of feeling compelled to solve problems abroad for which they never had viable solutions at home.[14] This feeling of global helplessness begins as a localized phenomenon for Payne, whose initial struggle involves trying to solve one crime (the murder of his wife and child) in one place (New York City), only to find that his suffering is rooted in corporate depredations on the public sector. When he finds himself unable to persist in the United States any longer, he encounters much the same thing: a wealthy family, the Blancos—who operate in real estate, politics, and human trafficking—seek individual gain at the expense of social institutions, and they intend to frame the outsider, Max, for their crimes in the process. The original personal trauma of the first two games fades in the face of these global concerns to the extent that the memory of his murdered wife becomes an afterthought in *Max Payne 3* (in a cutscene Payne remarks of his deceased wife, "We'd only been married a short time. By now she had been dead longer than I knew her"). The series thus charts the movement from purely individual trauma to a recognition of the broader social costs levied by global corporate capitalism and its erasure of public institutions.

While most of the game takes place in Brazil, flashbacks to his time in New York and New Jersey provide a bit of the classic noir color palette with nighttime scenes at a dive bar, a cemetery, and Max's putrid apartment littered with booze and pill bottles. The subtle political critique accompanying the classic noir of the earlier games, however, is largely absent. The third installment presents a fairly standard and largely un-self-critical white savior narrative. As is often the case of such narratives, Max ends up killing many, many people of color (especially ones living in poverty) while attempting to save a select few others (who are obscenely wealthy), most of whom he ends up failing to save anyway. The game also revels in racialized and classed depictions of sexuality: Max's foray into the favelas of Sao Paolo finds him employing his gumshoe talents by, curiously, following a young boy who is clearly tasked with leading white tourists to sites of sex work (and trafficking). It works out conveniently for Max—who immediately stumbles onto the trail he was seeking—and for the game developers—who get to titillate their imagined (teen and male) audience with plenty of close-ups on gyrating black and brown women's bodies. In short, *Max Payne 3* presents the worst of global capitalism (eroded or completely absent public institutions, massive inequality, racist exploitation of women for the benefit of wealthy white men) without much of a hint of critique. The game concludes with Max walking into the sunset, not exactly a noir staple. As he does so, a news story plays on a television screen showing that the corrupt government official who all along had been trying to frame Max has been found hanged in his jail cell, presumably murdered by the forces of corruption that will persist in this poor country comprised of people of color while the white savior hangs out at the beach.

Playing It Noir: Mods, Cheats, and Other Forms of Bad Play

If the series originates from a critical framing of noir affect as a response to the conditions of neoliberal capitalism and its devastation of public institutions, only to largely lose that criticality in the third game, we can trace a parallel move in the way that gameplay shifts from the first to last game. Studies focused on the relation between gameplay and affect are surprisingly uncommon, except in the realm of social science research.[15] That said, some game studies scholars have attempted to characterize the relationship between affect and play from the perspectives of cultural and affect theory. In Greg Singh's reading of Max Payne as neo-noir, he focuses on how the games' noir qualities prefigure particular modes of affective response. In his reading, however, he only briefly discusses the specifics of gameplay, arguing that the constraints of the largely linear single-player narrative correspond with "perhaps the most 'noirish' of affective responses—the sense of 'no way out.'"[16] In other areas of game studies, Christopher Moore has explored how game achievements and in-game character customization in *Team Fortress 2* revolve around considerations of affect. He argues that the activities of gamers should be seen as "always resistant, contestant, and nagging through play." For Moore gamers are akin to "digital dandies, flâneurs, flâneuse, and important figures in the malls of digital distribution, arcades of virtual environments, and the crowds of multiple social networks." While I would read many of the activities of gamers as more complicit in than resistant to the logic of capitalist success than were Benjamin's flâneurs, I nonetheless share Moore's sense that we ought to view gameplay as an arena where players have at least the opportunity to employ, in Michel de Certeau's terms, "tactical" forms of engagement against the top-down "strategies" encoded in the games themselves.[17]

Aubrey Anable's *Playing with Feelings: Video Games and Affect* is the first monograph devoted to a broader conception of the relationship between gaming and affect. She treats video games as "affective systems," an approach which allows for an expansive notion of both what constitutes games and what constitutes affects. Her interest lies as much in the feeling of frustration of playing *Candy Crush* while waiting for the subway as in more "serious" affective responses to "serious" games (crying at the emotional complexity of an indie game's lead character) which are used to justify gaming's cultural and artistic legitimacy. Her analysis of how these affective systems operate functions to critique the formalist approaches of "proceduralism," which tend to ignore issues of representation over and above understanding how the computational systems operate. The result of her approach is that she can "read across code, images, and bodies without reducing video games to either their representational qualities or their digital and mechanical properties."[18] My approach to understanding the Max Payne games similarly embraces such a nonreductionist approach, as well as her contention that in taking up games in this way, we can understand games as "more than just ideological training grounds for capitalism."[19] They also become mediums of resistance through their complex affective capacities.

What, then, can the Max Payne series teach us about gameplay and its relation to noir affect? To answer this question, I turn to a few examples of gamers playing in potentially resistant ways. Even though all three games provide limited freedom with respect to spatial exploration and alternative approaches to narrative progression, I differ from Singh's conclusion that those limitations create the affective response of "the sense of 'no way out.'" Quite the contrary, playing by adopting the game's strategies is precisely the *only* way out. By playing the "right" way, one progresses, one succeeds and receives awards in the form of achievements or trophies (depending on the platform), and ultimately one reaches a satisfying—even happy!—narrative conclusion. As mentioned above, *Max Payne 3* ends with a decidedly un-noir stroll into the sunset, and the straightforwardly tragic conclusion to *Max Payne 2* (with the death of love interest and femme fatale, Mona Sax) becomes a happy one (with Mona surviving) if the player completes the game on the hardest difficulty setting. In other words, if you're skilled enough at the game, then you get the happy ending. Playing the game well is at odds with the production of noir affect in the player. If you want to embody Max's affect, you have to play badly.

To invoke de Certeau's terminology again, playing "badly" means playing "tactically." It means drawing on the affordances of the gameplay environment in order to create a form of play that aligns with bad feeling. Jesper Juul writes about the significance of failure for an understanding of gaming, and particularly the *feeling* of failure we experience in the course of playing games. His analysis often returns to a logic of success, however, with failure as the thing from which we can learn, and the feeling of inadequacy caused by failure as an affective goad for us to self-improve.[20] What if instead we analyze failure as a good in itself, without the necessity of valuing it through its instrumentality? Juul's "art of failure" ends up being less art than technique. What it requires is the queering of failure that Jack Halberstam offers in *The Queer Art of Failure*. Halberstam offers a more radical notion of failure which does not treat it as something to overcome or improve upon: "To live is to fail, to bungle, to disappoint, and ultimately to die; rather than searching for ways around death and disappointment, the queer art of failure involves the acceptance of the finite, the embrace of the absurd, the silly, and the hopelessly goofy."[21] Such an impulse informing a culture of play just might be the best way to produce a noir affect that resists the logic of capitalist competition and success that so thoroughly permeates the world of mainstream gaming.

There are three kinds of practices I'll discuss with respect to the Max Payne series and what Alan F. Meades and other game studies scholars call "counterplay."[22] In *Games of Empire: Global Capitalism and Video Games*, Nick Dyer-Witheford and Greig de Peuter argue that the gaming industry operates on the logic of imperialism, always expanding, appropriating, and accumulating by dispossessing (as when, for instance, local practices and phenomena such as modding become coopted and monetized by corporate power). One strategy for resistance which they suggest is "counterplay" or "dissonant play"—when players deliberately resist the logics of the games they play.[23] Meades expands the definition of counterplay to include not just subversive modes of play within the diegetic space of games but also forms of disruptive activity outside of those spaces. While I agree with Meades that such forms of disruption deserve study, my focus here remains largely on play within the diegesis of the games.

In a manner analogous to the narrative shift away from critique and toward complicity which I identify above in the progression from the first two Max Payne games to the third, I suggest that the first two games also offer more potential for a critical gameplay experience. Partly this shift overlaps with general shifts in gaming culture from the early 2000s to the early 2010s, with console gaming displacing the primacy of PC gaming, and with greater controls placed upon software and hardware ownership and usage rights (through things like digital rights management mechanisms). In addition to those broader shifts into which this particular series fits, however, there are other variations specific to the games themselves that emphasize further the restrictiveness of play. In the early 2000s when the first two games were released, the culture of modding (short for "modifying") games was essentially allowed and supported by game development companies. The developers and publishers who created and owned the content enjoyed a symbiotic relationship with communities of modders. As long as developers made available software source code for modding, then the modders could work freely and help build the brand of the games they modded. (The classic example of this relationship from this period is *Counter-Strike*, a mod of *Half-Life*, which was purchased from its creators by Valve, the developer of the original game.[24]) In recent years some game companies have cracked down on modding, including Rockstar Games, the developer of *Max Payne 3*. In the summer of 2017 Rockstar created a brief crisis in the modding community when they took legal action against the developers of OpenIV, a popular modding tool for *Grand Theft Auto V*, but also for modding *Max Payne 3* (both Rockstar products).[25] After outcry that the corporate Goliath's lawyers had taken out the small open-source David, Rockstar relented and agreed to let modding of its titles continue (while its statement about modding, that the company "generally will not take legal action," still maintains a vague threat of potential legal action).[26]

Although there are mods of *Max Payne 3* despite Rockstar's less-than-accommodating approach to modding, there are far more mods of the first two games.[27] Modding, with any game, is not inherently subversive, critical, or transgressive. Some forms of modding are fully legal, and many (if not most) mods do not subvert the game's narrative, aesthetics, or gameplay. Rather, the vast majority of mods are meant to enhance the gaming experience in minor ways. Some popular mods for *Max Payne 2*, for instance, simply adjust or add to visual textures, weapons, or in-game effects (such as the appearance of ricocheting bullets). Indeed, in many ways modding functions as a sort of job training for those who desire work in video game development.[28] Although modding often fits into the logic of capitalist success, it also holds potential for practices of play and interaction that resist that ideological stance. One way that mods do so is through a playful and ironic approach. Such is the tactic of the "Max Payne 2 on Crack" mod, which adopts a seemingly random assortment of pop cultural references in the form of altered character models, level design changes, and narrative alterations. For instance, one encounters characters from the original game replaced by figures such as the Xenomorph of *Alien* fame, Deadpool from the Marvel comic, a T-799 cyborg from the Terminator series, Edward Elric from the *Fullmetal Alchemist* manga, and, for reasons that elude me (or, elude me to a greater extent than the other examples), the wrestler-turned-actor John Cena (who enters, of course, to his wrestling theme music). Such mods revel in a postmodern spirit of playful bricolage, but that is not to say that they necessarily subvert the logic of the source material in politically productive ways. With the "Max Payne on Crack" mod, the Mona Sax character sports the face of Max Payne, which might be understood to playfully nod toward the game's own obsession with the doppelganger motif (Mona is a twin whose sister dies in the first game; Max is mirrored by the "John Mirra" character discussed earlier). However, the writing over of Mona's face with Max's also traffics in homophobic attempts at humor that are endemic to the world of gaming culture.[29]

Speedrunning is another form of transgressive play where we might search for negative affect. And, indeed, there is something intensely masochistic about the cycles of repetition and disciplined practice required to perfect one's knowledge of the game and the necessary exploits to progress through the game as quickly as possible. However, that discipline ultimately serves the broader logic of success that Christopher A. Paul terms the "toxic meritocracy" of video game culture and design. For Paul, meritocratic values are widespread in games, and he argues that this "dependence on meritocratic norms . . . [has] the terrible impact of magnifying and excusing any structural inequalities among those playing video games."[30] Speedrunning exists primarily as a mode of competition, with speedrunners sharing their feats via YouTube and elsewhere (often with the goal of monetizing their play by logging enough views). Institutional bodies of a sort, like speedrun.com and speeddemosarchive.com, have begun to emerge in order to regulate and track records of different games and different kinds of speedruns. In short, these forms of play are certainly tactical and work against the grain of the systems in which they operate, as in the example of the "Dead Man Walking" glitch, which allows players at particular moments in the game to "trick" the enemies in the game into viewing Max as if he were a dead character (and thus they do not shoot at him, allowing the player to proceed through those parts of the game more quickly). Nonetheless, speedrunning as a form of play ends up reinscribing the same kinds of affirmative affect and corrosive ideologies endemic to the source material they seek to alter. The ideological assumptions about the universality of meritocracy underlying these forms of play serve to justify and empower some of the worst aspects of gaming culture (i.e., its misogyny, its toxic masculinity, its insistence on the positive affect of neoliberal selfhood).

My final example of counterplay is not a category but a specific instance of counterplay with the Max Payne series: JODI's *Max Payne Cheats Only* (2004).[31] JODI is the experimental collaboration between Joan Heemskerk and Dirk Paesmans, whose work transforms various instances of computational technologies (including video games, web-based interfaces, and mobile apps) into a kind of phantasmagoric reimagining of what we often view as all too natural objects. Much of their reputation is rooted in their web-based projects, but they have also created a variety of gaming-related pieces, including *Untitled Game* (2001), which alters the source code of *Quake* (1996) to radically shift the game from a horrifically violent and visually lush first-person shooter into a black-and-white, minimalist exploration of space and abstract lines and shapes. *MPCO* is a less radical alteration of the source material, and it is also not technically a mod, given that it does not rely on altering the software. It merely takes advantage of existing cheat codes present in the game code in order to create a dizzying representation of play that embraces negativity, futility, failure, and a resolute rejection of progress or progression. What emerges is a noir feeling rooted in a form of play, in a narrative and visual presentation of the noir genre, but ultimately capturing the underlying ideological strain of noir that the game and its narrative cannot fully produce through a straightforward approach to the playing of it.

Works by JODI always defy description to some extent—perhaps the best way to describe *MPCO* is that it visually represents what the game might look like if it were made primarily of glitches. The piece is organized around thematic "scenes" of a sort, such as the ninety-second clip of different character models (generic cops and criminals, along with some of the game's main characters) repeatedly running up a spiral staircase only to get stuck on the wall as it turns to the left, at which point the scene cuts to another character attempting the same with similar results. The cheat component is that the button to switch weapons has been reconfigured to switch from one character model to the next. As with many of the scenes in *MPCO*, the sonic component of the piece is part of its appeal. The repetition of the sound of the weapon-switch effect has a regular rhythm, and the sound of the characters' footfalls as they obsessively run into the wall becomes somewhat hypnotic. The soundtrack of another clip rises to the level of a legit techno track. It features Max's character repeatedly and rapidly engaging in the "melee" attack (essentially a pistol-whip). The sound effect of Max's clothing whooshing as he swings his arms combines with repeated percussive sounds as he hits different environmental materials with his handgun. The scene takes advantage of a cheat which allows the user to move the third-person camera around Max's body, such that we see him upside-down, rightside-up, from above and from below, and almost always directly in the character's face, such that we see through the polygonal shapes that make up the 3-D human figure. The quick movements also produce a blurring effect; when viewed from extremely close to Max's face, for instance, the character becomes a chaotic melding of ears and eyes wildly flailing about the screen. Never do we see Max heroically battling bad guys as he pursues the truth with his hard-boiled intensity. Instead when Max appears, he's stuck in a corner swinging his gun at walls and garbage cans. And yet, what emerges is an aesthetic of pleasure at odds with Max's usual bad feelings. If one is inclined toward music with repetitive, cacophonous sounds, one might find this particular scene toe-tapping.

Other scenes clearly engage in ideological and representational critiques of gaming. The series' femme fatale, Mona Sax, who appears in some sections of *Max Payne 2* as a playable character, appears in multiple scenes in *MPCO* sans clothing. In a cutscene in the game itself, Max encounters Mona at her apartment while she is showering, which leads to a steamy scene of sexual tension between the two as she unabashedly asks Max for a towel while approaching him in the buff. Because a naked Mona appears in the game, of course developers would make available a cheat which allows users to play as a naked Mona. JODI's take on this fact manifests in a critique of the prurient desire (often expressed with a juvenile tone) that animates so much of the toxic masculinity endemic to gaming. One scene features the nude Mona in a restroom performing backflips. It renders Mona's objectified body rather ridiculous as the close-up of her body produces the same effects seen in Max's techno number (i.e., one sees through the exterior of the body to the floor or wall behind it when the camera gets too close). It also turns out that Mona is in the men's bathroom, a fact which becomes clear when a male voice emerges from the toilet behind a closed door against which Mona keeps bumping as she does her backflips. In the regular playing of the game, this effect—knocking on the stall door—results in a cop repeatedly saying things like, "For crying out loud! Is it too much to ask for some privacy? I'll be out when it's done." Mona thus subverts the typical dynamics of male predatory behavior. And as the scene continues, she then jumps straight up next to the stall door such that the camera captures a shot of the male police officer sitting on the toilet. While such subversion of sexual power dynamics may not come across as exactly revolutionary—and some scenes featuring Mona's nude character are less obviously critical—the resistance to accepting the terms of playing the game on its own terms nonetheless carries with it a potential for affective transformation.

The web version of *MPCO* features a sequence of still images (not included in the installation video) which emphasize the logic of playing tactically while refusing any notion of playing for success. The images, organized in a sequence that can be followed by clicking on each image, show instructions written in bullet holes in walls and floors. On the surface, the final sequence functions as a sort of manual for users to use cheats within *Max Payne 2*. They mirror the "easter eggs" that developers themselves often place within the code of games, but in this case, after having watched a series of videos in which the cheat codes enable a play experience that embraces failure, it only makes sense to treat other players to the secrets of the game if they too intend to "cheat" tactically rather than strategically. Cheat codes, obviously, are supposed to make it easier for the player to succeed at playing a game. With *MPCO*, though, the game is not *played*, so much as *played with*. It becomes a software playground in which one can jump meaninglessly and create sonic atmospheres for the sheer aesthetic pleasure of so doing. *MPCO* is not failure toward success. Instead it represents a playing with the material that makes up noir affect. The affect can still be experienced, but in this altered form of play, it disrupts the cultural logics that would enable a specific circumscribed form of response to it. *MPCO* thus takes the bad feelings of the noir video game and dives deeper into them. It's not clear if the way out is through, but counterplay of this sort at least represents the possibility of something other than the "no way out" structure in which the games' narratives are rooted.

NOTES

1. *Max Payne* (Remedy Entertainment, 2001), PC. The version consulted for this essay is the PlayStation 4 emulation of the 2001 PlayStation 2 port, released in 2016.

2. *May Payne 2: The Fall of Max Payne; A Film Noir Love Story* (Rockstar Games, 2003), PC. The version consulted for this essay is the PlayStation 2 port (also 2003).

3. *Max Payne 3* (Rockstar Games, 2012), Xbox 360.

4. Sianne Ngai, *Ugly Feelings* (Cambridge, MA: Harvard University Press, 2005), 3.

5. While the concept in Teresa Brennan's work applies to how "emotions or affects of one person . . . can enter into another," her broader suggestion that with respect to affect "there is no secure distinction between the 'individual' and 'environment'" opens up the framework to other applications. In the realm of gaming, one can experience the transmission of affect as it relates to other actual people (say, a fellow gamer in the room or connected virtually to the play experience), to fictional people, and indeed to inanimate objects like the gaming system (to whom players might ascribe the affect of indifference when it refuses to accede to our demands). Teresa Brennan, *The Transmission of Affect* (Ithaca, NY: Cornell University Press, 2004), 3, 6.

6. Greg Singh makes the same comparison, noting *Double Indemnity* (and several other noirs) which employ a flashback structure of some sort. See Singh, "From Lonely Streets to Lonely Rooms: Prefiguration, Affective Responses and the *Max Payne* Single-Player," in *Neo-Noir*, ed. Mark Bould, Kathrina Glitre, and Greg Tuck (London: Wallflower Press, 2009).

7. Individualism is also central to the ideology of liberalism. One shift in that ideology under neoliberalism results from what Wendy Brown calls the "'economization' of political life and of other heretofore noneconomic spheres and activities," to the extent that "we are only and everywhere *homo oeconomicus*." The neoliberal subject, "as human capital, . . . is at once in charge of itself, responsible for itself, yet an instrumentalizable and potentially dispensable element of the whole." Brown's central argument about the effects of neoliberal ideology is that the "replacement of citizenship defined as concern with the public good by citizenship reduced to the citizen as *homo oeconomicus* . . . eliminates the very idea of a people, a demos asserting its collective political sovereignty." Wendy Brown, *Undoing the Demos: Neoliberalism's Stealth Revolution* (New York: Zone Books, 2015), 17, 10, 38, 39.

8. I follow David Harvey's account of neoliberalism, which characterizes it as a shift away from the "form of political-economic organization . . . referred to as 'embedded liberalism'" of the post–World War II era, which "signal[s] how market processes and entrepreneurial and corporate activities were surrounded by a web of social and political constraints and a regulatory environment that sometimes restrained but in other instances led the way in economic and industrial strategy." Neoliberalism, by contrast, "proposes that human well-being can best be advanced by liberating individual entrepreneurial freedoms and skills within an institutional framework characterized by strong private property rights, free markets, and free trade." The state and its public institutions thus serve only to "create and preserve an institutional framework appropriate to such practices." In implementation across a wide variety of contexts, the result has been that "Deregulation, privatization, and withdrawal of the state from many areas of social provision have been all too

common." David Harvey, *A Brief History of Neoliberalism* (Oxford: Oxford University Press, 2005), 11, 2, 3.

9. "Remedy Developers Visit New York!" 3D Realms, May 28, 1999, accessed August 8, 2018, http://legacy.3drealms.com/max/newyork.html.

10. James Naremore, *More Than Night: Film Noir in Its Contexts* (Berkeley: University of California Press, 1998), 11–27.

11. David Harvey also points out that neoliberalism is an international phenomenon, even if it has roots in Anglo-American politics and culture. By 2005 he writes that "Almost all states . . . have embraced, sometimes voluntarily and in other instances in response to coercive pressures, some version of neoliberal theory and adjusted at least some policies and practices accordingly." The situation in Finland in the 1990s was similar to that of Sweden, with shifts away from a traditionally strong welfare state through what Harvey describes as "'circumscribed neoliberalization.'" The Remedy designers thus visit the United States at precisely the time their own country was moving more toward the American model of neoliberal rule, which suggests a greater investment in understanding what might result from such a regime. See Harvey, *Brief History of Neoliberalism*, 3, 115.

12. See, for instance, "Gameplay Programmer," Remedy Games Careers, accessed August 8, 2018, https://remedygames-careers.jelpp.com/gameplay-programmer-5982cc76f3748d3071b58071/.

13. Ian Williams, "'You Can Sleep Here All Night': Video Games and Labor," Jacobin Magazine, November 8, 2013, accessed August 8, 2018, https://www.jacobinmag.com/2013/11/video-game-industry/. Williams suggests that the labor problems in the gaming industry are ones that we should expect to see in greater regularity in the future in other industries: precarity, lack of unionization opportunities, widening inequality in wages, crunch and burnout cycles, and so on. For a detailed account of trends in video game industry work, see Casey O'Donnell, *Developer's Dilemma: The Secret World of Videogame Creators* (Cambridge, MA: MIT Press, 2014), 135–166.

14. Like many developing countries, neoliberal structural adjustments were imposed on Brazil by the IMF in the 1980s. The kind of extreme inequality that one witnesses in *Max Payne 3* can be connected to neoliberalism, given that, as David Harvey argues, "The main substantive achievement of neoliberalization . . . has been to redistribute, rather than to generate, wealth and income" (*Brief History of Neoliberalism*, 159).

15. The moral panic over video games since they came into existence has been supported by various attempts to prove their deleterious effects through empirical research, but the consensus in recent years has taken shape around the notion that early panicked reactions tended to be overblown. For an overview of both the history of that panic and what social

science currently says about the issue, see Patrick M. Markey and Christopher J. Ferguson, *Moral Combat: Why the War on Violent Video Games Is Wrong* (Dallas: BenBella Books, 2017).

16. Singh, "From Lonely Streets to Lonely Rooms," 94.

17. I draw from Michel de Certeau's distinction between "strategies," which refer to the cultural apparatuses provided by those with power regarding how to operate in daily life (think of a corporate training exercise about workplace productivity), while "tactics" refer to the small modes of resistance which operators in the culture employ to resist such forces (think of a worker who checks Twitter during the corporate training exercise). See Michel de Certeau, *The Practice of Everyday Life*, trans. Steven F. Rendall (Berkeley: University of California Press, 1984).

18. Aubrey Anable, *Playing with Feelings: Video Games and Affect* (Minneapolis: University of Minnesota Press, 2018), xvi.

19. Anable, xiii.

20. Jesper Juul, *The Art of Failure: An Essay on the Pain of Video Games* (Cambridge, MA: MIT Press, 2013).

21. Jack Halberstam, *The Queer Art of Failure* (Durham, NC: Duke University Press, 2011), 187.

22. Alan F. Meades, *Understanding Counterplay in Video Games* (New York: Routledge, 2015).

23. Nick Dyer-Witheford and Greig de Peuter, *Games of Empire: Global Capitalism and Video Games* (Minneapolis: University of Minnesota Press, 2009), 194. The authors recognize that "dissonant development" is needed as well, and they also insist that they "don't exaggerate the subversion of dissident play or lower the bar on what counts as political engagement." Nonetheless, they maintain that "Just as in cinema, music, and literature ideologies are challenged, new subjectivities coalesce, and flashes of autonomy appear, so too sometimes with games" (194).

24. For a brief overview of the history of videogame modding, see Erik Champion, "Introduction: Mod Mod Glorious Mod," in *Game Mods: Design, Theory and Criticism*, ed. Erik Champion (Pittsburgh, PA: ETC Press, 2013), 9–26.

25. Many gaming blogs reported on the events as they unfolded over the course of a few weeks. For an overview, see Samuel Horti, "GTA publishers are leaving OpenIV alone after all," *Rock Paper Shotgun*, June 24, 2017, accessed January 29, 2018, https://www.rockpapershotgun.com/2017/06/24/gta-publishers-are-leaving-openiv-alone-after-all/.

26. "PC Single-Player Mods—Rockstar Support," Rockstar Games, August 7, 2017, accessed January 29, 2018, https://support.rockstargames.com/hc/en-us/articles/115009494848/.

27. Of course, there has been more time for modders to work with the first two games than with the third. And although these metrics are imperfect and merely suggestive, the popular website *Mod DB* (a database of mods for a variety of games across platforms) ranks *Max Payne* (112) and *Max Payne 2* (93) higher than *Max Payne 3* (219), with the rankings based on user game ratings and on the number of user visits to sites for each game and their mods. See Mod DB, accessed June 25, 2019, https://www.moddb.com/.

28. Gabe Newell, the president of Valve (a development company long supportive of modding), has advised those looking to enter the industry that they develop their skills by experimenting with modding. He also questioned the predictive value of "traditional credentialing" (like advanced degrees) when considering potential hires. See Andrea Peterson, "Gabe Newell on What Makes Valve Tick," *Washington Post* (blog), January 3, 2014, accessed January 29, 2018, https://www.washingtonpost.com/news/the-switch/wp/2014/01/03/gabe-newell-on-what-makes-valve-tick/.

29. No shortage of commentary in recent years has focused on the entanglement of gaming culture with misogyny, homophobia, racism, and other forms of hateful thinking and discourse. Particularly in the aftermath of GamerGate, which targeted game designers and critics such as Zoe Quinn, Anita Sarkeesian, and Brianna Wu with a campaign of online harassment in response to their efforts to merely speak against the toxic aspects of gaming culture. For a discussion of Sarkeesian's work in the web series *Tropes vs. Women in Video Games*, a series devoted to examining representations of women in games that led to Sarkeesian being harassed online even before she was targeted by GamerGate harassers, see Adrienne Shaw, introduction to *Gaming at the Edge: Sexuality and Gender at the Margins of Gamer Culture* (Minneapolis: University of Minnesota Press, 2014). Also see Anable, who, in her introduction to *Playing with Feelings*, situates some of the limitations within game studies with respect to the broader problems (around misogyny and racism) within gaming culture.

30. Christopher A. Paul, *The Toxic Meritocracy of Video Games: Why Gaming Culture is the Worst* (Minneapolis: University of Minnesota Press, 2018), 28.

31. *Max Payne Cheats Only* (hereafter cited as *MPCO*) appeared as an exhibition at Electronic Arts Intermix (EAI) in March 2005, but the publication date from EAI is listed as 2004. The exhibition format features a twenty-three-minute video. "Max Payne Cheats Only 1," Electronic Arts Intermix, accessed June 25, 2019, http://www.eai.org/titles/max-payne-cheats-only-1/. A version of the piece can also be accessed at http://maxpaynecheatsonly.jodi.org, although not in the form of the whole video. Users can click eight different links which lead to some of the materials that comprise the installation video.

CHAPTER 9

Chick Noir: Surveilling Femininity and the Affects of Loss in *Gone Girl*

Pamela Thoma

Faithful to the opening scene of Gillian Flynn's novel, David Fincher's *Gone Girl* (2014) begins with a filtered image of beautiful Amy Elliott Dunne (Rosamund Pike), lustrous blonde hair lovingly stroked by a hand, which the voiceover clarifies is that of husband Nick Dunne, played by Ben Affleck. Nick's narration, accompanied by a smoky musical score, quickly undercuts the romantic moment when he refers to his wife's head as a "skull," one that he would like to crack open to learn what Amy is thinking and feeling. Amy is classically enigmatic, an unsolvable riddle for Nick and immediately a mystery for the audience. We are also put on notice about their marriage when Nick asks what he characterizes as "the primal questions of every marriage: 'What have we done to each other? What will we do?'"

This inaugural scene makes use of noir iconography, including the dream-like close-up of a feminine face, which is immediately followed by shots of The Bar owned by Nick and his twin sister Margo, or Go, the down-and-out walking the shadowy dawn streets in North Carthage, Missouri, and Nick and Amy's mostly foreclosed, deserted suburb. The opening of *Gone Girl* also leans on the tropes and narrative conventions of detective fiction, setting up puzzles to be solved, promising mind-bending suspense. With its generic base in crime fiction and preoccupied with the corruptions of modern life, noir customarily shares the epistemological, ontological, and metaphysical concerns of detection reaching back to Poe, even if its origins are most closely associated with the American hardboiled novels of the 1930s.

As this volume attests, however, contemporary noir has more than one genealogy and wields widespread influence that lends itself to vibrant hybridity and robust adaptation. Of particular relevance here are noir's connections to the affectively complex narrative tradition in women's writing about marriage, family, and the home. Or, as Paula Rabinowitz explains the startling emergence of chick noir in the early twenty-first century and its swift uptake by readers: "the Gothic house is hardly new."[1] Specifically, we can draw a line from the psychological suspense based in the domestic sphere by authors such as Charlotte Brontë, Patricia Highsmith, Daphne du Maurier (a notable Hitchcock favorite), and Margaret Millar to contemporary works such as Flynn's *Gone Girl*, Paula Hawkins's *The Girl on the Train*, and Liane Moriarty's *Big Little Lies,* which some refer to as "domestic thrillers," or "marriage thrillers, or "neoliberal gothic."[2] I consider these texts "chick noir" to recognize that they update domestic noir of the postwar period and that their particular anxieties have an overlooked presence in contemporary chick lit. Chick noir departs significantly from the humorous remodeling of romance that chick lit, chick flicks, and feminized TV programming customarily offer as the "happy object" around which young women should orient self-making for proximity to and the promise of the "good life," neoliberal belonging, and future family happiness.[3] But if chick noir extends the generic portfolio of chick lit in a sideways or even queer direction, it also retrospectively curates the popular narratives of chick culture in a revealing way.

Gone Girl's narrative rigorously works against the heteropatriarchal marital embrace that preoccupies much feminized popular culture—texts that feature female protagonists and target a female audience. Indeed, chick noir may be understood in the terms of a reverse marriage plot, and in that way innovates but still depends upon the persistence of the romance narrative in contemporary culture, with *Gone Girl* elaborating the pattern through intense scrutiny of one unhappily married couple contending with recessionary era unemployment and diminished means. Further, *Gone Girl* centralizes a concern for reproduction, locating it as a rigidly gendered problem within heterosexual coupling and a challenge to be overcome by just about everyone. In short, postindustrial shifts in marriage and declines in the birth rate—the undoing of the repronormative, nuclear family—function as touchstones for the larger context of social decline and set the stage for the dramatization of the decidedly noir affects of loss.

This essay proceeds from the observation that *Gone Girl* represents negative affects associated with the personal loss of fractured relationships—sadness, grief, insecurity, and pessimism—predominately through a primary female character or, more specifically, through femininity. Just as importantly, *Gone Girl* dramatizes social loss and the attendant affective dynamics that characterize a shrinking public sphere in an era of expanding privatization and intensifying precarity. *Gone Girl* challenges audiences to consider the ways in which such losses may be simultaneously lamentable and laudable signs of social decline, with close links to gendered power relations and a specifically gendered model of selfhood. My discussion thus pays particular attention to the ways in which *Gone Girl* explores practices of surveillance as a characteristic feature of neoliberal governmentality. *Gone Girl* uses neoliberalism's technologies of surveillance, particularly popular cultural narrative, and contests a postfeminist model of feminine selfhood, which is tightly pinned to surveillance.

In the following section, I outline the development of chick noir, situating it in relation to chick lit broadly as a contemporary category of women's writing. Next, I contextualize the development of chick noir within postfeminism, a cultural discourse closely aligned with neoliberalism. Finally, I analyze *Gone Girl* for the ways in which the narrative textually produces—via the restaging of surveillant imaginaries—empathy, by deploying understanding and shared feelings of loss, and coercion, by circulating noir feelings of constraint or intimidation.

The Development of Chick Noir

In retrospect, the development of chick noir may have been anticipated, considering chick lit's recasting of popular romance fiction, which indicates changes in intimate relationships and the surprising "tenacity of notions of heterosexual romance given cultural and demographic changes including divorce, increase in single person households, and diversification of family forms."[4] Chick lit has recognized (and shaped) how coupling has become, in American marriage culture, a rather business-like endeavor in the decidedly unromantic trend of "a rationalized system for the procurement of a mate," as Suzanne Leonard analyzes.[5] Chick lit was defined initially as a humorous genre of fiction that "features single women in their twenties and thirties navigating their generations' challenges of balancing demanding careers with personal relationships."[6] Its realism wryly chronicles young women's struggles with increased demands for labor and consumption that have been added to long-existing expectations for normative family life. Further on, it is described as postmodern fiction: "Chick lit's success as a genre lies in its seductive bricolage of approximate dichotomies: independence and a husband, the writing life and married cohabitation, fine accessories and entry-level income."[7]

Despite its levity, in other respects chick lit is similar to noir, since it emerged as a popular rather than literary form; borrows liberally from melodrama and self-consciously from other diverse genres; migrates across media; continually remakes itself outside generic paradigms and travels globally; engages questions of gender, sexuality, class, and race; and comments, however ambivalently, on capitalist social relations and conditions. Indeed, when "consumption as a strategy for the production of the self" met an economy in crisis in the 2008 recession, the optimistic chants of workplace dramedy and romantic comedy gave way, and feminized popular culture underwent a makeover, rewriting tropes, archetypes, and narrative protocols in a decidedly somber direction.[8] Chick lit refashioned itself not only tonally, into slightly less smiley narratives of redemptive austerity predictably dubbed "recession lit"; but it also found in the adjacent cultural form of twentieth century noir a highly legible route to significantly renovate plot and residual affective impulses. Rather than chronicling anxieties about social conditions obliquely through symptom and satire, chick noir more directly acknowledges that all is not well with a model of female subjectivity that posits individual success through the primary ingredients of inspired wage labor and consumer choice. Driven not by aspiration, optimism, and happiness, but by negative affect, chick noir deals, as Lucie Whitehouse observes, "in the dark side of relationships, intimate danger, the idea that you can never really know your husband or partner or that home and relationship is threatened."[9]

Chick Culture in a Postfeminist Context

As a form of popular chick culture that borrows from noir, chick noir contributes to postfeminism, which scholars most frequently treat as a cultural discourse specific to the neoliberal era. Although the word *postfeminism* was first used in the United States in negative response to women's movement of the 1920s, it resurfaced in mainstream media in the 1980s in a similarly reactionary context.[10] It became prominent by the 1990s in popular culture in the United States and the United Kingdom, manifest in texts distributed through marketing categories that target and develop female audiences, an expanding source of consumers with disposable income, given shifts in labor force participation brought on by economic globalization and neoliberal social policies.

There are temporal and ideological dimensions to the concept, but most scholars do not engage postfeminism as a coherent political theory, so it is not treated as a feminist movement, stance, or even political identity category to which people attach. Instead, it is approached as an object of critique, a cultural "complexification of the backlash thesis," and a "re-negotiation" of feminist and antifeminist thought.[11] Still, this means considerable instability or slippage in definition because "postfeminist discourse deploys a variety of positions with respect to feminism, at times celebratory and at times laying blame for contemporary anxieties at the door of a past politics now felt to be misconceived."[12] Postfeminism's relationship to feminism has been characterized as a "double discourse" of evocation and rejection.[13] Similarly, Angela McRobbie writes of postfeminism's "double entanglement," in which feminism is "taken into account" in cultural texts, even posited as having succeeded in certain ways, expressly to then suggest it is "no longer needed," should be repudiated, and in any case is used against itself to dismantle feminist politics and disarticulate feminist alliances.[14] Texts thus symbolically showcase individualist figures of empowerment.

Ambivalence and contradiction clearly register in a highly patterned and popular narrative structure since the 1990s whereby postfeminist cultural texts customarily raise dilemmas, uncertainties, or dissatisfactions but then decline to address them through humorous deflections or "evasion, escape, and retreat."[15] In fact, postfeminist texts incorporate feminism in selective ways that overlap with the same disavowal of structural inequalities on display in post–civil rights and postracial discourse. This is abundantly evident in assumptions of whiteness and affluence and the general disregard for social differences across postfeminist culture; as Yvonne Tasker and Diane Negra point out, the construction of women as subjects only to the extent that they are able and willing to consume "is one of the contradictions at the core of postfeminist culture."[16]

Postfeminism is currently recognized as a generative cultural discourse with strong links to neoliberal efforts to regulate femininity and women by reshaping gendered political subjectivity, including feminist subjectivity. McRobbie describes this form of feminine citizenship or belonging as a new "sexual contract," one in which young women are called upon to "make good use of the opportunity to work, to gain qualifications, control fertility, and to earn enough money to participate in consumer culture."[17] Put another way, postfeminism adopts a neoliberal logic or rationality that relies upon and advances entrepreneurial selfhood. It is linked to other contemporary manifestations of feminism, including neoliberal feminism and most recently popular feminism, a networked form of empowerment or liberal feminism accessed through media visibility and in competing relation to popular misogyny, which is similarly networked.[18]

Through various cultural genres and platforms, including digital and social media, postfeminist texts function as technologies of gendered citizenship to displace the political subject-citizen and replace it with an aspiring subject-citizen who labors and consumes ostensibly according to their own choices but in neat alignment with market imperatives, which are to assume full responsibility for and independent care of the self, while relinquishing any social acknowledgment of or public support for structural disparities. If literary and cinematic manifestations may be more complex, narratively speaking, than reality television, Pinterest, or beauty apps, these forms all exhibit the hallmark ideological ambivalence toward feminist history and politics.[19] Certainly, as part of the broader "entertainment industry," postfeminist culture participates in the expansion of immaterial labor in the global economy since it is "focused on the creation and manipulation of affect," but it also indexes and even explores the affective dimensions of labor and subjectivity that are characteristic features of contemporary social life.[20]

Postfeminist texts regularly present "diagnostics of femininity," as Diane Negra puts it, "that take the place of [feminist] analyses of political and economic culture."[21] And these texts often involve matrimonial and maternal models of female subjectivity, which do not typically upset but rather reassure the status quo of gendered power relations and structures, both in the workplace and in the home. Given the degree to which women are hailed as and expected to be skillful entrepreneurs of the self, continuously involved in reinvention that nonetheless accommodates patriarchal, racial capitalism, the female subject has become the ideal or paradigmatic subject of neoliberalism.[22] Of course, such continuous reinvention requires prodigious labor, physical and affective, and significant outlays of capital, and it relies upon the commercialized and exploited labor of racialized and other minoritized women who disproportionately perform the services needed in makeover and self-care.

The Discontents of Chick Culture

In analyzing *Gone Girl* as chick noir, I join scholars who recognize the dissatisfactions legible in chick culture, rather than consign these fictions to facile celebrations of neoliberal economic citizenship as the route to achieving happiness. These observations provide understanding of the genre, including ethnic, diasporic, and transnational chick lit, that refuses a dismissal of popular texts for their "imbricated location within capitalism and neoliberalism."[23] Commenting on the pleasures of chick lit, Tania Modleski contends chick lit is less about female success than female disillusionment, with both capitalism and heteropatriarchal romance, so "women are still writing novels that point to their discontents, some of them explicit . . . some of them implicit." Promising what capitalism and patriarchy promise but have not or cannot deliver, "a fair number of chick lit novels have protagonists who live in a land of relative plenty (or shop as if they do), and who are faced with a cornucopia of 'choices' that a postfeminist society claims have been bestowed upon them."[24] Another view considers chick lit an affective fantasy of shared commercial intimacy, as part of a "mass genre" and long history of sentimental "women's culture" that substitutes for and contains political belonging.[25]

I observe that chick lit invites us to read for its emphasis on revision in the promises of consumer culture featured on its covers and in its storytelling, in the model of neoliberal subjecthood protagonists typically strive to emulate, and in the genre itself; it indexes the capitalist preoccupation with reinvention or makeover as a key feature of the neoliberal demand for women's flexible labor and as a condition of belonging.[26] Codified iconography, long established and highly legible narrative conventions, the regular production of subgeneric renovations, as well as reading patterns of enjoying several books a month on commutes to work all echo demands to continuously work on the self for improvements in employment and in the maintenance of normative, middle-class family life.

Implicit in the logics of continuous renovation, the unhappy realities of labor for women are at times explicitly chronicled in chick lit, despite a narrative pattern of dramatic comedy that is typically work-based.[27] Indeed, neoliberal "work societies" assume, demand, and even enforce waged and unwaged work, with work as much as anything else a dimension of subjectivity.[28] In representing the role of wage labor in the "dailiness of women's lives," the genre may provide critical commentary on the ways in which work has invaded personal life to an unprecedented degree and created "the consciousness of the always-present potential for engaging with work," what Melisssa Gregg has termed the "presence bleed" of the contemporary workplace.[29] Chick lit also elaborately registers the necessity of regulating one's affect to convey that work is meaningful, pleasurable, and rewarding, of a piece with how the contemporary workplace increasingly harnesses affects and consciously felt emotions for an economic system that depends upon forms of immaterial labor.[30] The labor of managing emotions at work, including about work, extends the increasingly intensified exploitation of caring and emotional labor that women in particular perform in social reproduction.[31]

Suzanne Ferriss has recently observed that, rather than high-paying glamorous careers, chick lit heroines are more properly understood as part of the precariat, where precarity is defined as a set of labor conditions of insecurity not only economic but also emotional: "'a much more widely felt mood and condition of unease and groundlessness.'"[32] I underscore that the genre of chick lit, especially in its shifting affective emphases, chronicles the structural processes of precaritization as a technology of neoliberal biopolitical governmentality: "contrary to the old rule of a domination that demands obedience in exchange for protection, neoliberal governing proceeds primarily through social insecurity, through regulating the minimum of assurance while simultaneously increasing instability."[33] Feminist scholarship has analyzed this process, including its impact specifically on mothering and the increasingly nonviable burdens of reproductive labor.[34] Chick noir brings the concerns in the genre about the neoliberal demands for women's flexible, immaterial, and largely unpaid labor, and the instability of contemporary work, to the surface, where they are manifest through anxieties and feelings of failure, decline, and loss that inevitably accompany impossible expectations or norms, including in characters who have relatively abundant resources for endurance and resilience.

Surveillance *and* Gone Girl

The indirect and the more direct treatment of precarity and of neoliberal demands for women's flexible labor in chick lit illustrate that the negative affects of loss, and specifically discontent with untenable conditions and fears about degeneration or decline, are embedded within and throughout postfeminist popular culture, as it chronicles in various ways the insufficiencies of contemporary social life. This approach to understanding chick noir follows from Gill's influential theorization of postfeminism as a set of attitudes, a "distinctive sensibility" made up of six interrelated tropes: "the notion that femininity is a bodily property; the shift from objectification to subjectification; an emphasis on self-surveillance, monitoring and self-discipline; a focus on individualism, choice and empowerment; the dominance of a makeover paradigm; and a resurgence of ideas about natural sexual difference."[35] If the rhetorics of individualism, choice, and empowerment ring cheerfully, postfeminism as a cultural discourse portrays, if not directly then certainly symptomatically, a deep concern for neoliberal-era subjecthood and the more somber affects that also play a fundamental role in people's lives at this conjuncture. As theorists such as Sara Ahmed and Lauren Berlant have established, affects and feelings, whether in response to cultural representations, aesthetic objects, commodities, or lived experience, are not homogenous—uniformly positive or negative—but depend upon ambivalence, contradiction, and paradox. Finally, affects are productive, so where we find feelings of happiness or optimism, we may also find disgust and despair. And when there is loss, both hopelessness and hope may emerge from what remains.[36]

Attentive to feminist and queer theoretical insights about the nonbinary and generative relations among affects, this analysis expands the contention that "one of postfeminism's key functions is to negotiate the failure of contemporary institutions and the prospect of social death."[37] However, rather than imagining femininity as "a state of vitality in opposition to the symbolically deathly social and economic fields of contemporary Western cultures" that is "empowered to recharge a culture defined by exhaustion, uncertainty, and moral ambiguity," *Gone Girl*, if not all of chick noir, imagines femininity, I argue, as a negative state of surveillance. Femininity is no longer only a form of "cruel optimism" or "the condition of maintaining an attachment to a significantly problematic object."[38] Instead, the femininity of primary female characters in such texts has fully adopted the technologies of power at work in neoliberal governance, turning its sights back onto failed institutions, rather than negotiating or managing them, while also maintaining the intense scrutiny of the female self that those same institutions have cultivated to devastating biopolitical effect, including the loss of vitality or life itself. Like the feminism of postfeminism, the femininity of chick noir no longer negotiates decline but rather dismantles itself as a thriving or vitalizing force.

Indeed, while the opening scenes of *Gone Girl* are identifiably noir—constructed through highly recognizable aesthetic, formal, and affective dimensions—they are also surveillance situations, characteristic scenes of late modernity. Fundamentally about seeing, watching, observing, and predicting future actions, as well as producing a coherent, sequential narrative from observed and anticipated behavior, these scenes emphasize connections between noir and surveillance, which precedes but informs and is even advanced by noir, principally through interests in detection. Noir shares with surveillance the concern for what is not evident or easily seen and known, for what is obscured by the divides between public and private, official and mundane, exposed and covert, especially when people or institutions are understood to be criminal or corrupt.

This chapter accepts as premise that surveillance is at the core of contemporary systems of power, knowledge, and subjectification, and it takes seriously the suggestion that narrative cultural forms—in this case chick culture—are important to understanding surveillance history and technologies. David Rosen and Aaron Santesso contend that the novel has been a site not only for representing surveillance but also for the "generation of Western forms of observation and assessment," especially of individual self or character, or the selfhood associated with Enlightenment thinking, liberalism, and the modern ideology of privacy.[39] The emergence of mass popular genres of literature "materialized during the crisis of observation, privacy, and realism" beginning in the middle of the nineteenth century to espouse "a far more fluid notion of privacy than most mainstream [literary] novelists would accept."[40] In particular, the appearance of the detective story was not random but became a key site for legitimizing the authority of surveillance and exploring various mechanisms that would effectively create knowledge about others' lives.

Similar claims about film point out that "surveillance techniques and technologies . . . and cinematic techniques and technologies . . . coalesce as *narrative logic*" and provide "a framework that organizes . . . subjective formations."[41] Surely, across popular mediums, cultural narrative engagements with surveillance provide a rich archive for understanding technologies and practices of surveillance in relation to conceptions of selfhood in neoliberal times. The importance of analyzing contemporary surveillance narrative lies not in producing intellectual knowledge about popular culture to validate texts, but in identifying possible contestations to conceptions of neoliberal selfhood and the culturally emergent or nonnormative self. For, as José Esteban Muñoz contends, the self of some fiction may well be a "disidentificatory self whose relation to the social is not overdetermined by universalizing theories of selfhood."[42]

With the faithful adaptation of Flynn's 2012 novel, the opening scene of Fincher's *Gone Girl* situates literature as an aesthetic form of popular mediated culture in close proximity to visual forms, a fact that highlights their shared concerns with seeing and interpretation. The *Gone Girl* of Flynn's novel and that of Fincher's film use and consider neoliberalism's technologies of surveillance and contest its model of selfhood, and they do this through a centralization of the affects associated with surveillance, routing them through a generic engagement with noir. Both texts stage contemporary surveillant imaginaries through narrative structure, as prevailing modes of observation through narrative focalization, and in the textual production of affect, in characters and in readers or viewers. Storytelling in these works is arranged through: (1) the observation of a scene's characters or a surveillant image; (2) the assessment or interpretation of observed characters' actions; (3) the ordering of observed actions into legible narratives; and (4) the primary affective force of surveillance or the structure of feeling created by surveillance and its logics. In short, these chick noir texts represent surveillance situations as narrative building blocks and layer them to create complex narratives containing multiple perspectives and multiple story lines, which intersect at certain, seemingly random points. This is not unlike how surveillance technology systems may record information about different moments of an observed subject's life, which is then ordered or arranged, in retrospect and typically after the fact of an event that needs to be understood, into a meaningful or coherent narrative. Further, narratives created in both surveillance situations in general and in these cultural texts specifically involve the production and circulation of feelings of empathy and constraint.

However powerful modern technologies of surveillance are depicted through and in *Gone Girl*, the novel and film suggest that surveillance practices are not all-controlling; they can and do produce a variety of ways of seeing, understanding, narrating, and feeling, including not only constraint or intimidation and threat through coercion but also understanding and sharing feelings of others through empathy. Rather than all of the power residing in the observer's hands, as discussions of "universalizing panopticism" suggest, power also lies "in the control of narrative, a control frequently in the hands of the person under watch."[43] Or, as Muñoz prefers, "The 'real self' who comes into being through fiction is not the self who produces fiction, but is instead produced by fiction."[44] In this sense, texts such as these shine further light on the role popular fictional narratives may play in developing or generating practices of surveillance and models of selfhood. The role for the observed would seem welcome, but this may assume that power or control in the production of narrative and specifically about character or selfhood is an unmitigated good. Concerned with this modern problematic, these texts present surveillance as fundamental to social decline, which may help us understand the negative disposition of chick noir or perhaps noir writ large.

In the story told by *Gone Girl*, the ability of the subject under surveillance to construct narrative and define selfhood is staged in several ways, and it is most often crafted to elicit empathy, although the object of empathetic feelings shifts depending on narrative point of view or focalization, and empathy often seems to be accompanied by threats or intimidation. For much of the film, it is actually Nick, rather than Amy, who is being watched, observed, and interpreted—by the police who suspect him of killing his missing wife, by the news media and audiences that are hungry for a gory and salacious spectacle, and by Amy, who also watches a televisually mediated Nick from her hideout. These scenes of surveillance, like the evening scene in which Amy sees Nick kiss his lover Andie outside The Bar, construct looking relations designed to generate empathy for Amy as a victim of Nick's infidelity and his emotionally and physically abusive treatment. Nick is slow to recognize any power to control the narrative constructed about him, so it is only near the end of the story that he begins to use the media to convey a message to Amy that he is sorry. This is not because Nick is remorseful and wants to reunite with his wife, as we learn from his conversations with Go and his own narration, but because Nick needs Amy to return and thereby exonerate him of murder charges. In other words, Nick aims to control the narrative produced through media surveillance for the purposes of anticipating and coercively influencing Amy's behavior.

Once it becomes clear that Amy is framing Nick and has been fabricating evidence against him, which in the book isn't until part two, when chapters told from Amy's first-person perspective in the present of the story allow her to share narrative control with Nick, empathy shifts toward Nick. Readers learn that Amy's narrative motivations are also coercive; in fact, Amy wants to punish Nick through incarceration or constant surveillance via the modern disciplinary institution *par excellence* of the prison.

To be sure, the narrative is more concerned with the ways in which Amy, the girl who is gone, is under surveillance and uses the scrutiny that she knows she and her marriage have always been under to shape and direct the investigation of Nick. The day Amy stages her own disappearance to exact revenge on Nick is their fifth wedding anniversary. As part of her elaborate framing of Nick for her presumed murder (she retreats from the original plan to commit suicide and instead flees), Amy plants clues in a treasure hunt that on previous anniversaries would simply lead Nick to a thoughtful gift. For their wood anniversary, each clue is coyly written and then placed in a location, such as in his office at the community college where he teaches creative writing and where he's had sex with his student lover, which reveals to the investigating detectives not only that Nick has been cheating on his wife but also that he is a possibly predatory man. Just to be certain, Amy also plants material evidence of irresponsibility in the clue sites, as in lingerie or expensive consumer goods they cannot afford.

For "the Nick and Amy Story" that Amy masterfully shapes and invites all to piece together, she writes a diary—strategically accurate but largely fictional—with over three hundred entries of revealing details and scenes from their marriage, providing another form of documentation or narrative evidence to incriminate Nick and persuade the authorities of his fundamentally abusive nature. Part one of Flynn's book alternates Nick's first-person perspective with Amy's faux diary installments, and it is only when chapters are no longer labeled "Diary Entry" that readers fully realize the misleading role of these installments in constructing the narrative they are reading. The film unfolds in a similarly misleading way because it dramatizes key fictional diary entries, scenes replete with dialogue and Amy's voiceover, to present and authenticate them, at least initially, as actual events.

Crucially, the most effective performance in terms of narrating the story of their collapsed marriage and in terms of the textual production of both feelings of empathy and coercion, may be the central scenes in which Nick and Amy argue over her suggestion that they start a family, which ultimately threatens both their marriage and their lives. As told by Amy, Nick accuses her of trying to "save their marriage" by having children, so Amy confronts him about the implication that their marriage has failed. A blow-up ensues and Nick forcefully shoves Amy, who falls and hits her head (fig. 1).

As her voiceover recounts, this was the moment when Amy realized not only that her marriage was over but also that Nick wanted to hurt her. A subsequent diary entry, dramatized in the film's very next scene, details Amy's attempt to purchase a gun for protection at the now bankrupt and deteriorating Riverway Mall (fig. 2). In the first scene, family making as salvation is named as both a possibility and a bad, desperate idea. It thus highlights ambivalence about reproduction as a problem in their marriage, and the next scene symbolically links that problem to the economic structural devastation of the recession. In this sequencing, the Dunnes' disintegrating marriage is connected to financial hardship in their personal lives, to various forms of violence, and to economic decay in society writ large.

Figure 1. A violent fight scene condemns Nick and the Dunne marriage.

Figure 2. Amy seeks protection at the crumbling Riverway Mall.

If the unnerving sequence seems to blame Nick, in another scene Nick tells Go that Amy was the one who did not want children, confirming at least that someone's ambivalence about reproduction led to the debacle that is their marriage. Regardless of which character did not want children, or their fertility treatments, the fact is presented as an impasse, both affectively and socially. While absent in the film, the book also features Amy's haunting by "the Hopes," the name her mother gives to several miscarriages endured before Amy was born. Similar to the fictional figure in her parents' *Amazing Amy* book series, these unborn or missing offspring—her siblings—and the child of the happy marriage and life she is expected to socially reproduce, represent to Amy a perfection she will never be able to achieve.

Finally, Amy demonstrates her ability to control narrative while under watch and via practices of surveillance when she stages her own rape by ex–high school boyfriend Desi Collings, whom she contacts after a robbery at her hideout leaves her in the "fucking noir" condition of "penniless and on the run."[45] Amy tells Desi that she needs him to rescue her from Nick's abuse and the unwanted limelight of scandal. Recovering in his luxurious lake home, Amy then uses the security system designed to protect personal property and privacy, a CCTV, to record a carefully scripted set of scenes, including her own bodily violation, which will help document a narrative of captivity, sexual assault, and self-defense. Amy murders Desi, but the recordings survive and provide a coherent narrative that becomes the most reliable forensic evidence the police have to explain Amy's disappearance and return after several weeks. Nick deciphers what Amy's done, and they speak directly about it. Still, they together perform a final act for the media watching public, one in which their love is reaffirmed and their salvaged marriage celebrated, primarily because Amy has revealed that she is pregnant.

Unlike the pregnancy that Amy fabricates to "package" herself "so people will truly mourn the loss" of her disappearance, this pregnancy, achieved via Nick's frozen sperm, appears to be embraced both by the public and the couple. In another conversation with Go that gives film audiences access to Nick's interior, he confides to his sister a sense of responsibility for the future child, sadly resigning himself to marriage with "that monster," as Go refers to Amy. At this point, however, both Amy and Nick recognize that the promise of happiness represented in normative family life is an especially effective way to gain public sympathies, since "America loves pregnant women." Not surprisingly, their story surfaces in new installments of *Amazing Amy*, which restores the couple's personal fortunes. Through projecting a narrative in which they ostensibly recover a lost desire for reproduction and the hope of futurity, Amy and Nick regain sanctioned middle-class standing, financial health, and social belonging.

Instead of recognizing how the processes of precaritization for women—emotional and economic tolls of insecurity that may easily produce anger and even rage—are brought about by social conditions of increased and unpaid reproductive labor alongside increased demands for wage labor, particularly in the context of the withdrawal of public supports for families and massive un- and under- employment, *Gone Girl* symbolically attributes precaritization to the missing child or the child whom the errant girl refuses to birth. The narrative echoes popular discourse that found myriad ways to blame women for an economy in crisis, as in Hannah Rosin's *The End of Men and the Rise of Women*. And while the context for this book and for the story in *Gone Girl* is clearly the recession, they share a troubling narrative that reinstalls as antidote the conventional gender relations and the failing institutions that are central to structural insecurity, effectively disregarding downturn conditions. As Negra has observed, postfeminist culture is both "expressive and repressive" of social problems, anxieties, desires, and struggles.[46]

If Amy and Nick's story of redeemed marriage is portrayed in the texts as credible with popular news media audiences, the unreliability of the two narrators that has been echoed and reinforced throughout the tale is of a piece with its depictions of a media industry that constructs consumable and sensationalist stories of them for a voracious public but is blithely unconcerned with relaying any accurate information about Nick, Amy, or their marriage. The finale is yet another installment in the mode of disingenuous storytelling that Flynn highlights, so the idea that a return to the repronormative family narrative will provide a happily ever after for this couple, a hallmark of romance fiction, and somehow restore social health for society writ large, is difficult to believe. Indeed, by the end of the novel and the film, readers and viewers know that these two characters are entirely untrustworthy storytellers. In detective drama that designs suspense specifically to resist closure, the truths that emerge at the end of the narrative maintain a provisional status, for detective narratives "betray premises such as evidentiary truth, verifiable identity and logical chronology upon which surveillance functions politically and socially."[47] Audiences also know that the noir narrative they have been consuming is manipulative, affectively speaking, because its structure of layered surveillance plays with audience feelings of empathy and constraint, jerking readers and viewers between two ultimately unlikeable perspectives and myriad contradictory focalizations.

Flynn's narrative toys, it seems, with the affective hypothesis of contemporary culture, which is the now widely accepted view, as Rachel Smith outlines, that "literature is at its most meaningful when it represents and transmits the emotional specificity of personal experience." In this consensus, texts "allow us direct contact with individuals who are like us but not like us; they allow us to feel what others feel; they provoke empathy; and they teach us how to understand what it means to be a unique human being."[48] So, just as "neoliberalism imagines the individual as an entrepreneur ... the affective hypothesis imagines the act of reading as an opportunity for emotional investment and return."[49] However, Flynn deliberately shows her characters to be unworthy or bad "investments," affectively speaking, and they do not provide an emotionally satisfying ending, but drift away as the plot flattens out and the presence of positive emotional words declines, a pattern that bestselling chick noir texts share.⁵⁰ While Amy and Nick may be read to make productive use of emotional ties, the narrative does not ultimately provoke empathy or teach us how to be empathetic people. Instead, Amy's and Nick's manipulations of other characters' empathy and the narrative's misleading engagement with reader sensibilities is far more likely to yield alienation or even disgust.

Despite moments of empathy in which audiences contending with austerity may understand characters' feelings: of failure when they lose their jobs as cosmopolitan journalists during the recession, loss when they sell their fashionable brownstone in New York City to move to an "ugly" neighborhood of foreclosed homes and shuttered malls, and sadness when their dream of marriage and family falls apart, their narratives, shaped through practices of surveillance, are both revealed to be similarly motivated by coercion. Further, Amy often frames her response to loss through the rhetoric of entitlement, conveying an intensely angry reaction to the loss of privileged whiteness in which a charmed life came crashing down. To be sure, these chick noir texts suggest that the narratives their characters produce create more violence and loss, in their own lives and in the lives of others, as they feature agents based on a model of selfhood that is most interested in instrumentalizing affect to possess feelings, control others' behavior, and advance personal goals.

While some media critics and spectators have taken issue with these texts for circulating myths about false accusations of abuse and rape and for the film's spectacular representation of sexual violence, Flynn as novelist and screenwriter layers so many misleading narratives that it would be unwise to focus on one, even if or especially because the one in question patently relies upon the primarily affective maneuvers of pornography and horror—specifically sexual arousal of the bodily sensations of desire or fear, respectively.[51] Instead, the layering of misleading and manipulative narrative points to larger questions about the production of narrative and especially its relation to practices of surveillance, which are, feminist studies scholars point out, "integral to many of the West's foundational structural systems of oppression" and which continue to be institutionalized.[52] Key to understanding Flynn's interrogative mobilization of noir detection are the ways in which femininity, embodied in the character of Amy, is figured as a site or state of surveillance, one that is both the object and the subject of surveillant scopophilia.[53]

Amy is, without a doubt, an expert observer of character and skilled storyteller. Her profession as a journalist has provided practice. But it was the dominant surveillant imaginary of Amy's childhood that has most rigorously schooled her in self-monitoring and that best prepares her for spinning moving tales as an adult. Growing up, Amy was the real-life basis for her parents' best-selling *Amazing Amy* children's book series, which provides the immediate backstory for public sympathies for Amy Elliott Dunne when she goes missing. Effectively, the storytelling in *Amazing Amy* functions as a central practice of parental surveillance and is the "Elliott bread and butter":

> My parents had worried that I'd take *Amy* too personally—they always tell me not to read too much into her. And yet I can't fail to notice that whenever I screw something up, Amy does it right. When I finally quit violin at age twelve, Amy was revealed as a prodigy in the next book. ("Sheesh, violin can be hard work, but hard work is the only way to get better!") When I blew off the junior tennis championship at age sixteen to do a beach weekend with friends, Amy recommitted to the game. ("Sheesh, I know it's fun to spend time with friends, but I'd be letting myself and everyone else down if I didn't show up for the tournament.") This used to drive me mad, but after I went off to Harvard (and Amy correctly chose my parents' alma mater), I decided it was all too ridiculous to think about.[54]

In describing the rationality of governance that creates docile bodies, Michel Foucault observes that constant surveillance, the central technique of modern disciplinary power, is initially directed toward disciplining the body but then includes the mind to induce a psychological state of "conscious and permanent visibility that assures the automatic functioning of power."[55] Amy's description of her self-monitoring in relation to a fictional better version in *Amazing Amy* conveys that she has both adopted and internalized a surveillant imaginary. While she disavows that *Amazing Amy* operates as a model of perfection to emulate during adulthood, suggesting that she grew out of the tutelage of *Amazing Amy*, *Gone Girl* tells a different story.

Amy's self-surveillance reveals a particularly gendered surveillant imaginary that aspires to produce a specific form of white, middle-class heteropatriarchal femininity. As Sandra Bartky has argued, within institutionalized heterosexuality, "self-surveillance is a form of obedience to patriarchy" that involves practices which aim to produce a certain body size and configuration; a specific repertoire of gestures, postures, and movements; and, crucially, display of the appropriately feminized body.[56]

Condensed for the film, the oft-cited Cool Girl passage of the novel, in which Amy recalls when she and Nick met, crystallizes for audiences her understanding of self-surveillance and self-making as foundations for their relationship; as Amy confides: "the way some women change fashion regularly, I change personalities":

> That night at the Brooklyn party, I was playing the girl who was in style, the girl a man like Nick wants: the Cool Girl. Men always say that as *the* defining compliment, don't they? *She's a cool girl.* Being the Cool Girl means I am a hot, brilliant, funny woman who adores football, poker, dirty jokes, and burping, who plays video games, drinks cheap beer, loves threesomes and anal sex, and jams hot dogs and hamburgers into her mouth like she's hosting the world's biggest culinary gang bang while somehow maintaining a size 2, because Cool Girls are above all hot. Hot and understanding. Cool Girls never get angry; they only smile in a chagrined, loving manner and let their men do whatever they want. Go ahead, shit on me, I don't mind, I'm the Cool Girl.[57]

Amy describes how Cool Girl became the new, modern standard: "Every girl was supposed to be this girl, and if you weren't, there was something wrong with you." Certainly, Amy's self is a particular studied and displayed affective version of herself—she performs and becomes Cool Amy or the woman who doesn't insist on her own desires and feelings, who eschews emotional intimacy, to attract Nick.

As McRobbie observes, the Cool Girl or "female phallicism" is a "thin tightrope to walk," one that asks women to perform masculinity without relinquishing the femininity that makes them desirable. "The phallic girl gives the impression of having won equality with men by becoming like her male counterparts. But in this adoption of the phallus, there is no critique of masculine hegemony," and she maintains a subordinate status, even allowing the denigration of her sexual agency for the maintenance of the sexual double standard.[58] Eventually, Amy comes to see Cool Girls as pathetic figures of femininity:

> They're not even pretending to be the woman they want to be, they're pretending to be the woman a man wants them to be. Oh, and if you're not a Cool Girl, I beg you not to believe that your man doesn't want the Cool Girl. It may be a slightly different version—maybe he's a vegetarian, so Cool Girl loves seitan and is great with dogs; or maybe he's a hipster artist, so Cool Girl is a tattooed, bespectacled nerd who loves comics. There are variations to the window dressing, but believe me, he wants Cool Girl, who is basically the girl who likes every fucking thing he likes and doesn't ever complain.[59]

After several years of dissonant detachment and propelled by the recessionary losses of career and urban lifestyle, Amy decides to become a different person, one who tries to meet the requirements of socially sanctioned, traditional femininity, namely those of affective bonds and domesticity. Nick is unwilling, however, to accept her makeover, much less reinvent himself for their relationship. Herein lies the more disturbing dimension for Amy of her considerable insights into and practices of surveillance. Self-policing includes "the reflection in woman's consciousness of the fact that *she* is under surveillance in ways that *he* is not, that whatever else she may become, she is importantly a body designed to please or to excite him."[60]

Cool Girl comes in fact with strict conditions, including the prevention and delay of reproduction. "So long as she does not procreate while enjoying casual and recreational sex, the young woman is entitled to pursue sexual desire seemingly without punishment."[61] But this is a ruse, with the new sexual contract, which requires that she reproduce in the most prudent ways.

Amy's ability to refashion herself, and her capacity to use technologies of surveillance to narrativize and display herself align to a great extent with postfeminism's ideal manifestation of the entrepreneurial female self whose empowerment is "entangled with the contemporary media savvy interactive subject."[62] This subject moves across media platforms to craft and broadcast a self, as part of the process of self-branding. Further, the cultivation of a self-brand through symbolic narrative that discloses this productive self is a moral duty or part of the proper care of the self, a form of immaterial and affective labor privileged in the neoliberal global economy that has shifted how consumers relate to products.[63]

Gone Girl depicts Amy as a virtuoso practitioner of surveillance who uses it to try to fulfill the terms of the new sexual contract. However, both Flynn's novel and Fincher's film recount how Amy recognizes these terms as either impossible or unrealistic when she turns cultural technologies of surveillance back onto the failing institutions of patriarchal heterosexuality and marriage and back onto neoliberal biopolitical governmentality, so these texts focus intently on Amy's production of a self-branding narrative in the story she tells to punish Nick. The process of creating a symbolic narrative to broadcast her brand—the imperative to display the appropriately feminized laboring and consuming self—nearly kills her and it threatens her participation in both biological and social reproduction.

Affective responses involve ambivalence, contradiction, and paradox. The coolness of chick noir, embodied in the figure of the Cool Girl who disavows intimacy, is not wholly outside or separate from the cuteness typically associated with feminized chick culture. Cuteness is both an aesthetic style of a commodified object and an affective judgment, description, and response to a cute object, Sianne Ngai theorizes. Moreover, if cuteness in contemporary US culture is customarily feminized, infantilized, and associated with toys, these items and especially luxury commodities of leisure signified by chick lit, activate complex social responses, including empathy and aversion, and at times also disgust.[64] The cute aesthetic of chick lit—visual and narrative—points to a contemporary structure of feeling that enables a variety of affective responses and a range of intimate or affective relationships with consumers as fans, readers, or viewers. As with the double-sided structure of all aesthetic categories, cuteness is based "on clashing feelings of tenderness and aggression."[65] Or, as Amy says to Nick when they give one another the same luxury cotton sheets for a second wedding anniversary gift, "We're too cute—I want to punch us in the face."

While Rosen and Santesso define surveillance as "the monitoring of human activity for the purposes of anticipating or influencing future events," and Mark Andrejevic considers it "the coupling of information collection and use with power," I have turned attention toward popular cultural narratives—chick noir—to explore what counts *for* surveillance and what counts *as* surveillance.[66] Surveillance practices, which include generating narrative logic and culture, that visualize bodies and bodily identities, or disappear them, "not only dismantle the coherent body but also remake the body, producing new ways of visualizing bodily identities in ways that highlight othered forms of racialized, gendered, classed, abled, and disabled bodies, as well as sexualized identities."[67] The visual languages and practices of surveillance used in popular cultural narrative may result in affectively violent spectacle, but they may also teach us much about prevailing and failing models of selfhood in neoliberal times.

NOTES

1. Paula Rabinowitz, "Tupperware and Terror: The Rise of Chick Noir," *Chronicle of Higher Education*, January 3, 2016, https://www.chronicle.com/article/TupperwareTerror/234716.

2. Carla Rodríguez González, "Geographies of Fear in the Domestic Noir: Paula Hawkins's *The Girl on the Train*," *Miscelánea: A Journal of English and American Studies* 56 (2017): 111; Emily Johansen, "The Neoliberal Gothic: *Gone Girl*, *Broken Harbor*, and the Terror of Everyday Life," *Contemporary Literature* 57, no. 1 (Spring 2016): 30–32; Victoria Kennedy, "'Chick Noir': *Shopaholic* Meets *Double Indemnity*," *American, British, and Canadian Studies* 28, no. 1 (June 2017): 19–21. Carol Goodman, "Motherhood

Noir," *CrimeReads*, May 10, 2018, https://crimereads.com/motherhood-noir/; Hillary Kelly, "The Villainous Bitch Has Become the Most Boring Trend in Literature," *Vulture*, January 16, 2019, https://www.vulture.com/2019/01/superficial-villainous-bitches-have-taken-over-novels.html.

    3. Sara Ahmed, "Happy Objects," in *The Affect Theory Reader*, ed. Melissa Gregg and Gregor J. Seigworth (Durham, NC: Duke University Press, 2010), 29.

    4. Rosalind Gill and Elena Herdieckerhoff, "Rewriting the Romance: New Femininities in Chick Lit," *Feminist Media Studies* 6, no. 4 (December 2004): 490.

    5. Suzanne Leonard, *Wife, INC.* (New York: New York University Press, 2018), 1–2.

    6. Suzanne Ferriss and Mallory Young, introduction to *Chick Lit: The New Woman's Fiction*, ed. Suzanne Ferriss and Mallory Young (New York: Routledge, 2006), 3.

    7. Stephanie Harzewski, *Chick Lit and Postfeminism* (Charlottesville: University of Virginia Press, 2011), 192.

    8. Yvonne Tasker and Diane Negra, introduction to *Interrogating Postfeminism: Gender and the Politics of Popular Culture*, ed. Yvonne Tasker and Diane Negra (Durham, NC: Duke University Press, 2007), 2.

    9. Lucie Whitehouse, "The Rise of the Marriage Thriller," *Guardian*, January 15, 2014, https://www.theguardian.com/books/booksblog/2014/jan/15/rise-marriage-thriller-couples-secrets-gillian-flynn.

    10. Harzewski, *Chick Lit and Postfeminism*, 8; Diane Negra, *What a Girl Wants? Fantasizing the Reclamation of Self in Postfeminism* (New York: Routledge, 2009), 5.

    11. Angela McRobbie, "Postfeminism and Popular Culture," *Feminist Media Studies* 4, no. 3 (2004): 256; Jane Gerhard, "*Sex and the City*: Carrie Bradshaw's Queer Postfeminism," *Feminist Media Studies* 5, no. 1 (March 2005): 41.

    12. Tasker and Negra, introduction, 8.

    13. Tasker and Negra, 8.

    14. Angela McRobbie, *The Aftermath of Feminism: Gender, Culture, and Social Change* (Los Angeles: Sage, 2009), 12.

    15. Negra, *What a Girl Wants?*, 7.

    16. Tasker and Negra, introduction, 2, 8.

    17. McRobbie, *Aftermath of Feminism*, 54.

    18. Sarah Banet-Weiser, Rosalind Gill, and Catherine Rottenberg, "Postfeminism, Popular Feminism and Neoliberal Feminism? Sarah Banet-Weiser, Rosalind Gill, and Catherine Rottenberg in Conversation," *Feminist Theory* (2019): 2, https//doi.org/10.1177/1464700119845555; Sarah

Banet-Weiser, *Empowered: Popular Feminism*, (Durham, NC: Duke University Press, 2018), 2–4.

19. Ana Sofia Elias and Rosalind Gill, "Beauty Surveillance: The Digital Self-Monitoring of Neoliberalism," *European Journal of Cultural Studies* 21, no. 1 (2018): 63.

20. Michael Hardt and Antonio Negri, *Empire* (Cambridge, MA: Harvard University Press, 2000), 292–293.

21. Negra, *What a Girl Wants?*, 5.

22. Rosalind Gill and Christina Sharff, *New Femininities: Postfeminism, Neoliberalism, and Subjectivity* (Basingstoke: Palgrave Macmillan, 2011), 4–5.

23. Pamela Butler and Jigna Desai, "Prologue: A Second Read: Further Reflections on Women-of-Color Chick Lit," in *Theorizing Ethnicity and Nationality in the Chick Lit Genre*, ed. Erin Hurt (New York: Routledge, 2019), 29.

24. Tania Modleski, *Loving with a Vengeance: Mass Produced Fantasies* (New York: Routledge, 2007), xxvvii, xxiv.

25. Lauren Berlant, *The Female Complaint: The Unfinished Business of Sentimentality in American Culture* (Durham, NC: Duke University Press, 2008), x.

26. Caroline Smith, *Cosmopolitan Culture and Consumerism in Chick Lit* (New York: Routledge, 2009), 6.

27. Elizabeth Hale, "Long Suffering Professional Females: The Case of Chick Lit," in *Chick Lit: The New Woman's Fiction*, eds. Suzanne Ferriss and Mallory Young (New York: Routledge, 2006), 103–105.

28. Kathi Weeks, *The Problem with Work: Feminism, Marxism, Anti-Work Politics, and Post-Work Imaginaries* (Durham, NC: Duke University Press, 2011), 5–8.

29. Ferriss and Young, introduction, 5; Melissa Gregg, *Work's Intimacy* (Cambridge: Polity, 2011), 2–3.

30. Pamela Thoma, *Asian American Women's Popular Literature: Feminizing Genres and Neoliberal Belonging* (Philadelphia: Temple University Press, 2014), 87–88.

31. Gregg, *Work's Intimacy*, 5, 13.

32. Suzanne Ferriss, "Working Girls: The Precariat of Chick Lit," in *Cupcakes, Pinterest, and Ladyporn: Feminized Popular Culture in the Early Twenty-First Century*, ed. Elana Levine (Chicago: University of Illinois Press, 2015), 181–182.

33. Isabell Lorey, *State of Insecurity: Government of the Precarious* (London: Verso, 2015), 2.

34. Julie Wilson and Emily Cheevers Yochim, *Mothering Through Precarity: Women's Work and Digital Media* (Durham, NC: Duke University

Press), 68–70; Laura Briggs, *How All Politics Became Reproductive Politics: From Welfare Reform, to Foreclosure, to Trump* (Berkeley: University of California Press, 2018), 17.

35. Rosalind Gill, "Postfeminist Media Culture: Elements of a Sensibility," *European Journal of Cultural Studies* 10, no. 2 (2007): 147.

36. David L. Eng and David Kanzanjian, eds., *Loss: The Politics of Mourning* (Berkeley: University of California Press, 2002), 2–3.

37. Tasker and Negra, introduction, 8.

38. Tasker and Negra, 9; Lauren Berlant, *Cruel Optimism* (Durham, NC: Duke University Press, 2011), 24.

39. David Rosen and Aaron Santesso, *The Watchman in Pieces* (New Haven, CT: Yale University Press, 2013), 10–11, 15, 107.

40. Rosen and Santesso, 145.

41. Catherine Zimmer, *Surveillance Cinema* (New York: New York University Press, 2015), 2.

42. José Esteban Muñoz, *Disidentifications: Queers of Color and the Performance of Politics* (Minneapolis: University of Minnesota Press, 1999), 20.

43. Rosen and Santesso, *Watchman*, 12–13.

44. Muñoz, *Disidentifications*, 20.

45. Gillian Flynn, *Gone Girl* (New York: Random House, 212), 319.

46. Negra, *What a Girl Wants?*, 21.

47. Zimmer, *Surveillance Cinema*, 3.

48. Rachel Greenwald Smith, *Affect and American Literature in the Age of Neoliberalism* (Cambridge: Cambridge University Press, 2015), 1.

49. Rachel Greenwald Smith, *Affect and American Literature*, 2.

50. Jodie Archer and Matthew L. Jockers, *The Bestseller Code: Anatomy of the Blockbuster Novel* (New York: St Martin's Press, 2016), 176–177, 229.

51. Carol J. Clover, "Her Body, Himself: Gender in the Slasher Film," *Representations*, no. 20 (Fall 1987): 189.

52. Rachel E. Dubrofsky and Shoshana Amielle Magnet, eds. *Feminist Surveillance Studies* (Durham, NC: Duke University Press, 2015), 7.

53. Dubrofsky and Magnet, 12.

54. Flynn, *Gone Girl*, 26–27.

55. Michel Foucault, *Discipline and Punish: The Birth of the Prison*, trans. Alan Sheridan (London: Penguin Books, 1991), 201.

56. Sandra Lee Bartky, "Foucault, Femininity, and the Modernization of Patriarchal Power," in *Feminism and Foucault: Reflections on Resistance*, ed. Irene Diamond and Lee Quinby (Boston, MA: Northeastern University Press, 1988), 81.

57. Flynn, *Gone Girl*, 223.

58. McRobbie, *Aftermath of Feminism*, 83.

59. Flynn, *Gone Girl*, 222.
60. Bartky, "Foucault," 81.
61. McRobbie, *Aftermath of Feminism*, 85.
62. Sarah Banet-Weiser, *Authentic: The Politics of Ambivalence in a Brand Culture* (New York: New York University Press, 2012), 56.
63. Banet-Weiser, *Authentic*, 60, 71.
64. Sianne Ngai, *Our Aesthetic Categories: Zany, Cute, Interesting* (Cambridge, MA: Harvard University Press, 2012), 73, 66.
65. Ngai, *Our Aesthetic Categories*, 44, 29.
66. Rosen and Santesso, *Watchman*, 10; Dubrofsky and Magnet, *Feminist Surveillance Studies*, x.
67. Dubrofsky and Magnet, *Feminist Surveillance Studies*, 9.

CHAPTER 10

Surplus Feelings: Neoliberal Noir and the Affective Economy of Debt

Alexander Dunst

In Nicolas Winding Refn's noir thrillers, as in life, we are always already in debt.[1] In the fourth quarter of 2017, US household debt increased by $193 billion—that is, over a period of three months. At the end of that same year, mortgages, credit card debt, and car and student loans combined were at $13.15 trillion. Even if you're lucky enough to have paid off your student debt or your mortgage, or can't afford one in the first place, you'll still find yourself in debt. If you're the citizen of practically any nation on earth, you will share in its deficit, a fact that holds true regardless of whether you are employed, still in school, are retired or have just been born. US national debt amounted to $19.8 trillion in November of 2016: that's roughly $60,000 per US citizen.[2]

Debt constitutes a personal obligation. To be more precise: debt is the financial measurement of a personal obligation.[3] In the early twenty-first century, most people are stuck with debt for life, chaining their future to past purchases and promises. As a consequence, debt enforces a specific temporality: debt is a loan we take out on the future—income, profit, or productivity that individuals or society at large hope to generate. Debt therefore also becomes a form of power: acting as a mechanism of control and all but guaranteeing that the future will bring more of the same. In this essay, I will think about the *affective* dimension of debt: the way in which our chronic indebtedness gives rise to specific structures of feeling. It's important to emphasize that our current economy of debt is a relatively recent phenomenon: until 1971, dollars were redeemable in gold, which limited how much money, and therefore debt, could be created. Since the end of the so-called "gold standard," levels of debt have risen exponentially—a process helped along by the abolition of US usury laws in 1980, which had put a limit on how much interest banks and loan companies could charge.

In discussing the cultural dimensions of debt, I will focus specifically on how film noir constructs what Sianne Ngai calls affective tone.[4] Like affect more generally, tone is not simply located *in* an aesthetic object or placed *within* the viewer; it arises from their interrelation. Feelings are arguably our most immediate response to cinema and the basis for further reflection: if a movie leaves us cold, we are less likely to keep thinking about it. However, as cultural critics, our impetus is sometimes to put our feelings aside as we analyze a film. In this practical sense, then, the main benefit of affect theory is that it impels us to take feelings seriously and to consider what cultural or ideological work they perform.

My argument plays out in two parts, followed by a few concluding remarks: the first part combines political economy and affect theory to analyze the affective consequences of neoliberalism. Here, I consider recent research in the anthropology of money and build on the thought of the young Karl Marx, Friedrich Nietzsche, and Jacques Lacan.[5] This discussion will help me to connect financial and affective economies—two areas of our lives that function on the basis of constant circulation, the movement of money and feelings. Affect theory claims that it rethinks the subject in a more materialist fashion, situating human agency in feelings and their physical embodiment rather than in an abstract cogito. Despite this ambition, contemporary affect theory usually fails to engage with the economy, which constitutes perhaps the most dominant aspect of our lives under neoliberalism.[6] Contemporary affect theory also has a tendency to look at affect in isolation from cognition and human action. While this focus counteracts a long tradition of ignoring feelings in favor of the cogito, it undermines the materialist recovery intended by affect theorists. My emphasis on affective and material *economies*, as well as the actions that evolve from them, is meant as a rejoinder to this tendency and a way of enhancing our understanding of the links between our economic and emotional lives under contemporary neoliberalism.

The second part looks at the affective tone of film noir and two films by Danish-American director Winding Refn: *Drive* (2011), adapted from James Sallis's eponymous novel, and *Only God Forgives* (2013), a sequel of sorts to *Drive*.[7] Both films exemplify the affective logic of debt, but they also tell us about the affective consequences and specificity of debt regimes. Our structural indebtedness demands a constant surplus of *jouissance*, or enjoyment, that underpins labor and consumption, yet simultaneously undermines it by confronting us with the fact that our enjoyment has always already been spent elsewhere. This impossible game of catch interrupts the transformation of desire, which orients humans toward future enjoyment, into positive emotional attachments, leaving us instead with the short-lived and destructive affects of anger and resentment, anxiety and fear. In analyzing these two films I also engage critically with Gilles Deleuze's concept of the affection-image to suggest that we need to look beyond an emphasis on image content and montage in our understanding of aesthetic tone and incorporate affect theory into the filmic analysis of color, sound, and time. Finally, I claim that we may fruitfully understand films associated with the subgenre of film noir as characterized by a logic of affective escalation.

Freudian psychoanalysis defines affect as the qualitative expression of the ebb and flow of human energy or drive.[8] The term *drive* lends depth-psychological meaning to the title of Refn's film, in which the protagonist embodies the autoreferentiality and destructiveness of the (death) drive.[9] Affects precede their integration into our identity, where they may become more stable emotions such as empathy or love.[10] Affects can also move between people—for instance, when we enter a room full of people dancing, or chance upon a couple having an argument, and feel the elation or tension that create the emotional atmosphere of these situations.

Money Is Debt, Debt Is a Feeling

Drive begins with two promises of a better future. The anonymous protagonist, who makes a living as a mechanic as well as a stunt and getaway driver in Los Angeles, falls in love with his neighbor Irene. Despite his traditional blue-collar profession, driver lives a typically precarious neoliberal life: he has to share his income from occasional gigs as a stuntman with his boss Shannon, who acts as a middleman and jokes about exploiting him. Meanwhile, Shannon's stunt car business barely pays enough for him to survive, and he dreams of finding a more profitable outlet for the driver's talents in racing. Soon enough, Irene's husband returns from prison and gangsters to whom he owes protection money threaten his family. When Shannon turns to mobster Bernie Rose for a favor, he too is reminded of old debts. Shannon's heavy limp, we learn, is the consequence of an unpaid loan.

Yet, what is debt?[11] We don't need to look far for an answer. Most of us carry around representations of debt, usually in the form of credit cards or cash. Crucially, credit and debt refer to the same interaction. If someone loans me a dollar on credit, I am in debt to them. A closer look at a dollar bill reveals it to be a representation of debt: "This note is legal tender for all debts, public and private." Money thus quantifies debts at specific values: 1, 5, 10, 20, or 100 dollars. On the bill's reverse side, we find the words "In God We Trust" above an image of the US Treasury. When we use money, we trust in a symbolic authority that guarantees its value. All of this is pretty banal. Curiously, the understanding that money constitutes a form of debt runs counter to mainstream economics. According to David Graeber, most economics textbooks repeat an old myth that harks back to Aristotle and Adam Smith's *The Wealth of Nations*. There, money is said to evolve from barter and is reduced to its function as a medium of exchange. Yet, historical evidence shows that money first appeared to account for debts, long before coins and bills ever existed. In other words: money is debt. Graeber explains the insistence on the "fantasy world of barter" with economists' deep-rooted belief in the division of state and so-called free market.[12] The myth of barter also hides the unequal obligations of debt behind a smoke screen of equal exchange. In so doing, economists replace debt's specific temporality, in which the future becomes bound to the past, with a homogenous present emptied of historical wrong.

In *Drive*, things start to go wrong when the anonymous driver and Irene's husband, Standard, rob a pawnshop.[13] They've agreed to this heist because Standard owes protection money from his time in prison. The heist ends with Standard's death, and the driver is left with a million dollars in cash. As the film emphasizes in its shots of the pawn shop, the million dollars represent yet another loan (fig. 1). Instead of helping to pay a debt, the protagonist has incurred another. The remainder of *Drive* consists of his attempts to return the money to the mob. As the driver learns, even the refusal of credit is impossible in an era of cheap money, in which risky loans can be sold and re-sold for profit, and capital is increasingly desperate for profitable investment opportunities. Debt thus breeds ever more debt. This interest or surplus is never purely financial but brings with it an excess of violence, as one murder leads to the next. The protagonist

Figure 1. The pawn shop in *Drive* as augur of debt.

thus initiates a movement over which he has little control but which depends on his participation for the cycle of violence to continue.

In its imagination of the shadow economy, *Drive* sides with an intellectual tradition that locates the origins of capitalism not in the marketplace but in debt. In recent years, sociology and anthropology have drawn on evidence that demonstrates that market economies arise from early city-states rather than functioning independently of state power.[14] In his notes on James Mill's *Elements of Political Economy*, the young Marx describes the subjective logic of debt.[15] Before providing a loan, the creditor makes projections about the future based on the debtor's past behavior. Social interactions form the basis of financial measurement. Therefore, debt shapes human individuality all the way into the "human flesh and human hearts."[16] The passage establishes a remarkable link between debt and the human body, on the one hand, and the body's physical and affective dimensions, on the other. We find similar language in Nietzsche's *On the Genealogy of Morality*. Nietzsche's polemic places the relationship between creditor and debtor at its center. Earlier societies, he claims, drew up detailed lists that made the amount of outstanding debt equivalent to "individual limbs and parts of [the debtor's] body."[17] After emphasizing the threat of retribution that underlies the creditor-debtor relationship, Nietzsche introduces a specific affect of debt: the creditor's "pleasure of having the right to exercise power over the powerless."[18]

Nietzsche's mythical fantasy of sadistic bankers was clearly intended to shock his readers. Winding Refn's *Only God Forgives* imagines a similar scene. Set in Bangkok, *Only God Forgives* concerns the global flow of illicit drugs—one of capital's most profitable investments and, not incidentally, one of society's central access points to pleasure. In the film Gosling plays

Julian, the expat owner of a Thai boxing club and drug trafficker who is haunted by fantasies of his own mutilation. It is only later in the film that we connect his visions of a machete to a rogue cop who takes justice into his own hands and cuts off the arms of his victims, ultimately realizing Julian's fears.[19] Julian's daydreams are at once nightmarish and highly eroticized: the first scene of this kind takes place during a slightly sadomasochistic encounter with a Thai sex worker. Winding Refn imagines pleasure as a liminal affect on the threshold of joy and pain; what Lacan calls *jouissance*. In *The Other Side of Psychoanalysis*, Lacan dissects the logic of contemporary capitalism in its affective dimensions. Nietzsche and Marx had already shown how debt functions as a form of power and even violence that shapes human bodies and feelings. Nietzsche further imagined the creditor's sadistic enjoyment. In *Only God Forgives*, the pain and pleasure of violence and sexuality move between Julian and the rogue police officer, Chang. Scenes that show Chang mutilate or murder his victims are contrasted with Julian's fantasies of the same scenario. What sets this this affective economy in motion?

For Lacan, human beings are distinguished by the fact that our lives lack a solid foundation. The institutions we use to build communities are not given by our biology but are acquired. This ultimate groundlessness leads to a search for fulfillment—a striving for enjoyment that fuels desire and a regime of production and consumption that converts affect into profit. Lacan writes: "Something changed . . . at a certain point in history . . . surplus *jouissance* becomes calculable, could be counted, totalized. This is where what is called the accumulation of capital begins."[20] Humanity's existential lack has long been understood as a primordial debt: we forever aim to pay back in labor, in desire, in pleasure, what can never be returned to us. Lacan adds to the repertoire of feelings that we experience in relation to debt: fear and pain, anxiety and pleasure become elements of a complex affective logic. His writings are also instructive because they understand affect as part of a larger cognitive-emotional system, countering what I described as its atomistic conception in contemporary affect theory.

Lacan's intervention concerns the specificity of feelings under contemporary capitalism. He pinpoints the ways in which affective and economic organization become linked by a process of financial calculation within a totality of economic relations. Lacan phrases this process in terms of a quantitative measurement of feeling (see previous quote). Capitalism's need to produce a financial surplus depends not only on the means of production, nor simply on an increasing amount of affective labor; rather,

Lacan asserts that capital accumulation may be thought of as a specific conversion of feeling, the production of a surplus of enjoyment that can be transformed into profit. What allows him to perceive this link between affect and profit is his understanding of the psyche as a social economy rather than an interiorized wellspring of emotion. Lacan is highly specific in his description of the affective components of capital accumulation: *jouissance*, a liminal pleasure, is neither equal to desire nor can it be described as a specific emotion. As the aim of desire, *jouissance* underlies productive labor and drives consumption, whose promise lies precisely in the enjoyment of commodities. *Jouissance* also sustains the manifold emotional attachments that allow humans to maintain social ties, a logic that is interrupted by the diversion of enjoyment toward capital accumulation. We see this latter process at work in the destructive consequences of debt portrayed in *Drive* and *Only God Forgives*, an escalation of physical violence and negative affects such as fear and anger, as well as the combination of violent action and cognitive-emotional assemblages that we know as revenge and paranoia.

Winding Refn's two films show how debt and credit act as economic incitements for the production of negative feelings. While credit may also be associated with positive affects such as elation and enthusiasm, by and large money as debt leads to negative expressions of psychic energy, such as fear, anger, anxiety, and resentment. The affective logic of debt may therefore be described in terms of its volatility and temporality. The first stems from the destabilizing effects these feelings tend to have. These are the consequence of debt's excessive demands, which force the debtor to provide interest in order to facilitate the production of surplus capital. Specific modes of violence accompany this form of power, from house foreclosures to the incarceration of debtors and a lack of food or health care.[21]

Debt's temporality, in turn, remains tied to the past even in its present and future dimensions. As McClanahan writes, debt functions as a "temporal fix" that "allows capital to treat an anticipated realization of value as if it has already happened."[22] In a sense, then, we can speak of a temporal destabilization that follows from the affective volatility of debt. The need to pay one's dues, which ties the present to the past, also impedes the formation of desire. Structurally, desire is characterized by an orientation toward the future. Lie's description of Refn's cinema as dominated by the logic of the death drive rather than desire can be seen as a consequence of the logic of debt, with its preponderance of negative affect and its emptying out of a horizon of possibility.[23]

Lacan's theoretical link between affective and financial economies is in need of further specification in an era of structural indebtedness. While his intervention came at a time of rising debt and and academic interest in the topic, his comments remained brief and allusive. In particular, Lacan's emphasis on the role of *jouissance* needs to be supplemented by a description of the specific affects that accompany the *jouissance* of the indebted. The dominance of the death drive over desire that Lie notes also speaks of a breakdown of social ties, a topic that Lacan paid much attention to in the final phase of his writings and which finds filmic expression in *Drive* and *Only God Forgives*.[24]

Affective Remainders

So far in this essay, I've used film as one critical discourse among others to make the argument that debt is not a purely financial phenomenon but has affective components that are central to its continued functioning. In this section, I turn toward a more detailed discussion of film noir, and Winding Refn's *Drive* and *Only God Forgives*. This analysis also necessitates a different approach to cinema: rather than being illustrative of certain conceptions of debt, I look at the role that specific negative affects play in noir and analyze how cinema as a cultural product participates in wider affective economies.

Both *Drive* and *Only God Forgives* are not just genre movies. Born in Denmark and raised and trained in the United States, Winding Refn's films combine elements of European arthouse and classical Hollywood cinema: they play tricks with continuity editing and indulge in what Kristin Thompson calls "stylistic excess": a counter-narrative "style for its own sake."[25] As a consequence, these films have been at least as successful with critics as with cinemagoers: *Drive* and *Only God Forgives* screened in the main competition at Cannes, and Refn won the award for best director for *Drive*. This critical recognition and their director's avant-garde leanings notwithstanding, it would be problematic to read the two films as subversive or resistant to neoliberal capital. Cinema depends on worldwide networks of funding, production, and distribution and is thus intimately tied to the globalized circuits of neoliberalism. In two essays on what she calls "default cinema," Rosalind Galt connects examples of global art cinema to the economic crises that periodically afflict capitalism and reads them as thwarting "the narratives of value that capitalist film culture demands."[26] Both *Drive* and *Only God Forgives* evince some of the same characteristics that Galt identifies as subversive: fantasies of escape from everyday existence, at times a willful refusal to signify, and, as a consequence, the destabilization of filmic diegesis.[27] Yet, in Winding Refn's films, these features are integrated into the framework of genre cinema and, in particular, the noir thriller: an aestheticization of extreme violence, the logic of revenge, and the performance of heteronormativity.

When we read movies as examples of film noir, several options present themselves. We can emphasize the uses of lighting or focus on cinematographic techniques that include extreme low or slanted angles. We can highlight specific plots or characters. In a more thematic vein, we might want to talk about social antagonism, gender, or class. Or we can note typical locales, temporalities, and forms of movement such as anonymous cityscapes, the flashback, and the importance of automobility for noir. I will comment on some of these aspects but will focus on understanding noir as a dramatization of *negative* affect.[28]

Noir has long been associated with feelings such as hate and suspicion, anger and guilt, resentment and betrayal. Affect theory therefore seems an appropriate framework for studying noir. Film noir's negative affects ask us to participate in feelings of suspicion and fear, anger and pain. Yet, these movies do so by first arousing our desire—drawing on the visual and auditory enjoyment we gain from aesthetic objects and sexualized bodies. In this sense, cinema too transforms affect into profit. The economy of cinema and the preponderance of negative feelings in film noir demand that we rethink the affective constitution of the present. Affect's function as a link between perception and action, in other words its constitution as the qualitative expression of the drives, often leads to an overemphasis on affect as potential. In part, this reductive understanding can be retraced to the impact of Deleuze's writings on contemporary affect theory. Noir can function as a crucial corrective. When Lauren Berlant sees a "cruel optimism" at work in neoliberal Western society, her theoretical framework leads her to posit an aspirational attachment to fantasy as a dominant structure of feeling. Contemporary noir films, however, are less concerned with a continued investment in desire than with a situation in which aspiration has been left behind, to be replaced with its affective remainders, from anger to resentment. Rather than performing attachment to a fragile sociality, noir imagines a deepening asociality.

One striking symptom of this asociality—the breakdown of internalized authority that institutes desire and much else—is the weakness of detection in *Drive*. Winding Refn has a point when he reduces the authorities to gangsters. Yet in their absence, the detective function morphs into vigilantism, an argument that the Western made a long time ago. If classical detective fiction aimed its totalizing energy at the constitution of society out of a cast of individuals, a process for which the crime provided narrative motivation, *Drive* turns this formula on its head.[29] Crime needs little to no detection because its presence makes itself known to the film's characters. The only way to escape from crime, after the identification of the criminal, then becomes the destruction of the social itself, the two terms *crime* and *society* becoming near synonymous in the process.

In my introduction, I spoke of affective tone, and the way in which cinema communicates feelings. In *Cinema 1: The Movement-Image*, Deleuze distinguishes three kinds of movement images: the perception image, the action image, and the *affection* image.[30] Deleuze explicitly conceives of the affection image (or *affect* image) as moving between subject and object: it is the "coincidence of the subject and the object in a pure quality" that characterizes the affective image.[31] Deleuze then identifies two types of affect image: the first is the close-up of a face or an entity that expresses emotion—the gleaming edge of a knife, for instance. The second he calls "any-space-whatever": a space filled with shadows or characterized by poetic abstraction.[32]

Both of these affect images feature in *Drive* and *Only God Forgives*. Refn has an intense liking for lyrical dissolves that produce the "any-place-whatever" that Deleuze refers to and expressive close-ups are, of course, a fundamental building block of cinema.[33] *Drive* and *Only God Forgives* are remarkable for the close-ups of their respective protagonists. At first viewing, both the anonymous driver and Julian appear almost expressionless: the blankness that Gosling lends to both characters has led critics to pronounce them as being without feeling altogether, or even as constituting the endpoint of Jameson's famous argument about the "waning of affect."[34] Affect theory has rightly taken umbrage with Jameson's thesis. If anything, the argument might have been more convincing had it been phrased as a waning of emotion.[35] A closer look at Gosling's performance reveals his character's affections for Irene. It allows us to perceive his facial expressions as moving between tension and the *jouissance* that accompanies his later acts of violence: an economic acting style, whose dramatic reduction pays attention to the shifting qualities that give meaning to libidinal energy. Arguably, though, Deleuze's account of cinematic affect remains limited by its focus on image content and composition. Color palette and lighting, soundscape, and continuity editing also contribute to the affective *tone* of Winding Refn's noir.

In an interview, cinematographer Newton Thomas Sigel mentions that the first film he watched with Winding Refn at the start of their collaboration on *Drive* was Kenneth Anger's *Scorpio Rising*. According to Sigel, Refn wanted to recapture the "sensual, sexual nature" of this 1963 experimental short film that combined an exploration of biker subculture and homosexuality with a soundtrack composed of dreamy pop songs.[36] On a narrative level, *Drive* replaces the homosexual desire of *Scorpio Rising* with heteronormative romance. But in addition to their use of pop music, the two films also share a fetishization of the male body and the gleaming metal of motorcycles and cars. Like the main character in *Scorpio Rising*, Refn's protagonist works in a garage when he isn't driving. The camera repeatedly pictures Gosling as he repairs car parts in a grimy T-shirt that emphasizes his muscular arms or, like Anger, cuts to individual elements of this interior space: disassembled mufflers and headlights that gleam brightly as they reflect the light. In the same interview, Sigel also mentions the color palettes of Kodachrome and Ektachrome film, the latter of which was used for *Scorpio Rising*, as an influence on his cinematography. Both film stocks are known for their high contrast and a rich, vibrant palette. Although it was shot on digital video with an Arri Alexa camera, *Drive* consciously aims to reproduce these visual qualities, which in turn imbue the film with a sensual charge. This affective tone gains a menacing edge in both films with the inclusion of the scorpion that lends *Scorpio Rising* its title and foreshadows the violent plot of *Drive*. The image of the scorpion that appears in different incarnations in the earlier film seems to have served as a direct inspiration for *Drive*. Throughout the movie, Gosling wears a jacket whose back features a remarkably similar stitched version.

More so than its close-ups or dissolves, *Drive*'s color palette and lighting sets the film's aesthetic tone. In contrast to individual close-ups that crystallize affect in isolated moments, a film's color palette defines its affective bearing in its entirety, suffusing a movie's atmosphere from the first to the last shot. Similarly, the fetishization of muscle and metal in *Drive* expresses the sexualized pleasure of looking, in a movie that begins and ends with Gosling. Bodily enjoyment, with its potential for pain and pleasure, powers the affective economy of debt and finds its continuation in these two films.

As several film theorists—from Carl Theodor Dreyer to Sergei Eisenstein and Deleuze—have noted, the defining quality of color in cinema is that it is constantly in flux.[37] In this discussion, I understand affect in similar fashion. The same may finally be said about sound. There are still images, but there is no still sound. *Drive*'s soundscape is noteworthy for being highly subjective—a quality that sound designer Lou Bender describes as motivated by the search for the film's "emotional truth": at times, the film almost completely excludes off-camera sounds to create a deliberately thin soundtrack.[38] At other points, the sound becomes intensely visceral: in an extremely violent scene, the driver and his accomplice Blanche (Christina Hendricks) hide in a motel room after the heist which led to Standard's murder. As soon as the driver learns that Blanche has revealed their location, the two are ambushed: over the next half minute or so, slow motion combines with background noise and the sound of the protagonist's breathing to give the impression that we are listening from *within* his body.

This aspect is emphasized even more clearly during a scene set in an elevator. The protagonist returns to Irene to explain the failed heist. On their way downstairs, they join a man who turns out to be a killer sent by the mob. What makes this episode remarkable is less the melodramatic kiss that precedes the violence but the scene's sonic intensity: the protagonist's heavy breathing and the translation of physical touch into sound as the driver smashes the head of his opponent, continuing long after the latter is left lying unconscious on the elevator floor. This sonic excess expresses a similarly excessive *jouissance* on the part of the protagonist and leaves Irene aghast, severing any bond of affection that remained between them after her husband's death. Thus, the soundscape's corporeal reality is at once highly affective: its evocation of fear and panic, violence and *jouissance* complements the affective tone communicated by *Drive*'s images. In contrast to Deleuze's taxonomy of the cinematic image, which divides action from feeling, action and affect combine in this scene to produce a highly charged cinematic experience.

Earlier I briefly discussed the temporality of debt. Chronic debt creates a future that constitutes itself as *more* of the *same* by forcing workers to produce labor and enjoyment that has already been absorbed into the economy. Debt produces a sense of stasis or repetition whose horizon is not the future but the future anterior, a time that has already been clocked. Debt restricts what may become but also demands a surplus, an increase in capital based on an increase in enjoyment. This cyclical temporality structures *Only God Forgives* from its very beginning. The opening shot depicts the sword that Julian will imagine as the instrument of his mutilation, a fear that comes true by the end of the film. In similar fashion, *Drive*'s settings evoke the 1950s, while the driver's car references the 1970s, and the font of the opening credits the 1980s: what we might call pastiche, or nostalgia film, emphasizes the absence of historical change.

This indistinction of past, present, and future also affects *Drive*'s diegesis: midway through the film, the driver has dinner with Irene and Standard. After a close-up of Gosling's face, the sequence shifts to him stealing a car, followed by a meeting with the gangsters to whom Standard owes money. What first appears to be a flashback turns out to be a flash forward—neither the car theft nor the meeting with the gangsters has happened at this point. As the viewer realizes later, the meeting with the gangsters also happens *before* not after the car theft. Winding Refn undermines the film's chronology not once but twice. This manipulation of continuity editing suggests that the past and future have become nearly indistinguishable but also that the film takes place as a sort of surplus: rather than leading to meaningful change, or a progression beyond the predicament in which they find themselves, the characters' feelings and actions appear as excess, an addition to a self-same present that comes at the price of their own destruction.

Given Deleuze's focus on the affect-image in *Cinema 1*, it seems surprising how little he has to say about the relationship between feeling and the time image in *Cinema 2*. In his preface to the English edition, Deleuze links the advent of the time image since 1945 to a postwar environment dominated by "any-spaces-whatever." These indeterminate landscapes had already constituted the affect-image in its spread beyond the single frame.[39] Yet, the collapse of the "sensory-motor schema," which allows for the progression from perception to affect and action and gives rise to a direct presentation of time's passing, occasions little reflection on the constitution of cinematic affect.[40] *Drive*, with its stark contrast between the ticking clock of the heist, lyrical dissolves, and indicators of temporal stasis may be said to embed its time images within an overall framework of the action image that constitutes part of its identification with the thriller genre.

This uneasy structure comes undone in *Only God Forgives*—one possible reason for its lesser success with audiences and critics.[41] Unlike the driver, Julian's role is primarily that of a seer: a character who becomes "prey to visual and sound situations."[42] Julian gives rise to hallucinations that remain indiscernible, scenes that are no longer clearly connected to the revenge narrative whose reluctant agent he becomes. The film's fragmentary quality can also be understood as its distance from the conventions of film noir. Among other things, this unmooring is indicated by the absence of the car from *Only God Forgives*, whose centrality to noir lies in mapping its locales within the modern city. In contrast, Julian either walks or appears in seemingly unconnected parts of greater Bangkok, only to meet his fate not in a parking lot, as the driver did, but in the countryside (fig. 2).

Figure 2. Julian meets his fate in *Only God Forgives*.

Conclusion: Who Forgives?

In both films, the attempts to repay a debt fail to stem the flow of violence. *Drive* and *Only God Forgives* descend into a series of murders. In a progression typical of film noir, the negative affects that motivate the characters lead to a narrative escalation: a cycle of betrayal, suspicion, anger, or hate spirals into ever more violent action and, in the process, strain the coherence of the plot.[43] *Drive* ends with the protagonist leaving the money behind in a parking lot and driving off—but only after he and Bernie Rose have stabbed each other, possibly to death. The driver's debt has been repaid, but at the cost of the complete breakdown of any social bond: the destruction of Irene and the driver's relationship and the death of most of the characters. In addition to its other characteristics, noir could thus be understood as an affective disposition or logic. Noir inflects narrative formula such as the melodrama and detective fiction and leads to a cycle of violence that destroys the social bond that connected its characters.[44]

The title of *Only God Forgives* both imagines moving beyond debt and limits debt forgiveness to a mythical power beyond human agency. Interestingly, the protagonists of both movies stop being the productive subjects that capitalism demands: the driver never drives his race car, and Julian neglects the family drug business. *Only God Forgives* imagines another payment for debt in the form of the sacrifice. Throughout the film, Julian baulks at his mother's thirst for revenge after his brother is killed following his own murder of a sex worker. During Julian's second meeting with

Chang, he challenges the much older and smaller man to a fight. In the end, Julian lands not a single punch: either because he is outclassed by the older man's skill or because he willingly offers up his own body as payment for his family's actions. Such physical violence seemingly returns us to Nietzsche's myth of a bodily equivalent for debt, in which flesh and limbs are measured against money owed. Yet, Julian's blood and bruises do not stem the flow of violence in *Only God Forgives*. The film's cyclical structure already indicated how hopeless Julian's attempt is: he envisions his own mutilation at the hands of Change long before he meets him, and the dream-like finale in which Julian willingly offers up his hands to Chang returns us to the opening shot. As in *Drive*, this ending remains ambiguous and may belong to the protagonist's fantasy space, may indicate his death and mutilation, or further payment and continuation of the debt economy. As McClanahan shows in *Dead Pledges*, the financialization of credit risk—in which, often unpayable, loans are sold and re-sold—means that keeping people in debt frequently represents a more profitable business venture than full repayment.[45] Sacrifice thus seems to have lost its ability to assuage the gods, its symbolic power subverted by the logic of equivalence. The failure of Refn's protagonists to extract themselves from the logic of debt indicates the challenges facing an ethics of refusal: labor or debt strikes demand collective, not individual, action and risk violence. Debt cancellation, in turn, only offers temporary relief if it does not lead to alternative practices of finance and trade. Winding Refn's films ultimately can't provide the complex social answers we need in order to achieve debt forgiveness.

The outlines of an answer may, however, be found in Graeber's book on *Debt*, which acknowledge debt's *affective* components: as he explains, precapitalist currencies were not used for precise quantification but rearranged strained relations between people or communities. After a war or other conflict, one group would make symbolic repayments to defuse violence—gifts that were unlike money but had symbolic value and served as a form of recognition.[46] Thus, we might imagine loans of art works between nations, or individuals committing to community service to repay loans. These alternatives move beyond debt by substituting recognition for precise repayment and imagine a future horizon for a shared society.

NOTES

1. Earlier versions of this essay were presented at the ACLA annual meeting in New York in 2014 and as part of the Cinema Studies Colloquium at

the University of Pennsylvania in February 2018. My thanks go to Emmanuel Bouju, Tim Corrigan, and the wonderful respondents I was lucky to have on both occasions.

2. That's not to say that debt is necessarily unethical. Public debt may be highly beneficial for societies if it is invested in the common good to ensure the conditions for repayment via future innovation. However, the rise in private debt over the past forty years mostly has been the consequence of stagnating or falling incomes and leads to economic crisis when these debts can't be serviced any longer. See, for example, Richard Duncan, "Interview: A New Global Depression?," *New Left Review* 77 (September–October 2012): 5–33.

3. My general argument is inspired by David Graeber, *Debt: The First 5,000 Years* (Brooklyn and London: Melville House, 2012); and Maurizio Lazzarato, *The Making of the Indebted Man: An Essay on the Neoliberal Condition*, trans. Joshua David Jordan (Los Angeles: Semiotext(e), 2012).

4. Sianne Ngai, *Ugly Feelings* (Cambridge, MA: Harvard University Press, 2005), 28–29.

5. Needless to say, those authors do not constitute an exhaustive overview of theories of debt. As Maurizio Lazzarato notes, the late 1960s and early 1970s saw a flourishing in theories of debt. In addition to Lacan, Michel Foucault and Gilles Deleuze also grappled with debt's role in Western economies. See Lazzarato, *Making of the Indebted Man*, 79–83. For a wider survey of recent studies on the topic, see Annie McClanahan, introduction to *Dead Pledges: Debt, Crisis, and Twenty-First Century Culture* (Stanford, CA: Stanford University Press, 2017), 1–18.

6. See, for example, Sara Ahmed, "Affective Economies" *Social Text* 79, No. 2 (Summer 2004): 117–139. Ahmed's article is limited to the circulation of feelings within the human psyche. See also, Lauren Berlant, *Cruel Optimism* (Durham, NC: Duke University Press, 2011); and Sianne Ngai, *Ugly Feelings* (Cambridge, MA: Harvard University Press, 2005).

7. James Sallis, *Drive* (Harpenden: No Exit, 2012). A detailed comparison of the two is beyond the scope of this essay. However, Winding Refn's film almost completely erases the explicit references to the novel's global migratory flows. Where, in the novel, Irene is a migrant whose son is sent back to Mexico after her death, her character is played by the Anglo-American actress Carey Mulligan in the movie adaptation.

8. See the entry on affect in: Jean Laplanche and Jean-Bertrand Pontalis, *The Language of Psycho-Analysis*, trans. Donald Nicholson-Smith (London: Karnac 1989), 13–14.

9. Sugi Lie follows this connotation to its logical conclusion and reads the film as situated within a contemporary society that is dominated by a

regime of the drive rather than desire. See Sugi Lie, "From *Shame* to *Drive*: The Waning of Affect; or, The Rising of the Drive Image in Contemporary Hollywood Cinema," *Social Text* 34, no. 2 (2016): 45–70.

10. Throughout this essay, I use the terms *affect* and *feeling* as near synonyms.

11. The following paragraph draws heavily on Graeber, *Debt*, 24–25.

12. Graeber, 23.

13. See *Drive*, directed by Nicolas Winding Refn (USA, 2011; Los Angeles: Sony, 2012), DVD.

14. Graeber, *Debt*, 50.

15. Karl Marx, "Excerpts from James Mill's *Elements of Political Economy*," in *Early Writings*, trans. Rodney Livingstone and Gregor Benton (London: Penguin, 1992), 259–278. Lazzarato makes generous use of this key text.

16. Marx, 264.

17. Friedrich Nietzsche, *On the Genealogy of Morality*, ed. Keith Ansell-Pearson, trans. Carol Diethe (Cambridge: Cambridge University Press, 2007), 41.

18. Nietzsche, 41.

19. *Only God Forgives*, directed by Nicolas Winding Refn (USA, 2013; Los Angeles: Radius, 2013), DVD. Refn's most recent movie at the time of writing, the psychological horror thriller *Neon Demon* (2016), continues his examination of affect, the economy and the physical flesh of the body as phantasmatic guarantee of value. For a Lacanian conception of the flesh and its relationship to social structure, see Eric L. Santner, *The Royal Remains: The People's Two Bodies and the Endgames of Sovereignty* (Chicago: University of Chicago Press 2011).

20. Jacques Lacan, *The Other Side of Psychoanalysis: The Seminar of Jacques Lacan*, Book XVII, trans. Russell Grigg (New York: W. W. Norton. 2007), 177.

21. Annie McClanahan's *Dead Pledges* criticizes the focus on the affective and personal dimension of debt over its structural violence. See McClanahan, *Dead Pledges*, 57. As I argue in this essay, both violence and affect are equally central to the logic of debt and can only be divided at the risk of misunderstanding its functioning under capitalism.

22. McClanahan, 13.

23. Lie, "From *Shame* to *Drive*."

24. See Jacques Lacan, *Le Séminaire de Jacques Lacan*, Livre XXIII: *Le Sinthome, 1975–1976*, ed. Jacques-Alain Miller (Paris: Seuil, 2005).

25. See Anna Backmann Rogers and Miklós Kiss, "A Real Human Being and a Real Hero: Stylistic Excess, Dead Time and Intensified Continuity in Nicolas Winding Refn's *Drive*," *New Cinemas: Journal of Contemporary Film*

12, nos. 1–2 (2014): 43–56; and Kristin Thompson, "The Concept of Cinematic Excess," *Cine-Tracts* 1, no. 2 (1977): 54–65.

26. Rosalind Galt, "Claire Denis and the World Cinema of Refusal" *SubStance* 43, no. 1 (2014): 105. See also Rosalind Galt, "Default Cinema: Queering Economic Crisis in Argentina and Beyond," *Screen* 54 (Spring 2013): 62–81. I'm grateful to Karen Redrobe for these references.

27. Galt, "World Cinema of Refusal," 106–107.

28. See also Christopher Breu and Elizabeth Hatmaker's introduction to this volume.

29. Joan Copjec, "The Phenomenal Nonphenomenal: Private Space in Film Noir," in *Shades of Noir: A Reader*, ed. Joan Copjec (London: Verso, 1993), 175.

30. Gilles Deleuze, *Cinema 1: The Movement-Image*, trans. Hugh Tomlinson and Barbara Habberjam (Minneapolis: University of Minnesota Press, 1986).

31. Deleuze, 65.

32. Deleuze, 109–112.

33. Deleuze, 107.

34. Caetlin Benson-Allett, "Generic Imperative," *Film Quarterly* 65, no. 3 (Spring 2012): 12; Lie, "From *Shame* to *Drive*," 46; and Fredric Jameson, "Postmodernism, or The Cultural Logic of Late Capitalism," *New Left Review*, no. 146 (1984): 61.

35. Jameson's argument was itself the unfortunate result of a simplistic understanding of Lacan's concept of psychosis, which mistook a different form of subjectivity for its fragmentation. See my *Madness in Cold War America* (New York: Routledge, 2016), 157–161.

36. John D. Witmer, "Road Warriors: Newton Thomas Sigel, ASC, and director Nicolas Winding Refn Craft a Violent Fairytale on the Streets of Los Angeles," *American Cinematographer*, October 2011, accessed January 25, 2018, https://theasc.com/ac_magazine/October2011/Drive/page1.html; and Kenneth Anger, "Scorpio Rising," in *The Films of Kenneth Anger*, vol. 2 (San Francisco: Fantoma, 2007), DVD.

37. See Wendy Everett, "Mapping Colour: An Introduction to the Theories and Practices of Colour," in *Questions of Colour in Cinema: From Paintbrush to Pixel* (London: Peter Lang, 2012), 7–38.

38. Anon., "The Sound of *Drive*: Soundelux Creates 'Emotional Truth' for Nicolas Winding Refn's Cerebral Action Film," *Marketing Weekly News*, October 15, 2011, 388.

39. Gilles Deleuze, *Cinema 2: The Time-Image*, trans. Hugh Tomlinson and Robert Galeta (Minneapolis: University of Minnesota Press, 2010), xi.

40. Deleuze, xi.

41. *Only God Forgives* failed to win a prize in the 2013 Cannes competition and was also less successful at the box office.

42. Deleuze, *Cinema 2*, 55.

43. In her now classic essay, Joan Copjec remarked upon a "progressive instability" in noir "that accounts not only for the regularity of the final, mutually destructive encounter between hero and femme fatale, but for the escalation of the violence in the *film noir* cycle as a whole" ("Phenomenal Nonphenomenal," 194).

44. For noir as an inflection of other genres rather than a genre in its own right, see Breu and Hatmaker's introduction in this volume.

45. McClanahan, *Dead Pledges*, 182.

46. Graeber, *Debt*, 60.

CHAPTER 11

Capitalism as Affective Atmosphere: The Noir Worlds of Massimo Carlotto

Andrew Pepper

This essay on the noir worlds of the Italian novelist Massimo Carlotto has two related starting points. First there is Carlotto's geographical universe and his Italian culture, notably the Veneto or the Nordest (which is also the title of one of his novels). Noir, in Carlotto's capable hands, owes a significant debt to its US forbearers (the English translation of *Nordest*, Carlotto's 2009 novel, is *Poisonville*, a direct reference to the town in Hammett's 1929 novel *Red Harvest*). But it is also implicated in a set of transnational networks extending out from the Veneto and Italy to the world. Following the current move to consider the global spread of noir beyond its foundational spatiotemporal moorings,[1] this essay posits Carlotto as one of the key practitioners of neoliberal or capitalist noir[2]—but without arguing for neoliberalism or capitalism in its neoliberal phase as totalizing systems that structure and determine all modes of existence and potentialities of life. The second related jumping-off point is more complicated and requires careful unpacking but for the purposes of summary, it can be explained through a simple paradox of contemporary existence: how life, on the one hand, necessarily exceeds attempts to order and control it and how, on the other, life becomes the target for increasingly far-reaching techniques of power.

The noir universe can in part be explained by or subsumed into the first element of this paradox: life in a Carlotto novel is typically violent, chaotic, unpredictable and indeterminate. People kill and are killed because Carlotto's universe is a violent, competitive one, but often his characters have no direct insight into their actions and motivations. In this sense, as this book as a whole and my essay want to demonstrate, there is a clear and compelling link between noir—however it is defined—and affect which "refers generally to bodily capacities to affect and be affected" and is typically understood as an autonomic or human bodily response to one's environment "in excess of conscious states of perception."[3] As such affect is both pre-conscious and pre-individual, a state where intentionality or causality is harder to map. As Patricia Ticineto Clough puts it, without exactly clarifying matters: "it refers to indeterminacy, metastability, where the unstable pre-individual forces . . . are neither in a linear nor deterministic relationship to the individuated molar body which these pre-individual forces nonetheless constitute."[4] If this sounds a lot like Carlotto's noir universe, defined by unpredictability and indeterminacy, and where this generalized sense of unpredictability and indeterminacy acts not on individuals but on worlds (what we might call "affective atmospheres"), this still requires us to think about the knotty problem of causality or intentionality. By this, I am referring not simply to the issue of whether or how far noir fiction disrupts the conventional linearity of other forms of crime fiction or indeed whether noir characters understand their own acts as intentional but rather the larger question of how we might conceive of the relationship between affect as nonconscious and nonsignifying and capitalism as an essentially determining and deterministic system; that is, the *affective atmosphere* of capitalism.

One of the shortcomings of my own account of Carlotto's work in *Unwilling Executioner: Crime Fiction and the State* (2016) is its willingness to use an unproblematized Marxian frame to account for the conjoined nature of the legal and illegal worlds and for the effects of a capitalist mode of production on the actions and moral capacities of Carlotto's characters.[5] Whether intended or not, the result is, in effect, a recalibrated ideological critique whereby Carlotto's novels—notably *Arrividerci amore, ciao* (2000), translated from the Italian by Lawrence Venuti as *The Goodbye Kiss* (2006)—critically interrogate and even demystify the devastating consequences of a generalized "logic of accumulation" and of "the unstoppable march of capitalism in its neoliberal phase."[6] Such an account might capture the extent to which capitalist forms are gradually and increasingly imposed on noncapitalist spheres but it misses the particular ways in which affect enters noir, or is always-already present within noir, as a nonsignifying bodily feeling outside of its objectification or object-targeting by power. If we see noir as a kind of unruly counternarrative to what Lauren Berlant calls the "good-life fantasies" (which are, in turn, central to her account of "cruel optimism"), then affect, like noir, "enters the description of the dissolution of the good-life fantasies not as a symptom of any mode of production or ideology's damaging imprint." Rather, "[its] strength as a site of potential elucidation comes from the ways it registers the conditions of life that move across persons and worlds."[7] Still, for my purposes, this last and perhaps overly general reference to the "conditions of life" does not quite come to grips with the particularities of power as it is envisaged by Carlotto—which is why I turn to the late work of Michel Foucault and its application by Ben Anderson in order to comprehend the paradoxical move in Carlotto, whereby his protagonists simultaneously exceed attempts to order them and yet become targets for new techniques of power.

Foucault's *The Birth of Biopolitics* (2008) traces the emergence of biopolitics as a way of managing and governing populations (or securing order through self-government or governmentality) in the context of the consolidation of capitalism. As Anderson explains, "Foucault's initial diagnosis of the emergence of forms of power that are 'bent on generating forces, making them grow, and ordering them' . . . was tied to a unique set of political-economic transformations, specifically the need for an expansion of the productive forces in capitalism."[8] Anderson finds a way of connecting "a specific economic ordering"—whereby "capitalist forms" are "imposed on a pre-existing, non-capitalist sphere," "value-creation becomes indistinct from social activity," and "surplus value is extracted throughout all of life"[9]—to a more general ordering of life (or the "strategic coordination of the multiplicity of forces that make up life"). Crucially, for his and indeed for my purposes, what "links this ordering of capital/life relations with a logic of governing is a problematization of life as contingent, as tensed between chaos and determination (as expressed through terms such as uncertainty, indeterminacy, discontinuity and turbulence)."[10] In other words, exactly those affects which characterize Carlotto's noir universe. Rather than limiting this universe to a consequence of economic determinism or indeed downplaying the effects of competition, accumulation by dispossession and the organization of life around the market, Carlotto's emphasis on both, by drawing attention to the violent, unruly contingencies and uncertainties that affect his characters, allows us to fully see the ways in which "affective life is imbricated in the working out of the neoliberal problem of how to organize life according to the market."[11]

In this essay, I focus on two novels featuring criminal-turned-restaurateur Giorgio Pellegrini—*The Goodbye Kiss* and *Alla fine di un giorno noioso* (2011), translated by Antony Shugaar as *At the End of a Dull Day* (2013)—and a "standalone" novel about the failures of the justice system called *L'oscura immensità della morte* (2004), translated by Lawrence Venuti as *Death's Dark Abyss* (2006). My intent is to reconfigure Anderson's formulation (e.g., "the working out of the neoliberal problem of how to organize life according to the market") in more straightforward terms as a problem of action. In Carlotto's noir worlds, taking bold and decisive action, which is the hallmark of his protagonists, is neither the unproblematic working out of individual agency in the face of new techniques of power nor a symptom of the subsumption of life by and into the market (whereby characters become unthinking and uncritical embodiments of, say, accumulation or competition). But this, I think, is where certain theories of affect—whereby the emphasis is also placed, as Anderson puts it, on "how affective life exceeds attempts to make it into an objective-target for forms of power"[12]— diverge from what we are calling "noir affect": to quote Breu and Hatmaker in their introduction, "a name for specific kinds of affect (loss, sadness, rage, guilt, shame, resentment, humiliation and refusal) and the name of a specific practice of narrative to dramatize such affects."[13] In other words, what Brian Massumi calls the hopeful dimension of affect whereby the uncertainty produced by complex organizational structures allow a "margin of manoeuvrability"[14] or Antonio Negri calls "biopower from below" (i.e,. "affective life is the non-representational 'outside' that opens up the chance of something new"[15]) is recast into its noir equivalent: action that is neither "becoming" nor subsumption by or into power but something darker, more agonistic, more inchoate. In the following sections I explore how Carlotto, across three exemplary novels, takes the possibilities inherent in these more hopeful accounts of affect (where bodies act as well as being acted upon) and recasts them into their noir equivalents (whereby the working out of the neoliberal problem of how to organize life according to market principles produces its own "noir affects": rage, anxiety, shame, and humiliation). At stake here is not the question of how the resulting narratives function as critiques of or are complicit with these new forms of power, but rather how or how far they are able to make connections between the violence which inevitably results from these noir affects and modes of accumulation, securitization (or objective-targeting) and value-creation that are ostensibly treated as "normal" and what the implication of these connections might be.

Noir Affect and Good-Life Fantasies: The Goodbye Kiss

In her book *Cruel Optimism* (2012), Lauren Berlant casts "that moral-intimate-economic thing called the good life"—or people's attachment to "conventional good-life fantasies" (e.g., enduring families and coupledom, stable, well-paid jobs, leisure time, economic opportunity, public justice)—as something that paradoxically acts as obstacle to one's flourishing (i.e., when an object or scene "that ignites a sense of possibility actually makes it impossible to attain the expansive transformation for which a person or a people risks striving").[16] As Breu and Hatmaker explain, cruel optimism is "a neoliberal affective state" whereby "discourses like self-help, postmodern management, and 'staying positive' function to cover over the exploited subject's anxious relationship to a neoliberal order that is systematically impoverishing them."[17] For Berlant, the contemporary "dissolution of optimistic objects/scenarios that once held the space open for the good-life fantasy" has in turn produced new forms—new "dramas of adjustment"—which are better able to trace the correlative anxieties of economic precariousness and affective distress.[18] But *The Goodbye Kiss* is not one of these new dramas, nor can it be, because rather than a "positive affect" that becomes "a negative phenomenon," Carlotto's noir begins with the assumption that affects are negative and life is unpredictable, dangerous, and anxious—and proceeds to show us how the attendant violence is intimately connected to the conditions of precariousness that result from the neoliberal subsumption of life by the market. The extent to which this puts pressure on Berlant's claims about the particular forms that cultural fantasies of affective distress caused by neoliberal precarity can take, and whether any kind of "affective solidarity" is possible, constitutes one of this essay's key lines of inquiry.

To claim that *The Goodbye Kiss* doesn't operate, on one level, as a cultural fantasy about "the good life" would be misleading. The first half of the novel traces the rise from petty and not so petty criminality to ostensible respectability and the "good life" of Giorgio Pellegrini who moves seamlessly and without any kind of perturbation from adventurer and proto-revolutionary to aspiring capitalist. In doing so Carlotto gives us an early hint that violent competition should be understood as the measure of all life. In one sense, there is nothing especially atypical about this: crime stories have long since been motivated the acquisitive ambitions of their protagonists and Carlotto's noir is no different. Having seen the wealth casually displayed on the Milanese streets—"I'd go to the centro and spend hours eyeing the people and cars. A tone of cash was floating around, and mostly everyone was oozing confidence"[19]—Pellegrini is made aware of his lowly status ("I was a marginal, an outcast . . . a bum") and what he needs in order to climb the social ladder and realize the good life: "Money. I needed money to lift myself from the dung heap I was stuck in. Then I'd establish a respectable position and stroll through the centro . . . flaunting the worry-free face of a winner" (*GK*, 29). Crime—and as the story progresses, increasingly violent crime, resulting in multiple deaths, imbued by the spirit of accumulation by dispossession and acquisitive competition— becomes the proverbial conveyer belt to wealth and respectability: once he has acquired a sufficient sum, Pellegrini is literally able to purchase his "rehabilitation" with the help of a Veneto lawyer and political fixer, although the lawyer, Sante Brianese, is quick to emphasize the performativity of respectability over the conspicuousness of consumption. "Around here it isn't important to know where the money originates. . . . But it mustn't stink of wrong-doing. On the contrary, it should carry the fragrance of hard work and a creative intellect" (*GK*, 100).

Where *The Goodbye Kiss* does its important political work is in its revelation of what Pellegrini finds once he enters respectable Veneto society ("the hunger for money was the same everywhere" and opens a restaurant, La Nena, frequented by the city's great and good. Not only is nothing at all different—as Carlotto tells us, "the legal and illegal economies were merged in a single system, offering the opportunity to grow rich and build a discreet position of power. . . . Business, crime and politics" (*GK*, 98, 108). More to the point, the legal economy works in exactly the same way and according to the same logics as the illegal one: so that the "skills" Pellegrini has learnt running a brothel or setting up an armored car robbery (logistics and planning, keeping costs down, exploiting staff, and being prepared to act decisively and with force if necessary) are the same ones he uses to run his restaurant and help out his new friends. "Your role is to protect our group of friends," [Brianese] once told me. "To restore legality. Ours, of course" (*GK*, 113). The idea that the legal world is every bit as competitive and cutthroat as the illegal world is not a new one, of course, but what Carlotto does so well, and what noir is able to show us so clearly, is that the good-life fantasies that drive the pursuit of crime in the first place are themselves imbricated in the networks of control and objective-targeting that reinforce neoliberalism's reordering of the social as well as economic domains. This may be akin to Berlant's "cruel optimism" insofar as the affective yearning (which is in one sense positive) has negative consequences, but Carlotto's "noir affect" takes and extends this formulation so that the desired-for (e.g., positive) good-life fantasy is stripped bare and violated to such an extent that its value as a goal or target is fatally undermined. Even the fantasy is baseless—subject, as it is, to the imperatives of accumulation by dispossession and violent competition.

In order to further his "rehabilitation" case, and to underscore his claims to respectability, Pellegrini marries Roberta after a whirlwind courtship in which Pellegrini traps her using the carefully calibrated language and actions of the good-life fantasy: "I acted as if I understood and tried to reassure her with banal speeches about the sincerity of my feelings. Finally I sent her a clear message, revealing my dreams and my plans to her. She seemed the image of my ideal woman. I escorted her to the door of her building, saying goodbye with a chaste kiss on the cheek" (*GK*, 118). Pellegrini may try—half-heartedly—to convince himself that he "loved her company" and that she "filled a hole in my life" despite the fact that he "really didn't know what to do with a woman who had no intention of giving me head or letting me fuck her in the ass" (*GK*, 119) But his pursuit of and marriage to her is part of the logic of acquisition whereby she, like the restaurant and other trappings or commodities of the good life, can be purchased and traded and where the fantasy is explicitly treated as fantasy— and as a game whose end goal is only ever Pellegrini's self-advancement: "To crown her soap-opera dreams, I took her to Venezia. . . . A great restaurant, a turn in the gondola, a serenade. In Piazza San Marco, I put a little box in her hand" (*GK*, 219). In Carlotto's noir universe, it isn't the case of Pellegrini's past returning to haunt him, although this would be one way of reading the turn of event: Roberta interrupts Pellegrini meeting with a dirty cop from his former life and when the cop is murdered (by Pellegrini of course) and the murder publicized, Roberta draws the appropriate conclusions and therefore puts herself in the crosshairs. Since there is no distinction between legal and illegal domains and therefore between Pellegrini's past and present, this is Berlant's good-life fantasy reconstituted as noir affect. There is no affective masking and no affirmative shadow lurking behind the negation: rather what we see is the "affective environment" of neoliberal capitalism turned inside-out in order to underline all that is specious, false, exploitative, violent and horrific about a logic and a moment where there is nothing (even or especially love) outside the market. In a deliriously noir inversion of romantic coupling, Pellegrini slips aspirin into his wife's food, knowing she is allergic and that the allergic reaction will kill her, and he even tells her this—"I put crushed aspirins in all the food you've eaten in the last twenty-four hours"—while he watches her lose consciousness and die before the ambulance he's called arrives. The novel concludes not with Pellegrini anxiously waiting to see whether he has evaded justice but rather with his successful rehabilitation at which point the noir-happy ending can take place (*GK*, 139). "I burst into tears. Of happiness. I'd done it. The nightmare was over. I could finally be like everybody else" (*GK*, 144). The irony of course is that insofar as "affective atmospheres" are shared rather than solitary—because affect acts not just upon individual bodies but also worlds—he is not *not* like everyone else which is another way of saying that everyone else is just like him. Not everyone, perhaps, would be capable of such grotesque cruelty but this is what happens when affect and affective life enter a noir universe that is itself "imbricated in the working out of the neoliberal problem of how to organise life according to the market."[20]

Creative Capitalism and Violence: At the End of a Dull Day

Carlotto's sequel to *The Goodbye Kiss*, *At the End of the Dull Day*, picks up Pellegrini's story a year later, once he has been fully assimilated into the Veneto's "respectable" social and business worlds. In doing so, it seeks, ostensibly at least, to reverse the narrative trajectory of the earlier novel (from criminality to "respectability") by moving Pellegrini in the opposite direction. Hence, when he is swindled by his lawyer and former friend, Sante Brianese, Pellegrini sets out to show his newfound acquaintances who he "really" is and what he is capable of: "They'd all known a different man, a man who was willing to do anything to please people and to be accepted. None of them had even the slightest idea of who Giorgio Pellegrini really was."[21] Of course, this is something of a misnomer or a misrepresentation, given that many of these same acquaintances have directly benefitted from the violence Pellegrini has dished out in their favor. But it speaks to or about the ways in which capitalism as a system typically obscures its predations and exploitative tendencies through claims to moral probity.[22] The noir *un*-masking of these same tendencies in Carlotto's sequel is foregrounded from the outset: we see how Pellegrini's social ascension ("I was now 'one of them.' And not just any one of them. I was a winner") is founded upon his violent exploitation of the foreign prostitutes he "works" as their pimp (*EDD*, 24). Just as David Harvey urges us not to distinguish between "extra-legal activities, such as robbery . . . predation, violence and coercion" and the accumulation of wealth "by legally sanctioned exchanges under conditions of non-coercive trade in freely functioning markets" (insofar as the capital has always "exhibited immense flexibility in its capacity to appropriate the common wealth"[23]), Carlotto wants us to see Pellegrini's activities not merely as criminal and predatory but also as constitutive of capitalism's capacity to smoothly appropriate or accumulate via dispossessing others of their labor and hence their wealth. The threat to the women may be physical—"we made sure they couldn't miss a pair of brass knuckles apparently left in plain view"—but in other ways the intent is to treat the women in such a way that they don't notice what is being done to them until it is time to dispose of them: "We sent them to live in comfortable, spacious homes, where Nicoletta [his partner] took personal charge of them. She taught them everything they needed to know about clothing makeup, perfume and etiquette" (*EDD*, 21). In other words, they are well treated not out of any benevolent intent demonstrated by Pellegrini and his partner but because it is in their commercial interest to do so. That exploitation girds and supersedes this benevolence is evidenced by the "knuckles" and manner in which the women are sold—like cattle—and shipped off to North Africa once their economic usefulness has been expended.

All of this requires careful elucidation about the precise nature of the relationship between noir and capitalism and between what we are calling noir affect and capitalism as "affective atmosphere." In one respect, as I have argued elsewhere, it is not entirely wrong to propose Pellegrini and his violence as symptom of the worst tendencies of accumulation (by dispossession), acquisition, and competition.[24] But it is the determining aspect of this relationship that is troubling, not least in light of work carried out by Berlant and others on affect that does not want to and indeed cannot treat a subject's affective life as "symptom of any mode of production's or ideology's damaging imprint."[25] At stake is the question of how to treat noir as an affective atmosphere and how to calibrate it to the obvious Marxian overtones of Carlotto's novel (i.e., whereby he *is* explicitly commenting on the exploitative practices of capitalism). Part of the problem for any account that might want to reduce Pellegrini to the sum of the forces acting upon him is that he doesn't, in Carlotto's own terms, cohere as a subject, even a determined one. For one thing, he is too unstable, too impulsive, despite his mendacious claim early in the novel that he had been able to lay "to rest those impulses [he]'d been unable to control in the past" and that "[he] no longer needed to get drunk on violence and cruelty in order to feel [he] was alive" (*EDD*, 38). Instead, the novel is fundamentally "about" Pellegrini's tortuous efforts to control these impulses (in effect to "know himself") and his inability to do so. More to the point, Carlotto wants us to understand that these efforts make no sense, rationally speaking, and are founded on the same exploitative practices as his business activities. Take, for example, his insistence upon watching his wife, Martina, both smear creams and ointments onto her face and body and pedal furiously on an exercise bike—ostensible to help her ward off "the aging process and keeping body and mind in tip-top shape" (*EDD*, 33). In actuality, this is a misogynistic power play that stands in lieu of "the intoxicating thrill of inflicting pain on others" and in doing so exposes (once again) the falsity of good-life fantasies (*EDD*, 46).

The broader point is that Pellegrini has little or no insight into who or what he is beyond an instinctive understanding of where his own violence might lead—and an implicit realization that he possesses little or no ability to control these tendencies. As he tells Brianese: "I must just be one of those unpredictable variables in your fucked-up system, Counselor, and I can promise you that I've shown considerable restraint and offered no more than a tiny demonstration of the extent of my professional skills in the field of inflicting violence" (*EDD*, 60). Rather than exhibiting the same capacities, and the same logic, then, as the system of graft and corruption that Brianese presides over (e.g., "The toxic leachings from a dump into the open sea . . . bribes paid to tamper with the health department statistics"), Pellegrini represents something "unpredictable" and even outré to this system (*EDD*, 61). To understand what this might mean we need to return to theories of affect, and more particularly of noir affect, because these too underscore the ways in which affects are "non-intentional, bodily reactions"[26] that align subjects for and against prevailing systems of power. This understanding of affect, derived initially from Spinoza, as "the power to affect and be affected," is interpreted optimistically by Brian Massumi insofar as it has positive political implications regarding our abilities to engage with the world and each other in potentially transformative ways: "To affect and be affected is to be open to the world, to be active in it and to be patient for its return activity. This openness is always taken as primary. It is the cutting edge of transformation."[27] Massumi's interventions have opened up space for Antonio Negri and other theorists to think about affect as "biopower from below," that is, "how affective life exceeds attempts to make it into an object-target for forms of power."[28] This is all well and good but noir is a contrary "heretical" genre, if indeed it is a genre,[29] and certainly one that is genetically disinclined to speak in optimistic ways about positive transformations of any kind. So the question remains: How is it possible for noir to avoid the trap of treating all human activity and emotion as trapped and determined (because affect, unlike emotion, is "a nonsignifying, nonconscious 'intensity' disconnected from subjective, signifying, functional-meaning axis to which more familiar categories of emotion belong"[30]) while at the same time thematizing the intensity and unpredictability of affective life in ways that negate rather than validate its "potentially emancipatory qualities" (because "noir affect" is first and foremost a negation)?[31] And how do all of this while still finding ways to critically interrogate the violent precariousness of life—affective or otherwise—as it is lived under neoliberalism?

In this section, I have tried to show how Carlotto's *At the End of a Dull Day* pulls off the first part of this formulation—drawing suggestive links between crime and capitalism and between Pellegrini's acquisitiveness and violent competitiveness and the everyday logic of business while emphasizing his unpredictability and unknowability even to himself. In the remaining part of this section, I show how Pellegrini's unpredictability does not validate affective life's "potentially emancipatory qualities" but rather is explained by the creative destruction and violence characteristic of what we might call capitalism in its neoliberal phase or moment.[32] After Pellegrini has been swindled by Brianese, his lawyer and a rising political star, he turns on his former mentor and subjects Brianese's wife to a horrific beating during what is intended to look to the world at large as a botched robbery (but where he reveals the truth to Brianese—to "persuade" the lawyer to pay back what he has stolen). By way of retribution, Brianese sets the Calabrian mafia, 'Ndrangheta, onto Pellegrini and his restaurant so that, initially, he has no choice but to let them use it as "washing machine" to launder their dirty money (*EDD*, 94). Therefore rather than treat the "famous 'locomotive' . . . the legal and illegal economies merged in a single system" as a monolith (*GK*, 108), Carlotto sets the "big beasts" of the conjoined domains of politics (Brianese as "lawyer and . . . parliamentarian of the Italian republic") and organized crime (as represented by the various figures of 'Ndrangheta including the local boss, Giuseppe Palamara) against Pellegrini who positions himself not as social bandit but rather as a new or "creative" economy entrepreneur selling his human capital in order to earn his freedom (*EDD*, 15). Indeed, this is precisely the language Pellegrini uses to frame his struggle with Brianese and especially the Calabrian mafia, which he portrays as the "crime" equivalent of General Motors or IBM, hierarchy-bound, procedure-heavy behemoths to his nimble, creatively inflected "start-up." His "creative criminality" venture, then, draws from the "astounding wave of creativity in every field, from music and film and art to crime" in an earlier epoch (the Situationists?)

and is set against not just "the dull, repetitive crimes committed by the capitalist establishment" but also by the various "international Mafias" that "moved in" aided by "globalization" and the decimation of "free market competition" so that "the spheres of illegal pursuits turned grey and humdrum like everything else" (*EDD*, 122).

There is of course something self-serving on Pellegrini's part in comparing "People like the Palamaras" to "dinosaurs who'd always lived in a culture devoid of imagination" and his own Marcuse-inspired "creative crime" venture premised on "Confusion. Chaos. Breakdown. Hurly-burly" that would "Blind them with imagination" (*EDD*, 122–124). Yet it is true that his plan to bamboozle Palamara and his henchmen by robbing a consignment of still-to-be-laundered money and cover his tracks with a series of elaborate stunts and carefully planned alibis ultimately succeeds in masking his culpability and his threat to Brianese's position is such that the lawyer-cum-politician agrees to pay back what he has stolen. Reflecting on where this leaves him, Pellegrini imagines his future criminal activities as a development of his creative endeavors ("I would no longer get bogged down in activities like the prostitution ring, which demanded a special dedicated logistical structure and organization" [*EDD*, 182]). But insofar as he claims that "flexibility would be the order of the creative local economy," it is striking how closely success here evokes, deliberately I think, the ways in which "neoliberalising processes attempt to harness the creative, inventive dimensions of life."[33] So where does this leave us? Should we see Pellegrini's exploits as success? Is this how Carlotto wants us to understand his protagonist's "creative criminality"?

Pellegrini is only able to broker a deal to ensure his survival (and hence success) once he has earned the backing of an elite member of the Veneto business establishment and only on the grounds that the status quo prevails. The situation, this nameless figure explains, may be "fluid" in the country at large "but there will never be any real change in the Veneto" (*EDD*, 176). Then we need to think about how far the violent, brutalizing logic that informs Pellegrini's victory ("I was born to ass-fuck my fellow man and it was something I really enjoyed. It made me feel alive") can be seen as endorsing neoliberalism's harnessing of creativity for its own ends (*EDD*, 179–180). "You're a monster," Brianese tells Pellegrini, a taint that requires careful consideration in light of the lawyer's accomplishments in the field of graft, violence, and corruption (*EDD*, 159). But is Pellegrini a monster and if so what informs or explains this monstrosity? Neoliberalism, like capitalism previously (to which of course neoliberalism is yoked) cannot be wheeled on as unproblematic explanation but Breu and Hatmaker are surely correct in their assertion that "the resurgence of noir proper in neoliberal noir . . . is organized around a new, present form of negativity, one that challenges the affirmative moral and commodified rhetoric of self-invention, self-investment, and self-maintenance as well as deserving winners and losers that is central to contemporary neoliberalism."[34] Perhaps the only qualification I would want to make is to think about how ambiguity enters into and unsettles any straightforward affirmation/negation formulation. As such, Pellegrini's creative criminality, informed by attendant techniques of privatization and responsibilization, is perhaps best understood as affirmation *and* negation: a maneuver that both draws from and challenges the affirmative logic of neoliberalism that proposes unproblematic freedom as an end result. What we find in *At the End of a Dull Day* is agonistic ambivalence: a central character who is both monster and successful entrepreneur, and violence that sets Pellegrini free and at the same time binds him into new and ever-proliferating forms of power. This leaves open the question of whether we as readers identify with Pellegrini's cunning and monstrousness which I will address in the next section.

Noir Justice as Abyssal Violence: Death's Dark Abyss

Death's Dark Abyss is perhaps the bleakest of all of Carlotto's novels because it takes a figure who should, unequivocally, command our sympathies as readers—far more so than the pathologically self-interested Pellegrini—and turns him into "a dangerous lunatic."[35] If Silvio Contin once enjoyed what we might call a good life rather than merely hankering after a good-life fantasy—"I was a sales agent for top-drawer wines. I had a secretary and tooled around in a Mercedes. I had a wife and son. Friends and relatives. Clara was a beautiful woman" (*DDA*, 19)—all of this is destroyed when his wife and son are killed in a botched robbery. In the present of the novel, Contin is living a hollow, diminished life mending shoes for a living and eating dinners in front of the TV when he is asked to show clemency to one of the robbers, Raffaello Beggiato, who was sentenced for thirty years but who has contracted cancer and is looking for a conditional release in order *not* to die in prison. His response is initially instinctive rather than rational or conditioned by "feelings": "The pain throbbed more intensely, and a twinge rose from his stomach to my throat. . . . That miserable fuck thought I was capable of noble gestures. To forgive you need to have feelings, a life" (*DDA*, 19). Here, feelings or emotions are not, in any straightforward sense, synonymous with pre-social, pre-individual "intensities" that we might associate with affect. If "feelings" for Contin are connected to the life he once enjoyed, what he "feels" in the present is more akin to what we are calling noir affect: those darker intensities that he doesn't understand and can't fully control. Carlotto characterizes these intensities not as rational—"I didn't possess the tools to confront death rationally" Contin admits, and then ruminates on "the loss that sometimes kept me from thinking rationally"—but rather as an abyssal sentiment that drives Contin to violently debase himself and others in pursuit of what he believes is justice (*DDA*, 23).

As with Pellegrini, then, there is much to contemplate in relation to Contin's intent and how far he acts, i.e., how successful he is at exceeding or evading attempts to control or order his existence or is acted upon, i.e., how far he is subject to the regulatory tug of power, whether associated with the state or more generally with a biopolitical management of populations. For his part, Contin believes, as much as he is capable of such thinking, that his actions in the present, premised as they are on denying Beggiato the opportunity to enjoy the fruits of his ill-gotten gains and uncovering the identity of Beggiato's accomplice who was never punished for the double murder, are premised on redress, if not exactly justice: so that when he finally locates the accomplice, he muses, "Before sending him to prison for the remainder of his life, I had the chance to make him understand the meaning of pain, anguish, loss" (*DDA*, 70). Contin may be capable of rational action and intent on one level, then, insofar as the clemency he ostensibly shows to Beggiato by not opposing his bail is a calculated ruse so he can follow Beggiato, once he has been released, back to his accomplice. But in other ways the fuel that motors his "murky plan" is "anxiety and pain" and a "howl that was difficult to repress" and that "ripped open [his] mind with its obsessive rhythm and plummeted straight to my chest" (*DDA*, 48, 51). In other words, this is "noir affect" as embodied state: those negative registers of loss, rage, anxiety, and humiliation that act on the body's central nervous system in order to produce certain behaviors that are of the opposite or negation of responsibilization and justice. So it is that Contin decides not to "run to the police" but follows his "instinct" which equates in his own mind to "death's dark abyss" and that perhaps explains his decision to kill the accomplice and his wife with an axe (*DDA*, 62, 65). I say "perhaps explains" because while the act is premeditated insofar as Contin first lays out plastic sheeting to cover up the crime, it also seems to come out of nowhere: "From the bag I grabbed an axe handle and hit her in the knees. She fell to the floor, and I kept swinging till she passed out" (*DDA*, 101).[36]

The bigger question, for me, is how to make sense of Contin's hate and the other negative or noir affects that "explain" his actions. One way would be to treat Contin's aberrance and eventually his violence as the product of what has been done to him individually or his own pathologized deviance (i.e., *what* he has done is explained by *who* he is). But if we are to identify the manifestations of "noir affects" in what he does and who he is, we also need to remember that "affective atmospheres are shared, not solitary, and that bodies are continuously busy judging their environments and responding to the atmospheres in which they find themselves."[37] For Sara Ahmed, meanwhile, affects are akin to emotions like hate which "*do things*": in "affective economies" they "align individuals with communities—or bodily space with social space—through the very intensity of their attachments."[38] Which begs the question: How might we begin to understand the affective atmosphere or affective economy of Carlotto's novel? And how is Contin's bodily space connected to the larger social space through the intensity of his hate? Here the novel's indictment of the Italian justice system and the failure of the state to adequately balance the protection and justice owed to victims with the human rights of perpetrators is brought into stark relief, but it is only when we think about Contin's animal cunning in relation to his condemnation of state praxis that the novel's larger concerns begin to make sense. As Anderson puts it, "not only is affective life always-already organised into collective affects such as state phobias but also neoliberal processes attempt to harness the creative, inventive dimensions of life."[39] In the case of Carlotto's noir worlds it is just that affective life and affective atmospheres are premised upon negation—whereby Contin's rage and anxiety is aligned with the social space he belongs to (e.g., state failure and neoliberal capitalism)—and where the "creative, inventive dimensions of life" are enacted through an instinctive urge towards destruction and violence.

Conclusion: Noir Affect as Political Unmasking?

In her book *Cruel Optimism*, Lauren Berlant contemplates the political implications of focusing on affect rather than ideology and seeks a way around Slavoj Žižek's suspicion that "a politics of affect is an oxymoron or worse, a bourgeois mode of sensational self-involvement masquerading as a radically ungovernable activity of being." As such, she asks whether "to talk about the activity of affect . . . in political terms is mainly to be mired narcissistically . . . or passively in the present?"[40] Conversely, we might ask, how might an ideological critique make sense of an activity or a behavior that is not first and foremost to be understood as the direct consequence or symptom of the means of production, where the primacy of capitalism as a mode of economic *and* social organization is either reinscribed or questioned? Is it possible to understand all of Giorgio Pellegrini's actions, even those that don't make full sense to himself (e.g., watching his wife "spin" on her exercise bike and rub creams into her body), or Silvio Contin's seemingly bottomless rage as being determined by the means of production? Can we easily see these novels as ideological unmaskings and if so, what ideologies precisely are being unmasked? Pellegrini, after all, would seem to be fully supportive of or beholden to the transformations ushered in by neoliberal rhetoric about creativity, responsibilization, and self-maximization. Nor, self-evidently, are these novels endorsements of new techniques of power and modes of behavior: Carlotto's politics—as evidenced in his claims about Mediterranean noir (e.g., "to tell stories with a wide swath; to recount great transformations; to denounce but at the same time to propose a culture of solidarity as an alternative"[41])—are leftist and clearly we are meant to see some kind of connection between Pellegrini's murderous inclinations, his acquisitive tendencies, and his competitive ruthlessness and the wider logic of capital.

These are not *protest* novels in which the conditions that force characters to act in particular ways are decried—Pellegrini acts with too much glee and a not insignificant amount of self-insight for *The Goodbye Kiss* or *At the End of a Dull Day* to be outraged at the state of the world. This is where the framing of his actions, and those of Silvio Contin, and Carlotto's noir worlds, in terms of affect is so instructive: it allows us to posit individual behavior as singular, complex, ambiguous, messy, and unruly (all of these descriptors would seem to apply to Pellegrini and Contin) while at the same time seeking to locate this behavior not as a direct product of what Berlant calls "the heuristic 'neoliberalism'" as "a world-homogenizing system" or the affect "of powerful, impersonal forces" but rather as acknowledgment that bodies and environments are constantly acting and acting on one another: that "affective atmospheres are shared . . . and . . . bodies are continuously judging their environments and responding to the atmospheres in which they find themselves."[42] For Berlant, the political work of such texts is done in their descriptions of dissolutions of good-life fantasies not as a symptom of ideology but in terms of the way they register "the conditions of life that move across persons and worlds, play out in lived time, and energise attachments."[43] But what of the noir aspect of "noir affect"? As this essay has demonstrated, noir in general and Carlotto's novels in particular are highly skilled at forensically dissecting good-life fantasies but they are less inclined than Berlant would like to show us how positive attachments are played out in lived time. Noir, after all, is first and foremost negation. That said, noir does not reduce human behavior to rage, hate, and violence; unease, ambiguity, and anxiety can and do flourish just as well in noir texts. Therefore the political work Carlotto's novels perform is, in part, at the level of moral rebellion on the part of readers (who see what or who Pellegrini is and strive to live different lives),[44] but this work also occurs in the glimpses we have of ourselves in Pellegrini and Contin (their frustrations and their capacities for action) and our careful delineations of what these identifications mean in terms of our own complicities with the same systems and world we have to negotiate on a daily basis.

NOTES

1. See, for example, Justus Nieland and Jennifer Fay, *Film Noir: Hard-Boiled Modernity and the Cultures of Globalization* (New York: Routledge, 2009).

2. On neoliberal noir, see Christopher Breu, "Work and Death in the Global City: Natsuo Kirino's Out as Neoliberal Noir," in *Globalization and the State in Contemporary Crime Fiction*, ed. Andrew Pepper and David Schmid (London: Palgrave Macmillan, 2016), 39–57. For "capitalist noir," see my *Unwilling Executioner: Crime Fiction and the State* (Oxford: Oxford University Press, 2016), 228–238. The relationship between neoliberal, capitalist, and affective noir is elucidated in this essay.

3. See Patricia Ticineto Clough, introduction to *The Affective Turn: Theorizing the Social*, ed. Clough and Jean Halley (Durham, NC: Duke University Press, 2007), 2; and Patricia Ticineto Clough, "The New Empiricism: Affect and Sociological Method," *European Journal of Social Theory* 12, no. 1 (2009): 48.

4. Clough, "New Empiricism," 48.

5. Pepper, *Unwilling*, 235–238.

6. Pepper, 236.

7. Lauren Berlant, *Cruel Optimism* (Durham, NC: Duke University Press), 15–16.

8. Ben Anderson, "Affect and Biopower: Towards a Politics of Life," *Transactions of the Institute of Geographers*, no. 37 (2012): 29.

9. Anderson, 33.

10. Anderson, 29.

11. Anderson, 40.

12. Anderson, 34.

13. See Breu and Hatmaker's introduction to this volume.

14. Brian Massumi, *Parables for the Virtual: Movement, Affect, Sensation* (Durham, NC: Duke University Press, 2002), 3.

15. See Anderson, "Affect," 34.

16. Berlant, *Cruel*, 2.

17. Breu and Hatmaker, introduction to this volume.

18. Berlant, *Cruel*, 3.

19. Massimo Carlotto, *The Goodbye Kiss*, trans. Lawrence Venuti (New York: Europa, 2006), 28. Hereafter cited in text in parentheses as *GK* and page number.

20. Anderson, "Affect," 40.

21. Massimo Carlotto, *At the End of a Dull Day*, trans. Antony Shugaar (New York: Europa, 2013), 74. Hereafter cited in text in parentheses as *EDD* and page number.

22. Famously in *The Communist Manifesto*, Marx describes how beneath or "veiled by religious and political illusions" lies "naked, shameless, direct, brutal exploitation." *Essential Writings of Karl Marx* (St. Petersburg, FL: Black and Red, 2010), 164.

23. David Harvey, *Seventeen Contradictions and the End of Capitalism* (London: Profile, 2015), 53, 54.

24. Pepper, *Unwilling*, 236.

25. Berlant, *Cruel*, 15–16.

26. See Ruth Leys, "The Turn to Affect," *Critical Inquiry* 37 (2011): 434–472, 437.

27. Brian Massumi, *The Politics of Affect* (Cambridge: Polity, 2015), ix.

28. Anderson, "Affect," 34.

29. David Schmid argues that noir "is premised on in its opposition to all cultural and political orthodoxies." Quoted in Andrew Pepper, "The American roman noir," in *The Cambridge Companion to American Crime Fiction*, ed. Catherine Nickerson (Cambridge: Cambridge University Press, 2010), 60.

30. Leys summarizing Brian Massumi's arguments in *Parables for the Virtual* in "The Turn," 441.

31. Leys, 441.

32. If we can tie the destructive potentialities of capitalism back to the revolutionary practices of the bourgeoisie (see *The Communist Manifesto*, chapter 1), what is particular about capitalism in its neoliberal phase, for my purposes, is the way in a privatization agenda and cuts to the welfare program resulting in widespread precarity that is felt hardest by the most vulnerable in society is reinterpreted as opportunity or freedom for the individual entrepreneur to sell his or her human capital without state stricture or intervention. For Anderson, Foucault's "*Homo Economicus*" is "a reorgan-

isation of the liberal subject" through "processes of privatisation, personalisation and responsibilisation" ("Affect," 38).

33. Anderson, "Affect," 39.
34. Breu and Hatmaker, introduction to this volume.
35. Massimo Carlotto, *Death's Dark Abyss*, trans. Lawrence Venuti (New York: Europa, 2006), 137. Hereafter cited in text in parentheses as *DDA* and page number.
36. Berlant frames this nonintentionality as follows: "Brian Massumi represents the nervous system as so autonomous that affective acts cannot be intended" (*Cruel*, 14).
37. Berlant, 15.
38. Sara Ahmed, "Affective Economies," *Social Text* 22, no.2 (2004): 119.
39. Anderson, "Affect," 39.
40. Berlant, *Cruel*, 15.
41. Massimo Carlotto, "Eulogy for Jean-Claude Izzo," in Jean-Claude Izzo, *Total Chaos*, trans. Howard Curtis (New York: Europa, 2005).
42. Berlant, *Cruel*, 15.
43. Berlant, *Cruel*, 16.
44. Barbara Pezzotti, *Politics and Society in Italian Crime Fiction: A Historical Overview* (Jefferson, NC: McFarland, 2014), 166.

Afterword: Melodrama, Noir's Kid Sister, or Crying in Trump's America
Paula Rabinowitz

Every day I wake up not screaming but with a knot in my stomach . . . I'm anxious. After Donald J. Trump's election, WNYC ran a radio series entitled the United States of Anxiety. It's the predominant affect these days. Once again, nuclear weapons figure in news reports: throw weights, ICBMs, megatonnage . . . a vocabulary familiar from my childhood as the daughter of an electrical engineer who designed radar; and natural disasters . . . hurricanes, floods, fires, now recognized as manmade, just like the bomb; over seventy million refugees fleeing war and famine and genocide . . . a repetition of the postwar years. These seem like throwbacks, to the heyday of noir, in the Great Depression's aftermaths: World War II and the Cold War. What could have happened while I slept in the city that never sleeps—encrusted now with the glittering detritus of a billionaire's empty lair on Fifth Avenue? This is the state of being humans have found themselves in since November 8, 2016. The day Donald Trump was elected president of the United States of (Not) America. The new United States of Noir Affect (USNA). But is now really another time of noir affect? Or has the flattening of affect necessary to go about one's business replaced it with something else, something that requires a new periodization of noir, one that looks at its afterword, its footnote, its kid sister—the weirdly lush melodramas of the late 1950s and early 1960s as a Technicolor extension from the bungalows and roadhouses of Raymond Chandler's Los Angeles into everywhere.

Tearjerkers have always been with us—cinema's history is littered with wet handkerchiefs—and like noir, melodrama waxes and wanes across national borders and decades. Its time and sensibility has come, again. These debased modes/genres take up a necessary chore of guiding and distilling the emotional undercurrent of a political or economic trauma into familiar territory, whether it be shattered by the harsh neon signs of noir or glowing with modern track lighting. Somehow, in the moment of #MeToo, with the groper-in-chief untouched by his declarations and others' accusations of assault, the sensations and sensibilities of noir feel (there's that word) slightly off. Of course, we are in the midst of a slimy world run by powerful and corrupt men; but these guys are above board—they own the police, as Evelyn Mulwray screams to J. J. Gittes about her father in *Chinatown* (1974); worse, they are the police. They rule the roost for now through a gold-plated corruption that's more frightening than any underworld criminality, no matter how slick Kirk Douglass appears in his Yosemite lodge in *Out of the Past* (1947). They succeed with daughters and sons and son-in-law; it's a family plot. We need a good cry, but it seems impossible to express the tears. What has become clear, according to Michael Goldfarb, is that "Donald Trump is a man of his class—the nouveau riche, country club class . . . the loudest voice at the country club: at Mar-a-Lago, in Bedminster, N.J." boasting of his brains and stability, and his sexual conquests.[1] And the genre most concerned with class and sexual transgressions and with preserving family name is called melodrama. It evokes the sickening chaos of perverse domesticity and family life—it's glimpsed *Written on the Wind* (1956). For all noir's repetitive claustrophobia, those closing in are not usually blood relatives: Whit (Douglass) comments to Jeff (Robert Mitchum), when Kathie (Jane Greer) returns; "She's back in the fold."[2] Not the family.

Since my 1950s girlhood spent devouring black-and-white movies on television (thinking then that all old movies were shot in black and white because of television), I viewed noir as the genre that prompted, even promoted, adulthood—a lesson plan for acquiring a cynical, sexually charged, and knowing stance that viewed the world with jaded eyeballs, sometimes, like Lee Remick's in *Anatomy of a Murder* (1959) from behind dark glasses. I was impatient to be a grown-up, finding childhood dull and predictable. I longed for the convoluted plots and intrigue, the canted, off-center emotions, found in B-movies. Could a protofeminist sink her teeth into these stories of degradation and violence in which defiant women often stood up to men only to die in the end? Obviously, yes. As Molly Haskell commented more than forty years ago, it's not the sappy endings meted out to heroines from 1940s women's pictures (some of which, like *Mildred Pierce* [1945], leak into noir), it's the immense shoulder pads of Joan Crawford filling the screen that stick in the imagination, firing our dreams.[3]

But can noir affect work now? One would think so; because of parallels between current anxieties and postwar ones, the thrill of noir—the tough but ultimately dim guy, the beautiful seductive and betraying woman, the one seemingly in control who gets it in the end—veers close to the tawdry politics of now. But not quite. And this slight difference creates an opening for another affective genre resonant today. Perhaps more apt is to think about noir and melodrama as necessary twins—one shoots and the other doesn't; one cries and the other doesn't. Despite a sleazy boss man in the White House, surrounded by his "work wives" as molls[4]—with Sarah Huckabee Sanders playing a pearl-necklaced "Ma" to mad "top of the world" Jimmy Cagney in *White Heat*—and despite the current resonance with the threat of nuclear annihilation depicted in the final scenes of that 1949 noir as well as others, such as *Kiss Me Deadly* (1955), as "Rocket Man" and the "Dotard" stage a standoff over the size of their respective "Buttons," the current darkness feels different.

Film noir of the 1940s was a delayed reaction formation to fascism, Depression and war ... a sublimation of the horrors of Auschwitz and Hiroshima, and in the United States, also a residual confrontation with racism,[5] deflected through the narrative and visual tropes of bad girls taking down doomed guys (who nevertheless thought they were smart and in control), and did so by deploying black-and-white cinematography and clipped dialogue to speak of or as a newly unionized white working class. But by mid-century, melodrama appears to take on a new set of concerns: ascendant capitalism ... personified by suburban mothers sporting New Look dresses over hour-glass figures, weak-kneed fathers and rebellious daughters straining to burst free from the pointy bras and ponytails that confine their future destiny. All living restrained, even repressed lives within a lush indoors full of colorful furniture and home accessories, giving set designers full rein to display the nuclear family housed within these wallpapered walls on widescreen. The heyday of the technicolor melodrama—the 1950s—overlaps with late noir. The US-Mexican border of *Touch of Evil* (1958) may be a continent away from *Peyton Place* (1957), but troubles at home resonate across state and national borders. Rape links the two places:

violence that has not yet been fully exposed, addressed, exorcised, so that women's lives can be whole.[6]

In 1950, Ida Lupino filmed *Outrage* starring Mala Powers as Ann Walton, a bride-to-be who is raped on the way home from a late night at work.[7] Its probing investigation of the psychological trauma, one whose name could not be spoken, places it on the cusp of time and genre. A vision of a sunny California town, Capitol City, as reeking with corruption as any big-city waterfront, it begins with nods to noir—the menacing coffee cup slung along the lunch-cart counter echoing *Detour* (1945), the looming circus posters closing in on Ann as she is stalked through the empty industrial lots recalling *Nightmare Alley* (1947). Lupino's performance in *Road House* (1948) as the torch singer Lily picked up by a crazed Richard Widmark—doing his wacko schtick to the nth degree—painted into her satin chemise moved the scene of noir from gritty Chicago into the North Woods; menacing pines replace venetian blinds as the chiaroscuro source of dread. Lily may be tough, appearing to be a classic femme fatale with her cigarette burning streaks into her piano and her husky voice to match, but she's not a killer.

Melodrama masked as film noir, and directed by one of Warner Bros' premiere femme fatales, *Outrage* straddles a line: morphing from claustrophobic scenes out of film noir to expansive landscapes of orange groves conveyed by sweeping musical refrains. Even these images of abundance and nature turn sinister as tall rows of orange crates containing luscious fruit pen the workers in. Ann flees her hometown, where she was a bookkeeper—an independent-minded working woman wearing tailored suits—because she is trapped by her shame and guilt. Found unconscious on a roadside after she hears a radio newscast at a bus stop diner reporting her as a missing person and takes off on foot, she ends up working at a ranch under an assumed name, Ann Blank (to be filled in later when it becomes Blake). Her new outfits—puffy-sleeved dresses with dirndl skirts fastened by ribbons resembling a Dutch milkmaid—and braids reminiscent of Judy Garland's in *The Wizard of Oz* (1939) figure her as a younger twin of her former self. This one, however, fights back. When a man attempts to kiss her and unravel her braids at a country dance, she grabs a heavy wrench and almost kills him.

Like Lupino's other films, *Outrage* opens up the family romance of Hollywood's bad girls to their kid sisters revealing how class and rape move from underground subtext to overt theme as the Cold War and the communist threat within replaced fascism and Nazi war without as sources of political horror. The femme noire was a venomous mixture of rage and lust seething along the surface of her tough exterior; her melodramatic baby sister cracks open the suppressed terror, anger and fear at a moment when the external threat of World War II was passing. Love—and its violent underpinnings within families striving to cross class borders—should have formed new family bonds. But these were always premised on lies about sexual violence. These younger siblings emerge from the Depression and war quietly spunky and defiant; but the ravages suffered by their mothers and older sisters mark them all—no amount of family normalcy can shake the past. Scenes of violence within the family and its middle-class community (for Ann, it's the town gossip and the prospect of marriage), take on an even darker cast than the shadowy corners and wailing sirens that make us shudder with pleasure and fear in noir. Melodrama may be noir's bad seed.

But step back. Take *The Big Sleep* (1946): When Philip Marlowe (Humphrey Bogart) gets involved with the Sternwood sisters, the dynamic between Vivian (Lauren Bacall) and her younger sister Carmen (Martha Vickers) portends the shift from noir violence to that of melodrama. Only in reverse order. During his investigation, Marlowe discovers that each sister hangs out with a group of sinister men. Their father, desiccated and perverse as he bakes amid his hothouse orchids, provides a roof but the two are motherless daughters, running wild. Carmen has shifted her sights downtown—joining a weird crew pushing pornography and drugs through a rare book shop. Bacall frequents a road house beyond the city borders gambling with a higher class of gangsters. Marlowe misdiagnoses Vivian as a femme fatale, still she turns out okay in Marlowe's book; Carmen is another case—a drug-addled teenager still sucking her thumb—"need[ing] to be weaned" from her dead mother. Extraneous to the dynamic of desire compelling the arcane plot driving Bogart and Bacall (the first movie they made together after their sexy encounter in *To Have and Have Not* [1944]), she is a precursor. The dumber, less sophisticated kid sister, who just longs to be cuddled or even seen, she will be brutalized in the process. In a way, she's far more dangerous to and within the family. Her older sister knows the score—men are shits but necessary if you want the goods—but Carmen is used to being indulged and seems to believe there is something called love; she finds Marlowe "cute," like a kitten. It does her in. The world of noir, jaded as it is, could not prepare her for the horrors of domesticity awaiting her at home. Noir's vicious tension plays out in smoky hotel rooms or sleek nightclubs; melodrama resides in nicely decorated bedrooms and living rooms and its dominant pose is oblivion to violation. A knowing oblivion, this oxymoron, governs melodramatic affect.

A young and very blond woman's incestuous rape connects a straitlaced small-town New Hampshire to a louche Mexican border town, but rape also stretches to Moscow where a rebellious dark-haired girl, Mala Powers's twin, is raped by her fiancé's brother during a bombing raid while her lover is fighting the German army in Stalingrad in *The Cranes Are Flying* (1957). In these and many late 1950s movies, the Cold War is sedimented under the hot one preceding it. Many of these films straddle the border between noir and melodrama, with the legacy of World War II playing out across the bodies of women who struggle to express love but are constrained by fears of pregnancy and subject to predatory men. If it takes about seven years for culture to metabolize political trauma, then these disturbing films foreground sexual violence, but also love's possibilities. Heirs to noir—with *Touch of Evil* signaling the dying of noir in the garbage-strewn mud of a Tijuana sewer[8]—they are working through postwar abundance. Women's sexuality, a dangerous disruption of class and family relations, is squelched even as it evokes such rage-filled lust among various men that the sunniest scenes darken and it all takes place in an ocean of tears, swelling music, self-sacrifice, and suppressed rage . . . the affective flip-side of the overt aggression and perverse desire that figures noir's emotional impact.

So, rather than dwell in the darkness of noir, I am taking a trip across town to the brightly lit living rooms of melodrama . . . the kid sister of noir . . . the goody-goody who knows more than she lets on. A close observer of her femme fatale older sister, she's no tramp; rather an almost wholesome naïf caught in another kind of crisscrossing web of desire and crime. That crime is rape, which cannot register as crime, not in the way theft or extortion or bribery or even murder can . . . a crime that dares not speak its name because the shame is all on the victim who must hide herself from the law, in effect becoming enmeshed in an even more corrupt world than that of noir: the nuclear family. Even more than the femme noire, who knows she's no good (probably because she too has been raped but that's long before the action), this feisty girl's got a disgraceful secret. Melodrama moves the action back to the teenager or young woman whose apparent innocence perpetuates a rot within the family, the community, the state.

The perverse sexuality underlying so much of noir—its strange forms of violence: the scalding coffee Vince Stone (Lee Marvin) hurls at Debby Marsh (Gloria Grahame) blistering her face in *The Big Heat* (1953); Ballin Munson's (George Macready) "friend," his deadly walking stick, impaling Johnnie's (Glenn Ford) attacker in *Gilda* (1946); Phyllis Dietrichson (Barbara Stanwyck) recounting to Walter Neff (Fred MacMurray) how her husband beats her as a prelude to off-screen sex in *Double Indemnity* (1944); Kathy's (Jane Greer) bizarre smile after she shoots Whit's flunky in *Out of the Past*; Bart Tare's (John Dall) fascination with Annie Laurie Starr's (Peggy Cummins) gun prowess in *Gun Crazy* (1950)—paradoxically operate in the oxymoronic register of explosive repression. What's done to both men and women within the world of noir is also what's done by them, to each other and to themselves. That's the essence of Robert Mitchum knowing better but still staying: "Baby, I don't care," when Kathy denies robbing Whit on the Acapulco beach before a torrential rain sends them running back to her bungalow. It's the message of Cora's (Lana Turner) lipstick case rolling under Frank Chambers's (John Garfield) foot in *The Postman Always Rings Twice* (1946). It's a thrill but a fear-inducing one that ends in death. Weird desire ultimately gets contained by the couple's mortality.

What is so uncanny about melodramatic affect is the straight out (and that is the right word), sexual violence at the core of the family, its foundation in the reproduction of daily life. A rape, often of a young woman or girl, often by a family member or close friend or admirer, leaves her not only victim but also tainted vixen—and her mother, if she is there, is complicit in maintaining a cloak of normalcy: all endure. That is melodrama and it's terrifying. Especially so in vivid color, where the saturated walls and dresses push the characters into the foreground, putting them on brutal display.

Some international examples: from the height of the Cold War; the Korean Peninsula divided and the Rosenbergs' executions a few years past in 1953, when the "Doomsday Clock" was first set by the Bulletin of Atomic Scientists at two minutes before midnight.[9] In 1957 the USSR had launched Sputnik and the United States was testing thermonuclear bombs in the Pacific. On the one hand, *Touch of Evil*—considered the endnote to the fifteen year heyday of noir—with Orson Welles framing, through his giant body, a plot of revenge (both in the film and against the genre) that anchors the affect of this mode/genre/style . . . whatever one wants to call it; on the other, *Peyton Place*, first a wildly popular novel soon appearing in paperback, then the Lana Turner vehicle, and then a television series, one of the first nighttime soap operas, shot on location in cinemascope in small towns of Maine and New Hampshire. And also *The Cranes are Flying*—a black-and-white Soviet melodrama which, like *Peyton Place*, looks back to World War II, featuring handheld camera sequences shot in the streets of Moscow and Siberia that hark back to early cinematic innovations by Dziga Vertov. Or *Cairo Station* Youssef Chanine's 1958 riff on Italian neorealism and pulp fiction that follows a day in the intersecting lives of peddlers and porters barely surviving, but full of fantasies fueled by rock music, girly magazine pin-ups and sensational news reports. Its over-the-top plot twists and chiaroscuro lighting bring in elements of noir's affect . . . murder and sexual perversity and, at its heart, the riveting body of a wild woman slithering across the train tracks and into warehouses with her bucket of cold sodas. But with its final shot of Hanuma (Hind Rostom), the girl in danger, pinned to the railroad tracks by her obsessed attacker (Chanine as the lame newspaper hawker, Qinawi), and her last-minute rescue by her lover, Abu Siri (Farid Shawqi), a union organizer, it sends us back to the earliest perils of Pauline. Snidely Whiplash from Rocky and Bullwinkle cartoons meets proletarian literature in Cairo.

Then there's Kenji Mizoguchi's *The Life of Oharu* (1952). Despite being set in seventeenth-century Edo-era Japan, it invokes a similar postwar story of thwarted love and class transgressions that result in the sacrifice of the beautiful wayward daughter (Kinuyo Tanaka), who dives from concubine to street walker to preserve a disgraced family after she is found entwined with her lover, a mere retainer (Toshiro Mifune). At his execution, he screams her name, and bequeaths her a command that she only marry for love. For love, how ridiculous! It's Japan and this is the Edo version of *Madame X* (1966), a late Hollywood melodrama, perhaps Lana Turner's greatest melodramatic role completing a cycle begun with Cora as femme fatale in *The Postman Always Rings Twice*, which mandates that the debased woman—the one who pursues her desires by transgressing class boundaries—must pay in exchange for salvaging the family's status. Like Oharu, Madame X degenerates before our eyes, this time to protect her son, only to die in his unknowing arms after collapsing in court during her murder trial.

Shot in Hugh Hefner's Playboy Mansion, it is a swan song to mid-twentieth-century melodrama, finalizing Turner's shift from femme fatale to mom fatale: a face lift for aging actress Constance Bennett, makeup to age forty-five-year-old Lana Turner twenty-odd years from a thirty-five-year-old proper (even if originally from across the tracks) Connecticut wife into a debauched drunk . . . absinthe and piano etudes shrouding her pain. *Madame X* is one of at least sixteen versions of Alexandre Bisson's play from 1908 (which starred Sarah Bernhardt in both the original Paris and New York shows) that demonstrates the historical flexibility of melodrama to assimilate political sensations of any given moment through the lens of a family romance.

Watching a woman go down the tubes and sacrifice herself for love (in this case of her son) provides a queasy pleasure . . . schmaltz, far removed from noir's shady pull, which is inevitably about masculine distress. I could not abide it as a girl or young woman; instead, I feasted on self-conscious bad girls. But these melodramatic fantasies fascinate me now as an older woman obsessively watching Trump's assaults on our psychic and political sanity. He, too, is a product of this pivotal moment when noir turned to melodrama, and from dread to anxiety, from murder to rape, from gang to family. My childhood, too: #MeToo. Lana Turner as Constance MacKenzie and her breathy creepiness around men still terrifies me. A frightening mother who breaks down on the witness stand at Selena Cross's murder trial, crying "I didn't understand," as she recounts how her daughter Alison had tried to explain the pressures she and her friend were under, psychologically and physically, trying to remain good girls in this wretched place. A mother who cannot see that girls get raped in their own homes.

Everything happens too fast in the United States of (Noir) Anxiety. One day an accountant decides to go to San Francisco, is poisoned by "luminous toxins," and next he's obsessively trailing his murderer, ending up, *D.O.A.* (1950). Only a decade after the dark visions of Nazis in the midst of a small New England town with its white-steepled church on the village green—in the 1946 noir thriller, *The Stranger*, where, in a reversal, Edward G. Robinson plays the Nazi hunter as the heavy against the smooth-talking Orson Welles intent on moving into the upstanding New England family—Peyton Place revealed that a seemingly sunnier small town could be infected by crime and viciousness even without Nazis insidiously appearing: a rich mill owner controls the lives of his son and workers; a depraved stepfather leers at his stepdaughter, blaming her for seducing him after he rapes her; repressive and repressed mothers force their children to leave home—one for New York in order to find love and work (as the mother had done during World War I); the other to join the paratroopers during World War II. Class divisions and then war's casualties saturate the scene: the mill owner's son runs off to marry his brassy childhood sweetheart whose father is a millworker (cross-class sex) just before enlisting, only to die in combat; the stepdaughter kills her stepfather when he returns for Christmas from the Navy (white-trash incest); the uptight bourgeois mothers find their children have blossomed into independent adults away from them and in the company of men from all walks of life (a generation of vipers, as Philip Wylie called them). The war, however, is abstract. Faraway, it is not waged against a named enemy. Like the radiation poisoning killing Frank Bigelow (Edmund O'Brien) in *D.O.A.*, what began in Germany—as the film had, with a screenplay by Billy Wilder and directed by Robert Siodmak, before either immigrated to America—has seeped into the fiber of even a regular guy, an accountant: this toxin, a convenient stand-in for Nazism or communism and fears of nuclear annihilation, invisible enemies within holding more terror than the actual wars, hot and cold, being fought over there. Melodrama continues to tell us that we are all dead men (and more important, women) walking. Violence has been thoroughly internalized, incorporated.

In the Soviet melodrama, *The Cranes Are Flying*, the war causes the deaths of Veronika's parents when bombs fall on Moscow. She is raped by her lover's brother during one air raid, after her fiancé is called to defend Stalingrad and march west into battle. There is a clear and overt cause: German fascist aggression. The turbulent intimacy of war and desire is conveyed through hand-held camerawork, a nod to Soviet avant-garde, Italian neorealism and low-budget American noir. Saving the nation is a family affair: Disgusted with herself but alone, Veronika marries her rapist and is sent to Siberia along with her husband, father-in-law and sister-in-law, both physicians, to work in a hospital. She is shunned by all of them and, hating her husband who spends his time with prostitutes, she holds out hope that her lover Boris is still alive. At the crescendo, despairing that Boris has died at the front and just as she is about to throw herself off a bridge into the frozen river below, she saves a small boy from an oncoming tram, also named Boris, abandoned by his parents at the train station. Besot, she takes the boy in. When peace arrives and the soldiers (though not her Boris) return to ecstatic crowds swarming the Moscow station, a new multigenerational family has formed—Veronika, her father-in-law, and the boy—and, along with the boisterous people to whom she hands out flowers from her bouquet, a new state.

This film, made after Nikita Khrushchev had revealed Stalin's crimes in 1956, looks back to the "Great Patriotic War" during which over twenty million citizens of the USSR perished, as a moment of domestic consolidation. But this unity, too, like the scrubbed suburban idyll of Peyton Place, is undergirded by a young woman's rape. Fascism lurks within the affect of noir—and *The Cranes Are Flying*, while schlocky and melodramatic to the hilt, nods at this noir sensibility, or at least its neorealist version, itself kin to noir, but it needs the melodramatic to express new social formations. Even more so, US melodrama shifted focus—just as the United States had—away from black and white and the fascist threat to the unspoken violence encrusting brightly lit home life.

Ida Lupino's bold examination of the aftermath of rape on a woman's psychic and social life in *Outrage* also moves from noir to melodrama and back in one of the rare deep disclosures within the film industry (not Hollywood as Lupino's film was produced independently) of the politics of rape and its effects. #MeToo before #MeToo. Rape is the violent act that cannot be assimilated—unlike gun fights in Westerns, or political and economic corruption in films noir—even when it is the undercurrent forcing the action of these genres: "a girl and a gun," as the saying goes. The forms of male-on-male violence—even when they are targeted at, or result from, violations of women's bodies or family integrity (as in *The Searchers* [1956] among Westerns; or films noirs: *The Big Sleep, Double Indemnity, The Postman Always Rings Twice,* or another John Garfield noir, *Force of Evil* [1948])—and the corresponding identification elicited both within the film and implicitly amid the audience is acceptable, truly perverse, but understandable.[10] We know how weird the sexual affect embedded within noir is and how it can seep into the core of those who come under its sway, as Frank Bigelow descends into a frenzied world of jazz and corruption after his poisoning, turning him to violence; but it is far stranger when the world seems transparently, excessively normal. All Ann can do after her rape is scream uncontrollably—then run away.

Martin Scorsese called *Outrage* "a subdued behavioral study that captures the banality of evil in an ordinary small town,"[11] oscillating, like Lupino's body (and her body of work), across the border of film noir and melodrama. This slippage makes clear the interconnections between the film genres' different, though related, affective powers. When the subject is sexual violence (as it is now), the cinematic mode of address and its evocation of emotion is likely melodramatic. Rape's aftermath needs exposition and explanation, as the town's doctor provides (after secretly giving Selena an illegal abortion) at her trial in *Peyton Place* and Doc, the Santa Paula minister, argues at Ann's hearing. To exonerate the women's violent reactions to assault, both men condemn a repressed and hypocritical social order that betrays women, but do so by outing them as victims in public; then sending the damaged young women under their care back to tainted heterosexual marriage. If film noir tracks the affective afterlife of racial barbarism—Nazis lurking within American society (*The Stranger*); Jews haunting a post-Holocaust Europe (in the French film *Panique* [1946]); and after the war, communists infiltrating American soil (*D.O.A.* obliquely; *Pickup on South Street* [1953] overtly)—through the omnipresence of dangerous sexuality, then melodrama unveils a corner of this tableau, hiding in plain sight: sexual violence within everyday family and community life. American as apple pie.

Innocent yet clear-eyed, the kid sister knows the score—and also the lyrics to "Lydia, the Tattooed"—as does Dinah Lord (Virginia Wiedler), Tracy Lord's (Katharine Hepburn) smart-aleck sister in *The Philadelphia Story* (1940). She holds a key to our despicable situation and pathetic attempts to change it. That is why we need to start crying again at the ravages besetting all melodrama's women, who, along with the ever-crucial femmes fatales, are also our older sisters now.

NOTES

This essay is pointedly about the gendered vision of family and national life in film and insists on the significance of using female pronouns as expressions of female siblings. For bringing a wide array of melodramas and their meanings into my view, I am indebted to the Film Society of Lincoln Center, which, during winter 2017–2018, screened "Emotional Pictures: International Melodrama," and to Rachel Schaff's PhD dissertation, "Melodrama and Memory: Historicizing Pathos in Czech Holocaust Films" (University of Minnesota, 2018). Like film noir, melodrama has been analyzed by scholars of literature, drama, music, and politics. I am indebted to the long history of feminist examinations of melodrama as a cultural, political, and psychological mode of address.

1. Michael Goldfarb, "From the Country Club to the White House," *New York Times*, January 19, 2018, A27.

2. *Out of the Past*, directed by Jacques Tourneur (USA, 1947; Los Angeles: Warner Archive, 2015), DVD.

3. All this was first pointed out in 1974 by Molly Haskell; see her *From Reverence to Rape: The Treatment of Women in the Movies*, 2nd ed. (Chicago: University of Chicago Press, 1987).

4. Jill Filipovic, "Donald Trump's Work Wives," *New York Times*, January 22, 2018, A21. On the role of Trump's wife/daughter as prop, see Paula Rabinowitz, "Los dos cuerpos de [las] Queens: o ¿es possible vivir con los Trump siendo feminist?" Spanish translation by Carlota Sánchez of "The Queens Two Bodies: Or, Living with the Trumps, Is It Possible for a Feminist?" *Pasajes: Revista de pensamiento contemporáneo* 3 (2017): 73–85.

5. See Dan Flory, *Philosophy, Black Film, Film Noir* (University Park: Pennsylvania State Press, 2008).

6. See "Women's Lives, Cut Short," *New York Times*, December 19, 2017, https://www.nytimes.com/interactive/2017/12/19/opinion/women-guns-domestic-violence.html. This article is part 3 of a nine-part editorial series about domestic violence and the murder of women and gun ownership.

7. *Outrage*, directed by Ida Lupino (USA, 1950). There is no version of *Outrage* in print.

8. See Jonathan Auerbach, *Dark Borders: Film Noir and American Citizenship* (Durham, NC: Duke University Press, 2011) for a thorough examination of the roles of Mexico and the atomic bomb as forces undermining the nation in late noir.

9. Sewell Chan, "End of the World Is a Bit Closer, Scientists Fear," *New York Times*, January 26, 2018, A9.

10. For more on how this dynamic of domestic violence plays out in some "Hollywood" novels, see Paula Rabinowitz, "America's Movie-Made Novels," *Letterature D'America* 38 (2018): 21–40.

11. In the documentary *A Personal Journey with Martin Scorsese Through American Movies* (1995); quoted in Bret Wood, "Outrage, 1950," TCM, http://www.tcm.com/thismonth/article/102732%7C0/Outrage.html (page discontinued).

CONTRIBUTORS

CHRISTOPHER BREU is professor of English at Illinois State University where he teaches contemporary literature and culture and critical and cultural theory. He is the author of *Insistence of the Material: Literature in the Age of Biopolitics* (2014) and *Hard-Boiled Masculinities* (2005). He also is the editor of a special section on "Materialisms" in *symplokē* 24, nos. 1–2 (2017).

ALEXANDER DUNST is assistant professor of American Studies at the University of Paderborn. His research and teaching focus on twentieth-century cultural history, the digital humanities, and contemporary visual narrative. He is the author of *Madness in Cold War America* (2016) and is currently writing a book on the rise of the graphic novel.

SEAN GRATTAN is lecturer of American literature at the University of Kent. He is the author of *Hope Isn't Stupid: Utopian Affects in Contemporary American Literature* (2017) and coeditor (with Christian Haines) of the special issue on "What Comes After the Subject?," *Cultural Critique* 96 (Spring 2017).

ELIZABETH A. HATMAKER was a poet, theorist, and teacher. She was instructional assistant professor at Illinois State University. She was the author of two books of poetry, *Infrastructures* (2015) and *Girl in Two Pieces* (2009). She passed away in 2015 due to complications from ALS.

PETER HITCHCOCK is professor of English at the CUNY Graduate Center and Baruch College of the City University of New York. His books include *Dialogics of the Oppressed* (1992); *Oscillate Wildly: Space, Body, and Spirit of Millennial Materialism* (1999); *Imaginary States: Studies in Cultural Transnationalism* (2003); *The Long Space: Transnationalism and Postcolonial Form* (2009); *The New Public Intellectual: Politics, Theory, and the Public Sphere* (2016; coedited with Jeffrey R. Di Leo); *Labor in Culture, or, Worker of the World(s)* (2017); and, most recently, *The Debt Age* (2018; coedited with Jeffrey R. Di Leo and Sophia McClennen).

JUSTUS NIELAND is professor of English at Michigan State University, where he teaches in the Film Studies Program. He is the author of *Feeling Modern: The Eccentricities of Public Life* (2008), *David Lynch* (2012), *Happiness by Design: Modernism and Media in the Eames Era* (2020), and *Film Noir: Hard-Boiled Modernity and the Cultures of Globalization* (2009), cowritten with Jennifer Fay. He is also coeditor of the Contemporary Film Directors book series at the University of Illinois Press.

ANDREW PEPPER is senior lecturer in English at Queen's University Belfast. He is the author of *Unwilling Executioner: Crime Fiction and the* State (2016) and *The Contemporary American Crime Novel: Race, Ethnicity, Gender, Class* (2000) and the coeditor of *Globalization and the State in Contemporary American Crime Fiction* (Palgrave 2016). He is also a coeditor of the forthcoming *Routledge Companion to Crime Fiction*. He is also the author of a series of crime novels set in nineteenth-century Britain and Ireland, including *The Last Days of Newgate* (2006) and *Bloody Winter* (2011).

PAULA RABINOWITZ is Professor Emerita of English at the University of Minnesota and serves as editor-in-chief of the Oxford Research Encyclopedia of Literature. Her publications include numerous essays and books on mid-twentieth-century American culture, including *Black and White and Noir: America's Pulp Modernism* (2002) and the prize-winning *American Pulp: How Paperbacks Brought Modernism to Main Street* (2014). She is currently working on a collection of essays titled "Into the Image" and a double biography of two fathers, "Cold War Dads: Family Secrets and the National Security State." She lives in Queens, New York.

BRIAN REJACK is associate professor in the Department of English at Illinois State University. He is the coeditor, with Michael Theune, of *Keats's Negative Capability: New Origins and Afterlives* (2019). He is also the author of "Toward a Virtual Reenactment of History: Video Games and the Recreation of the Past," published in *Rethinking History* (2007).

IGNACIO M. SÁNCHEZ PRADO is Jarvis Thurston and Mona van Duyn Professor in the Humanities at Washington University in St. Louis. He is the author of *Strategic Occidentalism: On Mexican Fiction* and *The Neoliberal World Market and the Question of World Literature* (2018) and editor of *Mexican Literature in Theory* and *Pierre Bourdieu in Hispanic Literature and Culture* (2018). His work focuses on the relationship between cultural institutions and aesthetics in Mexico and he has published over ninety articles and book chapters on questions of Mexican literature and cinema, world literature and cultural theory.

PAMELA THOMA is associate professor of English and the director of the Program in Women's, Gender, and Sexuality Studies at Washington State University. She specializes in Asian American literary and cultural studies and feminist media studies. She is the author of *Asian American Women's Popular Literature: Feminizing Genres and Neoliberal Belonging* (2014) and editor of a forthcoming volume on the fiction of Karen Tei Yamashita. Her essays have been published in *Contemporary Women's Writing* (2014), *Feminist Media Studies* (2009), and *Gendering the Recession: Media and Culture in an Age of Austerity* (2014), edited by Diane Negra and Yvonne Tasker.

KIRIN WACHTER-GRENE is assistant professor of Liberal Arts at the School of the Art Institute of Chicago. Her work focuses on African American literature and gender and sexuality studies and has been published in *African American Review*, *The Black Scholar*, *Callaloo*, *Feminist Formations*, *Legacy: A Journal of American Women Writers*, and more. She is guest editor of *At the Limits of Desire: Black Radical Pleasure*, a special issue of *The Black Scholar*, and is currently working on a book on Samuel R. Delany and transgressive African American literature.

INDEX

abjection, 14, 80–82, 86–87
abyssal violence, 253–255
Address Unknown, 181
adjustment, 36–37
Adorno, Theodor, 35, 147
aesthetics, 17–18, 53
affect: Ahmed on, 255; Brennan on, 127; circulation and, 133; contextualizing, 10–12; cyborg, 20–21, 159, 168, 170; debt and, 223, 228; Deleuze and Guattari on, 9, 12, 15–16; embodiment and, 15–16; Freud on, 12; gaming and, 186–187; ideology and, 255; industrial and biopolitical labor and, 9–10; Lacan on, 14; logic of capitalism and, 227–228; neoliberalism and, 243–244; positive, 7, 9, 245; posthuman, cyborg as, 157–158; as productive, 205; profit and, 227–228, 230; sad, 160; spectrum of, 128; Spinoza on, 12, 15; sticky, 133; Tomkins on, 16; waning of, 231. *See also* negative affect; noir affect
affect alien, 128
affect image, 224, 231
affective atmosphere, of capitalism, 242, 249
affective labor, 216
affective remainders, 229–234
affective solidarity, 245
affective systems, 186
affective tone, 223–224
affective turn, 11, 157
affect theory, 8–9, 12, 16–17, 156, 223, 230–231
African Americans, 65, 81–85
African American street lit, 78–79
Ahmed, Sara, 122, 128, 133, 205, 255
Alaimo, Stacy, 11
"Alfaville, Godard Apocalypse" (Bochner), 29–31, *30*

allegory, 60–61
Alpha 60 (character), 50–53
Alphaville, 18–19, 29–32, 46, 50–53, *52*
ambivalence, 63
American Century, 41–42
American Dream, 182
American Psychological Association, 87
Amy Elliott Dunne (character), 197, 208–216, *210*
Anable, Aubrey, 186
Anatomy of a Murder, 262
Anderson, Ben, 243–244, 255
Anger, Kenneth, 232
anthropology, 35–36
anti-communism, 125–126
Antinomies of Realism (Jameson), 169
antiracist struggle, 63, 65
anxiety, 14–15, 74, 261, 263, 269
Anxiety (Lacan), 14
any-space-whatever, 231, 234
Apartheid South Africa, 66
Argentine culture, 142
Arts Magazine, 29
asociality, 230
At the End of a Dull Day (Carlotto), 244, 248–253, 256
Auerbach, Jonathan, 44
Augé, Mark, 4
Aviña, Rafael, 145

Bacall, Lauren, 265
Baldwin, James, 87
Bannon, Ann, 123, 125–131, 133–134
Bartky, Sandra, 214
Barton Keyes (character), 33–34
Bass, Saul, 43
Basu, Biman, 87–88
Batou (character), 162–164, 171
BDSM, 19, 80–81, 85, 87–88, 90–92
Beck, Robert. *See* Slim, Iceberg

279

becoming, 9, 11–12, 15, 244
Beebo Brinker Chronicles (Bannon), 125–127, 130–131, 133–134
Bellmer, Hans, 164, 171–172
Bender, Lou, 232–233
Benjamin, Walter, 60, 170–172
Berlant, Lauren, 21–22, 205, 243, 255–257; on cruel optimism, 15, 70, 230, 245, 247
Berlin, 40
Bernal, Rafael, 149
The Big Sleep, 37, 265
The Big Sleep (Chandler), 123–124
biopolitical labor, 9–10
biopolitics, 243
biopower, 244, 250
Bioshock series, 179
The Birth of Biopolitics (Foucault), 243
black bodies, 85
The Black Dahlia (Ellroy, J.), 114
Black Dahlia murder, 113–114
black feminism, 82–83
black humor, 72
black kink, 19
black men, 81
black noir, 78
black pleasure, 83
black rapist, myth of, 68–69
Black & White & Noir (Rabinowitz), 102
black women, 81–85
Blind Man with a Pistol (Himes), 60
Bloch, Ernst, 51
The Blue Dahlia, 37
Bochner, Mel, 29–32, *30*, 52–53
bodies, 85, 157, 217, 232–233; embodiment, 15–16, 159, 169, 180, 226
Bogart, Humphrey, 265
Boltanksi, Luc, 50
Borde, Raymond, 1
Bracho, Julio, 143–144, 147
Brazil, 183–185, 194n14
Brennan, Teresa, 16, 61, 127, 193n5
Breu, Christopher, 133, 244–245, 252–253
Breuer, Joseph, 12–13
The Bride Wore Black (Woolrich), 112
Brigid O'Shaughnessy (character), 109–110
Brooks, Peter, 138
Brussels World's Fair (1958), 45–46, 49
Buñuel, Luis, 143–144, 147–148

bureaucracy, 33–35, 45–46, 49
Burger, Hanus, 40
Burgin, Victor, 68

Cain, James M., 3–4
Cairo Station, 267–268
Califia, Pat, 80
Call, Lewis, 80
Call Northside 777, 41
Camus, Albert, 4
Candy Crush, 186
capitalism, 7, 258n32; affective atmosphere, 242, 249; cinema and, 229; creative, violence and, 248–253; crime and, 251; globalized, 160, 185; industrial, 38; logic of, affect and, 227–228; Mexican, 20; neoliberalism and, 6, 203, 251–253
capitalist modernity, 140, 144, 151
capitalist noir, 22, 241–243
capitalist patriarchy, 169, 203
Carlotto, Massimo, 22, 257; Anderson on, 243–244; *At the End of a Dull Day* by, 244, 248–253, 256; *Death's Dark Abyss* by, 244, 253–255; *The Goodbye Kiss* by, 242, 244–248, 256; neoliberal noir of, 241; noir affect and, 242
Carter, Angela, 106–107
Cartesian duality, 159
Caruth, Cathy, 13
Certeau, Michel de, 186–187, 195n17
Chandler, Raymond, 37, 123–124, 139
characters, of noir, 122–123, 242
Chaumeton, Étienne, 1
Chauncey, George, 125
cheat codes, 192
chick culture, 21, 200–204, 216–217
chick lit, 199–200, 204, 217
chick noir, 21–22, 198–200; coolness of, 216–217; femininity of, 204–205; Gill on, 204–205; *Gone Girl* as, 203, 212–213; neoliberalism and, 204; surveillance and, 205–206
China, 149–50
Chinatown (1974), 101–103, *103*, 262
"Chinatown," 101–102, 116–118
Cinema 1 (Deleuze), 231, 234
Cinema 2 (Deleuze), 234
CIO. *See* Congress of Industrial Organizations
circulation, 133

classroom, 19–20, 105, 108–111, 113–118
Clemént, René, 17
Clough, Patricia T., 9, 242
"Coldness and Cruelty" (Deleuze), 106
Cold War, 39, 41, 45, 47, 64, 149
Coleman, Beth, 81, 88
collectivity, 116–117
The Color of Kink (Cruz, A.), 88
color palette, 231–232
communication, 33–39, 44–49
Communications Group, 35, 37
A Communications Primer, 46
communications technologies, 30
El complot mongol (Bernal), 149–150
computation, 47
computer, 50–51
Congress of Industrial Organizations (CIO), 65
connaissance (ego), 102
consensual sex, 69–70
Constantine, Eddie, 50–51
consumption, 200
containment narratives, 61–62
continental philosophy, 4
control, 46–47, 82, 84
Coole, Diana, 11
Copjec, Joan, 240n43
corporate power, US, 41–42
corpse, 107–108, 113–118
corruption, 146–147, 151
counterplay, 187
The Cranes Are Flying, 266–267, 270
creative capitalism, violence and, 248–253
creditors, debtors and, 226–227
crime, 145–147, 231, 251, 266
"crisis of man" discourse, 31–32, 50, 52
Cross, Noah, 102–103, *103*
Crossfire, 38
cruel optimism, 15, 70, 230, 245, 247
Cruel Optimism (Berlant), 255
cruising, 130
Cruz, Ariane, 88
Cruz, Roberto de la, 147
cultural anthropology, 35–36
the cultural front, 60
cultural imperialism, 41–42
cultural nationalism, Mexican, 143–144, 147, 149
culture: Argentine, 142; chick, 21, 200–204, 216–217; gaming, 178, 189–190, 196n29; gay, 125; marriage, US, 199–200; mass, 41
cuteness, 216–217
cybernetics, 46–47
cyborg: affect, 20–21, 159, 168, 170; embodiment, 159; in *Ghost in the Shell* films, 161–162, 165–173; noir resistance and, 160; as posthuman affect, 157–158
cynicism, failure and, 109

Daddy was the Black Dahlia Killer (Knowlton), 114
Damico, James, 2
The Dark Mirror, 38
Dassin, Jules, 5
Davis, Angela, 68
Dead Pledges (McClanahan), 236, 238n21
death drive, 70, 228
Death Mills, 40
Death's Dark Abyss (Carlotto), 244, 253–255
debt, 22; affect and, 223, 228; body and, 226; chronic, 233; in *Drive*, 224–226, 228–229, 233, 235–236; Marx on subjective logic of, 226; as money and feeling, 224–229; power and, 222–223, 226; public, 237n2; structural indebtedness, 229; temporality of, 228, 233; violence and, 225–226, 228, 235
debtors, creditors and, 226–227
deferred action (*nachträglichkeit*), 13, 60
Delany, Samuel R., 91
Deleuze, Gilles, 19, 104–105, 234; on affect, 9, 12, 15–16; on affection image, 224, 231; on sadism and masochism, 106–107
D'Emilio, John, 125, 130
denazification, 40
Denning, Michael, 47, 49, 60, 66
Derrida, Jacques, 152n12
Desi Collings (character), 210–211
desire, 91, 159, 228
despair, reparative, 70–73
Detective, as SMO, 108
detective fiction, 197–198, 231
Detour, 264
détournement, 31, *32*
Deux Hommes dans Manhattan, 42
Dewey, John, 100

Diagnostic and Statistical Manual of Mental Disorders: Fifth Edition (DSM-5), 87
Dick, Philip K., 172
Dimendberg, Edward, 4–5, 17, 31, 42
disciplinary power, 214
Discipline and Punish (Foucault), 81
dissonant play, 187
Distinto amanecer, 144, 146–147
D.O.A., 269–270
dolls, 164–165, 167–168, 170–171
Double Indemnity, 18–19, *33*, 33–34, 111–112, 122
dream-logic, 61
Drive, 22, 234; affect images in, 231; authorities and, 230–231; body in, 232–233; color palette, 231–232; debt in, 224–226, 228–229, 233, 235–236; genre cinema and, 229–230; *jouissance* in, 233; pawnshop in, 225, 226; *Scorpio Rising* and, 232; soundscape of, 232–233
drug trafficking, 226–227
DSM-5. See *Diagnostic and Statistical Manual of Mental Disorders: Fifth Edition*
Dunne, John Gregory, 114
Dunst, Alexander, 22
Dyer-Witheford, Nick, 187, 195n23

Eames, Charles and Ray, 46–47
Echeverría, Bolívar, 142–143
edgeplay, 90
education, 99–100
ego (*connaissance*), 102
Elements of Political Economy (Mill), 226
Ellis, Havelock, 96n36
Ellroy, Geneva, 114
Ellroy, James, 114
Ellul, Jacques, 51
Éluard, Paul, 51–52
embodiment, 15–16, 159, 169, 180, 226
emotion, 34, 228. See also affect; feeling
empathy, constraint and, 207, 212
"Employment of Homosexuals and Other Sex Perverts in Government" (US Senate report), 126
The End of a Primitive (Himes), 19; chimpanzee in, 65–66; the historical repressed in, 66–69; Kriss and Jesse in, 62–64, 66–67, 69–73; noir affect as sexualized rage in, 69–70; racism and sexism in, 67–68; reparative despair in, 70–73; *Today Show* in, 65
Ensayo de un crimen (Usigli), 147–148
the erotic, pedagogy and, 105
eroticism, 63
Ethics (Spinoza), 12, 15, 157
Evelyn Mulwray (character), 102–103
exchange, in kink theory, 86
exploitation, 83–84

failure: classroom and, 110; cynicism and, 109; gaming and, 187; gaze and, 111; trauma and, 116
failure/pain, of University discourse, 105–107
fantasies, 68
fascism, 31, 39, 47
Fay, Jennifer, 2–3
FBI, 49
feeling: debt as, 224–229; perception and, 8; of place, 122; ugly, 179–180. See also affect
female detectives, 108
female phallicism, 215
female subjectivity, 200, 202
femininity, 21–22, 204–205, 217
feminism, 80–81; black, 82–83; postfeminism and, 199–202, 205, 212, 216
femme fatale, 80, 101, 107, 109–111, 265–266
femme noire, 264–265
Fernández, Emilio, 143–145
Ferris, Suzanne, 204
figures of refusal, 10
filmic communication, 45, 47–48
film noir. See noir; *specific topics*
Film Noir (Fay and Nieland), 2–3
Fincher, David, 21, 197
Finland, 182–183, 194n11
Flanagan, Kieran, 139–140, 146–147
Flor Silvestre, 144
Flynn, Gillian, 21, 197–198. See also *Gone Girl* (Flynn)
Foote, Stephanie, 132
Fordism, 18–19, 34
Fordist era, 5–6, 10
A Foreign Affair, 40
Foucault, Michel, 81, 214, 243
Foundlings (Nealon), 126
France, 49–50

Frank, Adam, 128
Frank, Nino, 1, 17
Frankfurt School, 17, 35, 59
"Freaks and the American Ideal of Manhood" (Baldwin), 87
French New Wave, 4, 30–31
Freud, Sigmund, 12–13, 52, 105–106
Friere, Paulo, 100
From Caligari to Hitler (Kracauer), 38
Frost, Samantha, 11
Frye, Northrop, 2

Gallup, 38
Galt, Rosalind, 229–230
gameplay, 186–187
Games of Empire (Dyer-Witheford and Peuter), 187, 195n23
gaming: affect and, 186–187; console, 187–188; failure and, 187; modding and, 21, 188–189; negative affect in, 178–180; noir affect and, 185–187
gaming culture, 178, 189–190, 196n29
García Canclini, Néstor, 142
Garroway, Dave, 65
Gaslight, 41
gay bars, 125–130, 133
gay culture, 125
gay lounge time, 20
gay pulp, 20
the gaze, 111–113, 116, 118, 140–141
gender, 2, 63
gendered power dynamics, 79
gender relations, 211–212
General Assembly, UN, 42
genre cinema, 229–230
German occupation, by US, 41
El gesticulador, 147
Ghost in the Shell (1995), 159, 161–172, 174, 174–175
Ghost in the Shell (2017), 173–175
Ghost in the Shell 2: Innocence, 163–165, 164, 169–171, 173
Ghost in the Shell franchise, 20–21, 158–159, 168, 175
Gibson, William, 158
Gifford, Justin, 81–85
Gill, Rosalind, 204–205
Gilmore, John, 114
Giorgio Pellegrini (character), 244–254, 256–257
Glimpses of the U.S.A., 47

global communication, 39
globalization, 20
global modernity, 2–3
Global South, 143
Godard, Jean-Luc, 18–19, 29–32, 50–53
Goldfarb, Michael, 262
Gone Girl (2014), 21, 197–198; Amy seeking protection in, 209, *210*; fight scene, 209, *210*; gender relations and, 211–212; marriage in, 208–212, *210*; surveillance in, 206–208, 210–211
Gone Girl (Flynn), 21, 197–199; *Amazing Amy* stories in, 210–211, 214; as chick noir, 203, 212–213; Cool Girl passage of, 214–217; family narrative, 212; femininity in, 205; surveillance and, 205–208, 213, 216
The Goodbye Kiss (Carlotto), 242, 244–248, 256
good-life fantasies, 245–248
Gosling, Ryan, 231–232, 234
Graeber, David, 225, 236
Graham, Dan, 29
Grattan, Sean, 20, 71
graveyard, 116–118
Greenwich Village, 125–127, 130–131
Gregg, Melissa, 156, 203–204
Greif, Mark, 31, 41
Grieveson, Lee, 39, 44
Grossberg, Lawrence, 11–12
Grotesque, 15
Guattari, Félix, 9, 12, 15–16
Guillory, John, 33
gynoid, 163–164, 171

Halberstam, Jack, 187
Hank Quinlan (character), 47–49
Hanson, Harry, 113–114
Haraway, Donna, 169, 171, 176n9
Hardt, Michael, 9, 160
Hartle, Johan, 140, 152n12
Hartman, Saidiya, 83
Harvey, David, 194nn11,14
Haskell, Molly, 263
Hatmaker, Elizabeth A., 19, 73, 133, 244–245, 252–253
Hawks, Howard, 37
Hays, Will, 43
Heemskerk, Joan, 190
Hegel, G. W. F., 159
Heims, Steve, 44

Hekman, Susan, 11
Herman, Judith, 13
heteronormativity, 20, 124, 130, 133
heteropatriarchy, 123, 198, 203
heterosexuality, 129
Highsmith, Patricia, 18
Hill Collins, Patricia, 82
Himes, Chester, 19, 60, 62–65; in black noir tradition, 78; "Harlem Detective" novels, 79; noir historiography and, 73–74; reparative despair and, 71; Slim and, 78–79; unfinished novel, 74n3. See also *The End of a Primitive* (Himes)
The Hip Hop Wars (Rose), 81
Hirsch, Foster, 125
historical memory, 68–69
the historical repressed, 66–69
historical violence, 60
historicism: noir, 5–6, 13–14; temporality and, 5, 13–14
historiography, 60–61, 70–71, 73–74
Hitchcock, Alfred, 43, 50
Hitchcock, Peter, 20
Hollywood blacklist, 43–44
Hollywood Quarterly, 37
hommes fatales, 108
homophobia, 73, 75n17, 123–124, 128
homosexuality, 123–124, 126–129, 131–133, 232
homosociality, 108
Hoover, J. Edgar, 49
Houseman, John, 37, 39, 44–45, 47–48
House Un-American Activities Committee (HUAC), 43–44, 61–62
"How Does a Movie Communicate?" (Houseman), 45
HUAC. *See* House Un-American Activities Committee
humanism, 37–38, 50–51
human relations, 34
human resources, 34
Huston, John, 109, 145
hypersexuality stereotype, 84–85
the hysteric, 111–113

I Am a Woman (Bannon), 126–129
IBM, 46, 50, 52
ideology, 50, 255
If He Hollers Let Him Go (Himes), 60, 66
I Married a Dead Man, 1
immobile time, 50

imperialism, 187
incrementalism, 157
individualism, 204–205
industrial capitalism, 38
industrialism, 193n7
industrial labor, 9–10
industrial revolution, 46
information, communication and, 44
The Information Machine, 46–47
institutionalized racism, 71
intelligence, education and, 99–100
international relations, 44–45
Introduction to Feedback, 46

Jack Mann (character), 126–127, 130–131
Jake Gittes (character), 102–103
Jameson, Fredric, 4, 139, 142, 149–150, 152n12, 170; postmodernism and, 166–167, 169; on waning of affect, 231
Japan, 174
Japanese postwar cinema, 4
Jesse Robinson (character), 62–64, 66–67, 69–73, 75n17
Jezebel stereotype, 84–85
Jim Crow, 68
JODI, 190
Joe Gillis (character), 108
Johansson, Scarlett, 173–174
Johnston, Eric, 43–45
Jones, Howard Mumford, 36
Josiah Macy Jr. Foundation, 44
jouissance, 63, 87, 90–93, 96n51, 140–141, 224; in *Drive*, 233; Lacan on, 227–229
justice, noir, 253–255
Juul, Jesper, 187

Kantaris, Geoffrey, 148
Kawai Kenji, 165
Kepes, György, 43
Khrushchev, Nikita, 270
The Killer Inside Me, 12
kink: black, 19; play-slavery, 88–89, 91; pleasure and, 84; race play, 88
kink theory, 80, 86, 88, 91, 92
Kiss Me Deadly, 263
knowledge: adequate, 157; the erotic and, 105; identification and, 103–104; noir pedagogy and, 101–105; power and, 99–100, 103, 116; SHO relationship to, 112–113; subjective, 102, 104, 118

Index

Knowlton, Janice, 114
Kracauer, Siegfried, 35–40, 44–45, 47
Kriss Cummings (character), 62–64, 66–67, 69–73, 75n17
Kristeva, Julia, 14

labor: affective, 216; emotional, 34; industrial and biopolitical, 9–10; wage, 203–204
Lacan, Jacques, 14–15, 18–19, 61, 101–103, 223; discourses of, 107–108; on *jouissance*, 227–229
The Ladder, 126
Laplanche, Jean, 13, 19, 68, 105–106
Laswell, Harold, 35
Latin America, 142–143, 151
Laura (fictional character), 126–130
Lavender Scare, 125–126
League of Nations, 41
Lee Sang-Il, 3
leftists, on historical change, 59
Lemmy Caution (character), 30, 50–53
lesbian pulp fiction, 123
lesbians, 124, 126–127, 130, 132
LGBTQ community, 131–132
LGBTQ people, 127–128, 132–133
liberalism, 5–6, 45, 193n7
liberal racism, 64–65
The Life of Oharu, 268
Liu, Alan, 30–31, 34, 37, 53
Llámenme Mike, 150–151
The Lonely Crowd (Riesman), 46
The Lonely Crusade (Himes), 60, 66
The Long Night, 38
The Lost Weekend, 38
lounge time, 4, 6, 20, 129–130
Lupino, Ida, 264, 270–271
Lynch, David, 114

MacMurray, Fred, 33
Macy Conferences on Cybernetics, 44
Madame X, 268
maladjustment, 37–38
Maltby, Richard, 36
The Maltese Falcon, 41, 109–110, 145
management, 33–34, 46–47, 50
Mankiewicz, Joseph, 62
Marcuse, Herbert, 51–52
marriage, 208–212, 210
marriage culture, US, 199–200
Martin, Reinhold, 43

Martin, Theodore, 133
Martín-Barbero, Jesús, 148–149
Marx, Karl, 140, 223, 225–226
masochism: BDSM, 19, 80–81, 85, 87–88, 90–92; male, 106–107; sadism and, 19, 106–107, 116; S/M, 80, 87–88, 92, 105–107
masochistic hysteric object (MHO), 108, 110, 113–117
mass culture, 41
mass media, 31, 35
Massumi, Brian, 12, 160, 244, 250
materialism, 11, 159–160
materialization, 140, 144, 147
material trauma, 13, 68
material turn, 11
The Mathematical Theory of Communication (Shannon and Weaver), 31
The Mattachine Review, 130
Mattachine Society, 125
Max Payne, 178, 180–182
Max Payne 2, 178, 181–182, 186, 188–189, 191–192
Max Payne 3, 178–179, 183–186, 188
Max Payne Cheats Only (MPCO), 190–192
"Max Payne on Crack" mod, 188–189
Max Payne series, 21, 178; Finnish developers of, 182–183; New York City and, 182–184; noir affect and, 186; noir and, 179–185
May, Elaine Tyler, 64
Mayo, Elton, 34
McCarthy, Joseph, 61–62
McCarthyism, 64–66
McClanahan, Annie, 228, 236, 238n21
McCoy, Horace, 3–4
McRobbie, Angela, 201–202, 215
Mead, Margaret, 35–36, 39–40
Meades, Alan F., 187
media industry, 212
melodrama, 20, 138–139, 145, 235, 261–266, 271–272
The Melodramatic Imagination (Brooks), 138
Melville, Jean-Pierre, 42
Memento, 180
Menaul, Christopher, 10–11
Menzies (character), 48–49
meritocracy, 189–190
messianic time, 60

#MeToo movement, 23, 83, 262, 269, 271
Mexican capitalism, 20
Mexican cultural nationalism, 143–144, 147, 149
Mexican noir, 20, 143–151
Mexico, 142–143
Mexico City, 147–148, 150–151
Mex Noir (Aviña), 145
MHO. *See* masochistic hysteric object
Mike Hammer (character), 134n9
Mike Vargas (character), 48–49
Mill, James, 226
Miller-Young, Mireille, 83–84, 96n44
misogynist violence, 72, 86–87
misogyny, 79, 81–84
Mizoguchi, Kenji, 268
modding games, 21, 188–189
modernism, 3, 43, 52
modernity, 2–3, 33–34, 53, 140–144, 151, 204
modernization, 3, 138, 141–145
Mona Sax (character), 191–192
money, 223–229
Moore, Christopher, 185–186
More than Night (Naremore), 183
Morgan, Joan, 83
Motion Picture Association of America (MPAA), 43–45
Motoko Kusanagi (character), 161–164, 166–171, 173–175
MPAA. *See* Motion Picture Association of America
MPCO. See *Max Payne Cheats Only*
Mrs. Miniver, 40
Muggs, J. Fred, 65
Mulholland Drive, 114

nachträglichkeit (deferred action), 13, 60
Nadel, Alan, 61–62
The Naked City, 5
Naremore, James, 3–4, 137–138, 183
nationalism, Mexican, 143–145
"National Types as Hollywood Presents Them" (Kracauer), 45
national violence, 68–69
Natsuo Kirino, 5–7, 15
Nazism, 269–271
Nealon, Christopher, 126, 132
negative affect: anxiety as, 15; in gaming, 178–180; in *Gone Girl*, 199; of loss, 204; Ngai on, 17; noir as, 3–4, 7, 16, 230; in *Pimp*, 79–80; power of, 9; queer theory and, 81; situating, 15–17; in *Touch of Evil*, 49–50; trauma and, 13; as ugly feeling, 179–180; women and, 16
negative power, of affect, 9
negativity, 3, 7–9
Negra, Diane, 202, 212
Negri, Antonio, 9, 160, 244, 250
the "Negro Problem," 63
neoliberalism, 9–10, 15, 20, 193n8, 256; affect and, 243–244; capitalism and, 6, 203, 251–253; chick noir and, 204; cruel optimism in, 70, 230; Max Payne series and, 179, 183–184; selfhood and, 217; surveillance and, 199
neoliberal noir, 6, 10, 241, 252–253
Neon Demon, 238n19
neo-noir, 6, 102, 185
network society, 158
new materialisms, 11
new sexual contract, 201–202, 216
Newton, Esther, 125
New World Economic Order, 41
New World Information Order, 41
New York City, 182–184
Ngai, Sianne, 17, 21, 29, 179–180, 217, 223
Nick Dunne (character), 197, 208–216
Nieland, Justus, 2–3, 18–19
Nietzsche, Friedrich, 15, 223, 226–227
Nightmare Alley, 264
noir: affect theory and, 230; anxiety and, 14–15; capitalist, 22, 241–243; characters of, 122–123, 242; "Chinatown" of, 101–102; classical film, 140–141; dangerous women in, 82; as elusive, 1; feeling of place in, 122; female detectives in, 108; Fordist, 6; gender, class, race and, 2; genesis of, 3–4; heteropatriarchal violence in, 123; historiography, 70–71, 73–74; Lacan's discourses and, 107–108; mass media in, 31; in Max Payne series, 179–185; melodrama and, 138–139, 145, 235, 261–266, 271–272; Mexican, 20, 143–151; narratives, distortion by, 61; narratives, in 1950s, 61–62; as negative affect, 3–4, 7, 16, 230; negativity of, 3, 7–9; neoliberal, 6, 10, 241, 252–253; perverse sexuality of,

Index 287

266–268; plots, 1–2; practices of, 4; proximity to the real, 17–18; qualities of, 1–2; in range of media, 7; reading, 18–23; S/M and, 107; sociological, 139, 144, 149, 151; space and time, 3–5, 60–62, 140; spaces of, 4–5, 231, 234; spatiality, 31; students, 101–105, 116, 118; texture of, 122; UN, 39–50; *veçu* in, 17; Žižek's Lacanian account of, 14. *See also specific topics*
noir aesthetic, 17–18
noir affect: ambivalence in, 63; bureaucratization of, 33, 45–46; Carlotto and, 242; "crisis of man" discourse in, 50; gaming and, 185–187; good-life fantasies and, 245–248; Greif on, 31–32; Liu on, 31; Max Payne series and, 186; as political unmasking, 255–257; posthumanism and, 160; of postwar Berlin, 40; power and, 250; sad, 160; sexualized rage as, 69–70; space, time and, 3–5; understanding, 6–10; violence and, 244–245. *See also specific topics*
Noir Anxiety (Oliver and Trigo), 14
noir communication, 33–39
noir fantasy, 107–108
noir form, 139, 144, 147–149
noir historicism, 5–6, 13–14
noir humanism, 37–38
noir justice, 253–255
noir mediascape, 137–141, 144–147
noir pedagogy, 73–74, 101–105, 116, 118
noir time, 13–14
noir video games, 21, 178–179
nonplace, 4–5
nontime, 4–5
North by Northwest, 43
No Way Out, 62
Noyes, Eliot, 46
nuclear family, 266

Odd Girl Out (Bannon), 126
Office of War Information (OWI), US, 40, 43
Oliver, Kelly, 14–15, 61
Los olvidados, 147–148
One-Dimensional Man (Marcuse), 51
on-location filming, 5
Only God Forgives, 224, 226–231, 233–236, 235

On the Genealogy of Morality (Nietzsche), 226
open admission, 100
oppression, of women, 81–82
Orbaugh, Sharalyn, 158
organizations, 31–32, 50
Orientalism, 101, 124
Oshii Mamoru, 159, 161–163, 165–168, 170–172, 174–175
other/Other, 103–104, 106, 108–113, 115
The Other Side of Psychoanalysis (Lacan), 227
Out, 5–7
Out of the Past, 262
Outrage, 264, 270–271
OWI. *See* Office of War Information, US

Packer, Vin, 126
Paesmans, Dirk, 190
Parables for the Virtual (Massumi), 12
patriarchy: capitalist, 169, 203; heteropatriarchy, 123, 198, 203; self-surveillance and, 214; sexuality and, 80–81, 83
Paul, Christopher A., 189
pedagogy, 105. *See also* noir pedagogy
Pepper (character), 85–87, 89, 92
Pepper, Andrew, 22, 242
perception, feeling and, 8
perverse sexuality, 266–268
perversion, 87, 107
Peters, John Durham, 35
Pettey, Homer B., 138
Peuter, Greig de, 187, 195n23
Peyton Place, 263–264, 267, 271
Philip Marlowe (character), 37, 109, 123–124, 265
Phyllis (character), 89–92
Phyllis Dietrichson (character), 111–112, 122
Piccato, Pablo, 145–146
Pimp (Slim), 19, 78; asymmetrical power dynamic, 86; BDSM power dynamics in, 80–81, 85, 88, 90–93; black women characters in, 81–85; kink theory on, 80; negative affect in, 79–80; Pepper in, 85–87, 89, 92; Phyllis in, 89–92; play-slavery kink in, 88; sex work in, 83–86
pimp identity, 82, 85
pimps, power and, 88

place, feeling of, 122
Playing with Feelings (Anable), 186
play-slavery kink, 88–89, 91
pleasure, 83–86
Plein Soleil (Clemént), 17
poetry, 51–52
political correctness, 71–72
Popular Front, 47
positive affect, 7, 9, 245
possibility, becoming and, 9, 11–12
postfeminism, 199–202, 205, 212, 216
post-Fordist production, 10
posthuman affect, cyborg as, 157–158
posthumanism, 160, 166–167, 175
The Postman Always Rings Twice, 267–268
postmodernism, 11, 166–167, 169
postmodern neo-noir, 6
postwar Berlin, 40
postwar France, 50
postwar Hollywood, 43
postwar international organizations, 44–45
Pound, Ezra, 107
power: debt and, 222–223, 226; desire and, 91; disciplinary, 214; dynamics, BDSM, 80–81, 85, 88, 90–92; Foucault on, 81; knowledge and, 99–100, 103, 116; life and, 241–242; masochistic males and, 106–107; noir affect and, 250; pimps and, 88
Prime Suspect, 10–11
proceduralism, 186
profit, 227–228, 230
Project for a Scientific Psychology (Freud), 12–13
propaganda, 31, 35–36, 40, 45, 47
"Propaganda through Entertainment" memo, 40
propping, 105–106
proximity to the real, 17–18
"Psychiatry for Everything and Everybody" (Kracauer), 37–39
Psycho, 43
psychoanalysis, 12–14, 36, 60, 68, 224
Psychological Warfare Division, of US Office of War Information, 40, 47
psychologism, 37–38
Psychology of Industrial Behavior (Smith, H. C.), 36–37
public debt, 237n2
Public Sex (Califia), 80

pulp fiction: African American, 79; gay, 20; lesbian, 123; queer, 128, 131–133
Puppet Master (character), 161, 166–167, 172
The Pursuits of Happiness (Jones), 36

Quake, 190
The Queer Art of Failure (Halberstam), 187
queer characters, 123–125
queer pulp fiction, 128, 131–133
queer theory, 80–81, 205
queer youth, 128

Rabinowitz, Paula, 23, 102, 198
race, 2, 63
race play kink, 88
racism: antiblack, psychosexual dimensions of, 88; institutionalized, 71; liberal, 64–65; misogynist violence and, 72; repetition and, 70–71; sexism and, 67–68, 73–74; whitewashing, 173–174
Ramírez Berg, Charles, 143
Randolph, A. Philip, 65
rape, 263–264, 266, 270–271
rationality, ideology of, 50
reading, 128, 131–132
the Real, 17–18, 101–102, 108, 139
Rejack, Brian, 21
Rendezvous in Black (Woolrich), 112
reparative despair, 70–73
repetition, 14, 70–71
repression, 61–62, 64, 66–69, 266–267, 271
Resistance, 42
retroactive meaning (*nachträglichkeit*), 13
Riesman, David, 36, 46
Road House, 264
Robinson, Edward G., 33
robots, 170
Rockstar Games, 188
Roger O. Thornhill (character), 43
Rose, Tricia, 81, 83
Rosen, David, 206, 217
Rosin, Hannah, 211
Ross, Kristin, 50

sad affect, 160
Sadian woman, 106, 109
sadism, 19, 38–39, 106–107, 116
sadistic hysteric object (SHO), 111–113, 115

Index

sadistic master object (SMO), 108–110, 112, 114–117
sadomasochism (S/M), 80, 87–88, 92, 105–107
Sallis, James, 224
Sam Spade (character), 109–110
Sánchez, Fernando Fabio, 146–147
Sanchez Prado, Ignacio M., 20
Sanders, Rupert, 173–174
Santesso, Aaron, 206, 217
Sarlo, Beatriz, 142
savoir (subjective knowledge), 102, 104, 118
Schrader, Paul, 137–138
Scorpio Rising, 232
Scorsese, Martin, 271
Scott, Darieck, 81–82
screen memory, 68–69
Security Index Card File, 49
Sedgwick, Eve Kosofsky, 16, 71, 128
Seigworth, Gregory J., 156
self-branding, 216
selfhood, 206–208, 217
self-surveillance, 205, 214–215
Senate, US, 126
seriality, 162, 167, 169–170
Severed (Gilmore), 114
sex, 63, 70, 80, 84–85, 216
sexism, racism and, 67–68, 73–74
sex play, 85
sexual abuse, 12–13
sexual agency, 81–82
sexual enjoyment, 106
sexual exploitation, 82
sexual freedom, 81
sexual fulfilment, 63
sexual identity, 80, 89
sexuality, 62; of black women, 82–83; patriarchy and, 80–81, 83; perverse, 266–268; propping and, 105–106; transgressive, 80, 84–85; trauma and, 68; of women, 266
sexualized rage, as noir affect, 69–70
sexualized violence, 82–83
sexual need, 70
sexual violence, 68
sex work, 83–86
Shadow of a Doubt, 38
Shannon, Claude, 31
Shirow Masamune, 158, 165–166
SHO. *See* sadistic hysteric object

Shoot the Piano Player, 5
Short, Elizabeth, 113–115
Sigel, Newton Thomas, 232
Silverman, Kaja, 52
Silvio Contin (character), 253–255, 257
Singh, Greg, 185
Siodmak, Robert, 41
situatedness, 133
slavery, US, 82–83
Slim, Iceberg, 19, 78–79. *See also Pimp* (Slim)
S/M. *See* sadomasochism
Smith, Adam, 225
Smith, Henry Clay, 36–37
Smith, Rachel, 212
Smithson, Robert, 29
SMO. *See* sadistic master object
Sobchack, Vivian, 4–5, 129–130
the social, subjectivity and, 9
society, crime and, 231
sociological noir, 139, 144, 149, 151
La sombra del caudillo, 146
Some Like It Hot, 47
Sommer, Doris, 139
sound design, 232–233
South Africa, 66
space and time, of noir, 3–5, 60–62, 140
spaces, of noir, 4–5, 231, 234
spatiality, noir, 31
spatialization, 5
the specter, 140
speedrunning, 189
Spellbound, 38
Spillane, Mickey, 124–125, 134n9, 150–151
Spillers, Hortense, 83
Spinoza, Baruch, 12, 15, 157–160, 172, 250
The Spiral Staircase, 38, 41
Spring Fire (Packer), 126
sticky affect, 133
The Stranger, 269
Strangers on a Train (Highsmith), 18
street lit, 78–79, 81
structural indebtedness, 229
structuralism, 2
students: creative, 100–101; as MHO, 115–116; noir and, 101–105, 116, 118; SHO, 111–113; SMO and, 109–110; the University and, 103–105; within structures of power, 100

"Studies on Hysteria" (Freud and Breuer), 12–13
subject, 11, 102
subjectification, 73
subjective knowledge (*savoir*), 102, 104, 118
subjective logic, of debt, 226
subjectivity: female, 200, 202; the social and, 9; split, 111
submission, desire and, 91
subordination, 86–87, 89
Sunset Boulevard, 108
surveillance, 199; bodies and, 217; chick noir and, 205–206; Foucault on, 214; in *Gone Girl*, 205–208, 210–211, 213, 216; self-surveillance, 205, 214–215; technologies, 206–207
Suspicion, 41
Susan Vargas (character), 48

Taft-Hartley Act (1947), 61–62
Tarzan, 50–52
Taylorism, 34
Team Fortress 2, 185
technocracy, 50
technological reproducibility, 170–172
The Technological Society (Ellul), 51
technostyle, 31
temporality: in *Alphaville*, 51; of debt, 228, 233; historicism and, 5, 13–14; lounge time, 4, 6, 20, 129–130
"Terror Films" (Kracauer), 47
texture, of noir, 122
therapeutic adjustment, 36
Thoma, Pamela, 21
Thompson, Jim, 12
Thompson, Kristin, 229
"Those Movies with a Message" (Kracauer), 39
time: immobile, 50; lounge, 4, 6, 20, 129–130; messianic, 60; noir, 13–14; space and, 3–5, 60–62, 140
#TimesUp, 83
"Today's Hero" (Houseman), 37
Today Show, 65
Tomkins, Silvan, 16–17
Tom Ripley (character), 122–123
tone, 17, 231
totalitarianism, 31–32
Touch of Evil, 46–50, 263, 266–267
toxic meritocracy, 189

transgressive sex, 80, 84–85
trauma, 12–14, 61, 63–64; failure and, 116; material, 13, 68; MHO and, 115–116; sexuality and, 68; victimization and, 117
traumatic Real, 139
Trigo, Benigno, 14–15, 61
True Confessions (Dunne), 114
Truffaut, François, 5
Trump, Donald, 23, 261–263, 269
Turner, Fred, 44–45
Turner, Lana, 267–269
Twin Peaks, 181
two deaths, 14
Two Men in Manhattan, 42

ugly feelings, 179–180
Ugly Feelings (Ngai), 17
UN. *See* United Nations
un-Americanness, 44, 49
the uncanny, 14–15
UNESCO, 41, 44–45
United Nations (UN), 39–50
United States (US): corporate power, 41–42; debt in, 222; FBI, 49; marriage culture, 199–200; mass culture, 41; neoliberalism and, 183–184; noir novel, in 1950s, 61–62; occupation by, 40–41; OWI, 40, 43; Senate, 126; slavery, 82–83
universities, 100–101
the University, 103–107, 109–111, 118
Untitled Game, 190
Unwilling Executioner (Pepper), 242
US. *See* United States
Usigli, Rodolfo, 147–148
utopia, 135n17

Vance, Carol, 80
veçu, 17
Vengeance is Mine (Spillane), 124, 134n9
Vernet, Marc, 1
Vertigo, 43
victims, trauma and, 117
video games, 21, 178–179, 186, 194n15. *See also* gaming
Vighi, Fabio, 147–150
Villain, 3
violence: abyssal, 253–255; creative capitalism and, 248–253; debt and, 225–226, 228, 235; in gendered power

Index

dynamics, 79; heteropatriarchal, 123; historical, 60; misogynist, 72, 86–87; national, 68–69; noir affect and, 244–245; of racism and sexism, 72–74; sexual, 68; sexualized, 82–83
visibility, 131
Von Braun, Natacha, 51–52

Wachter-Grene, Kirin, 19
wage labor, 203–204
Walter Mulwray (character), *33*, 33–34, 112, 122, 180
waning of affect, 231
Weaver, Warren, 31
Welles, Orson, 46–49
Welsh, Irvine, 79, 90
WFMH. *See* World Federation for Mental Health
White Heat, 263
white masculinity, 67–68
whitewashing, 173–174
Wiegman, Robin, 68
Wiener, Norbert, 44

Wilder, Billy, 18–19, 33–35, 40, 47
Williams, Raymond, 157
Winding Refn, Nicholas, 22, 222, 224, 226, 228–232
Wolfenzon, Carolyn, 147–148
womanhood, 64
women: black, 81–85; dangerous, in noir, 82; exploitation of, 83–84; *femme fatale*, *See* 80, 101, 107, 109–111, 265–266; negative affects and, 16; oppression of, 81–82; Sadian woman, 106, 109; sexuality of, 266
women's culture, 203
Woolrich, Cornell, 1, 3–4, 112
Work Progress Administration (WPA), 63
World Federation for Mental Health (WFMH), 44
WPA. *See* Work Progress Administration
Written on the Wind, 262

Žižek, Slavoj, 3, 14, 107, 140–141, 255

www.ingramcontent.com/pod-product-compliance
Lightning Source LLC
Chambersburg PA
CBHW030435300426
44112CB00009B/1013